THE REAL HISTORY

OF THE

American Revolution

THE REAL HISTORY
OF THE

American Revolution

A NEW LOOK AT THE PAST

Alan Axelrod

STERLING

New York / London
www.sterlingpublishing.com

STERLING and the distinctive Sterling logo are registered trademarks of Sterling Publishing Co., Inc.

Library of Congress Cataloging-in-Publication Data Available

10 9 8 7 6 5 4 3 2 1

Published by Sterling Publishing Co., Inc.
387 Park Avenue South, New York, NY 10016
© 2007 by Sterling Publishing, Inc.
Text © 2007 by Alan Axelrod
Distributed in Canada by Sterling Publishing
$^c/o$ Canadian Manda Group, 165 Dufferin Street
Toronto, Ontario, Canada M6K 3H6
Distributed in the United Kingdom by GMC Distribution Services
Castle Place, 166 High Street, Lewes, East Sussex, England BN7 1XU
Distributed in Australia by Capricorn Link (Australia) Pty. Ltd.
P.O. Box 704, Windsor, NSW 2756, Australia

Book design and layout: Oxygen Design, Sherry Williams/Tilman Reitzle

Printed in China

Sterling ISBN-13: 978-1-4027-4086-2
ISBN-10: 1-4027-4086-7

For information about custom editions, special sales, premium and corporate purchases, please contact Sterling Special Sales Department at 800-805-5489 or specialsales@sterlingpub.com.

For Anita and Ian

"Tyranny, like hell,
is not easily conquered;
yet we have this consolation with us,
that the harder the conflict,
the more glorious the triumph."

Thomas Paine, "*The Crisis,* No. 1," 1776

CONTENTS

The Real History of the American Revolution

PART ONE

The Pursuit of Happiness

PART TWO

Drumming Up a War

Dramatis Personae

Adams, John (1735–1826)
An organizer of the Revolution, who was a negotiator of the Treaty of Paris and the nation's first vice president and second president.

Adams, Samuel (1722–1803)
Master propagandist of the Revolution, who was the principal figure in the Massachusetts independence movement.

Allen, Ethan (1738–89)
Connecticut leader of the Green Mountain Boys.

André, John (1750–80)
Major in the British army who served as liaison with the American traitor Benedict Arnold and who, arrested while carrying plans of West Point supplied by Arnold, was executed as a spy.

Arnold, Benedict (1741–1801)
Bold Continental army general who turned traitor.

Attucks, Crispus (c. 1723–70)
Runaway slave, who, a victim of the Boston Massacre (1770), is generally considered the first fatality in the fight for independence.

Beaumarchais, Pierre Augustin Caron de (1732–99)
Best remembered as the author of the comic plays *Le Barbier de Séville* (1775) and *Le Mariage de Figaro* (1784), which served as the basis for the Rossini and Mozart operas. Beaumarchais also brilliantly masterminded a French-backed scheme to covertly finance the American Revolution.

Boone, Daniel (1734–1820)
Most celebrated American frontiersman during the colonial, revolutionary, and early Federal periods, Boone was instrumental in the settlement of Kentucky as well as its defense during the war.

Brant, Joseph (1742–1807)
Mohawk political and military leader, who was Britain's most skillful and effective Native American ally.

Burgoyne, John ("Gentleman Johnny") (1722–92)
British general disastrously defeated at Bemis Heights in the Saratoga campaign (1777).

Carleton, Guy (1724–1808)
British general and governor of Canada, who repelled the American invasion of 1775.

Clark, George Rogers (1752–1818)
Patriot commander in the far frontier.

Clinton, Henry (1738–95)
Second in command under British commander in chief William Howe, whom he succeeded in May 1778.

Cornwallis, Charles (1738–1805)
Often victorious British general who lost the culminating battle of the war at Yorktown, Virginia (September 28–October 17, 1781).

de Grasse, François Joseph Paul, comte (1722–88)
French admiral who contributed to the American victory in the Yorktown campaign (September 28–October 17, 1781).

Deane, Silas (1737–89)
Controversial American representative instrumental in securing financial aid from France.

d'Estaing, Charles Hector Théodot, comte (1729–94)
Inept French admiral.

Dickinson, John (1732–1808)
Author of "Letters from a Farmer in Pennsylvania" (1767–68), which challenged the right of Parliament to tax the colonies.

Franklin, Benjamin (1706–90)
Colonial renaissance man who was instrumental in negotiating the French alliance and was the principal negotiator of the Treaty of Paris (1783).

Gage, Thomas (c. 1721–87)
Royal governor of Massachusetts and commander in chief of British forces in North America; replaced as military commander by William Howe.

Galloway, Joseph (c. 1731–1803)
Pennsylvania attorney and legislator who unsuccessfully sought to avert the Revolution with his "Plan of a Proposed Union between Great Britain and the Colonies" (1774), a proposal for home-rule government.

Gates, Horatio (c. 1728–1806)
Stodgy Continental army commander, given credit for the Saratoga victory (September 19 and October 7, 1777), but ignominiously defeated at the Battle of Camden (August 16, 1780).

George III (1738–1820)
King of England during the American Revolution.

Germain, George Sackville, Lord (1716–85)
British secretary of state for the American colonies, ultimately responsible for prosecuting the war.

Greene, Nathanael (1742–86)
Major general in the Continental army who distinguished himself as commander of the Southern Department beginning in October 1780.

Grenville, Lord George (1712–70)
British first lord of the treasury whose Revenue Act of 1764 and Stamp Act of 1765 triggered the events that led to the American Revolution.

Hale, Nathan (1755–76)
Connecticut schoolmaster turned Patriot spy, famed for his reputed final words: "I only regret that I have but one life to lose for my country."

Hamilton, Alexander (c. 1757–1804)
Dashing Continental army officer and aide to Washington; instrumental in organizing the Constitutional Convention; served President George Washington as the nation's first secretary of the treasury; killed in a duel with Aaron Burr.

Hancock, John (1737–93)
Revolutionary organizer and president of the Continental Congress; first and most conspicuous signer of the Declaration of Independence.

Henry, Patrick (1736–99)
Electrifying orator, who declared in March 1775, "give me liberty or give me death."

Herkimer, Nicholas (c. 1728–77)
American militia general fatally wounded at the Battle of Oriskany (August 6, 1777).

Hopkins, Esek (1718–1802)
First commander in chief of the Continental navy.

Howe, Richard (1726–99)
British commander in chief of Royal Navy forces in America, and brother of William Howe.

Howe, William (1729–1814)
Replaced Thomas Gage as commander in chief of British forces; brother of Admiral Richard Howe.

Jay, John (1745–1829)
New York attorney and founding father who served as the U.S. minister plenipotentiary to Spain (1779) and was one of the commissioners who negotiated the Treaty of Paris (1783), ending the American Revolution; Jay became the first chief justice of the U.S. Supreme Court (1789–95).

Jefferson, Thomas (1743–1826)
Revolutionary radical, principal author of the Declaration of Independence, governor of Virginia, and third president of the United States.

Jones, John Paul (1747–92)
Scottish-born American naval hero.

Kalb, Johann (Baron de Kalb) (1721–80)
German volunteer officer serving in the Continental army, fatally wounded at the Battle of Camden.

Knox, Henry (1750–1806)
Continental army artillery chief who served as the nation's first secretary of war.

Knyphausen, Wilhelm von (1716–1800)
Commander in chief of the "Hessians."

Kosciuszko, Tadeusz (1746–1817)
Polish patriot and military engineer who served at Saratoga (September 19 and October 7, 1777), helped to fortify West Point (1780), and fought with distinction under Nathanael Greene in the South (1780–81).

Lafayette, Marie Joseph Paul Yves Roch Gilbert du Motier, Marquis de (1757–1834)
French aristocrat and most celebrated of the foreign officers in the American service.

Laurens, Henry (1724–92)
One of the American negotiators of the Treaty of Paris.

Lee, Arthur (1740–92)
Problematic American representative in Europe.

Lee, Charles (1731–82)
George Washington's second in command, who was suspended after poor performance at the Battle of Monmouth Courthouse (June 28, 1778).

Lee, Henry ("Light-Horse Harry")
(1756–1818) Dashing American cavalry commander.

Lincoln, Benjamin (1733–1810)
Continental army commander who served well at Bennington and Saratoga, was taken prisoner when Charleston fell in 1780.

Marion, Francis ("Swamp Fox")
(c. 1732–95) Patriot guerrilla leader in the Carolina backcountry.

Montague, John, 4th Earl of Sandwich
(1718–92)
First lord of the British Admiralty

Morgan, Daniel (1736–1802)
Brilliant American commander considered the only military genius of the Revolution.

Morris, Robert (1734–1806)
Known as the "financier of the American Revolution."

Moultrie, William (1730–1805)
Continental army general successfully defended Fort Sullivan against the British assault on Charleston in 1776.

North, Frederick, Lord (1732–92)
Prime minister under King George III.

Otis, James (1725–83)
Massachusetts attorney who, in 1761, coined the phrase (and the concept), "Taxation without representation is tyranny."

Paine, Thomas (1737–1809)
British-born Philadelphian whose pamphlet *Common Sense* (1776) galvanized the cause of independence and whose later series of essays, collected as *The Crisis* (1776–77), were instrumental in preserving and nurturing the revolutionary spirit.

Pitt, William, "the Elder" (1708–78)
British politician who effectively served as prime minister (1756–61 and 1766–68) during much of the French and Indian War (1754–63) and who championed the cause of American liberty during the 1760s, urging the repeal of the Stamp Act (1765) and other repressive policies governing the colonies.

Pulaski, Casimir (1747–79)
Polish officer instrumental in creating a Continental cavalry force; fatally wounded at the Battle of Savannah.

Putnam, Israel (1718–90)
Continental army major general who was a principal commander at Bunker Hill (June 17, 1775).

Revere, Paul (1735–1818)
Silversmith and courier for the Massachusetts Committee of Correspondence, whose "Midnight Ride" roused the Minutemen before the battles of Lexington and Concord in 1775.

Riedesel, Baron Friedrich (1738–1800)
Hessian commander.

Rochambeau, Jean Baptiste Donatien de Vimeur, comte de (1725–1807)
French general who, with Washington, was co-victor of Yorktown (September 28–October 17, 1781).

Rodney, George Brydges (1718–92)
British admiral who achieved numerous victories against the Spanish and French during the American Revolution.

Schuyler, Philip (1733–1804)
Veteran of the French and Indian War (1754–1763) and delegate to the Continental Congress; was commissioned one of four major generals of the Continental army in 1775 but, after the fall of Fort Ticonderoga to the British (1777) was relieved of command.

Steuben, Baron Friedrich Wilhelm Augustus von (1730–94)
Prussian officer instrumental in training the Continental army.

Sullivan, John (1740–95)
Continental army major general who served widely and led the destruction of Iroquois villages in upper New York.

Tarleton, Banastre (1754–1833)
Boldly unconventional British officer, notorious for his ruthless command of Tories.

Townshend, Charles (1725–67)
British chancellor of the Exchequer whose policies for taxing and otherwise regulating the Anglo-American colonies (1767) galvanized early revolutionary sentiment in the colonies.

Vergennes, Charles Gravier, comte de (c. 1719–87)
French foreign minister under Louis XVI instrumental in negotiating the Franco-American alliance during the American Revolution.

Ward, Artemas (1727–1800)
Highest-ranking officer at the outbreak of the Revolution; one of the two commanders at Bunker Hill (June 17, 1775).

Warren, Joseph (1741–75)
Massachusetts physician who was a prominent activist in the independence movement and who served as a major general at the Battle of Bunker Hill (June 17, 1775), where he was killed.

Washington, George (1732–99)
Commander in chief of the Continental army and first president of the United States; the "Father of His Country."

Wayne, Anthony ("Mad Anthony") (1745–96)
Skillful and daring American general, whose greatest triumphs were Stony Point (1779) and the Battle of Green Spring (1781).

Author's Note

This book is intended to be an answer to the question, "What's a good basic book on the American Revolution?" The approach is purposely concise and, while authoritative, it is nonacademic—meaning that I do not hesitate to resolve controversies with straightforward explanations of the significance of key events. *The Real History of the American Revolution* does not go out of its way to be revisionist, but neither is it a traditional celebration of flag-waving patriotism. This said, I hope the book leaves the reader with an appreciation of just how extraordinary the American Revolution was. History offers many revolutions, but precious few that leave a people unambiguously better off than they were before the revolution. The American Revolution did just that. Moreover, whereas most revolutions become civil wars, resulting in bitter struggles between or among competing factions—struggles that typically outlast the revolutions—the American Revolution produced a nation. It is a nation beset with many problems, to be sure, but unified to a remarkable degree. Finally, the American Revolution brought something unique to the world: an entirely new kind of nation. It was not founded on the claims of some hereditary ruler or as the result of a religious passion or because of some tribal affiliation, but on the basis of a set of ideas articulated in a document: the Declaration of Independence. No nation had ever before come into existence on such a basis.

Is this the only book you need to understand the American Revolution? Of course it isn't. But it is the only book you need to begin this understanding.

PART ONE

The Pursuit of Happiness

Chapter 1

THE CAUSES OF A REVOLUTION

Why Our Founding Fathers Fought Our Mother Country

WE AMERICANS LIKE TO TALK ABOUT OURSELVES in superlatives. The biggest this. The greatest that. The most whatever. Surprisingly enough, a lot of the talk turns out to be true. For instance: We are the most idealistic as well as the most cynical people on the planet. Americans really do believe in life, liberty, and the pursuit of happiness as inalienable (Jefferson actually wrote "unalienable") rights. That's what the American Revolution was all about, right?

Right. But don't walk away after you get that answer. Keep the conversation going long enough, and you'll be sure to hear something to the effect of: Well, yes, there's what Jefferson wrote in the Declaration of Independence and what Patrick Henry (whoever he was) said in a speech about liberty or death (Do I really *have* to choose?), but, you know, when all is said and done, the Revolution was finally all about money, because a bunch of rich colonial merchants and plantation owners got tired of paying their taxes.

Where, exactly, is the truth?

Idealism is often a rosy-colored glass, but that doesn't mean the cynical view is automatically the real truth. And besides, why can't a wealthy merchant or a rich planter have the good of his fellow citizens at heart? After all, life, liberty, and the pursuit of happiness are a lot easier to enjoy with a full wallet. Conversely, when you've got your rights guaranteed it's a lot easier to fill your wallet. So let's begin with an open-minded look at what the fighting, from 1775 to 1783, was all about.

AS TYRANTS GO, WAS KING GEORGE III ALL THAT BAD?

DESPERATION DRIVES MOST REVOLUTIONS. Why else fight, kill, and die? Take the French Revolution (1787–99), for instance. The people of France were hungry, and the nation couldn't feed them. The French king and queen seemed utterly indifferent to the condition of the people and were, in fact, often downright oppressive. There was an important new middle class growing up in France, well-to-do and intelligent, but almost completely excluded from political power. The country had also just raised a crop of cutting-edge political thinkers, the philosophes, who started publishing theories of radical reform.

Or there's the Russian Revolution of 1917. The people of Russia were hungry, and the nation couldn't feed them. The peasantry (the agricultural working class) and the proletariat (the industrial working class) had been excluded from all power, political and economic, for centuries. The czar seemed utterly indifferent to the condition of the people and was often harshly oppressive. Russia had raised a brand-new crop of political leaders, including Lenin and Trotsky—who were inspired by the German social thinkers Marx and Engels—and who had quite a way with people. They gave political and intellectual direction to a collective feeling of despair and desperation.

The French Revolution and the Russian Revolution were complex historical events that took many twists and turns, but, at bottom, they both came to this: the mass exercise of an instinct for survival. In France and in Russia, conditions had become so bad that change, immediate and violent, seemed the only hope. The engine of these revolutions was desperation.

REALITY CHECK:

British for Independence?

The British government was by no means solidly opposed to American independence. A significant liberal minority in Parliament favored it, arguing that it was not only the right thing to do, but that England would continue to enjoy all the benefits of trade with America but without the financial burden of governing and protecting it.

Now, just how desperate were the Americans at the start of the last quarter of the eighteenth century?

No doubt about it, the economics as well as the physical reality of life in the frontier regions were tough. Despite this, no one seems to have been really hungry, let alone starving, there. King George III, his ministers,

New York City revolutionaries tore down a statue of King George III on July 9, 1776, but the highly imaginative Parisian artist who created this print was no eyewitness. Although the statue did depict the king on a horse, surely the revolutionaries were not half-naked slaves wearing turbans.

and many in Parliament were politically stubborn, often inept, sometimes just plain dumb, and, yes, certainly unfair, but neither the Crown nor the government was terribly oppressive in the treatment of the American colonies. Compared to the other major colonial powers of the time—Spain and France—the Brits seemed downright enlightened. Besides, in contrast to the kings of these countries, George III was reined in by a strong national constitution based on the Magna Carta and a tradition of very liberal common law. No wonder that, even after the American Revolution had begun, most Americans continued to feel toward the king at least some loyalty and even affection. In any case, they didn't hate him. In fact, stubborn and imprudent as it could be, the British government showed a significant if grudging willingness to compromise with the colonies and give them a lot of what they asked for.

Look at the list of ingredients that went into the French and Russian revolutions. They are just about identical, and they are powerful. But, face it, the stuff that went into the American Revolution doesn't seem nearly as strong. So what drove our nation's fight for independence?

The Absentee Landlord Problem

"Character," the Greek philosopher Heraclitus declared, "is destiny." If he could have hung around another 2,300 years or so to witness the American Revolution, he might have also said: "Geography is destiny."

Between America and England is the Atlantic Ocean, which was not easily, quickly, or cheaply crossed by the wind-powered wooden ships of the eighteenth century. For that reason alone, the New World and the Old World were very different, very separate worlds. And if it was difficult and slow for people and goods to move back and forth between these worlds, it wasn't any easier or quicker to send letters or documents back and forth. With travel and communications both risky and cumbersome, government was difficult indeed. To govern a country effectively requires recognizing and responding to the needs and wants of the people and to enforce laws and policies upon them. How do you do that when you can't see or hear or talk to those people on a regular daily basis? Does absence make the heart grow fonder? Not in the case of America and England during the eighteenth century. Over the years, as the Americans born in America came to outnumber those who sailed over from England, it became increasingly difficult for the mother country to identify with its distant subjects and for those subjects to feel a compelling affinity for the mother country. As time passed, geography promoted a separate and unique identity for the colonies.

For quite a while, none of this much mattered. The Crown and Parliament, absentee landlords, were just happy to possess in the American colonies a profitable source of raw materials to import and a ready market for manufactured goods to export. Historians say that the mother country practiced a policy of "salutary neglect" toward the colonies, collecting no taxes from them and pretty much leaving them to govern themselves.

THE FRENCH AND INDIAN WAR

WHAT CHANGED THIS HAPPY SITUATION was a series of wars fought from the late seventeenth through the mid-eighteenth centuries in North America between the continent's two principal colonial rivals, England and France, and also involving Indians allied with one power or the other. These wars culminated in what many historians consider the first "world" war. In Europe, India, and even the Pacific, it was called the Seven Years War, but in North America, where it started in 1754, it was called the French and Indian War, and it struck England's North American colonies as an unprecedented catastrophe.

NUMBERS:

The French and Indian War: Troops, Casualties

20,000: Number of British soldiers and sailors serving

13,400: Number of fatalities suffered by British army

Unknown: Number of British wounded

80: Number of months war lasted

The colonists had no choice but to look to the mother country for protection, and that changed everything. On the British side, the military contribution to the French and Indian War created a greatly increased feeling of possessiveness toward the colonies. The Crown suddenly wanted a tighter grip on what it had fought to defend, and there was a sense within much of the British government that the colonists now owed a greater degree of allegiance to the mother country. On a more urgently practical level, prosecuting a major war across an ocean had produced an enormous debt, so that neither King George III nor Parliament was willing to continue the practice of salutary neglect toward the colonies. The government wanted the colonies to help defray the cost of their defense.

This political cartoon accompanied an editorial by Benjamin Franklin calling for American colonies to band together for protection against Indians and the French. First published in the Pennsylvania Gazette *on May 9, 1754.*

These two major shifts in attitude began quickly unknotting the bonds of affection and loyalty that had stretched so thinly across the Atlantic from England to America. Moreover, while the French and Indian War contributed to the patriotic pride some colonists felt in being English, the overall effect of England's military intervention in the war was to create an impression of the mother country's general ineptitude and indifference. Many colonists, especially those who fought or served as officers in colonial militia units (George Washington conspicuous among these) judged British military aid as having been stingy and inadequate. Moreover, British military commanders treated colonial authorities with disrespect and even contempt. They answered to London, not to local officials and certainly not to the American people.

THE KING TRIES TO STUNT COLONIAL GROWTH

THE FRENCH AND INDIAN WAR saved British North America from the French, only to begin losing it for the English. If the war inserted a wedge between England and its colonies, what happened next drove that wedge home.

By the King.

A PROCLAMATION.

GEORGE R.

WHEREAS We have taken into Our Royal confideration the extenfive and valuable acquifitions in America, fecured to Our Crown by the late definitive Treaty of Peace, concluded at Paris, the tenth day of February laft; and being defirous that all our loving fubjects, as well of our Kingdoms as of our Colonies in America, may avail themfelves, with all convenient fpeed, of the great benefits and advantages which muft accrue therefrom to their commerce, manufactures and navigation; We have thought fit, with the advice of our Privy Council, to iffue this our Royal Proclamation, hereby to publifh and declare to all our loving fubjects, that We have, with the advice of our faid Privy Council, granted our Letters Patent under our Great Seal of Great Britain, to erect within the Countries and Iflands, ceded and confirmed to Us by the faid Treaty, four diftinct and feparate Governments, ftiled and called by the names of QUEBEC, EAST FLORIDA, WEST FLORIDA and GRENADA, and limited and bounded as follows, viz:

On October 7, 1763, George III issued a proclamation setting the lawful limit of western settlement at the Appalachian Mountains.

Victory in the French and Indian War wrested control of North America from the French, but the fighting did not stop. The frontier continued to blaze with war between Indians and settlers, perpetuating the drain on the king's purse and army. To put a stop to this, on October 7, 1763, George III issued a proclamation setting the lawful limit of western settlement at the Appalachian Mountains.

> *"It is just and reasonable and essential to our interest and the security of our colonies that the several nations or tribes of Indians with whom we are connected, and who live under our protection should not be molested or disturbed."*
>
> King George III, Proclamation of 1763

At first, the Proclamation of 1763 seemed to work admirably well. It quickly ended the very bloody coda to the French and Indian War known as Pontiac's Rebellion, a seventeen-month conflict in which the Ottawa, Delaware, and Iroquois Indians, loosely led by the Ottawa chief Pontiac, fought colonial British forces in an effort to reclaim lands they lost in the French and Indian War. Yet even as it pacified the Indians, it enraged the settlers. They took the Proclamation Line as something of a royal dare, crossing it in droves to defiantly push settlement into and beyond the forbidden mountains. Predictably, this provoked Indians to raid the trans-Appalachian frontier, and, just as predictably, the Indian raids sent settlers howling for help from royal authorities. The reply of these authorities was that the king had forbidden settling the West, so, in effect, such settlers were on their own.

As a result of the Proclamation of 1763, an interesting change began to occur in North America. By and large, the southeastern coastal region of the continent, known as the Tidewater, contained the most well-established and wealthiest portion of the population. Normally, wealth is associated with conservatism, a desire to maintain the status quo—which, after all, looks pretty good to people who have gold in their pockets. However, the coastal population was also most directly connected with the rest of the world, including the latest in ideas on philosophy, science, and government. This introduced a strong current of liberalism, even radicalism, into the Tidewater. The inland region, the frontier, known as the Piedmont, was poorer and substantially less well established than the Tidewater. While have-nots are usually less conservative than haves—because the status quo has not treated them nearly so well—in pre-Revolutionary America this was not the case. The frontier, isolated from the latest ideas, tended toward both religious and political conservatism. That was before the Proclamation of 1763, which spurred the people of the Piedmont to rebellion in the form of crossing the line. When Indian raids followed the violation of the Proclamation Line, and both the Crown and the Tidewater colonial administration failed to intervene to stop the raids, the hitherto conservative Piedmont became even more radicalized. Royal limits and royal indifference to danger alienated the frontier both from the mother country and from the fat-and-happy "establishment" perched on the Tidewater coast.

A Question of Loyalty

If things were tough in the Piedmont, they were no picnic in the Tidewater, either. As the center of colonial government, the Tidewater, in the years following the Proclamation of 1763, found itself torn between the outcries of the frontier and the demands for obedience that came just as loudly from England. At first, the decision concerning which voice to heed was fairly simple. George and

REALITY CHECK
Biological Warfare or Myth?
Pontiac's Rebellion occasioned an early instance of biological warfare. On June 24, 1763, when a war party of Delawares demanded the surrender of Fort Pitt, the acting commander, Simon Ecuyer, summoned the Delaware chiefs to a conference and presented them with the gift of a handkerchief and two blankets—both from the fort's smallpox-ridden hospital. Ecuyer then revealed what he had done, which prompted the Delawares to retreat. A smallpox epidemic subsequently did sweep through a portion of the tribe, but it is by no means certain that the infected handkerchief and blankets caused it, since the disease was endemic in North America. Some records suggest that the epidemic was already under way before the encounter with Ecuyer, and it is known that the two Delaware chiefs who actually handled the infected items were hale and hearty a month after contact.

his Parliament were the side of the bread that had all the butter. But as the Piedmont and even the regions to its west became more populous, they became more powerful, making the call of king and mother country fade by comparison. Many Tidewater leaders turned away from Europe and toward the West. During much of the earlier English colonial period, the Piedmont had defined itself in opposition to the Tidewater. Now, however, the two regions discovered more and more in common, even as the authority of a distant king came to seem increasingly arbitrary and even tyrannical.

In 1764, the Sugar Act was passed by the English Parliament to offset the war debt brought on by the French and Indian War and to help pay for the expenses of running the colonies. This act increased the duties on imported sugar, textiles, coffee, wines, and indigo dye. It doubled the duties on foreign goods reshipped from England to the colonies and also forbade the import of foreign rum and French wines.

Identity Crisis

Children cling to their parents. Adolescents often run from them— yet, usually, many years will pass before they claim full independence. In contrast to childhood on the one hand and adulthood on the other, adolescence is a period of identity crisis, as the individual, suspended between two stages of life, struggles to define himself or herself. So it was with the American population between the French and Indian War and the Revolution. If the Proclamation of 1763 made settlers angry and brought calls for reform of government, it did not yet provoke demands for outright independence. The fact is that throughout most of the eighteenth century and even during the early years of the American Revolution itself, the majority of colonists thought of themselves not as Americans but as English men and women who happened to live in America. This mind-set created a kind of colonial paradox—really, a profound emotional crisis: While protest, let alone outright revolt, seemed a betrayal of one's very heritage, the colonists were also painfully aware that, while they were expected to be loyal English men and women, they were not being accorded the full rights and privileges of English subjects. We'll get into the details of this in just a minute (and also later in this book), but, for now, we just need to note that, as the colonists saw it, if they were denied rights that their countrymen in Europe had enjoyed since King John signed the Magna Carta in 1215, they were, by definition, victims of tyranny.

An Overly Possessive Mother

Remember, unlike the masses who would fight the French and Russian revolutions, the colonists were not starving, nor were they being oppressed and tortured in the manner of those people. Nevertheless, after the Proclamation of 1763, they began to think of themselves as victims of tyranny. And what king and Parliament did over the next decade or so repeatedly seemed to confirm this impression.

The end of "salutary neglect" not only included the imposition of the Proclamation Line, but also a whole host of new duties and taxes. The first was the Stamp Act of 1765, which required that every paper document, ranging from legal contracts to playing cards, bear a revenue stamp purchased from a royally appointed colonial stamp agent (see page 47). The Stamp Act was only the first and most hated in a series of revenue laws enacted to force the colonies to bear some of the cost of the recently ended French and Indian War. Most of these acts were not taxes as such, but were very restrictive laws regulating and limiting colonial free enterprise by compelling Americans to sell their goods exclusively *to* England and to import other goods exclusively *from* England.

In itself, the negative economic impact of the new taxes, duties, and regulations was bad enough, but the attitude behind these measures made them even worse. Colonists perceived indifference and arrogance. They didn't merely feel financially burdened, they felt abused. That feeling was intensified by the Quartering Act of 1765, which required colonial governments to furnish barracks and provisions for royal troops, the very people charged with enforcing the hated new revenues and regulations. If the taxes and the regulations seemed tyrannical, how much greater a manifestation of tyranny was the presence of armed troops, for whom (to add insult to injury) the colonists were expected to pay?

Just when it seemed impossible to make matters worse, Parliament enacted laws to enhance the enforcement of the odious revenue laws. The new statutes declared that violations of the Stamp Act and the other revenue acts were to be tried not in local colonial

---

ALTERNATE TAKE
United States of England?

If George III and Parliament had chosen not to end the policy of "salutary neglect," Americans would almost certainly have been content to remain English men and women. For the colonists, the concept of tyranny was tied to the feeling of being economically oppressed. Without an economic incentive, the issue of parliamentary representation would likely have remained a mere abstraction, too weak to serve as a motive for war. Living under salutary neglect, the thought of revolution simply may not have occurred to the colonists, and there would have been little reason for the colonies to unite, let alone rebel against the mother country.

DETAILS, DETAILS
Magna Carta

Signed under duress by England's King John in 1215, the Magna Carta was hardly intended as the revolutionary document it is often portrayed as being. It resulted not from a dispute between the king and the common people, but from a disagreement between the Pope and King John on the one hand and the English barons on the other. John and the Pope thought a king should have absolute power, whereas the barons wanted the king to be bound by law. By renouncing certain rights and pledging to respect certain legal procedures, John gave his barons more power. The Magna Carta gave no rights to commoners, but because the king was forced to bend his will to the law, the document was the first step in a very long process that finally produced the supremacy of constitutional law—including, ultimately, the principle of government by consent of the governed. Despite the limited scope and conservative pedigree of the Magna Carta, the document came to acquire, in the course of history, something of the status of a Bill of Rights, as if it really were a guarantee of liberty and justice for all English men and women.

In a none-too-subtle expression of disapproval, this chamber pot is decorated with a portrait of King George III. The photograph shows a reproduction of an authentic pot mounted under a "chair of ease." During the eighteenth century, such decorated chamber pots were common expressions of political satire.

courts, but in vice-admiralty courts, which answered to the Crown rather than to the people of America. Had most colonists of the era truly identified themselves as Americans, this would have been outrageous. But because most still identified themselves as English men and women, it was even worse. For no right was more sacred in English law than trial by a jury of one's peers. It was in the Magna Carta!

TAXATION WITHOUT REPRESENTATION

WE WERE A LONG WAY, IN THE MID 1760s, from the Declaration of Independence of 1776. At the time, the vast majority of colonists were by no means ready to argue that King George and Parliament were attacking their basic human rights. In fact, to most colonists, "human rights" would have been a meaningless phrase. But what was stunningly clear to them was that they were being called upon to behave as loyal British subjects even as they were being denied the rights of English men and women.

On February 24, 1761, a well-respected Boston lawyer named James Otis made a speech against something called "writs of assistance," commands compelling colonial officials to cooperate with royal officers in curbing customs and duties violations. Otis declared that "Taxation without representation is tyranny." John Adams, who heard the speech, wrote to his wife that the impassioned Otis "burned with a fire of flame," and, suddenly, the American colonies had a phrase that put into words the very kernel of their cause. What "Remember the Alamo," "Remember the *Maine,*" and "Remember Pearl Harbor" would be to later generations of Americans, "No taxation without representation" was to this earliest generation— a battle cry. Suddenly, more and more people realized that it wasn't so much the new taxes or even the laws intended to enforce them that made for tyranny, it was the imposition of these things in the absence of any voice in the government that imposed them. Without give and take, there is only theft. When the thief is government, the theft is called tyranny, and no English man or woman could be expected to tolerate it. England was governed, after all, by a hard-won and much-treasured system of parliamentary monarchy, the cardinal principle of which was that Parliament, not the king, levied taxes. And this was crucial, because the people were represented in Parliament and, therefore, the people, through their representatives, determined what taxes could be justly levied and, through their representatives, consented to pay those taxes. Not a penny was extorted by the king. That would be slavery.

The idea that taxation without representation is tyranny prompted some colonial leaders to do nothing more than lobby Parliament for representation. Parliament's reply was the lame theory that, although members of Parliament were elected from geographical districts, they really did not represent the districts that elected them, but each member represented *all* English subjects—even the colonists, who could not vote. In itself, this was hardly a convincing answer to the taxation-without-representation problem. But some colonists went beyond this. They argued that even if king and Parliament *did* agree to some form of colonial representation—which they did not seem about to do—true parliamentary representation for the colonies was a practical impossibility. There was, first of all, the matter of the Atlantic Ocean. Great distance was a barrier to effective representation. Furthermore, the interests of the colonists were often very different and very remote from those of the people of the mother country. Finally, Parliament could never give the growing colonies justly proportional representation—that is, representation that would be fair both to the colonists and to the people of England.

To those colonists with the courage to accept it, the notion that parliamentary representation was simply impossible must have been both disturbing and exciting. Accept that proposition, and what follows is pretty intense: If taxation without representation is

The pro-independence Bickerstaff's Boston Almanack of 1770 featured on its cover this portrait of Boston lawyer James Otis, who coined the influential phrase, "Taxation without representation is tyranny."

TAKEAWAY

Rights of Man

The American Revolution did not begin because the colonists wanted independence from England, but because they believed they were being denied their rights as English men and women. More than anything else, it was the repressive measures King George III, his ministers, and Parliament took against the colonies that finally united them to oppose the mother country.

necessarily tyranny, and representation is impossible, then the only two alternatives are continued acquiescence in a kind of slavery—or independence. And if the Crown would not voluntarily grant that independence, then the only course open would be revolution.

Of Many, One

The designers of every U.S. coin always find a place to stamp the national motto *E pluribus unum,* Latin for "Of many, one." From their creation in the seventeenth and early eighteenth centuries, the colonies never had any trouble getting the "many" part right, but the "one" was of little interest to them. In terms of trade and land acquisition, the colonies competed rather than cooperated with one another. Except in time of major Indian war, the colonies had no reason to unite. Beginning with the Stamp Act and the legislation that followed, however, the Crown and Parliament gave the colonies that reason. United protest against the Stamp Act, in the form of an all-colony boycott of British trade, got the obnoxious law repealed in less than a year. And although other taxes and duties were enacted, *all* of them were repealed by 1770—except, as we'll see in Chapter 4, for the hateful and fateful tax on tea.

The mother country's attempt to coerce compliance from her errant children created a new family, from which the mother was excluded. Protest motivated colonial leaders to develop systems of communication, cooperation, and coordination among the thirteen colonies. It was all for one and one for all, as whatever the royal government did to chastise or punish a particular colony at a particular time was instantly elevated to an event of "national" importance and consequence, something that affected everyone. Through a program of unwise taxes and regulations, the British king and his Parliament unwittingly forged a nation out of a collection of separate, competitive, and often disputatious colonies. The American Revolution was started, really, by the very people who most wanted to prevent it.

Chapter 2

COLONIAL LIVING

The Background of the North American Colonies, with Emphasis on How the English Colonies Grew and Competed with One Another

THE RENAISSANCE, THAT PERIOD OF EUROPEAN HISTORY SPANNING THE LATE FOURTEENTH THROUGH THE MID-SIXTEENTH CENTURIES, was just what the French-derived name says it was: a rebirth of the learning and curiosity that had been more or less dormant during the medieval period preceding it. With rebirth came restlessness and discontent with the status quo. For many people, from commoners to kings, Europe began to feel cramped. Medieval society had been rigorously divided into a tiny aristocracy and a vast peasantry, but now a new social class was growing up, a "middle class" of merchants and artisans. For them, prosperity depended on their finding new and greater sources of import goods as well as markets for what they produced. Within Europe, however, both supply and demand were limited.

That was a real problem for the middle class. But, these days, even the aristocracy was feeling thwarted. Aristocratic Europe was dominated by a system of primogeniture—meaning that a family's eldest son generally inherited all

ALTERNATE TAKE

Vikingland?

In 986, Norse voyager Bjarni Herjólfsson sighted Newfoundland, but didn't bother to land. Around 1000, Viking Leif Eriksson explored the northern coast of what he dubbed "Vinland" (its true location is a matter of debate among historians, who have sited it anywhere from Labrador to New England). Eriksson established a rude settlement at a place in Newfoundland now called L'Anse aux Meadows. His brother-in-law Thorfinn Karlsefni settled in Vinland from 1007–9, and his wife, Gudrid, gave birth to the first Euro-American child— a son named Snorro. Leif the Lucky was from Greenland, which his Norwegian father, Erik the Red, had settled. As Newfoundland was remote from Greenland, so Greenland was remote from Europe, and no one in the Old World seems to have paid any attention to what the Vikings were doing so far away. If they had, European colonization of the New World might have gotten a five-hundred-year head start and have begun up north instead of in the Caribbean.

or most family titles and property on the death of the father. It was a fantastic deal for the firstborn, but it left younger sons to fend for themselves in a Europe pretty well used up, with most noble titles taken and virtually all property claimed.

As for the lowest class, the peasantry, well, the prospects— never good—were dimmer than ever.

COLUMBUS AND COMPANY

BY THE SO-CALLED HIGH RENAISSANCE—the late fifteenth century— what Europe desperately needed was a *new* world. It would be convenient to say next that a Genoese seafarer, Cristoforo Colombo, suddenly offered to find one. Yet, although he may have heard tales about a western realm called Vinland (modern Newfoundland) far across the "Ocean Sea," discovered some five hundred years earlier by the Norseman Leif the "Lucky" Eriksson, Columbus did not propose discovering a new world, but simply finding a new way to get to another part of the old. As everyone who's ever sat through a school pageant knows, in 1492, Colombo—better known to history by his Latinized name, Columbus—persuaded Spain's Queen Isabella and King Ferdinand to finance a voyage to pioneer a sea route to gold-rich and spice-laden Asia. Understanding that the world was round, Columbus wanted to sail west to reach

the East—not as some stunt, but because this route would be much shorter, faster, safer, easier, and cheaper than either sailing all the way down to the stormy southern tip of Africa, then swinging all the way up to the ports of Asia or traveling many thousands of perilous miles via overland caravan, across Europe and the Asian land mass.

This late nineteenth-century classroom chromolithograph (early color print) depicts Christopher Columbus taking possession of "the new country." Fanciful though the image is, its inclusion of priests and soldiers accurately depicts the experience of the Spaniards, who sought to conquer America with a Bible and a sword.

When the lookout aboard Columbus's flagship, the *Santa María,* sighted land on October 12, 1492, Columbus assumed he had reached part of Asia. The Arawak natives he found there—whom he dubbed "Indians," because he was in India, right?—called the place Guanahani, but Columbus christened it San Salvador.

Only after two more voyages—Columbus made four in all—did the Great Navigator conclude that he had found a New World. At first, he and his patrons were disappointed, but, soon enough, the leaders of Spain, Portugal, England, France, the Netherlands, and even Sweden sent out expeditions to claim pieces of this New World.

In 1493, Pope Alexander VI issued a bull that divided a large part of the New World between Portugal and Spain, effectively excluding Portugal from any claim to territory in what would later be called North America. Beginning in the early sixteenth century, the Spanish *conquistadores*—conquerors—swept through much of South and Central America, as well as into what is now the southeastern and southwestern United States. They came, as the saying goes, with a sword in one hand and a Bible in the other, subjugating the Native Americans they encountered even as they sought to save their souls by converting them from heathen error to Catholic truth. Initially, the conquistadores sought gold, which they believed to be abundant in the New World. When this proved illusory, they exploited native labor to harvest the agricultural riches

REALITY CHECK
Samana Cay Theory

In 1882, Gustavus V. Fox, former undersecretary of the navy, presented research supporting Samana Cay, an island in the Bahamas sixty-five miles south of San Salvador, as the site of Columbus's landfall. In 1884, one James B. Murdock pointed out that the Samana Cay theory was not supported by Columbus's log. It was believed that Watling Island (which was even renamed San Salvador in 1925) was the true Guanahani. The Watling–San Salvador theory held sway until 1986, when Joseph Judge and the staff of the *National Geographic* made new calculations based on the Columbus logs and pronounced Samana Cay the most likely landfall after all. The issue remains unresolved.

As this 1685 English map shows, even by the end of the seventeenth century, America was largely a blank unknown, except for those portions that had been explored and claimed by the English or the Spanish.

POP CULTURE
The Black Legend

Bartolomé de Las Casas, a Spanish priest who accompanied the first conquistadores, published in 1552 *A Short Account of the Destruction of the Indies,* in which he documented the atrocities committed by his countrymen. A few years later, he amplified these eyewitness accounts in his *History of the Indies,* bequeathing to the world what became the popular image of Spanish cruelty in America. Based in truth, Las Casas's portrayal was exaggerated over the years into a cultural stereotype of the tyrannical Spaniard known as the "Black Legend," which colored the negative Anglo-American view of Hispanic America. The Black Legend certainly contributed to overwhelming popular support for the U.S.–Mexican War of 1846–48 and the Spanish-American War of 1898.

of the vast region, creating vast *ranchos* over which the dispossessed second and third sons of the Spanish nobility might rule.

ENTER THE ENGLISH

IN 1496, KING HENRY VII commissioned a Genoese seafarer, Giovanni Caboto, whom he called John Cabot, to find what Columbus had not found: a "Passage to India"—a direct route to the spice-rich Indies. This was especially important to England, because, of all European nations, it was the farthest from the traditional avenues of the lucrative Asian trade. Cabot landed in Newfoundland on June 24, 1497, explored probably as far south as Maine, then returned to assure Henry that he had reached the northeast tip of Asia. The king packed him off on a second voyage, and, with two hundred men in five ships, he disappeared at sea.

After Cabot, the Frenchman Jacques Cartier and the Britishers Sir Francis Drake, Martin Frobisher, John Davis, Henry Hudson, Thomas Button, Robert Bylot, and William Baffin all searched in vain for a "Northwest Passage" connecting the Atlantic and Pacific through America. Determined to find the passage, English adventurer Sir Humphrey Gilbert decided to finance exploration by securing a charter from Queen Elizabeth I to settle any lands not already claimed by Christians. Gilbert sailed and claimed Newfoundland in 1583, but, his ship overloaded, sank on the way back to England. His charter passed to his half brother, the dashing Sir Walter Raleigh, a favorite of Queen Elizabeth.

The Enigma of Roanoke

Raleigh sent a reconnaissance fleet in 1584 to what would one day be called Croatan Sound in the Outer Banks of North Carolina. When the fleet returned with glowing reports of a land inhabited by "most gentle, loving, and faithful" Indians who lived "after the manner of the Golden Age," Raleigh dubbed the new land Virginia, after his patroness, Elizabeth the Virgin Queen. Then, in April 1585, he sent Sir Richard Grenville back with a small group of would-be settlers, who landed in June. Grenville returned to England, leaving Ralph Lane in charge of the colony. Visiting in 1586, Sir Francis Drake found them starving and brought them back to England. Raleigh tried again later in 1587, sending three ships with 117 men, women, and children to what is now Roanoke Island, off the coast of North Carolina. Their leader John White planted them in a swamp and went back to England to fetch the supplies Raleigh had promised but had not sent. White's return to the colony was delayed by the attack of the Spanish Armada against England (the same reason why the promised supplies had not been shipped), and he did not get back to Virginia until 1590. What did he find? No one. And nothing except for some rusted hardware and the word "CROATOAN" mysteriously carved into a tree trunk. White speculated that this was a message, indicating that the colonists had fled to Croatoan Island—or had been abducted to it by hostile Indians.

John White returned to his Roanoke colony—in what is today North Carolina's Outer Banks—and discovered that all of the colonists vanished without a trace, save for "CROATOAN" carved into a tree trunk.

Jamestown Takes Root

It was April 1606 before two groups of merchants, the Virginia Company of London (sometimes called the London Company) and the Plymouth Company, secured from King James I another charter to establish a colony in the territory of Raleigh's patent, which was held to encompass whatever portion of North America had not been claimed by Spain. The Virginia Company was granted a charter to colonize southern Virginia, while the Plymouth Company was given rights to northern Virginia.

The Virginia Company recruited 144 settlers, moneyed gentlemen as well as poorer folk (the latter having purchased their passage and right of residence by becoming "indentured servants," binding themselves to labor for the Virginia Company for a period of seven years), who left England in December 1606 aboard the *Susan Constant,* the *Discovery,* and the *Goodspeed.* One hundred five survived the Atlantic passage, arriving on May 14, 1607, at the mouth of a river they named the James, where they cobbled together the small settlement of Jamestown. Historians call it the first *permanent* English colony in the New World—although, soon sick and starving, half the colony was dead within months. Nor did conditions improve anytime soon. The colonists themselves referred to 1608–9 as "the starving time." Unable to grow adequate crops, they resorted to cannibalism, even looting their own fresh graves as well as those of Indians.

Doubtless, those Indians—the Powhatans—debated whether simply to allow these sorry newcomers to die off or to help them. In the end, they decided to help, and it was largely thanks to Chief Wahunsonacock and his Powhatans that Jamestown survived, took root, and even began to prosper as the people cultivated a remarkable plant to which the Indians had introduced them: tobacco.

A great fondness for that weed took Europe by storm, giving Jamestown—and America—its first profitable export commodity. Many of the indentured servants survived to satisfy their seven-year obligations, received ownership of the land they had worked, and became successful tobacco farmers. For the Spaniards, gold had been an elusive lure to the New World. For the English of Virginia, it was tobacco, thanks to which the English presence in America became at last a sure thing.

This nineteenth-century color print depicts the arrival of the Jamestown colonists on May 14, 1607. After enduring two nearly lethal winters, the tiny colony took root and became the first permanent English settlement in America.

Plymouth Pilgrims

Unlike the Spanish, the English settlers of Virginia came neither as conquerors nor as religious zealots, but as people seeking alternatives to the scarcity of economic and social opportunity in the Old World. We might say that they came in search of commercial freedom. Up the coast came a different breed of English settlers, who sought neither conquest nor commerce, but religious freedom. They were the Pilgrims, and the land they claimed is still called New England.

King Henry VIII broke with the Roman Catholic Church in 1534, yet the Church of England he established remained quite similar to the Roman Catholic Church in doctrine and practice. As early as the reign of Henry's daughter Elizabeth I (1558–1603), a group of Anglican priests, most of them graduates of Cambridge University, began to voice their belief that the Church of England was failing in the true reform of worship. By the early seventeenth century, these dissidents were called Puritans (because they wanted to purify Anglicanism of Roman practices), and the Puritan reform movement grew in popularity, especially among England's less affluent, who resented the rich display of the mainstream Anglican Church. William Laud, the Anglican Archbishop during the reign of James's successor, King Charles I, persecuted the Puritans, some of whom fled the country for Holland, a haven of religious tolerance. Others remained in England, where, led by Oliver Cromwell, they waged two civil wars—1642–46 and 1648–51—and beheaded Charles I.

The Puritans who left England before the first civil war were called Separatists and were mostly poor farmers who had nothing to lose by leaving the mother country. However, after living in Holland for a dozen years, they were both poorer and, far worse, deeply distressed that their children were growing up more Dutch than English. These problems drove them to take the radical step of going to America. With help from Sir Edwin Sandys, treasurer of the Virginia Company, they obtained patents authorizing them to settle in the northern part of the company's American territory. On September 16, 1620, 102 immigrants, fewer than half of them Separatists, left Plymouth on the *Mayflower*. The "Pilgrims"—as the Separatists' first historian, William Bradford, later labeled them—sailed to Cape Cod Bay and an advance party landed on December 21, 1620; the rest of the settlers followed on December 26.

Like the first settlers of Virginia, those who landed at the place they named Plymouth had managed to find a most uncongenial spot and time for planting a colony. The season was winter, and the flinty New England soil was at best marginally fertile. More than

FORGOTTEN FACES
Manteo

When Captains Philip Amadas and Arthur Barlowe, the mariners Sir Walter Raleigh sent in 1584 to scout a site for an English colony in North America, returned to England from the North Carolina coast, they carried with them some tobacco plants, potatoes, and two Croatoan Indians, Manteo and Wanchese. Manteo was Christianized in London, and he returned to the Roanoke colony in 1587, where he served as liaison and interpreter between the colonists and the Croatoans. Manteo is commemorated in the name of the North Carolina, town of Manteo.

DETAILS, DETAILS
Powhatans

It was the English who referred to the confederacy of some thirty tribes living in the Virginia Tidewater, the eastern shore of Chesapeake Bay, and part of southern Maryland as the Powhatans, a name derived from the throne name of Chief Wahunsonacock—Powhatan. The name means waterfall and was also the name given to the village of Wahunsonacock's birth, which was near a waterfall.

LINK

Precursor to the Constitution

On November 21, 1620, as the *Mayflower* rode at anchor in Provincetown Harbor, the Pilgrim and the non-Puritan passengers (whom the Pilgrims called "Strangers") drew up the Mayflower Compact, an agreement to cooperate in a "civill body politick . . . for the generall good of the Colonie." The document is considered the first American constitution, anticipating the Constitution under which the United States operates by 168 years.

half the colony was dead before spring. As the Powhatans had helped the Jamestown settlers, so the Wampanoags took pity on the Pilgrims and showed them how to plant and fertilize crops and improvise shelters. Yet while both the New Englanders and the Virginians were English, the Plymouth settlers were made of sterner stuff. Neither moneyed gentlemen nor indentured servants, they were mainly yeoman farmers, unafraid of hard work and fiercely protective of their liberty. In 1627, eight of the most prosperous Pilgrim leaders acquired a six-year monopoly on the local fishery and fur trade in exchange for assuming the colony's obligations to the Virginia Company investors. Thus freed from the enterprise that had backed its founding, the colony took a step toward independence. In 1639, it also made a move toward democracy by creating a representative body of deputies elected annually by the men of the growing colony's seven towns.

Inspired by the example of Plymouth, another group of Puritans, slightly less radical than the Plymouth Separatists, established the Massachusetts Bay Colony in 1630, and during the next dozen years about twenty thousand immigrants arrived, most of them Puritans. The Massachusetts Bay Colony soon overtook the Plymouth settlement in size and prosperity.

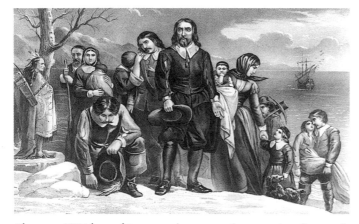

The year 1876 brought the centennial of American independence and, with it, a rush of patriotic Currier & Ives prints, including this highly popular imagining of the Pilgrims' landing at Plymouth, Massachusetts, on December 21, 1620.

The Spirit of Independence

Although the Puritans were revolutionaries who had struggled for religious freedom and who created a genuine form of representative government, they were also intent on enforcing a strict Puritan orthodoxy. When one of their number, the Reverend Roger Williams—who had immigrated from England in 1631—voiced his opinion that lands chartered to Massachusetts and Plymouth actually belonged to the Indians, that a civil government had no authority to enforce religious laws, and that religion flowed from individual conscience and perception, not the Bible or the authority of any clergyman, he and his family were exiled from the Massachusetts Bay Colony in October 1635. Together with a handful of followers, Williams found refuge, in January 1636, among the Indians on Narragansett Bay and purchased from them a modest tract on which he founded a town he called Providence. It was the first settlement in Rhode Island. For the next four decades, Williams welcomed to Rhode Island people of all religious persuasions and created a representative government founded on the principle of religious freedom.

> *"Coerced religion stinks in God's nostrils."*
>
> *Roger Williams*

The Massachusetts Puritans might have been happy to be rid of the likes of Roger Williams, but they were dismayed by the prosperity of heterodox Rhode Island. Even more distressing to them was the colony called Mary Land, which had been founded by Cecil Calvert, Second Baron Baltimore. On March 25, 1634, Calvert and two hundred English Catholics had landed on an island at the mouth of the Potomac, which they named St. Clement's Island (modern St. Clement's Island State Park). Mary Land—later Maryland—not only became a haven for Catholics (who were persecuted by Anglicans and Puritans alike), but when its colonial assembly passed An Act Concerning Religion in 1649, it became the first American colony to guarantee by law freedom of worship (provided, of course, that it was Christian worship).

Diversity and independence of religion in America were extended even further when members of another persecuted sect, the Society of Friends—more familiarly called Quakers because some believers shuddered and quaked during worship—settled in Pennsylvania under the leadership of William Penn in 1682. The Quakers believed in the absolute "immediacy" of Christ's teachings and were persuaded that knowledge of God could not be mediated through Scripture, ceremony, ritual, or clergy. Revelation came to each person individually in the form of an "inward light." Whereas most nations adopted warlike Latin mottoes to adorn their official seals, Penn designed a seal inscribed with the words "Mercy, Justice, Truth,

POP CULTURE
The First Turkey

In 1621, the Pilgrims and the Wampanoags signed a treaty of peace at Strawberry Hill in Plymouth. Later, the settlers and the Native Americans shared a harvest meal, which some historians cite as the predecessor of the modern Thanksgiving holiday. It is possible that wild turkey was on the menu, but goose and duck were far more likely. The colonists' Wampanoag guests—who outnumbered their hosts by about ninety to fifty—almost certainly brought venison, fish, eel, and shellfish. Beer was the drink of choice. Cranberry sauce and pumpkin pie were nowhere to be had. Nor was this Thanksgiving over and done with in a single day. The feast seems to have occupied about one week.

The early twentieth-century American painter Jean Leon Gerome Ferris depicted William Penn in 1682 being greeted by the inhabitants of his proprietary colony, Pennsylvania.

Peace, Love, Plenty" and quickly drew up "a treaty of friendship" with the local Indians. Penn also promulgated the "Great Law" of Pennsylvania, which extended the right to vote to any man (women were excluded) who professed a belief in God and met modest property requirements. The Great Law also abolished most imprisonment for debt and restricted capital punishment to cases of treason and murder. Fully a century before the Bill of Rights was added to the United States Constitution, the Great Law decreed that no person could be deprived of life, liberty, or estate (property) without an impartial jury trial.

Despite profound differences from the other colonies, especially Puritan New England, Pennsylvania shared with those other settlements the hope of creating a better life. In founding Georgia in 1732–33, James Edward Oglethorpe had an even more explicitly utopian purpose. Not only did he intend to create a haven of religious freedom, but also an alternative for debtors imprisoned in England and for others convicted of certain criminal offenses. Oglethorpe believed that the colony would give the debtors a fresh start and rehabilitate the criminals. He enacted laws prohibiting the sale of rum, forbidding slavery, and limiting individual land holdings to fifty-five-acre farms in order to promote equality. Oglethorpe's bold experiment soon faltered, unfortunately, as each of the utopian laws was abandoned.

Colonies Disunited

Assailed by one disappointment after another, James Oglethorpe left Georgia and returned to England. What most grieved him was the introduction of slaves into his colony. By the time Georgia had been fully established in 1733, slavery in America was already more than a century old. The first twenty African slaves had been imported by Dutch traders at the behest of the Virginia tobacco farmers in 1619, barely a dozen years after Jamestown had struggled into being. These first unwilling immigrants to America were regarded as neither of higher nor lower class than white indentured servants, but as southern plantations became larger and larger, the demand for African slavery grew and became an important part of the entire colonial economy.

The slave trade was one leg of what historians call the "triangle trade," a pattern of commerce in which ships leaving England with trade goods landed on the African west coast, traded the merchandise for slaves, then transported their living cargo to the West Indies or the mainland English colonies. In these places, the slaves were traded for the very agricultural products—chiefly sugar, tobacco, and rice—that slave labor had produced. The final leg of the triangle was the return voyage to England, by ships laden with New World produce to trade for English manufactured goods.

Despite the fact that all of the colonies shared in the triangle trade—and thus reaped the economic benefits of slavery—the keeping of slaves on a large scale became increasingly associated with the large southern plantations, which required a lot of cheap labor. In contrast, the small farmers to the north had little use for slave labor. Over the years, in the North, these economic facts combined with moral objections to slavery and contributed to a growing alienation between the southern and northern colonies. Along with the various religious differences among the colonies, the fierce economic competition among them, and the competition for possession of western lands, slavery was one of the issues that divided rather than united the colonies. During the seventeenth century and through at least the first half of the eighteenth, the English colonists thought of themselves first and foremost as English men and women, then as Virginians, Georgians, New Englanders, and so on. The one thing they did not consider themselves was Americans.

NEW FRANCE

AND THE COLONISTS PROBABLY would have continued in disunity had it not been for competition of another kind. At about the time that the English scratched out their precarious toehold in Virginia, the French started exploring the continent. Although "Black robes"—Catholic missionaries—followed close behind the French explorers, religion was not as compelling a motive for French settlement as it was for the Spanish or among many of the English. Rather, Cardinal Richelieu, the power behind the throne of the weak-willed King

DETAILS, DETAILS
Thomas Hooker

Born in Leicestershire, England, in 1586, Thomas Hooker became a Puritan pastor and, like many other Puritans, fled to Holland to avoid persecution. He then immigrated to the Massachusetts Bay Colony in 1633 and, three years later, led a group of followers to Hartford, Connecticut. Hooker objected to limiting voting rights to church members and, to the Connecticut General Court in 1638, he protested that the right of the people to elect their magistrates was a gift of God, not the church. For this view—and for his Fundamental Orders for Governing Connecticut (1639), which advocated liberalized church and civil government—Hooker has sometimes been called "the father of American democracy."

The intrepid French explorers of the Mississippi, Father Jacques Marquette (standing) and Louis Joliet (or Jolliet) descend the river in 1673. This wood engraving is from the nineteenth century.

NUMBERS
Population Count

By the beginning of the eighteenth century, the population of the English colonies was about 250,000 and growing rapidly, whereas that of New France was 25,000 in Quebec, the center of French colonial population.

Louis XIII, saw New World territory as a source from which France could finance its bid for dominance among European nations. Richelieu sponsored seven voyages by Samuel de Champlain between 1603 and 1616, during which the explorer mapped the Atlantic coast from the Bay of Fundy to Cape Cod, established settlements, and founded the French fur trade. He also made alliances with the Algonquin and Huron tribes against the tribes of the powerful Iroquois League, which would prove of great importance in the military struggles between the French and English in North America spanning the late seventeenth through the mid-eighteenth centuries. In 1608, Champlain founded Quebec and ultimately secured the entire St. Lawrence valley region for France.

Champlain proved worthy of his wily patron Richelieu. Even as he enthusiastically promoted Canada to the cardinal and the king, he discouraged full-scale colonization because his aim was to operate Quebec as his exclusive trading post. Thus it was 1628 before New France had its first farmer, and the development of the colony lagged far behind the colonies of England. This was a situation Louis XIII's son and successor, Louis XIV, sought to remedy. He saw New France not merely as a source of quick trade profit, but as the anchor of a worldwide empire, and, beginning in the mid-seventeenth century, he encouraged rapid colonization. For him, that meant establishing farms, not pushing exploration westward. Nevertheless, Louis XIV's *intendant* (chief administrator) in Canada, Jean Baptiste Talon, defied royal policy by sending a fur trader named Louis Joliet, in company with a Jesuit priest named Jacques Marquette, to travel west in search of the ever-attractive, ever-elusive Northwest Passage.

In the end, although he failed to find the passage, Joliet did reach the Mississippi River and claimed for France a vast portion of what one day would be the United States. Wisely, in a gesture intended to placate his sovereign, Joliet called the great territory Louisiana, which encompassed (as Joliet and Louis saw it) all that lay between the Appalachian and Rocky mountains. On any map, the expanse now claimed by France dwarfed that claimed by England; however, whereas the English territories bristled with cities and settlements, even by the end of the Sun King's long reign in 1715, New France consisted of just a handful of precarious outposts sown over vast spaces in Nova Scotia, along the St. Lawrence River, and in Louisiana.

NEW NETHERLAND

TRADITIONAL EUROPEAN RIVALS, the French and the English would inevitably square off against each other in America as well. Both powers, however, faced competition from a third. In 1609, an Englishman, Henry Hudson, sailed in the Dutch service up the river that now bears his name in search of—what else?—the Northwest Passage. Although he failed to find it, his voyage as far as the site of modern Albany nevertheless gave the Netherlands a claim to the richest fur-bearing region of North America south of the St. Lawrence River. In the beginning, only a handful of Dutch sea captains visited the newly claimed region to trade for furs with the Indians, but, in 1621, the Dutch West India Company was founded. This financial powerhouse backed the creation of New Netherland in 1623. The following year, the company built a trading post at Fort Orange (Albany), and Peter Minuit arrived as first director-general of the Dutch colony. On August 10, 1626, Minuit purchased Manhattan Island from the Manhattans, a band of the Delaware tribe, for trade goods that a nineteenth-century historian valued at the equivalent of $24. He built a fort at the tip of the island and called it New Amsterdam, a bustling place that soon became the nucleus of the fur trade.

In contrast to the Spanish, English, and French, the Dutch were initially far more interested in trade than in acquiring land. This avoided most of the deadly conflicts with Indians that often afflicted the other colonial contenders. Only after the local supply of beavers dwindled did the Dutch begin to stake out farms, and, with this, the Dutch colonists and the Indians fell to fighting.

As the expenses of war replaced the profits of trade, the Dutch West India Company in 1645 recalled to Holland the brutal and inept governor, Willem Kieft, and replaced him with a tough, peg-legged son of a Calvinist minister, Peter Stuyvesant. He saw his job as simultaneously suppressing the Indians while whipping the colonists into shape. Stuyvesant set about building a defensive wall to protect New Amsterdam from Indian raids (the site of this structure is modern Wall Street) and instituted a campaign of persecution against Quakers and Lutherans (whom he thought likely to foment a rebellion).

Eyewitness

Governor Willem Kieft used terror tactics in an effort to intimidate and dominate the Indians who lived in the vicinity of New Amsterdam. In February 1643, he turned the Mohawks—important trading partners of the Dutch—loose on the Wappingers, who fled to Pavonia (today Jersey City, New Jersey) after the Mohawks had killed seventy of them and enslaved others. David Pietersz de Vries, a Dutch "artillery master," had dinner with Kieft on February 24. As de Vries sat "at table with the governor, Kieft began to state his intentions, that he had a mind to wipe the mouths of the Indians," by which de Vries understood that Kieft intended to let loose a general massacre on the Wappingers who had taken refuge at Pavonia. "Stop this work," deVries pleaded. "You wish to break the mouths of the Indians, but you will also murder our own nation."

De Vries's words fell on deaf ears. During the night of February 25, Kieft sent Dutch soldiers across the Hudson River into Pavonia. Most of the refugees there were women and children, whom the Mohawks had been reluctant to harm. The night of mayhem that ensued became infamous throughout the colonies as the Slaughter of the Innocents. The troops returned to New Amsterdam bearing the severed heads of eighty Indians, which soldiers and citizens used as footballs on the streets of New Amsterdam. Thirty prisoners also taken were tortured to death for the public amusement. De Vries recalled:

> I remained that night at the governor's, sitting up. I went and sat in the kitchen, when, about midnight, I heard a great shrieking, and I ran to the ramparts of the fort, and looked over to Pavonia. Saw nothing but firing, and heard the shrieks of the Indians murdered in their sleep. . . . When it was day the soldiers returned to the fort, having massacred or murdered eighty Indians, and considering that they had done a deed of Roman valour, in murdering so many in their sleep; where infants were torn from their mother's breasts, and hacked to pieces in the presence of the parents, and the pieces thrown into the fire and in the water, and other sucklings were bound to small boards, and then cut, stuck, and pierced, and miserably massacred in a manner to move a heart of stone. Some were thrown into the river, and when the fathers and mothers endeavoured to save them, the soldiers would not let them come on land, but made both parents and children drown,—children from five to six years of age, and also some decrepit persons. Many fled from this scene, and concealed themselves in the neighbouring sedge, and when it was morning, came out to beg a piece of bread, and to be permitted to warm themselves; but they were murdered in cold blood and tossed into the water. Some came by our lands in the country with their hands, some with their legs cut off, and some holding their entrails in their arms. . . . At another place, on the same night at Corler's [Corlear's] Hook on Corler's plantation, forty Indians were in the same manner attacked in their sleep.

Not surprisingly, New Amsterdam and its outlying dependencies were plunged into war with no fewer than eleven Indian tribes. De Vries reported: "When now the Indians destroyed so many farms and men in revenge for their people, I went to Governor William Kieft, and asked him if it was not as I had said it would be, that he would only effect the spilling of Christian blood. Who would now compensate us for our losses? But he gave no answer."

Relations between New Netherland and New England became strained as the colonies fiercely competed for Indian loyalty and trade. Although both England and France lost a good deal of revenue to Dutch competition, New Netherland soon found itself on the verge of self-destruction. Stuyvesant's despotism did not tend to create loyalty among the citizens of his colony, and the system of settlement imposed by the Dutch West India Company created even greater discontent. In contrast to English and French colonists, who owned their land and therefore had an immediate personal stake in their colonies, the Dutch settlement was subject to the patroon system, by which land grants were made to absentee landlords who installed tenant farmers. Thus New Netherland was a colony of tenants rather than owners, and, on September 8, 1664, when a fleet of British warships sailed up the Hudson to seize New Netherland, the Dutch colonists offered no resistance. A fuming Stuyvesant had no choice other than surrender. In this way, New Netherland passed bloodlessly to the British, who renamed both the colony and its chief town New York, after the Duke of York (the future King James II). As for the Dutch residents, their lives continued much as they had before, living now in peaceful coexistence with English colonists. Even Peter Stuyvesant retired peacefully to his *bouwerij,* the old Dutch word for farm (the road that led to his farm is the site of present-day Bowery Street).

Try as he might, Peter Stuyvesant, the crusty peg-legged governor of New Netherland, could not rally Dutch colonists to resist the British takeover of the colony in 1664. In this early twentieth-century painting, colonists plead with Stuyvesant not to fire on the British ships in what would become New York Harbor.

FIRES IN THE WILDERNESS

WITH THE ABSORPTION OF NEW NETHERLAND, the English now dominated the eastern seaboard below Canada. Yet the English colonial merchants were hardly free agents. England's colonies existed under what historians have labeled the mercantile system, which was a form of economic nationalism in which the colonies were held to exist solely for the enrichment of the mother country. That is, the colonies would furnish England with gold, silver, raw materials, and markets. Trade with other nations was either prohibited or strictly limited, and, at that, was subject to taxation for the benefit of the mother country.

As we will see in the next chapter, the policies and legislation that grew out of the mercantile system were the most immediate causes of the American Revolution. But why did the colonists wait so long to fight for economic freedom?

Well, they had a lot on their plates.

War was the colonies' constant and unwelcome companion. The early wars were between the Indians and the colonists, but, beginning in the late-sixteenth century, a series of conflicts erupted between the two great North American colonial rivals, France and Britain (with some involvement by Spain), and were conducted in large measure through Indian proxies. The early wars—between colonists and Indians—were almost always provoked by land disputes; the wars between the colonial powers likewise put territorial control at stake, but they were also direct extensions of European conflicts. They were, in effect, the New World theater of Old World wars.

King William's War

The first of these conflicts in North America was King William's War, named for Britain's William III, who, shortly after he ascended the throne, formed the Grand Alliance on May 12, 1689, with Austria and the Netherlands. This coalition opposed France's Louis XIV, who had invaded the Rhenish Palatinate (southwestern Germany) on September 24, 1688. In Europe, the war that broke out was a nine-year struggle known as the War of the Grand Alliance or the Nine Years War. Although the Rhenish Palatinate was a very long way from North America, the European conflict nevertheless enflamed the chronic hostilities between the French and English colonists.

King William's War pitted the French and Abenakis (of northern New England and southeastern Canada) against the English colonists and their Iroquois allies. The result was a long and bloody series of guerilla engagements, mostly on the frontier. Although King William's War was officially ended in September 1697 by the Treaty of Ryswick—which concluded the War of the League of Augsburg in Europe—sporadic fighting continued, connecting King William's War with the next major conflict, Queen Anne's War.

Eyewitness

In September 1694, Indians raided Deerfield, Massachusetts. One of the survivors, John Williams, the town's minister, wrote a harrowing account of the raid, typical of the colonial wars in which Indians were employed both by the English and the French as instruments of terror:

> They came to my house in the beginning of the onset, and by their violent endeavors to break open doors and windows, with axes and hatchets, awaked me out of sleep; on which I leaped out of bed, and, running towards the door, perceived the enemy making their entrance into the house. I called to awaken two soldiers in the chamber, and returning toward my bedside for my arms, the enemy immediately broke into the room, I judge to the number of twenty, with painted faces, and hideous acclamations. I reached up my hands to the bed-tester for my pistol, uttering a short petition to God. . . . Taking down my pistol, I cocked it, and put it to the breast of the first Indian that came up; but my pistol missing fire, I was seized by three Indians, who disarmed me, and bound me naked, as I was in my [night]shirt, and so I stood for near the space of an hour. Binding me, they told me they would carry me to Quebeck. . . .

> I cannot relate the distressing care I had for my dear wife, who had lain in [given birth] but a few weeks before; and for my poor children, family, and Christian neighbors. The enemy fell to rifling the house, and entered in great numbers into every room . . . The enemies . . . insulted over me awhile, holding up hatchets over my head, threatening to burn all I had; but yet God, beyond expectation, made us in a great measure to be pitied; for though some were so cruel and barbarous as to take and carry to the door two of my children and murder them, as also a negro woman; yet they gave me liberty to put on my clothes, keeping me bound with a cord on one arm, till I put on my clothes to the other; and then changing my cord, they let me dress myself, and then pinioned me again. Gave liberty to my dear wife to dress herself and our remaining children.

> There followed a three-hundred-mile winter march to Quebec, which the reverend's wife (from whom he became separated on the journey) did not survive: "I asked each of the prisoners (as they passed by me) after her, and heard that, passing through [a river], she fell down, and was plunged over head and ears in the water; after which she travelled not far, for at the foot of that mountain, the cruel and bloodthirsty savage who took her slew her with his hatchet at one stroke, the tidings of which were very awful."

Queen Anne's War

Like King William's War, Queen Anne's War was the American the-
ater of a larger European conflict. In 1701, England, the
Netherlands, and Austria, fearful of an alliance between France and
Spain, formed a new anti-French Grand Alliance a year after King
Charles II of Spain, a Hapsburg, died, having chosen a Bourbon as
his successor. The French supported Charles's nominee, Philip of
Anjou, a grandson of Louis XIV, whereas England, Holland, and
Austria favored the second son of Hapsburg emperor Leopold I, an
obscure Bavarian archduke named Charles.

The War of the Spanish Succession was declared in Europe on
May 4, 1702. In America it took its name from the reigning queen of
England and began on September 10, 1702, when the South Carolina
legislature authorized an expedition to seize the Spanish-held fort
and town of St. Augustine, Florida. When the fort successfully
resisted a siege, the English colonial troops sacked St. Augustine,
pillaging and then burning it. The destruction of nearby Indian
villages brought retaliatory Indian raids, to which South
Carolinians responded by
sending a mixed force of
militiamen and Chickasaws
to ravage the territory of
the Appalachee tribe of
western Florida and to
destroy the Spanish missions
in the country. This opened
a path into the very heart
of the Louisiana territory,
prompting the French
to recruit allies among
tribes in the South as
well as the North.
From Nova Scotia to
the Gulf of Mexico,
the North American
frontier was in flames,
as French-allied Indians
fought the English and

*Currier & Ives's nine-
teenth-century print
depicts England's King
William III, for whom
King William's War
(1689–97) was named.*

British merchant captain Robert Jenkins displays his severed ear to Prime Minister Robert Walpole (seated and apparently none too eager to examine the item), claiming that Spanish coast guards had cut it off. This scene never actually took place, but Jenkins's claim (which most historians dispute) triggered the War of Jenkins's Ear (1739) between England and Spain, leading to the War of the Austrian Succession (1740–48) in Europe and, in North America, the overlapping King George's War (1744–48), in which England squared off against the colonists of France and Spain.

English-allied Indians fought the French and both sets of Indians fought one another. The war was not marked by European-style battles between great armies, but was a dreary chain of raids and counterraids, which did not end until the Treaty of Utrecht was concluded in that Dutch city on July 13, 1713. The treaty gave Hudson Bay and Acadia to the English, but the boundaries between French Canada and the English colonies remained unsettled and continued to loom as a cause of war.

After Britain and Spain made peace in Queen Anne's War, Britain was granted an *asiento,* a contract that permitted the English to trade with the Spanish colonies in goods and slaves. No sooner was this agreement made, however, than British traders abused its privileges, provoking a Spanish crackdown on smugglers. One English sea captain, Robert Jenkins, claimed that Spanish coast guards cut off his ear during an interrogation. As the Brits saw it, a missing ear was worth a war, and in 1739 the "War of Jenkins's Ear" erupted between England and Spain. In less than a year, this conflict merged with a much greater war, called in Europe the War of the Austrian Succession (1740–48).

King George's War

The new war had been provoked by the death of Holy Roman Emperor Charles VI in 1740, which brought a number of challenges to the succession of his daughter Maria Theresa as monarch of the

REALITY CHECK
Blade or Brawl?

Historians do not doubt that Captain Jenkins lost an ear, but most scholars are persuaded that he had lost it in a barroom brawl rather than to a Spaniard's blade.

Hapsburg lands. Wanting to advance his claim to the Hapsburg territories, King Frederick the Great of Prussia invaded Silesia. France, Spain, Bavaria, and Saxony sided with him, while Britain came to the aid of Maria Theresa. As usual, the fight ignited war in North America, where it was called King George's War, after King George II of England.

Georgia's James Oglethorpe made the first offensive move, leading an invasion into Spanish-held Florida during January 1740. Aided in the west by the Creeks, Cherokees, and Chickasaws, Oglethorpe captured Fort San Francisco de Pupo and Fort Picolata, both on the San Juan River. From May through July, he laid siege to St. Augustine, but withdrew when Spanish forces menaced him from behind. He made a second attempt to capture St. Augustine in 1743, failed, and withdrew from Florida altogether. In the meantime, up north, the British managed to capture Louisbourg on Cape Breton Island, Nova Scotia, with its formidable fort that guarded the approach to the St. Lawrence River. Apart from this engagement, however, King George's War was like the other colonial wars before it, a succession of frontier raids and retaliations, of brutal murders rather than formal military battles, most of them carried out by Indians. In the end—and the end came with the European Treaty of Aix-la-Chapelle on October 18, 1748—King George's War achieved little for either the British or the French in North America, except to establish some enduring alliances with Indian tribes. By the end of the war, the Iroquois tribes (especially the Mohawks) had grown close to the English, while many of the non-Iroquois, Algonquian-speaking tribes sided with the French. These alliances would be crucial in the last great North American conflict before the American Revolution: the French and Indian War.

THE FRENCH AND INDIAN WAR

ON MARCH 27, 1749, less than a year after signing the Treaty of Aix-la-Chapelle, King George II granted huge tracts of wilderness land to a group of investors calling themselves the Ohio Company. English settlers now began penetrating regions, mainly in southwestern Pennsylvania, that the French regarded as their exclusive province. To block the English advance, the French built a chain string of forts through the far frontier, stretching from New Orleans up to

Montreal. The forts alarmed the British colonists, among whom war fever began to spread. In London, the king's minister, Lord Halifax, was not immune to the contagion and declared that, by trading with Indians in the Ohio valley, France had invaded Virginia. The governor of that colony, Robert Dinwiddie, commissioned a twenty-one-year-old Virginia militia major named George Washington to carry an ultimatum to the French invaders: Leave or be evicted by force.

Accompanied by a small force, Washington delivered the message to the commandant of Fort LeBoeuf (modern-day Waterford, Pennsylvania) on December 12, 1753. When Washington reported to Dinwiddie that the Frenchman had rebuffed the challenge, the governor ordered the erection of a British fort at the "forks of Ohio," the junction of the Ohio, Monongahela, and Allegheny rivers—the site of present-day Pittsburgh—considered the gateway to the western frontier.

The French calmly watched the building of the fort, then, in April 1754, they attacked and, on the seventeenth, seized the rude stockade from its British builders, improved it, and called it Fort Duquesne. Unaware of this reversal, Dinwiddie sent Washington—now a lieutenant colonel—with a few hundred men to reinforce the fort. Along the way, on May 28, Washington surprised a thirty-three-man French reconnaissance party, ambushed them, and killed ten.

This fifteen-minute skirmish must be counted as the first "battle" of the French and Indian War. But Washington did not have long to savor his victory. Aware that the French would retaliate in force, he cobbled together a makeshift stockade at Great Meadows, Pennsylvania, where he planned to make a stand, hoping to hold off the attack until the arrival of reinforcements. He dubbed it Fort Necessity.

The anticipated attack came on July 3. On the very next day—July 4—Washington, having lost half his command, surrendered. He and the other survivors were permitted to leave, save for two hostages, who were taken back to Fort Duquesne. It was the first of many bitter English defeats in the French and Indian War, the worst of which came when British brigadier general Edward Braddock led about 2,500 men, mostly British regular troops, in a campaign to retake Fort Duquesne. On July 9, 1755, an advance guard of 1,459 officers and men—including Washington and a regiment of

This contemporary engraving depicts the defeat and death of British general Edward Braddock in the Battle of the Wilderness (July 9, 1755).

Virginians—was camped near the fort, preparing to assault it. With no more than 72 French regulars, 146 Canadian militiamen, and 637 Indian allies, the French made a preemptive surprise attack. Braddock's regulars made no attempt to adapt European combat tactics to the wilderness. Like good soldiers, they tried to stand neatly in their ranks and fire. And it was in this attitude that they were mowed down like so many sheaves of standing wheat.

Panic ensued. It was said that many redcoats huddled together, sheeplike, awaiting the inevitable blow of a hatchet. Braddock himself was mortally wounded, and of nearly 1,500 men engaged, only 462 returned—among them George Washington, who had had two horses shot from under him and now owned a coat pierced through by four bullets.

"Who would have thought it? We shall do better next time."

Edward Braddock's dying words

NUMBERS
The Seven Years War: Casualties

Historians estimate that military deaths in the Seven Years War (including those in the French and Indian War) totaled 868,000 from battle and from disease.

Steadily, during 1755–56, the situation in North America went from bad to worse for the English, who lost more and more territory to the French. Only after William Pitt (the Elder) became British secretary of state for the southern department—a post that put him in charge of American colonial affairs—did the colonies receive more skillful British officers and larger contingents of troops, both of which helped turn the tide. The British now became increasingly committed to a North American war, which had merged with a much larger conflict that engulfed most of Europe and European colonies as far away as India. What was called in America the French and Indian War became in Europe the Seven Years War. Although the English suffered defeat at Lake George, New York, in 1758, as well as at Fort Ticonderoga in the same colony, they retook Fort Duquesne. The following year, Fort

Niagara fell to the English, and then, on September 14, Quebec was lost to the French in a fifteen-minute battle between two young generals, Britain's James Wolfe and France's Marquis de Montcalm, both of whom died in the struggle.

The loss of Quebec spelled the end of New France. In triumph, England declared war on France's ally Spain in 1762, successfully attacking Spanish outposts in the Caribbean and Cuba. The French and Indian War was ended by the Treaty of Paris on February 10, 1763, which also concluded the Seven Years War. France yielded all of North America east of the Mississippi River (save New Orleans), and Spain ceded eastern and western Florida to the English, in return for being allowed to keep Cuba.

A Lesson of War

Britain had won but was left with a crippling war debt, which prompted the government to levy unprecedented taxes on the colonies during the next several years. As the Crown and Parliament saw it, this was only just. The colonies should help pay for their own defense. For some colonists, the Anglo-American victory in the French and Indian War was a source of pride and did, in fact, produce gratitude toward the mother country and a sense of obligation to her. But many others saw the victory as having been achieved not thanks to, but in spite of, British regular officers and troops. Victory had been, they believed, a feat of *American* arms. Instead of focusing on the culminating British triumphs in the war, these colonists remembered the long string of British defeats, humiliations, and disasters that had come before.

Defense had long been a principal reason for loyalty to the mother country. Now a growing number of Americans were asking: *Why should we depend for our defense on the likes of the British army?* And the question that followed was even more pointed: *Why should we endure increasingly burdensome taxes to pay for such a defense?* In the years that followed the end of this culminating war for domination of North America, many Anglo-American colonists could find only one answer to both questions: *We should not.* For them, that answer was the lesson of the war and a reason to seek independence.

TAKEAWAY
Seeds of Unity
The English colonies in America faced many dangers, including competition from Indians and the colonies of other European powers. Yet the English colonies were slow to unite, and only after the mixed performance of the British military in the French and Indian War, together with the increasingly oppressive British taxes that followed the war, did large numbers of colonists think about uniting for independence.

Chapter 3

HARD ACTS AND SHOCKING IDEAS

*How British Policies after the French and Indian War
Created Fertile Ground for an American Revolution*

J HE FRENCH AND INDIAN WAR GOT THE COLONISTS THINKING. Some, to be sure, were grateful to Britain for defending them against the French and, even more, against the Indians, but a growing number were coming to believe that the colonial militia and volunteers had done a better job of fighting than the British regulars and that maybe, just maybe, the colonies had outgrown their need for a mother country.

GEORGE, BE A KING!

FREDERICK LOUIS, THE PRINCE OF WALES, was the firstborn son of King George II. He did not please his father, who called him "the greatest beast in the whole world," adding, "and I most heartily wish he were out of it"—the antecedent of "it" being "world." When he came of age, this unloved son married Princess Augusta of Saxe-Gotha and sired, in 1738, the baby who would become George III, one of nine offspring, none of whom seemed terribly promising.

"Had he been born in different circumstances, it is unlikely that he could have earned a living except as an unskilled laborer."

British historian J. H. Plumb, about George III

The British historian J. H. Plumb called young George "a clod of a boy whom no one could teach," and notes that his mother repeatedly scolded him, "George, be a king!" But no one expected that he would have to be a king anytime soon. However, one day in 1751, while playing tennis or cricket, George's father, the Prince of Wales, was struck by an errant ball, never recovered from the blow, and was dead within two weeks. This suddenly put Frederick Louis's son in line behind George II. When George II died on October 25, 1760, twenty-two-year-old George III was crowned king.

Perhaps with his mother's words still ringing in his ears, George III was eager to prove himself a king. One of his very first concerns was to raise money to defray the ruinous cost of the French and Indian War/Seven Years War, still three years away from ending. Accordingly and with little thought, he boldly approved enforcement of a series of Navigation Acts, quite venerable laws (the first of which had been on the books since the mid-seventeenth century) that simply had never been enforced. The Navigation Acts regulated colonial imports as well as exports, specifying that the colonies had to buy most goods exclusively from Britain and could export many commodities (called "enumerated articles") only to Great Britain or other British colonies.

King George III— "The New England governments are in a state of rebellion, blows must decide whether they are to be subject to this country or independent," the king said to his prime minister in November 1774. "The people are ripe for mischief. . . . We must either master them or totally leave them to themselves and treat them as aliens."

REALITY CHECK

Farmer George: Simpleton or Sophisticate?

Histories of the American Revolution often treat King George III as a simple-minded, loutish tyrant. While it is true that, as a child, he was a slow learner, he exhibited a remarkable intellectual curiosity as he matured, developing a keen interest in botany and agriculture (earning him the nickname "Farmer George") and cultivating a sophisticated court that encouraged and patronized music and art. At least from his eighteenth year onward, George did study hard in an effort to prepare himself for the throne. Far from enjoying the self-assurance of the truly stupid, he was tormented by self-doubt and feelings of inadequacy. Clearly, he wanted to be a good king.

An End to Salutary Neglect

Remember, neither George III nor the Parliament that sat during his reign created the Navigation Acts. They just decided to enforce them, thereby ending a long period during which (as historians have put it) the British government practiced a policy of "salutary neglect" toward the colonies. In effect, Crown and Parliament had been giving the colonies a free ride. In 1760, at the king's urging, the free ride had come to an end.

The king and Parliament began by resurrecting a law enacted under George II in 1755, which authorized royal customs officers to issue "writs of assistance" to local colonial authorities, compelling their cooperation in nabbing smugglers and others who tried to evade the Navigation Acts. As colonists saw it, this was bad enough, but, even worse, a writ of assistance allowed royal officials to search warehouses and even private homes without a court order. Outraged though many colonists were, they were also at the time embroiled in the French and Indian War, so they were in no position to resist enforcement of the Navigation Acts.

The Colonial Cash Cow

George III was pleased that he had found a source of income in the colonies, but not all of the king's ministers thought milking the colonial cash cow was a good idea. William Pitt the Elder, who functioned unofficially as prime minister during 1756–61, thought the new policy was too harsh, would retard colonial development, and (worst of all) would spark disloyalty. Finding Pitt's objections unwelcome, the king engineered his ouster in October 1761 and chose as his replacement as chief adviser the conservative Lord Bute, a man George admired far beyond his actual attainments. Parliament never got on well with Bute and forced his resignation in 1763.

It was bad enough that the king rejected Pitt's moderate advice, but it was even worse that, during the final years of the French and Indian War and its aftermath, when both Britain and her colonies needed a strong, sure, and unified government, George and Parliament managed to create inconsistency verging on political chaos. Bute was followed by Lord Grenville, who was quickly replaced by the Earl of Rockingham, who was in turn supplanted by the return of Pitt—who, however, was almost immediately forced to retire, not by king or Parliament, but by the ravages of mental illness. For two years, during most of 1766–68, Britain was without a prime minister because George decided to keep the post vacant in the hope of Pitt's recovery. He returned to office very briefly, but stepped down again and then became a member of the opposition.

William Pitt the Elder served unofficially as Britain's prime minister during 1756–61 and 1766–68. A champion of liberty for the North American colonies, he opposed the Stamp Act and other onerous taxes on the colonies.

In 1770, the king settled on Sir Frederick North, who would serve as prime minister for the next dozen years. He was precisely what George wanted—but hardly what Britain needed—a royal yes man, who found it quite easy to drown any of his own original ideas or personal convictions in whatever the king willed. A royal servant rather than a genuine statesman, North earned enemies on both sides of the Atlantic. He saw to it that the king and the conservatives in Parliament could continue to milk the colonial cash cow, no matter what this did to the colonies or how it eroded transatlantic relations.

DRAWING THE LINE

TAXATION WAS NOT THE ONLY CRITICAL ISSUE in the decade following the French and Indian War. The French and Indian War was ended not in some American town, but in far-off Paris, with the Treaty of Paris, which concluded the Seven Years War on February 10, 1763. Although the French quit fighting in America, not all of the Indians did. Pontiac, war chief of the Ottawas, called a grand council of Ottawa and other tribal leaders, including those from the Delaware, Seneca (as well as elements of other Iroquois tribes), and the Shawnee. He persuaded the chiefs to mount an attack on Detroit and many of the other western outposts the French had just surrendered to the

MEDICAL MATTERS
The Madness of King George

Like his minister Pitt the Elder, George III was destined to suffer a severe mental collapse, which resulted in frank insanity by 1788. Although the stresses of leadership, including the loss of the American colonies, may have been responsible for the king's breakdown, most modern medical historians believe that he suffered from a physiological ailment, porphyria, in which porphyrins, a constituent of hemoglobin, are overproduced and excreted, intoxicating the nervous system and causing great pain, mania, paralysis, and delirium—symptoms that suggest madness. George recovered and relapsed at least three times before sinking into complete and violent insanity in 1811, whereupon his son ruled as regent until he ascended the throne as George IV on his father's death in 1820.

English. The spasm of violence that tore at the frontier was, if anything, even more brutally concentrated than the French and Indian War had been. It was, however, brief. Soon persuaded that the supply of British and colonial troops was inexhaustible, Pontiac and the others came to the peace table, where they found that the government of George III had something very promising to offer.

In 1758, during the height of the French and Indian War—when the British were struggling—the Treaty of Easton was instrumental in turning the tide against the French. By this treaty, Britain and its colonies promised the Delaware—who had been powerful allies of the French—that white settlement would go no farther than the Allegheny Mountains. Persuaded that the English no longer wanted to invade their western lands, the Delaware abandoned the French.

The Ottawa chief Pontiac rallied the leaders of other tribes to resist English incursions into Indian lands. The result was Pontiac's Rebellion (1763–66), a bloody coda to the French and Indian War.

As it turned out, the Anglo-Americans almost instantly violated the Treaty of Easton by pushing settlement beyond the Alleghenies; however, George III and his advisers believed that the intent of the Treaty of Easton had been correct and effective. Create a buffer zone between the Indians and the colonists, and peace could be maintained—without the expense of war. Acting on this insight, on October 7, 1763, George issued a proclamation that pushed back the limit of western settlement from the Allegheny Mountains to the eastern part of the Appalachian Mountains. Presented to Pontiac and the others, the Proclamation of 1763 ended the bloody "rebellion" on the part of the Indians.

Unfortunately for king and kingdom, although the Proclamation Line placated the Indians, it stirred rebellion among some colonists, who heeded the Proclamation Line along the Appalachians as little as they had the Treaty of Easton line along the Alleghenies. This time, however, when settlers ventured across the forbidden hills, the Indians, responding to the betrayal of a promise, let loose their fury all along the trans-Appalachian frontier. This prompted the settlers to call on royal authorities for military aid. Understandably, all pleas received a chilly reception. How could they expect soldiers of the king to help them violate a proclamation of the king?

The refusal of Crown officials to protect the trans-Appalachian settlers alienated many who lived on the frontier, a region that was traditionally conservative and fiercely loyal to king and country. Perhaps even more acutely, the Proclamation Line crisis put the colonies' more established coastal region, called the Tidewater, in a very uncomfortable position between the anguished outcry of the frontier on the one side and demands from the mother country for greater loyalty and obedience on the other. The people of the frontier might grow to resent the government in London, but they could more immediately strike at the much nearer colonial governments on the East Coast, and this had colonial officials worried. At first, the decision as to which way to lean—east toward London or west toward the Appalachians—was an easy one. King George and the Parliament were very powerful, whereas the frontier was weak. But as more and more settlers flowed into the Appalachian and trans-Appalachian West, an increasing number of Tidewater leaders directed their gaze away from the Atlantic. Within months of the Proclamation of 1763, colonial governors began refusing to enforce the settlement line and some even encouraged settlers to cross it.

POP CULTURE
American Frontiersman

Most famous of all those who transgressed the Proclamation Line was Daniel Boone, a very real person who became one of the giants of American mythology and popular culture. Bankrolled by Richard Henderson, a North Carolina land speculator, Boone pioneered the early settlement of Kentucky, the first major English colonial outpost west of the Appalachians. Boone heard about Kentucky while he was serving under George Washington during General Edward Braddock's disastrous campaign against Fort Duquesne. Toward the end of the French and Indian War, he made the Kentucky trek, then started leading groups of settlers into the land, placing them around the town he had founded, Boonesborough.

The eighteenth-century English cartographer Thomas Kitchin published this hand-colored "new and accurate map of the British dominions in America" in 1763, following the defeat of the French in the French and Indian War.

TAXATION WITHOUT REPRESENTATION

THE PROCLAMATION LINE CRISIS simmered and roiled within the context of growing colonial discontent over issues of taxation. George Grenville became Britain's first lord of the treasury and chancellor of the exchequer in April 1763. Grenville was, in fact, admirably suited to the position in that he was an acknowledged master of finance; however, during this most unstable period of British government, Treasurer Grenville also effectively functioned as Premier Grenville, with extraordinary powers that should have been managed by a skilled prime minister, not a clever accountant. Comfortable with cash, Grenville was thoroughly inept where people were concerned.

George III eagerly endorsed Grenville's program for raising revenue from the colonies and summoned all his majesty to usher through Parliament the first in a series of new colonial taxation acts, the so-called Grenville Acts, in 1765. These hefty import and export duties—we'll detail them in a moment—were piled on top of the once dormant, now active, Navigation Acts, as well as another set of early eighteenth-century revenue laws, also recently reactivated, called the Acts of Trade.

For most colonists, the new laws, especially as heaped upon the old, were all just too much. Burdensome in themselves, the duties came at an economic low point for the colonies, which were being beaten down by a business recession in the aftermath of the French and Indian War. This was bad—even ruinous for many—yet few colonists objected, at least in principle, to taxation. What really rankled was being taxed without the benefit of parliamentary representation. In fact, this issue steadily emerged as the central cause of the Revolution.

Popular interpretations of the American Revolution portray it as a contest of the colonists against a dictatorial King George III, who insisted on oppressing them with taxes. In fact, no English king, George included, had possessed the power to levy taxes since 1215, when the English barons coerced John I into signing the Magna Carta. From that point on, it was Parliament that held the purse strings, and only Parliament could levy taxes. To proud English men and women, this spelled the difference between tyranny and good government; Parliament, after all, represented the English people.

ALTERNATE TAKE
Forestalling a Revolution

Historians and others have often wondered whether the American Revolution could have been forestalled had King George and Parliament continued to pursue the policy of salutary neglect. The answer is yes, at least for a time. Taxation without representation was unquestionably the catalyst for revolution; however, even without taxes, it is inevitable that, sooner or later, some other issue would emerge—whether or not to go to war with another country, for example—that would highlight the absence of colonial representation in Parliament. Representation was the key. Without it, loyalty to a government or a king is all but impossible.

The American colonists considered themselves, above all else, English men and women. And therein lay the problem, which, as mentioned in Chapter 1, was suddenly crystallized on February 24, 1761 when a distinguished Boston lawyer named James Otis—who had just resigned from a well-paid position as the king's advocate general of the vice-admiralty court at Boston—spoke out against the writs of assistance, which had been designed to enforce the collection of duties and taxes, and which, as the king's advocate general, Otis had been expected to issue and to administer. His conscience would not let him do so, and he explained why: "Taxation without representation," he said, "is tyranny."

Otis's speech articulated a popular theory that was rapidly gaining currency in the colonies—that the colonists were as English as anyone living in England, but that, unlike them, the colonists were not represented in Parliament—and his ringing phrase soon found an echo in another, *No taxation without representation,* which would become a rallying cry for revolution.

So just what were the taxes that caused so much trouble?

Massachusetts lawyer James Otis resigned a royal office in 1761 rather than serve the blanket search warrants known as writs of assistance. This nineteenth-century engraving shows him accepting the cheers of Bostonians as he leaves town hall.

Acts of Trade

Added to the revived Navigation Acts of 1645, 1649, 1651, and various additional Navigation Acts passed between 1660 and 1696, there were the Acts of Trade, which included:

The Wool Act (1699)—prohibited exporting wool products from the colonies to protect the British domestic wool industry.

Naval Stores Acts (1709–74)—reserved colonial raw materials needed by the Royal Navy and the British merchant marine, especially timber.

The Hat Act (1732)—barred the export of hats from one colony to another.

The Molasses Act (1733)—fixed high duties on sugar and molasses imported into the colonies from French and Dutch

islands. This act was especially damaging to the colonial economy, because the New England rum industry depended on
imported molasses, and the French and Dutch islands were
key markets for British colonial goods, which could be traded
for molasses as well as hard currency.

The Iron Acts (1750 and 1757)—retarded the development of
the colonial iron industry by fixing Britain as the exclusive
market for colonial export iron.

Grenville Acts

The Grenville Acts were imposed on top of the Navigation Acts and
the Acts of Trade.

The American Revenue Act or Sugar Act (1764)—ostensibly
reduced the 1733 duty on foreign molasses, but it simultaneously raised the duties on foreign refined sugar as well as on
a roster of products imported from countries other than
Britain, including textiles, coffee, indigo dyestuff, iron, hides,
raw silk, and potash (for soap and other products).

The Currency Act (1764)—revamped the colonial customs
system, creating a new vice-admiralty court that gave royal
officials, not locally elected people, absolute jurisdiction over
all matters of taxation and customs.

On May 24, 1764, a Boston town meeting proposed that the
colonies fight the Grenville Acts by signing a Non-Importation
Agreement, pledging themselves to boycott most English goods.
Before the year was out, a number of colonies had signed on to
the boycott.

The Stamp Act

The colonial boycott of 1764 was significant for its impact on British
trade, but it was even more important as a danger signal. The boycott was an act not of this or that colony, but of colonies united.

Remember, religious differences and economic competitiveness had always tended to separate the colonies. The colonials thought of themselves first and foremost as English men and women, then as New Yorkers, New Englanders, Virginians, Carolinians, and so on. *Americans?* The concept did not take root before the 1760s, when the actions of the British government began drawing the colonies together in a new identity, an *American* identity.

Parliament should have understood the significance of a united boycott and taken heed of the warning. Instead, Parliament approved the most infamous of the Grenville Acts: the Stamp Act of March 22, 1765.

The Stamp Act effectively taxed all manner of printed material by requiring that a royal tax stamp be affixed to newspapers, legal documents, and even dice and playing cards. As with the other taxation measures, the purpose of the Stamp Act was to defray the cost of colonial defense, which included maintaining British soldiers in the colonies. Now that the French and Indian War was over, an increasing number of colonists had no use at all for redcoats in their midst, and they resented even more being asked to pay for soldiers they did not want. There was a growing sentiment that George and Parliament were demanding that colonists pay for an army sent to occupy their own country. Added to the bitterness over this was the provision that any violation of the Stamp Act was to be tried in the vice admiralty courts by royal magistrates instead of by locally elected or appointed officials. Taxation was beginning to be seen as a synonym for tyranny.

The response to the Stamp Act was even more intense and widespread throughout the colonies than the responses to previous Grenville Acts. Taking note of how the colonists were organizing and uniting, one Isaac Barré, a parliamentary liberal who had opposed passage of the Stamp Act, made a speech in which he called the colonists "these sons of liberty." A former Boston brewer, bankrupt businessman, and brilliant political agitator named Samuel Adams came across this phrase in a newspaper and found it magnetic in its appeal. He organized one of the first of many secret societies that sprang up in the colonies. His group, like many of the

Protest against the Stamp Act of 1765 took many forms. Like all other colonial publications and documents, the Pennsylvania Journal and Weekly Advertiser *was required to bear a royal tax stamp. Defiantly, on October 31, 1765, it printed a skull and crossbones to indicate where the hated stamp was to be affixed.*

Revolutionary rabble-rouser (and failed brewer) Samuel Adams is shown here in a nineteenth-century engraving, after a portrait by John Singleton Copley.

others that quickly followed it, called itself the Sons of Liberty. The members embarked on a mission: to pressure, harass, and even terrorize the royal stamp agents responsible for selling tax stamps and enforcing their use.

They were most effective. Every stamp agent the Sons of Liberty approached resigned. And they approached every stamp agent. Even more important, John Adams, the Harvard-educated attorney who had been so moved by Otis's 1761 speech, drafted a Stamp Act protest on behalf of his hometown of Braintree, Massachusetts. His "Instructions to the Town of Braintree" was circulated all the way to the colonial assembly in Boston and became the model other towns followed for protesting the Stamp Act. In this way, local protests coalesced into a movement that was continental in its breadth.

No Quarter

Along with the Stamp Act, Parliament passed the Mutiny Act of 1765, which included a provision for quartering troops in private houses. At first, colonists evaded the quartering requirement by denying that it applied to Britain's overseas possessions. Parliament blocked this dodge by passing the Quartering Act, which did shed the requirement that private homeowners billet soldiers, but it also explicitly required colonial authorities to furnish barracks and supplies for British troops at the public expense. The following year, the act was extended to require that taverns and inns board troops and seek reimbursement from local governments. Colonial legislatures dealt with the new act simply by refusing to allocate funds for the support of troops.

A Congress Convenes

The refusal to allocate funds for quartering was an act of defiance, but James Otis proposed an even more momentously defiant step: the convening of a Stamp Act Congress. From October 7 through October 25, 1765, delegates from South Carolina, Rhode Island, Connecticut, Pennsylvania, Maryland, New Jersey, Delaware, and New York (Virginia, New Hampshire, North Carolina, and Georgia declined to participate) gathered in New York City and drew up a fourteen-point Declaration of Rights and Grievances. Chief among them were the propositions that Parliament had no right to tax the colonies and that the Crown's vice-admiralty courts had no proper jurisdiction in the colonies.

Having drawn up the declaration, the delegates sent copies to King George III and to both houses of Parliament. William Pitt warmly embraced the Declaration of Rights and Grievances and led in Parliament a movement to repeal the Stamp Act. Even conservative members, who had favored the Stamp Act, were now under pressure from merchants among their constituencies, who wailed that the colonial boycott had caused a 25-percent decline in exports. In the meantime, while Parliament debated, every colonial government except that of Georgia simply refused to enforce the Stamp Act — and even in Georgia, enforcement was spotty and half-hearted.

The dense and implacable Grenville called for the deployment of regular troops to enforce the Stamp Act. This prompted Benjamin Franklin to speak up. Born in Boston, Franklin accumulated a fortune as a Philadelphia printer and entrepreneur. He had served in the Pennsylvania Assembly, was postmaster general of the colonies, and also served as a commercial agent for Pennsylvania. The latter job put him in London, where he represented the business interests of his home colony. Franklin possessed in abundance all the people skills Grenville utterly lacked, and when he pointed out to the many British politicians and officials with whom he was friendly that the colonies neither *should* pay nor *could* afford to pay the Stamp Tax, they listened. And they listened even more closely when he warned that British military intervention would almost surely provoke outright rebellion. On March 18, 1766, the Stamp Act was repealed.

The repeal was a great triumph for the colonies—yet the celebrations were short lived as Parliament, on the very day of the repeal, passed the Declaratory Act, which asserted that body's sovereign authority to make laws binding on the American colonies.

In some places, colonists protested the Stamp Act by burning copies of the proclamation promulgating it, as depicted in this postcard from 1903.

LINK

If This Be Treason . . .

While New Englanders were intimidating the stamp agents, Patrick Henry, a member of Virginia's House of Burgesses (the colonial legislature), introduced seven resolutions known to history as the Virginia Resolves of 1765. The seventh of these was the most important, because it declared that Virginia, by right, enjoyed total legislative autonomy and was not, therefore, subordinate to Parliament. More than a decade before July 4, 1776, it was a declaration of independence.

A successful attorney, Henry was blessed with a silver tongue. He launched the Virginia Resolves with a provocative speech that concluded: "Caesar had his Brutus—Charles the first, his Cromwell—and George the third—may profit by their example." When some conservative burgesses, appalled, raised cries of "Treason! Treason!" it is believed that Henry calmly replied: "If this be treason, make the most of it." The resolves were passed on May 30, 1765.

THE WEATHERCOCK CROWS

IF ANYTHING, CHARLES TOWNSHEND was proud of his reputation for deftly changing direction with whatever political wind prevailed. He was dubbed the "Weathercock"—a sobriquet he had bestowed on himself. He replaced Grenville as chancellor of the exchequer in 1766, after William Pitt resumed the reins of government. However, when Pitt suffered a mental collapse later that very year, Townshend took control of the cabinet and shoved through Parliament three major acts named for him. These so-called Townshend Acts included the Revenue Act, an act that created a new system of customs commissioners, and an act suspending the New York Assembly.

The Revenue Act imposed duties on lead, glass, paint, tea, and paper imported into the colonies, and stipulated that these tax revenues would be used to defray military expenses in the colonies and to pay the salaries of royal colonial officials. The latter provision was especially significant because it took from colonial legislatures the power of the purse, thereby making most colonial administrators independent of local government and answerable only to the Crown.

The new customs regulations Townshend introduced unleashed an army of royal customs commissioners, whose main purpose was what the historian O. M. Dickerson called "customs racketeering." Typically, the commissioners bided their time, refraining from enforcing the complex technicalities governing the import and export duties. Then, suddenly, they would crack down, summarily seizing merchant vessels not in compliance with the regulations they themselves had delayed enforcing. The commissioners would effectively ransom the seized vessels and goods by assessing enormous fines. Of all funds collected, a third went to the royal treasury, a third to the royal governor of the colony, and a third to the customs commissioner who had made the seizure. And if the merchant could not pay, the ship and its cargo were sold at auction, the proceeds divided in those same thirds.

Letters of Liberty

Besides reviving the anti-British boycott, the Townshend Acts provoked the Massachusetts General Court (the colony's principal legislative body) to inform the other colonies of steps it was taking to oppose the acts and to invite the other colonies to take similar steps.

Composed by James Otis and Sam Adams, the "Massachusetts Circular Letter" was approved by the court on February 11, 1768, and circulated to the dozen other colonies. It presented three frankly revolutionary propositions: First, that the Townshend Acts constituted "taxation without representation"; second, that governors and judges must be answerable to the colonial legislatures, not Parliament and the Crown; and, third, that Americans not only had no parliamentary representation, but that they could *never* be represented in Parliament.

It was the last point that was the most directly and literally revolutionary of all. Back in 1761, Otis had protested the absence of parliamentary representation. Since then, the position had become even more radical, holding that representation was at best impractical for a colony distant from the mother country. Even if distance were not a factor, given the size of the colonies— and their continued growth—justly proportioned parliamentary representation for the colonies would eventually dwarf parliamentary representation of England itself. The people of Great Britain, of course, could not be expected to accept such a situation. Therefore, colonial representation in Parliament was not just impractical, but impossible. And this proposition left no alternative to independence.

As if the ultimate implication of the "Circular Letter" were not revolutionary enough, the document concluded with a call for the colonies to submit plans for active and concerted resistance. Responding to this call, the royal governor of Massachusetts dissolved the colony's General Court on the grounds of sedition. But the message had already been sent, and New Hampshire, New Jersey, Connecticut, and Virginia each announced their endorsement of the document, while the Massachusetts House of Representatives voted overwhelmingly against rescinding it.

Even as the "Massachusetts Circular Letter" circulated, the Pennsylvania political theorist John Dickinson published his own set of letters. "Letters from a Farmer in Pennsylvania to Inhabitants of the British Colonies" appeared in serial form during 1767–68, in

John Dickinson's "Letters from a Farmer in Pennsylvania to Inhabitants of the British Colonies" (1767–68), widely published throughout the colonies, turned public opinion against the Townshend Acts of 1767.

TAKEAWAY

Ill-Advised Policies

By abandoning salutary neglect for a colonial policy of taxation and trade restriction, King George III and Parliament united the hitherto competitive colonies in protest first against taxation and then against taxation without representation. More than anything, the independence movement was the product of Britain's unwise colonial policies rather than that it grew from any indigenous hunger for liberty.

a magazine called the *Pennsylvania Chronicle*. They were copied and widely republished throughout the colonies and in Great Britain as well. Whereas the General Court of Massachusetts had written as a government, Dickinson wrote person to person. Aimed at the common folk, his "Letters" argued that Parliament had no right to tax the colonies solely for revenue and that suspending the New York Assembly (which Townshend had done) was an unjust blow against liberty. But Dickinson didn't merely argue that taxation without representation was wrong, he made a plainspoken yet airtight case for its being contrary to British law. The power of his "Letters" was his argument that the revenue laws did not just violate colonial rights, they were an affront to the rights of all English people. So compelling was this argument that Dickinson succeeded not only in helping to rally colonial unity, but also in garnering widespread popular and parliamentary support in England for a more liberal colonial policy. Beyond even this, Dickinson's "Letters" published the situation of England's colonies to the entire world, ushering onto the global stage the cause of American liberty.

Had Townshend purposely intended to goad the colonies into rebellion, he could not have come up with a more effective means than the Revenue Act, the customs commissioners, and the suspension of the New York colonial assembly (in retaliation for its refusal to authorize funds mandated by the Quartering Act). Yet "Champagne Charlie"—as Townshend's parliamentary colleagues called him because of his playboy lifestyle—was not fated to witness the effect of his handiwork. He contracted typhus and died the very year his legislation was enacted. For their part, the colonies, now accustomed to taking united action, renewed their boycott of British goods. It proved so devastating to British merchants that all of the Townshend duties were repealed on April 12, 1770. All but one. It was the tax on tea.

Chapter 4

INVITATION TO A TEA PARTY

The Revolutionary Movement Gets Organized

THE IDEAS THAT DEFINED THE AMERICAN REVOLUTION—taxation without representation is tyranny, the American colonies could never be represented in an English parliament, the colonies should stand united—were formulated, expressed, and circulated in the cities and towns of America, but it was on the frontier that the first militant revolutionary acts took place.

THE REIGN OF THE REGULATORS

IN VENTURING BEYOND THE FAMILIAR safety of the coast, the colonial frontiersman was by definition and necessity courageous and unconventional. But he was also conservative, living far from the cutting-edge ideas of liberty and revolution that were beginning to circulate in the cities. Despite resentment over the Proclamation Line royally decreed in 1763, the frontiersman of this period felt more loyalty to King George III than to the colonial governors and legislators based in the coastal towns. To the frontier dweller, these men seldom seemed to cast their glance westward. Colonial law and colonial wealth largely neglected the frontier, and when frontier folk began to feel that they derived no benefit from their government, they began to take the law into their own hands.

About 1768, a North Carolinian named Herman Husbands organized a militant protest group he called the Regulators. As the urban colonists had begun to protest lack of parliamentary representation, the rural Regulators protested lack of representation in the provincial assembly. They were also enraged over the embezzlement of public funds by officials of the Crown. When—as expected—the colonial powers turned a deaf ear to their protests, on April 8, 1768, seventy Regulators rode into the settlement of Hillsboro, North Carolina, and liberated a horse that had been seized from a local man for nonpayment of taxes. To drive their point home, they also shot up the house of Edmund Fanning, the local tax collector and Crown official. Fanning secured permission from Governor William Tryon to arrest Husbands and another Regulator leader, William Butler. No sooner did he do this then, as if by magic, not seventy but seven hundred Regulators materialized. When this small army headed for the jail, Fanning wisely turned his prisoners loose.

William Tryon, royal governor of North Carolina, acted to suppress the Regulators' Revolt of 1771, considered a prelude to the American Revolution.

Governor Tryon was not about to sit still for such lawlessness. In September 1768, he personally led fourteen hundred colonial troops against thirty-seven hundred Regulators. Despite their superior numbers, the Regulators saw that they were outgunned and therefore prudently retreated, contenting themselves over the next few years with performing vigilante acts against local thieves and rowdies, to whom colonial authorities seemed quite indifferent. But then, early in 1771, the Regulators again lashed out at Fanning. A mob seized him, horsewhipped him, ran him out of Hillsboro, and then burned his house down. This moved the North Carolina Assembly to pass the so-called Bloody Act, which declared the Regulators guilty of treason, a capital crime.

On May 16, 1771, Governor Tryon led a thousand colonial troops to the Alamance Creek, near which some two thousand Regulators were camped. Aware that the Regulators had backed down before, Tryon sent them a warning to disperse or be fired upon—which they mocked. He attacked. After about an hour of shooting, the Regulators withdrew from the field. Each side had lost nine men (some authorities report twenty Regulators dead), and many more were wounded. On May 17, James Few, one of the Regulator leaders, was executed. Twelve more were later convicted of treason. Six were hanged on June 19; the other six, together with sixty-five hundred settlers in the area, were compelled to swear an oath of allegiance to the royal government. After the Battle of Alamance, many Regulators migrated across the Alleghenies.

"Fire and be damned!"

*A Regulator's response to
Governor Tryon's order to disperse*

URBAN OUTBREAK

THE REGULATOR UPRISING in North Carolina was the most visible episode in a Regulator movement that swept across the frontier in the decade before the American Revolution. Protests in towns were more peaceful—at first.

Battle of Golden Hill

When the New York Assembly refused to authorize funds to support the Quartering Act, the Crown retaliated by suspending the assembly on October 1, 1767, whereupon a new assembly was elected. It also refused to vote the necessary funds and was duly dissolved. At last, in January 1769, a third assembly bowed to the demand of the Crown and granted £2,000 to fund the quartering of royal troops. By this time, the controversy had divided New York—a generally conservative colony—between those who supported the king and Parliament and those who called for greater colonial autonomy. On December 16, 1769, Alexander McDougall, a prosperous city merchant who led the New York chapter of the Sons of Liberty, published a provocative broadside titled "To the Betrayed Inhabitants of the City and Colony of New York." The broadside

DETAILS, DETAILS
State of Franklin

It is believed that the Battle of Alamance and its aftermath sent about 1,500 former Regulators west, many of them along the trail pioneered by Daniel Boone. They were among the settlers, who, led by James Robertson, made homes along the Watauga River (in present Tennessee). These individuals created in 1772 the Watauga Association for their mutual protection. The association's government consisted of a five-man court, but when this proved inadequate, the Watauga settlers in 1776 sought and secured the protection of North Carolina. After the American Revolution, the Wataugans, again discontent, seceded (with others) from North Carolina to form in 1785 the brand-new state of Franklin (named after Ben, whose support they solicited), which today is the northeast end of Tennessee. The United States government declined to admit Franklin to the union, its government faltered, and it became part of Tennessee when that territory became a state in 1796.

incited a number of clashes between citizens and soldiers after the New Year. At Golden Hill (the site of present-day John Street, a few blocks north of Wall Street in lower Manhattan), Sons of Liberty members and sympathizers erected a "liberty pole," a traditional symbol of the defiance of authority recalling the maypole of earlier times. Such symbols were increasingly becoming part of the American landscape.

On January 13, 1770, British troops tried to bring down the pole, but were driven off. They succeeded on the seventeenth, however, which provoked a new flurry of rebellious broadsides and, on January 19, a riot at Golden Hill. Royal authorities dispatched thirty or forty troops to disperse the rioters, who had armed themselves with swords and clubs. In the clash that ensued, several were wounded, but no one was killed. McDougall, however, was arrested on February 7, 1770, charged with having written the first broadside. He declined to post bond, and his cell was filled with visiting supporters and well-wishers.

LINK

Village Lore

Alexander McDougall is commemorated—albeit with an alternate spelling—in the lovely Macdougal Street of Greenwich Village in lower Manhattan.

The *Liberty* Incident

Although Alexander McDougall became a local celebrity—and later, a major general in the Continental army—nothing immediate came of the Battle of Golden Hill. Little wonder, since New York had more Loyalists than rebels. Boston was another story.

Like Alexander McDougall, Bostonian John Hancock was a prosperous merchant and a Son of Liberty. Unlike the New Yorker, however, Hancock was not by inclination a rabble-rouser. His dispute with the royal government was more personal than political. He found the royal customs officials arrogant, and he took every opportunity to frustrate and annoy them. It was, in fact, a kind of game. Hancock scrupulously obeyed the letter of the law even as he repeatedly found ways to demonstrate his contempt for those who enforced the law. One day, customs inspectors descended below decks of Hancock's provocatively named sloop *Liberty*. Aware that the law required inspectors to obtain permission from the ship's master before going below decks, Hancock ordered his crew to eject them without ceremony.

John Hancock, a prosperous Boston merchant who defied royal taxes and trade restrictions, was one of the fathers of the American independence movement and became the first signer of the Declaration of Independence in 1776.

Hancock's ill manners provoked a complaint to the attorney general of the colony, whose ruling that Hancock had been within his rights made customs inspectors all the more determined to "get" this arrogant fellow—next time.

"Next time" came on May 9, 1768, when *Liberty* sailed into Boston with twenty-five pipes (about 3,150 gallons) of Madeira wine. Hancock paid the required duty, unloaded the cargo, and took on a new cargo of tar and whale oil. The law required a ship's owner to post bond for a new cargo before loading it, but, in practice, customs commissioners delayed the bond until the ship had cleared port. In a rare lapse, Hancock followed customary usage rather than the letter of the law, a slip-up that Joseph Harrison, the chief collector of customs, gleefully noted. He also noted that the declared cargo was far below the ship's capacity and suspected that Hancock was actually carrying more. Harrison decided that he had ample legal reason to seize *Liberty*.

As fate would have it, just as Harrison was getting ready to make his move, two British warships, *Romney* and *St. Lawrence,* sailed into Boston Harbor. In need of crew members, *Romney*'s skipper sent a "press gang" ashore to "impress"—that is, abduct and *press* into naval service—any able-bodied locals unfortunate enough to cross the gang's path. Impressment was standard operating procedure in the Royal Navy, but it had been outlawed in American waters for more than a century. This clearly did not discourage the *Romney*'s master; however, when the press gang grabbed an American sailor (Furlong by name) out of a wharfside tavern, the waterfront crowd responded by pitching stones at the press gang, mobbing them, and rescuing Furlong. After the gang returned to the *Romney* empty-handed and much abashed, the captain beat to quarters (signaled preparation for battle) and trained his guns on the growing mob. He held his fire, and the Bostonians held their ground.

The official seal of the United States Army prominently features a Liberty Cap atop a Liberty Pole—both popular symbols of America's revolutionary activists.

REALITY CHECK

Rejection of Ejection Theory

Although most historians report that Hancock ordered the customs inspectors ejected, Hancock biographer H. L. Allen (*John Hancock: Patriot in Purple,* 1948) writes that Hancock's crew sent one official home drunk, while they shoved the other into a cabin and nailed the door shut until the ship had been unloaded.

It was precisely during this standoff that Harrison decided to seize Hancock's *Liberty*—using a boatload of armed sailors from none other than HMS *Romney.* Seeing this, the quayside crowd rushed to block the *Romney's* longboat, but could not reach it in time to prevent its lashing onto the *Liberty* and towing it alongside the British warship below all of its menacing guns. Thus thwarted, the mob turned its rage on Harrison, his son, and another customs official, Benjamin Hallowell, rushing and then clobbering all three. Harrison senior managed to wriggle away, but the mob dragged his son by the hair through the streets, and Hallowell was left unconscious in a pool of his own blood. From here, the mob turned to the homes of Harrison, Hallowell, and John Williams, inspector general of customs, breaking the windows of all. Taking the hint, other customs officials fled first to refuge aboard the *Romney* and then to the royal fortress in Boston Harbor known as Castle William.

Anxious to head off a general rebellion, Massachusetts royal governor Francis Bernard pledged an end to impressment and ordered the customs officials to return Hancock's ship and duties. For his part, Hancock had not planned to be thrust front and center into the contest for American liberty, but now he was quite willing to seize the opportunity events presented. No, he declared, he would not accept the offer. He demanded that the *Liberty* affair run its course through the courts. On March 1, 1769, in one of the precious few prudent decisions it made, the Crown responded by dropping the case—but not before customs officials reported Massachusetts to be in a state of insurrection. In response, the Crown sent two regiments of British infantry to Boston. They landed in October 1768.

Anatomy of a Massacre

They were not welcome. Bostonians saw British soldiers as the agents of tyranny, but they were also tyranny's victims. Treated brutally by their officers, they were paid far less than a subsistence wage. So it was no wonder that, on a cold, gray March 5, 1770, an off-duty redcoat showed up at Grey's ropewalk—a wharfside maker of ship's ropes—in search of part-time work. In better times, no one would have begrudged the soldier a job. But times were bad. Boston, like the rest of the country, was struggling under the recession that followed the French and Indian War, and jobs were hard to come by. What the small crowd that gathered at the ropewalk saw was a British soldier—sent to oppress them at their expense—trying to snatch a job that by rights should go to one of them.

It was quite enough to touch off a minor riot. And when that was over, the crowd just never went home, but continued milling about the streets. At about nine in the evening, some sixty Bostonians gathered around Hugh White, a redcoat sentry on guard outside the Customs House.

What had drawn the crowd to Sentry White was the complaint of one Edward Garrick, who loudly announced to White that his company commander had not paid his master for a wig he had ordered. Apparently unwilling to hear his commanding officer spoken ill of, White called on the accuser to step forward. Garrick did, whereupon White struck him in the face with the butt of his musket. Clasping his injured face, Garrick ran, pursued by another redcoat at the point of a bayonet.

It was a very good way to start another, bigger, riot.

The mob grew and began pelting White and other soldiers with icy snowballs. Commanding officers arrived, but were unable to gain control of their men or of the crowd. Captain Thomas Preston rounded up seven soldiers to rescue Sentry White. Henry Knox, owner of the popular London Book-Store and destined to become first a general in the Continental army and later President Washington's secretary of war, approached Preston: "For God's sake, take care of your men. If they fire, they die!"

"I am sensible of it," Preston quietly replied, then turned and barked an order to White: Fall in with the seven-man detail he led. White was only too willing to obey, but the people of Boston surged forward to block his departure. Unable to penetrate the mob, Preston ordered his troops to form a defensive line where they stood.

To the Bostonians, this came as yet another provocation. Hurling more ice balls, they shouted taunts, daring the soldiers to open fire.

At a loss, Preston summoned Justice of the Peace James Murray and asked him to read the Riot Act. Perhaps a recitation of the severe penalties for public disorder would sober the mob. Instead, it

REALITY CHECK
Put Your John Hancock Here

Most people today know John Hancock through his iconic signature on the Declaration of Independence—a signature so famous that the phrase "John Hancock" has become a synonym for any official signature. Hancock was the first to sign the document, and he did so in a hand more ornate and considerably larger than any of the other signatures. Legend has it that he announced his intention to sign big enough and bold enough that King George III could read it without his spectacles. To be sure, Hancock enjoyed tweaking authority figures, and perhaps he made such a remark, but surviving examples of his signature on other documents are virtually identical to his Declaration signature.

served only to provoke a fresh volley of ice balls—this time against Murray.

Suddenly, a different sort of projectile flew from the Bostonian mass. It was a heavy wooden club, which knocked Private Hugh Montgomery off his feet. He rose and, without uttering a word, cocked his musket and fired.

The wild shot hit no one, but it did provoke Richard Palmés, merchant, to strike out at Montgomery with the billet of wood he gripped in his fist. Montgomery lunged back with his bayonet, sending Palmes into rapid retreat.

The legendary silversmith and rider Paul Revere first entered the history of the American Revolution in 1770, when Sam Adams and Joseph Warren asked him to engrave a depiction of the Boston Massacre for mass distribution. Revere portrayed the British captain Thomas Preston with upraised saber, ordering his men to fire on the unarmed Bostonians. Preston, of course, did no such thing—he tried to prevent the shootings—yet generations of Americans came to know the Boston Massacre through Revere's work of graphic fiction.

Now the contagion was loose. Private Matthew Killroy leveled his musket at Edward Langford and Samuel Gray.

"God damn you, don't fire!" Gray called out.

But Killroy did, sending a musket ball into Samuel Gray's brain.

At almost the same instant, another musket sounded. It was a single report, but the nervous soldier must have accidentally loaded two balls. For two rounds buried themselves in the chest of Crispus Attucks, a forty-year-old fugitive slave from Framingham, killing him where he stood. Gray was the first man hit—he died later—but Attucks, a black slave, died instantly and was therefore the first man killed in this overture to a war for liberty.

The fall of Crispus Attucks was followed by more shots and the deaths of three more Bostonians—two killed instantly and a third mortally wounded. Then came a silence broken only by the neatly choreographed click-click-click of well-drilled soldiers reloading. The Bostonians, undaunted, pressed forward again. Again, the soldiers leveled their muskets. But this time, Preston strode along the line of men, reflexively knocking each musket barrel toward the sky.

"Don't fire!" he commanded sharply.

COLONIAL JUSTICE

Captain Preston and six of his men were indicted by a Massachusetts court on charges of murder. His majesty's soldiers had ample reason to believe that they would be delivered into the hands of mob justice. Surely, Sam Adams and his fellow Son of Liberty, Dr. Joseph Warren, did all they could to stoke the fires of Boston's fury. But not everyone was willing to be consumed. A pair of prominent local attorneys, Josiah Quincy and John Adams, volunteered to defend the accused. The last thing John Adams wanted to see among a people aspiring to become citizens of a free country was mob justice. On behalf of their clients, the two attorneys argued justifiable homicide by reason of self-defense. It is a testament both to the quality of the lawyers and to the character of the people of Boston that the juries acquitted Preston and four of his men. Two others were found guilty not of murder, but of the lesser crime of manslaughter. Their punishment was nothing more than discharge from military service with a brand on the thumb.

> *"Council ought to be the very last thing an accused person should want [be denied] in a free country."*
>
> —
>
> *John Adams, on volunteering to defend the British soldiers accused of the Boston Massacre, 1771*

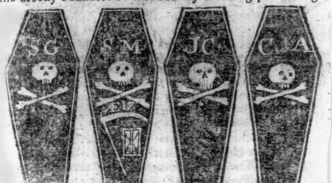

Laſt Thurſday, agreeable to a general Requeſt of the Inhabitants, and by the Conſent of Parents and Friends, were carried to their *Grave* in Succeſſion, the Bodies of *Samuel Gray, Samuel Maverick, James Caldwell,* and *Crispus Attucks,* the unhappy Victims who fell in the bloody Maſſacre of the Monday Evening preceeding!

On this Occaſion moſt of the Shops in Town were ſhut, all the Bells were ordered to toll a ſolemn Peal, as were alſo thoſe in the neighboring Towns of Charleſtown Roxbury, &c. The Proceſſion began to move between the Hours of 4 and 5 in the Afternoon; two of the un-

Sam Adams and other rabble rousers did their best to fan the flames of the Boston Massacre into outright revolution. At Adams's behest, Paul Revere engraved these four coffins for the Boston Gazette *and* Country Journal *(March 12, 1770). The coffins bear the initials of those killed in the Massacre: Samuel Gray, Samuel Maverick, James Caldwell, and Crispus Attucks.*

MAKING A REVOLUTION

DESPITE THE PROPAGANDA EFFORTS of Sam Adams and Dr. Warren, the Boston Massacre (as Sam Adams called it) failed to touch off a larger rebellion. If anything, the trials of the redcoats that followed served to quell revolutionary passions. Moreover, in April 1770, the hated Townshend Acts were repealed, and it began to look as if the mother at last sought reconciliation with her rebellious offspring. But the Sons of Liberty, which had come into being with the Stamp Act in 1765, never really went away after the act was repealed the following year, and it remained active even after the outrage of the Boston Massacre had faded.

Back in 1765, Sam Adams and other revolutionary activists had understood that the key to opposition of the Stamp Act was unity, and unity was still the key to building a full-scale revolution. For a short time, it looked as if the Boston Massacre might become the nucleus around which that colonial unity would crystallize, but the passions associated with the event faded. Yet before the fires of revolution sputtered into embers, a ship called the *Gaspee* burned.

The *Gaspee* Affair

With an abundance of coves and inlets, Narragansett Bay, off Rhode Island, was a paradise for smugglers—people who did not necessarily protest oppressive taxes, but simply did not pay them. Late in the spring of 1772, Lieutenant William Dudingston of the Royal Navy sailed the schooner *Gaspee* into the bay in search of smugglers. Dudingston was very good at his job, and his patrols soon cut a deep slice out of Rhode Island smuggling. From the colonial point of view, that was bad enough, but Dudingston also had a talent for adding insult to injury. His arrogance finally provoked Rhode Island's locally elected governor, Joseph Wanton, to threaten to arrest Dudingston. The lieutenant responded by reporting the threat to the fleet admiral, who, in turn, exchanged heated letters with the governor.

The HMS Gaspee, *a Royal Navy revenue schooner, patrolled the waters of Narragansett Bay in search of colonial smugglers attempting to avoid trade regulations and import duties. The burning of the* Gaspee *on June 9, 1772, was cheered by those who favored independence.*

On June 9, Dudingston's luck broke. While pursuing a smuggler who was sailing close to shore, the *Gaspee* ran aground on a sandbar near Providence. One witness to this incident was Sheriff Abraham Whipple, a colonial official whose sentiments were identical to those of Governor Wanton. He hurriedly assembled a flotilla of small boats and surrounded the *Gaspee* that night.

Lieutenant Dudingston called out: "Who comes there?"

"I am the sheriff of the County of Kent, God damn you," Whipple replied. "I have a warrant to apprehend you, God damn you—so surrender, God damn you."

Predictably, Dudingston refused, whereupon the sheriff and his men forced their way aboard the *Gaspee*. Dudingston leveled his sword at one of the boarders, who responded by shooting the lieutenant in the groin. After surgeons hurriedly mended the skipper's wound, Whipple bundled him and the rest of his crew into boats. With everyone disembarked, Whipple put His Majesty's Ship *Gaspee* to the torch.

Thanks to the communication network Sam Adams and others had created, news of the "*Gaspee* affair" blazed through the colonies, creating great excitement, and when the Crown made a half-hearted attempt to bring Whipple and the other arsonists to justice, Sam Adams organized the first "Committee of Correspondence" to ensure that information was quickly disseminated and action fully coordinated. Other Committees of Correspondence sprang up throughout the colonies. These were so similar to the original Sons of Liberty that the names were used interchangeably. In the face of such well-organized colonial opposition, the Crown dropped its case against Whipple and the others.

Oh, *That* Tea Party

But dropping the case was hardly sufficient to halt what had now begun. As we saw in the previous chapter, in 1770 the Townshend Acts were repealed, which meant no more odious taxes on import commodities—except for one. It was King George III who personally insisted on retaining the tax on tea because he believed that "there must always be one tax" in order to preserve Parliament's right to tax the colonies. Yet the fact was that the tea tax could be evaded quite easily by purchasing smuggled tea from Dutch

REALITY CHECK
Premeditated Assault?

Traditionally, Sheriff Whipple's assault on the *Gaspee* has been portrayed as a spontaneous act of rebellion. In fact, the British Admiralty—in charge of suppressing smugglers—employed loyalist spies. One of the spies wrote a letter to the Admiralty on June 16, 1772, strongly suggesting that the attack on the British ship was not impromptu, but had been very well planned. The spy reported that the raiders blacked their faces and arms—presumably to reduce their visibility and enhance the element of surprise—and that six, perhaps seven boats embarked from Providence while another boat came from Bristol. The attack, therefore, appears to have been quite thoroughly coordinated, suggesting the degree to which the spirit of rebellion had developed in Rhode Island.

sources. Ironically, therefore, the tea tax was harder on the financially ailing East India Company than on the colonists.

By the 1770s, the East India Company was a business that deserved to die. This creaky cartel of British merchants and shippers was both inefficient and thoroughly corrupt. But it was also very cozy with Lord Frederick North, who functioned as George's prime minis-

Many Britons believed that the policies of George III's prime minister Lord North were unjust to the American colonies. This British political cartoon from May 1774 shows Lord North pumping water from a fountain adorned with the head of King George III, the water flowing onto the prostrate bodies of Britannia and a Native American figure representing America. Some ministers look on approvingly while others protest.

ter. Whenever the company had a problem, it called on its man in government, and, right now, it had a very big problem. If it could not ship to America at least some of the 17 million pounds of Indian tea languishing in its London warehouses, the whole lot would go rotten. How, the company asked Lord North, could America be compelled to buy its tea instead of the smuggled Dutch product?

North had an answer. He understood that the East India Company actually paid two taxes, one when it landed tea in Britain, whether for sale or transshipment elsewhere, and another when it landed a shipment in America. By means of the Tea Act (May 10, 1773), Lord North forgave the first tax and retained the lesser three-penny-a-pound duty due on landing in America. The net result would be a reduction in the price of East India tea below that of the Dutch-smuggled tea. North reasoned that, at bottom, economics was quite simple. People bought whatever cost the least. Surely, then, the colonists would now buy English tea.

Simple? Not quite. North assumed that the Tea Act would buy off rebellion—and cheaply, too—even as it kept the East India Company afloat. What it actually did, however, was drive hitherto moderate American merchants into the camp of the revolutionary radicals. The problem was that, under the Tea Act, the East India Company did not wholesale its product to colonial merchants, but sold exclusively to specially designated consignees in the ports of New York, Charleston, Philadelphia, and Boston. The American merchants, cut off and cut out, could not compete.

As the Sons of Liberty had intimidated royal stamp agents, so now the Committees of Correspondence sent toughs to intimidate the consignees. The consignees in Philadelphia, New York, and Charleston folded almost instantly. Moreover, American captains and harbor pilots refused to handle the East India Company cargo, and tea ships were turned back to London from Philadelphia and New York before they could unload. A ship was allowed to land in Charleston, but the tea was impounded and lay in a warehouse until 1776, when the Continental Congress auctioned it off to help defray the costs of war.

In Boston, as usual, things went differently. When three Tea Act ships landed at Boston Harbor, the agents of the Committee of Correspondence prevented their being unloaded and demanded that the ships return to England. Thomas Hutchinson, the royal governor of Massachusetts, refused to issue the permits that would allow the ships to leave the harbor.

For America's growing ranks of revolutionaries, a standoff was always an opportunity for a meeting. At a December 16, 1773, convocation of the Committee of Correspondence, Sam Adams and other leaders sent Captain Francis Rotch to Governor Hutchinson with a most earnest plea that he issue the exit permits. While awaiting Rotch's return with the governor's reply, a crowd of some seven thousand spilled into the street from Boston's Old South Church.

Rotch returned at six in the evening. The governor, he reported, was standing firm. The ships would stay.

Samuel Adams climbed the Old South pulpit. "This meeting can do nothing more to save the country," he pronounced. Clearly in response to this cue, an eerie imitation of the Mohawk war cry rose from the crowd outside the church.

Three troops of colonists, fifty men to each troop, their faces painted in the manner of Mohawk warriors, marched to Griffin's Wharf, where they clambered into boats and rowed out to the three tea ships. The operation was executed with military precision, as each troop boarded a ship simultaneously. The ship's crews offered no resistance as, with quiet efficiency, the counterfeit Mohawks threw into the harbor a total of 342 tea chests valued at £10,000 (almost $1.7 million today). Their mission completed, the "Indians" returned to their boats and rowed ashore.

Boston Tea Party

These political songs, commemorating the Boston Tea Party, were popular with New Englanders in 1773.

In protest of the new taxes, American patriots tar and feather the excise-man (royal tax collector), while men dump tea into Boston Harbor. This print was published in London in 1774, a year after the Boston Tea Party.

Revolutionary Tea

There was an old lady lived over the sea,
And she was an Island Queen;
Her daughter lived off in a new country,
With an ocean of water between.
The old lady's pockets were full of gold,
But never contented was she,
So she called on her daughter to pay
   her a tax
Of three pence a pound on her tea,
Of three pence a pound on her tea.

"Now mother, dear mother," the
   daughter replied,
"I shan't do the thing you ax;
I'm willing to pay a fair price for the tea,
But never the three penny tax."
"You shall," quoth the mother, and
   reddened with rage,
"For you're my own daughter, you see,
And sure 'tis quite proper the daughter
   should pay
Her mother a tax on her tea,
Her mother a tax on her tea."

*On the evening of December 16, 1773, three compa-
nies of fifty men each, masquerading as Mohawks,
passed through a tremendous crowd of spectators,
went aboard the three ships in Boston Harbor, broke
open their cargo of tea chests, and heaved them into
the harbor. The event, shown here in a 1903 postcard,
was instantly dubbed "The Boston Tea Party."*

Tea, Destroyed By Indians

YE GLORIOUS SONS OF FREEDOM, brave and bold,
That has stood forth——fair LIBERTY to hold;
Though you were INDIANS, come from distant shores,
Like MEN you acted ——not like savage Moors.

Chorus
Bostonians SONS keep up your courage good,
Or Dye, like Martyrs, in fair Free-born Blood.
Our LIBERTY and LIFE is now invaded,
And FREEDOM'S brightest Charms are darkly shaded:
But, we will STAND——-and think it noble mirth,
To DART the man that dare oppresses the Earth.

Bostonians SONS keep up your courage good,
Or Dye, like Martyrs, in fair Free-born Blood
How grand the scene!——(No Tyrant shall oppose)
The TEA is sunk in spite of all our foes.

A NOBLE SIGHT——-to fee th' accursed TEA
Mingled with MUD——-and ever for to be;
For KING and PRINCE shall know that we are FREE.

….Bostonians SONS keep up your courage good,
And sink all Tyrants in their GUILTY BLOOD.

A Lady's Adieu to Her Tea-Table

FAREWELL the Tea-board with your gaudy
    attire,
Ye cups and ye saucers that I did admire;
To my cream pot and tongs I now bid adieu;
That pleasure's all fled that I once found
    in you.
Farewell pretty chest that so lately
    did shine,
With hyson and congo and best double fine;
Many a sweet moment by you I have sat,
Hearing girls and old maids to tattle
    and chat;
And the spruce coxcomb laugh at nothing
    at all,
Only some silly work that might happen
    to fall.
No more shall my teapot so generous be
In filling the cups with this pernicious tea,
For I'll fill it with water and drink out
    the same,
Before I'll lose LIBERTY that dearest name,
Because I am taught (and believe it is fact)
That our ruins is aimed at in the late act,
Of imposing a duty on all foreign teas,
Which detestable stuff we can quit when
    we please.
LIBERTY'S the Goddess that I do adore,
And I'll maintain her right until my
    last hour,
Before she shall part I will die in the cause,
For I'll never be govern'd by tyranny's laws.

The Boston Tea Party galvanized support for the movement toward independence not only in the colonies, but among liberal elements in Britain as well. There was a call in Parliament for the final repeal of all taxes and coercive acts in restraint of trade. Yet the liberal voices were drowned out by the diehard din of the conservatives. King George himself sputtered, "We must master them or totally leave them to themselves and treat them as aliens." It was a strange and extreme thing to say, as if the king himself—not some colonial firebrand—were declaring a war for independence.

*"Leave the Americans as they anciently stood. . . .
Do not burthen them with taxes; you were not
used to do so from the beginning."*

*Edmund Burke, speech before the House of Commons,
after the Boston Tea Party*

INTOLERABLE

So far, coercion had served only to drive the colonies closer to rebellion. King George III and Parliament should have learned that lesson. Instead, they responded to the Boston Tea Party with what they themselves called the "Coercive Acts" and the colonists christened the Intolerable Acts. These included:

Closure of the port of Boston;

Curtailment of representative government; members of the upper chamber of the Massachusetts Assembly would henceforth be royal appointees, not popularly elected representatives;

Appointment by the royal governor of previously elected local officials;

Restriction of town meetings to a single annual session;

Reduction of local judicial jurisdiction, with all capital cases to be
    tried in England or in another colony;

Extension of the Quartering Act, preparatory to the permanent
    quartering of British troops in Boston.

In addition to approving the Coercive Acts, King
George III, in 1774, appointed General Thomas Gage, a
veteran of the French and Indian War, to serve both
as royal governor of Massachusetts and as commander in chief of all British forces in America.
In effect, the king installed a military government in the colony.

Gage arrived in Boston on May 13, 1774.
After disembarking on the seventeenth, he
found a reception as chilly as the cold rains of
early spring. Week after week, Boston's church
bells tolled as if for the dead, and Bostonians wore
black badges of mourning. Gage, however, let it roll off
his back. On June 1, he clamped down by implementing the
harshest of the Intolerable Acts, the Port Act, which closed Boston
not only to overseas traffic but to seaborne shipments from other
colonies as well.

It seemed only to make the people stronger.

When Gage ordered the capital moved from Boston to Salem,
the General Assembly defiantly convened in Salem with a bold new
name, calling itself the Provincial Congress. When Gage ordered
this body dissolved, the delegates barred the doors against his messenger while voting a proposal to convene a Continental Congress,
with delegates drawn from all of the colonies.

*General Thomas Gage
was commander in
chief of all British
forces in North
America and served as
military governor in
Massachusetts from
1774–75. His inept
attempts to enforce
upon the colonists the
onerous taxes and
policies of George III
hastened the coming
of the Revolution.*

PART TWO

Drumming Up a War

Chapter 5

THE FLAME KINDLED

How the War Began in New England

$\mathcal{T}$HE "PATRIOTS," THE "REBELS," THE "AMERICANS"—whatever we choose to call them—did not start the American Revolution, at least not on their own. They had a lot of help from King George III and the Parliament of Great Britain. If the Boston Tea Party hadn't been followed by the Coercive—or Intolerable—Acts and the arrival of a military government led by General Thomas Gage, it might have faded from history as mere vandalism. But the Intolerable Acts were passed and Gage was sent. Indeed, the Crown seemed perversely intent on proving itself to be what Sam Adams and other rabble-rousers said it was: tyrannical.

The king and his ministers thought they could *coerce* the colonies into obedience. Instead, they made obedience *intolerable*. And just when it seemed impossible to make the crisis any worse, George found a way to make it much worse.

ROYAL SELLOUT

ON JUNE 22, 1774, GEORGE III signed into law the Quebec Act, which extended the Canadian province of Quebec all the way down into the Ohio Valley and the country of the Illinois. Canada had been a British possession since the end of the French and Indian War, so, in a sense, George was merely reshuffling his colonies a bit. Yet, even though the people of Quebec were now subjects of the English king, they spoke French, they abided by laws founded on French rather than English tradition, and they worshipped not in the Church of England but in that of Rome. Their flag might now be British, but they themselves were and would always be French men and women. In the Quebec Act, George III recognized this. He decreed that in the territory covered by the act, French would be spoken, French law would prevail, and the Roman Catholic Church would be sanctioned by the government.

From the point of view of overall colonial policy, the Quebec Act was not a bad idea. In fact, it was an admirably tolerant and enlightened way of dealing with the many ethnic French colonials who still populated Canada. Typically, British imperialism showed little regard for the ethnic, cultural, and religious traditions of a conquered people, but just as George had sought to avoid trouble with the Indians by drawing the Proclamation Line of 1763, so now he tried to placate the French Canadians by letting them continue to live as *French* Canadians. The trouble was that, just as the Proclamation Line mollified the Indians at the cost of enflaming the people of the colonial frontier, so the Quebec Act pandered to the French Canadians at the cost of outraging the people of the thirteen lower colonies. The Quebec Act gave to these people the very territory the Protestant, English-speaking, British colonists saw as their future: the West. Now, while it was true that the Quebec Act did not bar

In effect, the Quebec Act preempted the western expansion of English-speaking, Anglican-professing colonists, and thereby further alienated Britain's colonies from the mother country. This 1774 British political cartoon shows four Anglican bishops joining hands to dance around a copy of the Quebec Bill as Lord Bute (on the bagpipes) and Lord North look on approvingly, the devil hovering behind them.

Anglo-American colonists from sharing the region with the French Canadians, it forced them to do so on French Canadian terms. This seemed to abrogate nothing less momentous than the Magna Carta, which guaranteed that every English man and woman would always be governed by *English* law.

COMING TOGETHER

EVERYTHING KING GEORGE AND HIS MAN IN BOSTON, General Gage, did in an effort to suppress rebellion served instead to incite rebellion. Each new law seemed to cut another tie with the mother country even as it forged link upon link between colonies that never before had much reason to join forces.

The Port Act, most odious of all the Intolerable Acts, was meant to beat radical Boston into submission while also cutting it off from the rest of America, as if to quarantine the contagion of rebellion. Precisely the opposite occurred. A blockade is an act of war, intended to starve a place and a people. With Boston's ports closed, the other New England colonies rallied round and arranged to ship foodstuffs into the city overland. And it was not just Boston's neighbors that did this. From as far as low-country South Carolina came rice, trundled in over almost nonexistent colonial roads. More remarkably, Quebec—beneficiary of the misbegotten Quebec Act—sent down huge quantities of wheat.

A Continental Congress

Bread is essential, of course, but the colonists well knew that man does not live by bread alone. Even as the colonies saw to the physical sustenance of Boston, they heeded the call of the Massachusetts Assembly for something more: a "Continental Congress." The phrase had a magnificent ring to it, one that was also rich with meaning—that already, in effect, proclaimed independence. For it was not a *colonial* congress—a phrase that would have signified political subordination to Britain—but a congress encompassing the continent, a continental congress, a phrase asserting a geographical fact and acknowledging allegiance to no power beyond that fact.

Fifty-six delegates from twelve colonies—the Georgians stayed home—convened at Carpenters' Hall, Philadelphia, on September 5, 1774, and got a great deal accomplished in a very short time.

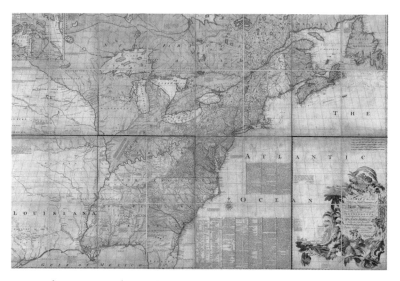

This 1774 map is titled "A map of the British and French dominions in North America, with the roads, distances, limits, and extent of the settlements." In the tiny print in the center of the map, the map-maker explains the map's purpose: "After the first Drawing of this Map in 1750, it was again corrected and improved, before it was published, and I have since taken Care to procure & examine all the Information I could get in order to render it as correct & usefull as possible; which has given occasion this Second Edition of it; in which I have likewise inserted all the Observations I believe we have for the Geography of N. America, since I find them grossly misrepresented by others."

The Congress began by endorsing the "Suffolk Resolves," which had been drafted by Sam Adams's compatriot, the young physician Joseph Warren. The resolves condemned the Intolerable Acts as unconstitutional and urged Massachusetts to form an independent government, which would withhold taxes from the Crown until the acts were repealed. In the meantime, the resolves exhorted citizens to arm themselves and to adhere to a general boycott of English goods. After having been adopted by a convention held in Suffolk County, Massachusetts, the resolves were rushed to Philadelphia and the Continental Congress in the saddlebag of a Sons of Liberty courier, prominent silversmith by trade named Paul Revere.

"On the fortitude, on the wisdom and on the exertions of this important day, is suspended the fate of this new world, and of unborn millions."

from the Suffolk Resolves, 1774

The Continental Congress also debated a document drawn up by one Joseph Galloway, a leading Philadelphia lawyer, vice president of the prestigious American Philosophical Society, and good friend of Benjamin Franklin. "Galloway's Plan of Union," as it is known, proposed solving the problem of home rule for the colonies by giving them something like dominion status within the British Empire. Under Galloway's plan, the colonies would be governed by a "grand council," whose members would be popularly elected to three-year terms—except for the president-general, who would be a royal appointee and who would have veto authority over the council. In this way, the colonial government would always be inferior to the royal government, but it would hardly be powerless. It would have direct authority over commercial, civil, criminal, and police matters when more than a single colony was involved, and it would have authority to veto parliamentary legislation affecting the colonies. The First Continental Congress gave very serious thought to "Galloway's Plan of Union," in the end defeating it by just a single vote.

The Continental Congress formally denounced the Intolerable Acts and the Quebec Act, as well as other repressive measures, declaring a total of thirteen acts of Parliament (passed since 1763) unconstitutional. Moreover, each of the delegates pledged their colony's absolute support of a boycott against Britain until all thirteen acts were repealed.

The congress drew up a set of ten resolutions, enumerating the rights of colonists. These documents, which anticipated the Bill of Rights—the first ten amendments to the U.S. Constitution, adopted in 1791—were especially important because they implied that it was the business of government to guarantee individual rights, *human* rights— something the government of King George III had failed to do.

On October 20, 1774, the delegates to the Continental Congress signed the "Continental Association," sometimes simply called the "Association," which was an official pledge of adherence to a total boycott against trade with Britain, Ireland, and the British West Indies. It was also a prelude to formal union.

In its final acts, the congress drew up addresses to the American people and to the king. Delegates agreed to reconvene on May 10, 1775, if their grievances had not been adequately addressed. They adjourned on October 26.

DETAILS, DETAILS
Location, Location

Carpenters' Hall had just been completed earlier in 1774 as headquarters of the Carpenters' Company, a Philadelphia guild of master builders, when it was used to house the First Continental Congress. Carpenters' Hall is not to be confused with the State House— today called Independence Hall—just a block away. Why did the First Continental Congress meet in a guild hall instead of the State House? The State House was considered to be a nest of Loyalist and Tory sympathizers.

Chaplain Jacob Duché leads the delegates of the First Continental Congress in prayer as they convene in Philadelphia's Carpenter's Hall in September 1774. This mezzotint was published in 1848.

OPENING MOVES

PERHAPS MORE THAN ANY OTHER REVOLUTION before or since, the American Revolution was a revolution of ideas, ideas expressed in language of great and compelling eloquence. But, as in any revolution, words could go only so far. While the Continental Congress met and talked, General Gage set about assembling and consolidating his troops. On September 1, 1774, he sent a detachment of redcoats from Boston to nearby Cambridge and Charlestown to seize cannon and powder from colonial arsenals there. In response, the newly renamed "Provincial Congress" of Massachusetts, now meeting in Salem instead of Boston, appropriated £15,627 to buy new military supplies. It also authorized John Hancock to head a central Committee of Safety and further authorized him to call out the militia. A portion of the Massachusetts militia had adopted a name that had been used in the colonies as early as 1756, during the French and Indian War. They called themselves "Minutemen," because these citizen-soldiers pledged themselves to be armed, assembled, and prepared for battle on a minute's notice.

Paul Revere's First Ride

Paul Revere put a lot of mileage on his horse in the lead-up to the American Revolution. He had carried the Suffolk Resolves all the way from Massachusetts to Philadelphia during the First Continental Congress, and now, on December 14, 1774, he rode out to warn John Sullivan—who had been a delegate to the Continental Congress and was a major of the New Hampshire militia—that General Gage planned to send reinforcements to secure a large cache of munitions stored at the poorly guarded Fort William and Mary in Portsmouth Harbor, New Hampshire.

Duly alerted by the indefatigable Revere, Sullivan tapped militia captain John Langdon to accompany him in leading a band of volunteers to the fort. The handful of redcoats who were guarding the munitions in anticipation of Gage's arrival were so stunned by the appearance of Sullivan and his well-organized—not to mention well-armed—men that they surrendered without firing a shot. Sullivan and Langdon collected the guns and powder and carried them off for safekeeping and eventual distribution.

The Quickening Pace of Rebellion

At this point, General Gage was not so much alarmed by what was going on around him as he was befuddled by it all. The organization, coordination, and speed of colonial action were dumbfounding. In rapid succession, the Massachusetts Provincial Congress had appropriated funds to purchase military supplies, had called up the militia, and had set up a central Committee of Safety. All that Gage could think of doing was to pronounce these acts treasonable. But by the time he even issued this proclamation, the Provincial Congress, having enacted the foundation for revolution, promptly dissolved itself and evaporated on December 10, 1774, leaving Gage no body of traitors to arrest.

Not that the general stood idle. While the colonists armed and organized, he deployed his troops, positioning and preparing them—only to find himself repeatedly on the receiving end of the deeds of colonial saboteurs. His supply barges mysteriously sank. Straw laboriously stockpiled for soldiers' bedding inexplicably burst into flame. Wagons, mustered to carry the multitude of heavy baggage a conventional army far from home required, suddenly turned up wrecked and ruined. Everywhere he turned, New Englanders were drilling, and when they weren't practicing for war, they were stealing for it. Crown munitions dwindled and disappeared from arsenals and armories.

Soon, acts of rebellion were so numerous and widespread that Gage scarcely knew what to attend to next. He reasoned, however, that there could be no rebellion without arms and ammunition, so his first priority had to be putting a halt to the theft of munitions. Accordingly, at midnight of February 25, 1775, he sent Colonel Alexander Leslie with the 240 men of the 64th Foot Regiment from Castle William, Boston Harbor, to Salem, Massachusetts, where, he had heard, the rebels had squirreled away some stolen cannons and powder.

Occurrence at Salem Bridge

As he landed his troops at Marblehead, Massachusetts, from where he planned to march to Salem, Colonel Leslie had no idea that one John Pedrick, another Sons of Liberty courier, had already ridden out to Salem with word of his approach. Gage's intelligence was

DETAILS, DETAILS
Sixty Seconds or Less

The term *Minutemen* not only described the ready-in-a-minute status of the Massachusetts militia, but was also used to distinguish the militia organizations created in the fall of 1774 from existing organizations, which included large numbers of Tories or Loyalists. In September, the resignation of all officers in Worcester's militia was demanded, and the three original regiments were re-formed into seven new ones, with new officers elected. These officers were instructed to choose one-third of the men in each new regiment to be ready to assemble under arms on a minute's notice. Throughout the rest of the fall, other Massachusetts militia units followed Worcester's example.

correct: nineteen cannon had been secreted in Salem. More precisely, nineteen cannon *barrels* were stored in the town. The plan had been to take them across a drawbridge to a forge, where they would be mated with carriages. Pedrick's timely warning, however, prompted citizens to move the barrels elsewhere. Presumably to cover this removal, Patriot colonel Timothy Pickering assembled his forty Minutemen at the open drawbridge, just in time to meet Leslie and his 240 redcoats.

As a crowd of Salem residents gathered, Leslie demanded that Pickering lower the bridge. Pickering refused, and both sides seemed ready to open fire. At this point, a Salem preacher stepped out of the crowd and suggested a compromise. He persuaded Pickering to lower the draw on condition that Leslie's troops advance no farther than thirty rods (495 feet) into the town, satisfy themselves that there were no cannon here, turn around, then march right out. With both sides agreed on this, the redcoats advanced, looked, found nothing, and, true to their word, left.

It was another non-battle, like that at Fort William and Mary, and it might have been lost to history had not the redcoats, returning to Boston via a town called Northfields, encountered one Sarah Tarrant. This lady threw open the sash of her window and called down to the passing column: "Go home and tell your master he has sent you on a fool's errand and broken the peace of our Sabbath. What, do you think we were born in the woods, to be frightened by owls?"

Her words were significant for two reasons. First, they were spoken by someone who knew all about what had just happened at Salem. Clearly, the colonists were communicating with one another much more quickly than soldiers were able to march. Second, her words were sufficient to provoke one soldier to unshoulder his musket and point it at her. "Fire," Sarah Tarrant taunted him, "if you have the courage—but I doubt it." He lowered his weapon, shouldered it again, and trudged on.

Give Me—Liberty!

Did Sarah Tarrant gamble that a British soldier would not dare shoot an unarmed woman? Or was she willing to be killed in the name of liberty? We cannot know, but her brief, homely speech carved into history its modest niche nevertheless.

Down in Virginia, no one ever accused Patrick Henry, a prosperous lawyer renowned for his silver tongue, of anything modest. Whether defending an accused criminal or prosecuting a lawsuit, he was given to big speeches propelled by brilliant wit. A member of Virginia's House of Burgesses since 1765, he led his fellow legislators to a meeting at Raleigh Tavern on May 27, 1774, after the colony's royal governor, John Murray, Lord Dunmore, dissolved the assembly for talking rebellion. During one of these meetings-in-exile, on March 23, 1775, Patrick Henry rose in speech:

Patrick Henry's famed "Give me liberty, or give me death" speech of March 23, 1775, was depicted by Currier & Ives in a lithograph published during the nation's first centennial, 1876.

> There is no retreat but in submission and slavery! Our chains are forged. Their clanking may be heard on the plains of Boston! The war is inevitable—and let it come! I repeat it, sir, let it come!
>
> It is in vain, sir, to extenuate the matter. Gentlemen may cry, "Peace! Peace!"—but there is no peace. The war is actually begun! The next gale that sweeps down from the north will bring to our ears the clash of resounding arms! Our brethren are already in the field! Why stand we here idle? What is it that gentlemen wish? What would they have? Is life so dear, or peace so sweet, as to be purchased at the price of chains and slavery? Forbid it, Almighty God! I know not what course others may take, but as for me, give me liberty or give me death!

Unlike Sarah Tarrant, Patrick Henry was not looking down the barrel of a musket, yet no one doubted that he meant what he said—that the choice had come down to one of two courses: liberty or death. And, with each passing week, more and more colonists—more and more *Americans*—were beginning to see the situation in just that way.

Revere Rides—Again

Even if the nineteenth-century American poet Henry Wadsworth Longfellow hadn't written the words "Listen my children, and you shall hear / Of the midnight ride of Paul Revere," his name would still be well known to passionate collectors of early American silver. By the early 1770s, Paul Revere was the most famous silversmith in the country, admired for his exquisite work in silver as well as gold, including fine tableware, precisely crafted surgical instruments, spectacle frames, and even replacements for missing teeth.

The "Liberty Bowl," fashioned in 1768 by Patriot silversmith Paul Revere, is engraved with the names of the Massachusetts legislators who signed the "Massachusetts Circular Letter," urging the other colonies to join in a boycott of British goods until the Townshend taxes were repealed.

Paul Revere was an artist and an artisan. He was no orator and certainly not a politician. However, he was the son of one Apollos Rivoire, who had immigrated to America when he was thirteen years old, just one of thousands of Huguenots (French Protestants) fleeing the religious persecution they suffered at home. Rivoire became the apprentice of Boston silversmith John Coney and, later, apprenticed his son Paul to himself. Paul Revere proved an apt pupil—and he was also both personable and popular, earning a reputation as someone who could never bring himself to refuse a dare. Hungry for danger, he served two years with a Massachusetts regiment in the French and Indian War, then returned to Boston to make his way as a silversmith. Besides his trade, he doubtless also learned from his Huguenot father the true value of liberty, and perhaps it was this that drove him to make friendships among the movers and shakers of Boston politics. Sam Adams, John Adams, John Hancock, James Otis, and Dr. Joseph Warren—all knew and admired Paul Revere. Did they dare him to dress up as a Mohawk and join other similarly attired Bostonians in dumping tea into Boston Harbor? Did they dare him to ride as fast as he could when he carried the Suffolk Resolves from Boston to Philadelphia—or when they sent him off on his other horseback errands for the Sons of Liberty? Or was it his love of liberty that moved him to volunteer whenever a swift messenger was needed?

POP CULTURE
Precious Metal

Paul Revere prospered as a silversmith in his lifetime, but, in 1863, long after his death—but just after Longfellow published "Paul Revere's Ride"—the value of authentic Revere silverware skyrocketed. Wall Street tycoon J. P. Morgan offered Mrs. Marston Perry $100,000—the equivalent of millions today—for a Revere punch bowl commemorating the Sons of Liberty. The Longfellow poem also gave rise to a rumor that Revere made a set of dentures for George Washington. True, Revere made false teeth; true, Washington had false teeth; but there is no evidence that the Boston silversmith made dentures for him.

On Sunday, April 16, 1775, Joseph Warren sent Revere to warn John Hancock and Sam Adams that General Gage was sending troops to arrest them. The reason? On March 30, 1775, George III assented to Parliament's New England Trade and Fisheries Act. Popularly called the New England Restraining Act, it limited New England's trade to Britain and the British West Indies, prohibiting trade with other nations, and it barred New England ships from the North Atlantic fisheries. This prompted Massachusetts to revive the Provincial Congress, which then called on Dr. Warren and his Committee of Safety to begin the transformation of the colony into an armed camp. On April 12, General Gage responded by imposing martial law and issuing a blanket indictment against the colonists, declaring everyone to be "in treason." This notwithstanding, he offered full and free pardons to everyone—with the exception of the ringleaders, Samuel Adams and John Hancock. Thus Revere rode off to Lexington, Massachusetts, and told the two men that they must prepare to flee.

Paul Revere's "midnight ride" on April 18, 1775, to alert the Patriot militia between Boston and Lexington to the march of the redcoats on the eve of the battles of Lexington and Concord, has been depicted in countless popular images. This one, from about 1870, was intended to decorate a bank note.

—and Again

In addition to riding hard, fast, and far, Paul Revere was spymaster in a ring of Boston citizen-spies. The ring had observed Gage preparing his grenadiers and light infantry, as well as repairing a flotilla of whaleboats, leading Revere to conclude that a British raid on Concord (where a cache of Patriot arms and ammunition was stored) was probably imminent. As soon as he returned to Boston from

FORGOTTEN FACES
Sybil's Ride

Paul Revere was not the Revolution's only rider of note. Sixteen-year-old Sybil Ludington lived in the small Putnam County, New York, village named for her family, Ludington Mills, the daughter of a Patriot militia colonel. On April 26, 1777, a messenger appeared at the Ludingtons' door, warning of the approach of the British. Colonel Ludington had little time to summon and organized his militiamen, who lived miles apart from one another across the countryside. The messenger and his horse were spent, and the colonel had to remain at home, planning the regiment's action. It fell to Sybil, a strong and capable rider, and her horse, Star, to make a thirty-mile circuit through the night and rain sounding the alarm: "Muster at Ludingtons!" The people of Carmel, New York, erected a statue of her, astride Star, as a monument to the courage of a faithful daughter and courageous Patriot.

Lexington, therefore, Revere put his spies on high alert. He arranged for a signal that would alert the Charlestown countryside to the movement of Gage's troops. He stationed his friend, John Pulling, in the steeple of the North Church. If Pulling saw troops marching out of Boston by land, he would show a single lantern from the steeple. As immortalized in the excerpt below from Longfellow's poem, if he saw that they had boarded the whaleboats to take them across the Back Bay water, he would shine two lanterns—and Revere would know that they were embarking to attack Concord:

> He said to his friend, "If the British march
> By land or sea from the town to-night,
> Hang a lantern aloft in the belfry arch
> Of the North Church tower as a signal light,—
> One if by land, and two if by sea;
> And I on the opposite shore will be,
> Ready to ride and spread the alarm
> Through every Middlesex village and farm,
> For the country folk to be up and to arm."

Henry Wadsworth Longfellow, "Paul Revere's Ride," 1863

Paul Revere had a female counterpart in sixteen-year-old Sybil Ludington of Putnam County, New York, who rode thirty miles to muster the local Patriot militia on April 26, 1777.

On April 18, Gage dispatched mounted officers along the road to Concord to clear it of rebel couriers. After nightfall, the sergeants were sent to rouse the light infantrymen and grenadiers from slumber. These men—six hundred to eight hundred of Gage's elite troops—were quickly and quietly mustered on Boston Common. They were entrusted to the command of Lieutenant Colonel Francis Smith, assisted by Major John Pitcairn of the Royal Marines. By half past ten, they were ready to march—and they made straight for the whaleboats.

Pulling watched the troops and knew what to do. He opened the slides on two lanterns, which shone from the North Church steeple. Seeing this, Revere and another Sons of Liberty courier, William Dawes, set out from Boston to raise the alarm throughout the countryside. The British were heading, across the bay water, for Concord.

Dawes and Revere split up, Dawes taking the longer overland route to Concord, via Boston Neck to Cambridge and Menotomy (modern Arlington), then west to Lexington and Concord, while Revere rowed over to Charlestown, took horse there, and galloped off by eleven.

It was not a stealthy ride, but a loud one—as loud as Revere could make it. Over and over again he shouted: "The regulars are out!" And if a window was dark or a light failed to go on, he threw a fistful of pebbles against the glass for good measure.

Revere reached Lexington about midnight and rode up to the house of Parson Jonas Clark, where John Hancock (the parson's cousin) and Sam Adams had taken refuge. Militiaman William Munroe stood guard.

Breathless, Revere yelled to Munroe: "Open the door!"

"Please!" Munroe whispered hoarsely. "Not so loud! The family has just retired and doesn't want any noise about the house."

"Noise!" Revere exploded. "You'll have noise enough before long. The regulars are out!"

Now it was Munroe himself who burst into the house to wake Hancock and Adams.

"What a glorious morning this is!" Sam Adams proclaimed as he stepped out into the midnight. And when Hancock looked at him incredulously, he added: "I mean for America."

REALITY CHECK
Crying Out Loud
Revere's warning cry was "The regulars are out!"—not, as popular lore has it, "The redcoats are coming!"

About an hour behind Revere, Dawes rendezvoused with him in Lexington, and the two rode on together to Concord. En route, they were joined by Dr. Samuel Prescott, who had spent most of the evening courting his intended bride. Now he, too, lent his voice to rousing the countryside from slumber.

As Prescott and Dawes paused to wake a certain house, Revere rode on—only to be stopped by a knot of redcoats.

"God damn you, stop!" one of them ordered. "If you go an inch farther you are a dead man."

All three men were arrested, but Prescott immediately escaped, and Dawes slipped away soon afterward. Only Revere was held. An officer rode up to him.

"Don't be afraid," the officer said, indicating his blustering men. "They will not hurt you."

Revere betrayed no sign of alarm. "You've missed your purpose," he said.

The officer explained that he and his men were hunting for deserters.

"I know better. I know what you're after," said Revere. "You're too late. I've alarmed the country all the way up. I should have five hundred men at Lexington soon."

This captured the young officer's attention, and he sent off for his commander, a Major Mitchell.

Mitchell was in no mood for provincial impertinence. Cocking his pistol, he put the muzzle against the silversmith's temple and quietly demanded to know the truth, the whole truth.

In reality, it did not require a gun to the head to prompt Paul Revere to reveal that the entire countryside was prepared and eager to fight.

According to some sources, Mitchell responded by ordering Revere to mount, then handed the reins to one of his men and ordered him to lead Revere off. After a mile or so, as if realizing that the damage had already been done, the redcoat let Paul Revere ride into what was left of the night. Other sources report that Revere was released without a horse and returned on foot, barely in time to witness part of the battle on the Lexington Green.

TOWARD MORNING

Revere rode back to Clark's house, where he was flabbergasted to find Adams and Hancock still arguing about what they should do.

Revere settled the debate with a single word: *Flee!* And he accompanied the pair to a crossroads, pointed them toward Philadelphia, and told them to start riding.

It was April 19, 1775, but still hours from dawn of that day. As Adams and Hancock began the long trip to Philadelphia, Gage's regulars lifted themselves out of the whaleboats that had taken them from Boston to Lechmere Point. Ahead of them, they knew, was a sixteen-mile march to Concord, the still-dark morning wet and cold, their clumsy muskets long (thirty-nine inches) and heavy (fourteen pounds). They knew it would not be a pleasant march—but, suddenly, it got a whole lot worse. No sooner had they clambered from their boats than shots rang out from unseen shooters and church bells tolled from every steeple. The whole countryside, it seemed, knew they were on their way to Concord.

Chapter 6

OPENING SHOTS

*Lexington, Concord, and
the Other Early Battles*

THE BOUNDARY SEPARATING AN UNEASY PEACE from outright war was about to be crossed. Despite all they had seen and heard of colonial solidarity and determination, neither the British officers nor the enlisted soldiers doubted they would easily crush any rebellion. They insisted on regarding the Yankees as little more than a rabble. And what chance did a rabble have against the finest soldiers of Europe?

*"I am satisfied that one active campaign, a smart action,
and burning two or three of their towns,
will set everything to rights."*

*Major John Pitcairn, Royal Marines, April 1775,
just before the battles of Lexington and Concord*

LONG ODDS—BUT JUST HOW LONG?

HAVING DEFEATED FRANCE AND SPAIN in the French and Indian War (as well as in the European theater of that war, known as the Seven Years War), Britain was now the most powerful country on the planet. No nation had a standing army superior to that of Britain, and its navy was without peer. In contrast, the colonies had no army—just militia units, including the Minutemen—and certainly no navy. It is little wonder that King George and the conservative forces in Parliament had no real fear of an American Revolution. After all, how could a handful of upstart colonists hope to prevail against a world power?

The Americans understood Britain's position in the world. Many were even proud of it. Yet those increasingly bent on achieving home rule—or even total independence—were nevertheless contemptuous of British soldiers' skill at arms. Yes, the French and Indian War had been won, but many a colonist remembered how the redcoats under General Edward Braddock had simply panicked, blundered, and died at the Battle of the Wilderness (1755) early in that war.

Ever since the French and Indian War, the colonists had had plenty of opportunity to watch redcoats march and drill, which the troops were certainly good at. Yet the colonists also saw that the individual British soldier was an indifferent marksman at best. This was not due to a deficiency of aptitude, but was a product of training. British officers, like officers in all European armies, regarded their men as brutes, rogues, and criminals to be whipped into sufficient shape to enable them to march mindlessly and in perfect unison. Under fire, their job was to stand and shoot until they were killed or the battle was won. The skill of the individual marksman was unimportant when one line of soldiers faced another at fifty yards' distance. All that really counted in this situation was the ability of the men to fire a simultaneous volley, move to the rear without tripping over one another, reload, and fire another volley. It was the unbroken tempo of massed fire that counted, not the accuracy of any individual shot.

In contrast to this, the Yankee farmer used his weapon to hunt and typically prided himself on marksmanship (especially since shot and powder were costly, hard to come by, and had to be conserved). What little military experience most colonists had was in

DETAILS, DETAILS
What's in a Name?

Modern historians generally refer to the revolutionary activists as *Patriots,* with a capital *P.* The term was certainly used before and during the American Revolution, but it was not the only name by which the revolutionaries were identified. They were also called *Whigs,* after the liberal party in the mother country, Conversely, the Loyalists were often called *Tories,* after the British conservative party. British troops and officers, as well as British Tories, usually referred to the revolutionaries as rebels (lowercase *r*), whereas British Whigs, who favored the independence of the American colonies, called them *Americans.* Few revolutionaries referred to themselves as Americans, however. Even after banding together, colonists—Patriots and Tories alike—typically identified with their home colony, calling themselves Massachusetts men, New Yorkers, Virginians, and so on.

REALITY CHECK
Spare the Rod . . .

There is truth in the judgment that the Patriots enjoyed a "home field" advantage over the British regulars. Whereas the militiamen and other volunteers fought for their liberty and homeland, the redcoats, far from home, fought because they had been ordered to. Yet the officers of both sides relied heavily on corporal punishment and the brutal threat of it. In 1775, militia captain Parker warned, "The first man who offers to run shall be shot down," and in 1776, at the ill-fated Battle of Manhattan, General George Washington was seen rallying his panicked troops not with inspiring words, but with the flat of his saber smartly laid across backs and backsides.

combat against Indians. Such fights were not confrontations between two neatly arrayed lines of troops, but a matter of one man against another. Miss your mark, and you gave your enemy an opportunity to kill you. Those who survived skirmishes with Indians were generally very good shooters.

This is not to say that most Americans were Indian fighters. Few colonists had ever fired a weapon in anger, and the majority of town dwellers never handled a gun at all. Still, few were impressed by the British "regular." Nor was this low opinion strictly a matter of marksmanship. Schoolbook histories teach us that the colonists called the British soldier "redcoat." In fact, the more common name for him, at least in New England, was "lobsterback," a mocking slur inspired by the sight of the bare back of the typical British regular, which was striped with angry scars and scarlet welts, the evidence of a military policy that mistook brutality for discipline. In the British army, the smallest infraction was "corrected" with the lash, and Thomas Gage earned a reputation (among fellow officers) for leniency because he reduced the generally accepted penalty for desertion from execution by hanging to the administration of a thousand lashes. Moreover, since he understood that a thousand lashes given all at one time was invariably fatal—not to mention exhausting to the sergeant who administered the punishment—Gage decreed that the lashes were to be meted out at the rate of 250 per week over four weeks. Lenient? The fact was that British soldiers deserted in droves, especially in America, and to have hanged them all would have thinned the ranks to an unacceptable level.

To colonists, the lobsterbacks were slaves—or worse: the willing victims of British tyranny. They were not perceived as British patriots, loyal to the Crown, so much as cowering men mindful of the whip. Aware of the low morale prevailing among the regulars, colonials routinely enticed individuals to desert, even giving them a piece of land and a fresh start in America in exchange for their services as trainers of green militia companies.

Viewed from a distance, it was absurd to think of the armyless, navyless colonies engaging the mighty British Empire in battle. Close up, however, the odds were not quite so long as they at first appeared.

. . . Back at Lexington

As described at the end of Chapter 5, musket fire and peal of church bells greeted the British grenadiers and light infantrymen as they disembarked at Lechmere before dawn on April 19, 1775. It was enough to prompt Lieutenant Colonel Smith and Major Pitcairn to send riders back to Boston to summon reinforcements. Clearly, the element of surprise had been lost, and they were going to need all the help they could get.

As the red-coated regulars left their boats at Lechmere Point, militia captain Jonas Parker dressed the ranks of the seventy or so citizen-soldiers he had been able to muster on the green at Lexington, which fronted the Concord road, along the British line of march from Boston to Concord.

Perhaps these militiamen passed the predawn hours trading jibes about the lobsterbacks, but one can imagine their thoughts once they actually glimpsed the approach of Pitcairn's advance guard: scarlet-coated marines, smartly crossed cartridge belts, meticulously whitened with pipe clay, catching the morning sun, a "Brown Bess" musket on each shoulder. We know that one of Parker's men was heard to murmur, "so few of us. It is folly to stand here." And we also know that Parker roared back: "The first man who offers to run shall be shot down."

Parker and his men were about to confront a superior British force—superior in numbers, superior in equipment, and superior in conventional military training—on terms that favored the British. For they were not fighting in the wilderness—the crafty American frontiersmen hiding behind rocks or concealed by forest growth—but were meeting in the open, as on any European field of battle. Pitcairn ordered his reluctant men to form their line of battle—a standard shooting formation, two men deep—to allow the front line to fire a volley, then move to the rear and reload as the second line fired its volley. It sounded easy enough, but handling the cumbersome Brown Bess was by no means easy, especially under fire—the barrels were almost four feet long!

Tories, also called Loyalists—those who remained loyal to the king—were subject to all manner of abuse at the hands of Patriots, ranging from intimidation to murder. In between these extremes was tarring and feathering—shown here in a 1795 print—in which the victim was painted with hot tar onto which loose chicken or goose feathers were thrown. The treatment caused potentially serious burns, but its principal purpose was to make the victim look ridiculous.

Line of Fire

"Brown Bess" was the familiar name for most firelock muskets of the eighteenth century, including those used by British and American forces in the American Revolution.

MORE OFFICIALLY, THE ROYAL ARMY referred to it as the Long Land Pattern Service Musket. No one knows for certain where the familiar name came from. The origin of the "Brown" part is easy enough to guess, since the walnut gunstock was typically brown. The source of "Bess" is more obscure. Some speculate that it might refer to Queen Elizabeth I, although that seems unlikely, since the Long Land Musket entered service a full century after the death of Good Queen Bess. Others have claimed that the musket was named after a legendary highwayman (bandit) who used a musket and rode a horse named Black Bess. Linguistically minded authorities suggest that "Bess" is a corruption of the Dutch buss, meaning gun barrel, or the German Büchse, gun. Finally, some suggest that "Bess" is an expression of the soldier's intimate relationship to his weapon, which he hugs as he would a wife or lover. Even today, soldiers sometimes christen their weapons with the name of a girlfriend or—yes—mother.

A British Manual of Arms during this period prescribed no fewer than a dozen precise motions for loading, aiming, firing, and reloading the Brown Bess. Getting through all twelve steps meant that the average soldier could squeeze off two shots a minute. An excellent soldier (and

the troops under Smith and Pitcairn were the best in Britain) could get off as many as five shots in those same sixty seconds.

Experienced officers such as Smith and Pitcairn knew what they could expect from their lines of fire. They knew, for example, that the first volley was invariably the most effective, because the troops had had ample time to load their powder and the bullet carefully, ensuring that both were properly tamped down with the ramrod. Once the fight heated up, however, fire became increasingly less dependable—especially with a fourteen-inch bayonet fixed in place, which made manipulating the ramrod and shoving it down the barrel very awkward indeed. As reloading became more hasty, shooting became less effective. Many muskets misfired or propelled the ball at a lower velocity, which meant it was both less accurate and less destructive.

This British grenadier stands with his "Brown Bess" musket, a name possibly derived from the color of the weapon—although it is true that, during the American Revolution, gun stocks were often painted in a variety of colors, not always brown. Metal gun barrels were often "russetted," or coated with a brown rust-inhibitor; again, however, the British army generally left their barrels untreated, so that they were bright gunmetal rather than brown.

The famed American illustrator Howard Pyle, in 1898, painted this representation of the redcoats advancing up Breed's Hill during the Battle of Bunker Hill, which illustrates the machine like precision of a line-of-fire formation.

Experienced officers left to chance as little as possible. The ideal was to transform men into the components of a machine. After the front rank fired, its men, with crisp movements, retired behind the second—or third—rank to reload. As it reloaded, what had been the second row fired, and while it reloaded, the third fired—by which time the original front row had rotated back to the front, and, having reloaded, fired again. None of this was expected to come off spontaneously. Each movement—loading, ramming, cocking, priming the pan, and firing—came in response to an order barked by a sergeant or an officer. If the machine was working the way it should, a volley was fired every fifteen seconds.

The really hard thing was to keep the machine running smoothly while its all-too-human components were taking fire from the enemy machine arrayed against them. The effective maximum range of the Brown Bess was no more than one hundred yards, but no competent officer would open fire at that extreme end of the weapon's effectiveness. Instead, he would close with the enemy to about half that distance, fifty yards, and if he were a really good commander, he would withhold the order to open fire until after the enemy had started shooting. To be sure, this meant that you would suffer the first losses, but when you returned fire, you would have the advantage of about one-third greater firepower—assuming a three-rank line of fire—because you had three ranks ready to fire, whereas the enemy had just two (as long as it took the first rank to reload). Moreover, while the enemy had been standing to fire, your men were still advancing, which meant that your first volley would be fired at closer range than that of the enemy and so would be that much more devastating.

Such tactics were simple in concept, but difficult in execution. Opposing forces approached each other in two masses, each a perfect target for the other. Men would fall on both sides, but the side that fired, reloaded, and fired again at the faster rate inflicted more casualties while sustaining fewer losses. That side, therefore, was the victor.

It was just such a mass that tramped toward the line arrayed on Lexington green.

"Stand your ground. Don't fire unless fired upon. But if they want to have a war, let it begin here!"

Such is the account of Parker's words that has been passed down to us. The words are tailored so neatly to the requirements of history that most modern historians suspect fabrication after the fact. Whatever it was that Parker said—or failed to say—a number of the Lexington militiamen, beholding the approach of the scarlet wave, blinked, shrugged, and simply walked away.

Seeing this, Pitcairn brought his men close, halted them, withheld his order to fire, and instead called out to the militiamen who remained on the green: "Lay down your arms, you rebels, and disperse!"

Captain Jonas Parker had a choice. He could respond in the manner of a conventional European officer and order his men to give battle. In that case, outnumbered, outgunned, and outtrained, he and his men would have been cut down. Alternatively, he could surrender on the terms Pitcairn commanded: order his men to lay down their muskets and walk away. Instead of doing either, Parker ordered his militia company to fall out—but to take their weapons with them.

Pitcairn was having none of it. He repeated his demand that they lay their weapons down.

Parker's refusal either to fight or to surrender created a kind of vacuum of anarchy. Without orders on either side, someone fired. A British regular was slightly wounded in the leg, and two balls grazed Pitcairn's horse. Were the shots from a British or an American musket? No one knew—or knows. But they were enough to prompt a British officer to order a volley. No sooner was the volley loosed than Pitcairn ordered a ceasefire.

"Form and surround them," Pitcairn commanded.

To his stunned dismay, instead of forming as ordered, his men fired a second volley. Perhaps all those months of anxious waiting in Boston under the endless taunts of the city's citizens had taken their toll. Whatever the reason, discipline dissolved.

Those militiamen who had not already run off returned fire, not in a volley, but catch-as-catch-can. Undisciplined fire is ineffective fire—except that, in this instance, it stirred the hornet's nest. Apparently without orders, the redcoats, their bayonets already fixed, charged what remained of the American line. All but

Parker now fled. He had been wounded in the first or second volley, but was still standing, quite alone now. He was struggling to reload when the British bayonets cut him down.

On Lexington green, eight militiamen, including Captain Parker, lay dead. Ten more writhed with the agony of their wounds. Except for the British regular hit in the leg, Pitcairn's men suffered no casualties. Such was the Battle of Lexington, which most historians consider the first battle of the American Revolution.

Britons were eager for news of the American Revolution. This map, published in 1775, shows Boston and environs, including Lexington and Concord sites "of the late engagement between the King's troops & the provincials."

HEARD 'ROUND THE WORLD

SOME OF THE BRITISH AT LEXINGTON may have taken note of Captain Parker's heroism. Or perhaps they saw his death as that of a misguided rebel who didn't have the sense to run. In any case, based on this first encounter, the redcoats had little reason to fear the American fighting man as they resumed their march on Concord.

What they did not know is that word of the engagement at Lexington traveled to Concord and the surrounding communities much faster than they could march. Militia companies poured in— so many that no one knows just how many Americans were ultimately involved in the Battle of Concord. Some have guessed as many as twenty thousand, but that number hardly seems credible. The most reliable computation is that, before the battle was over, 3,763 Patriots had fought—but never more than about half this number at any one time, since, as fresh militiamen arrived, others, exhausted with battle, their supply of forty or so rounds spent, left the field.

By the time the British arrived in Concord—and the arrival was initially unopposed—just about four hundred militiamen, commanded by James Barrett, a local resident who bore the lofty

REALITY CHECK
Drummer, Private

Many histories of the American Revolution describe Abner Hosmer as a "drummer boy," which calls to mind the youngster in Archibald Willard's classic painting *The Spirit of '76*. In fact, Hosmer was twenty-one years old when he fell at Lexington, and, while he was a drummer, he also carried a musket. He was born in Acton, Massachusetts, on August 21, 1754, the third son of Jonathan and Martha (Conant) Hosmer.

rank of colonel, had mustered on a ridge overlooking the town. In the town below, Lieutenant Colonel Smith took no notice of them, but casually entered a local tavern with his staff officers and purchased dinner and libations while his grenadiers began searching house to house for hidden munitions.

They were turning up much less than they had anticipated—mostly bullets; however, they discovered a number of gun carriages, which they instantly put to the torch. Seeing the flames, one of Barrett's officers pointedly asked: "Will you let them burn the town down?"

Barrett apparently said nothing by way of reply, but calmly ordered the militia down from the ridge to march to the defense of Concord. He cautioned his men to hold fire unless and until fired upon.

The first to see Barrett's men approach was the captain of the British light infantry. Stunned, he hastily formed up his men into two ranks. It was the standard drill, of course: the first rank would fire a volley then slip behind the second rank to reload while the second rank, now up front, fired. Yet something went wrong. The well-drilled maneuver faltered and failed. The resulting volley was ragged, broken, and the men stumbled over each other as they moved behind the second rank. Most of the shots fell short,

This eighteenth-century engraving by Cornelius Tiebout depicts the Minutemen firing on the British at the Battle of Lexington. Note the wife, at lower right, reluctant to let her Patriot husband join the fight.

Emerson's Hymn

When he wrote the poem below, Emerson was on the verge of his early fame as a philosophical essayist, but he still possessed enough of the common touch to pen popular patriotic verse. His "shot heard round the world" was early evidence of his gift for crafting memorable aphorisms, which would come to include "Whoso would be a man must be a nonconformist," "Things are in the saddle and ride mankind," "The only way to have a friend is to be one," "Hitch your wagon to a star," "To be great is to be misunderstood," and "Build a better mousetrap, and the world will beat a path to your door," among many others.

Hymn Sung at the Completion of the Concord Monument, April 19, 1836

By the rude bridge that arched the flood,
Their flag to April's breeze unfurled,
Here once the embattled farmers stood,
And fired the shot heard round the world.

The foe long since in silence slept;
Alike the conqueror silent sleeps;
And Time the ruined bridge has swept
Down the dark stream which seaward creeps.

On this green bank, by this soft stream,
We set to-day a votive stone;
That memory may their deed redeem,
When, like our sires, our sons are gone.

Spirit, that made those heroes dare
To die, and leave their children free,
Bid Time and Nature gently spare
The shaft we raise to them and thee.

—*Ralph Waldo Emerson*

rippling the surface of the river like so many cast pebbles. Two did find marks. Militia captain Isaac Davis fell dead, as did one private, Abner Hosmer. These casualties did not dishearten the Americans, who, in contrast to the little band at Lexington, marched like soldiers.

According to the most popular account, the first American shots came when an officer called out: "Fire, fellow soldier! For God sake, fire!"

"Fellow soldier" was, of course, a fellow citizen, a militiaman, and not a professional warrior. Years later, in his "Hymn Sung at the Completion of the Concord Monument, April 19, 1836," the philosopher-poet Ralph Waldo Emerson would write of Concord's "embattled farmers," one of whom fired the first shot—"the shot heard round the world."

Victory at Concord

In that first exchange of fire, three British soldiers died, and nine more were wounded. The light infantry hastily withdrew into the town, eliciting from Barrett's men loud cheers.

That jubilation was evidence that the militiamen were, after all, civilians first and soldiers second. Had they been professionals commanded by a professional, they would not have stood and cheered, but pressed forward. A retreating force is always vulnerable—you can't shoot backwards—and good soldiers don't let such a force get away. Yet instead of pursuing the retreating British, no one but a single militiaman, ax in hand, even ventured as far as North Bridge, where the light infantry had left its dead and wounded. As the militiaman crossed the bridge, one of the prostrate redcoats stirred, whereupon the "embattled farmer" buried his ax in the man's skull.

Among those who witnessed this act of gratuitous brutality were the grenadiers, who were just that moment marching back from having searched none other than Colonel Barrett's house. They had heard rumors that, during the French and Indian War, some Americans fought like Native Americans. Now they gasped. An *American* had scalped a *British* soldier! Instead of exciting in them a desire for vengeance, the grisly spectacle chilled them with terror and apparently took the fight out of them.

The first engagement at Concord was over by ten o'clock in the morning. Colonel Smith set about collecting his wounded and prepared to leave Concord to return to Boston. About an hour before this, in Boston, drums were beating and fifes were piping. It was a tune that had become familiar to Bostonians, a tune with words about a fellow named Yankee Doodle who went to town "riding on a pony." The British intended the ditty to mock the bumpkin rebels. Later, those rebels would adopt it as their own, but right now it was the marching song of about fourteen hundred British soldiers (including 460 Royal Marines), who drew behind them 2 six-pound cannons. Led by thirty-three-year-old Lord Hugh Percy, they marched over Boston Neck and through Roxbury on their way to reinforce the expedition sent to Concord.

These reinforcements were surprised at how silent the countryside was. True, some saboteur had pried out the planks of the

Yankee Doodle Dandy

The lyrics to "Yankee Doodle" are attributed to Dr. Richard Schuckburgh, a British army surgeon during the French and Indian War, who intended to ridicule the provincial American volunteers. Historians still debate the roots of the tune—some believe it dates back to fifteenth-century Holland, where it was sung as a harvesting song. In the sixteenth century, the British supposedly changed the lyrics to make it a derisive song about Oliver Cromwell. By the time of the American Revolution, "Yankee Doodle" had accumulated as many as 190 verses. The below excerpt dates from after George Washington assumed command of the Continental army in June 1775.

Yankee Doodle

Father and I went down to camp
Along with Captain Gooding
And there we saw the men and boys
As thick as hasty pudding. . . .

Chorus
Yankee Doodle, keep it up
Yankee Doodle dandy

Mind the music and the step
And with the girls be handy.
And there was Captain Washington

Upon a slapping stallion
A-giving orders to his men
I guess there was a million.

The Farmer and his Son's return from a visit to the CAMP.

FATHER and I went down to camp,
   Along with Captain Gooding,
And there we fee the men and boys
   As thick as hafty pudding.
Yankey doodle keep it up, yankey doodle
   dandy,
Mind the mufic and the ftep,
And with the girls be handy.

And there we fee a thoufand men,
   As rich as fquire David,
And what they wafted every day,
   I wifh it had been faved.
        Yankey doodle, &c.

The 'laffes they eat every day,

And ftuck a crooked ftabbing iron
   Upon the little end on't.
        Yankee doodle, &c.

And there I fee a pumpkin fhell,
   As big as mother's bafon,
And every time they touch'd it off,
   They fcamper'd like the nation.
        Yankee doodle, &c.

I fee a little barrel too,
   The heads were made of leather,
They knock'd upon 'ith little clubs,
   And call'd the folk together.
        Yankee doodle, &c.

And there was captain Walhington,

We call the most famous song of the American Revolution "Yankee Doodle," but its original title was "The Farmer and His Son's Return from a Visit to the Camp." The song originated with the redcoats and was meant to make fun of the unpolished, untrained, and ill-equipped Patriot militiamen, but was soon taken up by the very objects of the intended ridicule. This broadside from 1775 is one of the earliest extant versions of the song.

Charles River Bridge, which slowed the advance of the column, but there was no other sign of resistance. The village of Cambridge, whose citizens routinely made a sport of taunting British soldiers, was utterly silent, deserted.

Where was everybody? Lord Percy and his men were about to find out.

From every village and every farm between Boston and Concord, militiamen suddenly materialized. These men did not deploy themselves in neat lines of battle, but instead took up positions behind stone walls and trees—some crouched inside houses—so that the road to Concord became a gauntlet of shots fired from unseen snipers. Lord Percy's men began falling, one here, another there.

Amos Doolittle's contemporary (1775) line engraving depicts the entrance of the British troops into Concord, Massachusetts, on April 19, 1775.

*"There was not a stone-wall or house,
though before in appearance evacuated,
from whence the Rebels did not fire upon us."*

Lord Percy to Thomas Gage,
April 20, 1775

Still, Percy marched on, toward Smith and Pitcairn's detachment, which had already begun their retreat from Concord. Militiamen now poured into the village and the surrounding area. They were not well organized, and Smith's light infantry was able to mount a number of blistering counterattacks against isolated militia bands. When they surprised some of the militia lying in wait in local houses, the British not only killed the men, but torched the houses as well.

Despite this, the militia continued to arrive, and as the British slipped by them, withdrawing from Concord, the Patriots took up sniper positions on either side of the road, setting up a crossfire that claimed more and more of the retreating column.

If any of the militiamen were veterans of the French and Indian War, they had seen all this before: how even the best British soldiers, beaten into disciplined marchers, able to form, stand, and fire on command, simply did not know what to do when the fire came from snipers unseen. Smith's troops were terrified, exhausted, and—mostly—bewildered. They began to fall apart. Recognizing this as they approached Lexington, Smith ordered a halt so that he could re-form his columns. As he set about this business, he sent Pitcairn with a marine patrol to chase off any militiamen who might take a notion to attack the halted troops.

Once again, Smith underestimated the Americans, who suddenly descended on Pitcairn's patrol, engulfing it, then driving the marines back against Smith's re-forming soldiers. Smith could do nothing but order the retreat to resume—and on the double-quick, too.

"I am of the opinion, that when once these rebels have felt a smart blow, they will submit; and no situation can ever change my fixed resolution, either to bring the colonies to a due obedience to the legislature of the mother country or to cast them off!"

George III to the Earl of Sandwich, July 1, 1775, after receiving a report on the battles at Lexington and Concord

NUMBERS
Battle of Concord: Troops, Casualties

When the count was taken in barracks, 73 regulars were confirmed dead and 26 listed as missing, presumed dead. Another 174 had been wounded. The cost to the Americans was 49 killed, 5 missing, and 41 wounded.

By this time, Lieutenant Colonel Smith's soldiers had been marching, fighting, or fleeing for nearly twenty hours. When they finally stumbled into Lexington, it was not as an army, but as a refugee band, ragged, bleeding, and spent. When they were met in town by Percy's reinforcements, the most any of them could manage was a feeble cheer. As for Percy, he had just spent many miserable miles exposed to Yankee snipers, and the only way he could think of to keep the militiamen at bay was to open up on them with his six-pounders.

Although the cannon fire did not stanch the influx of militiamen, there was no one to organize them. That was the great weakness of militia. Each company might be well enough commanded, but there was no one in charge overall. Had the militia been better led—or led at all—they might have wiped out virtually all of Smith and Percy's eighteen hundred men. A coordinated army would have bottled them up in Lexington, then closed in for the kill. In the end, however, those who fought the British on this day were not an army, but a body of "embattled farmers." Initiative and courage they had in abundance. Discipline and training they lacked, and so the forces of Percy and Smith were able to leave Lexington at about three in the afternoon and resume their retreat. Militiamen continued to snipe at and harass the withdrawing columns, and the British retaliated as best they could against the mostly unseen foe. They put to the torch many houses along the way, and if they ran across a knot of Patriots in the open, they vented on them with all of their wrath.

Yet the running—or trudging—battle continued all the way back to Charlestown, where Smith and Percy finally found refuge within cover of the range of the cannon that bristled on the British men-of-war riding at anchor in the harbor.

The Curtain Rises

While the battles of Lexington and Concord were being fought, the Continental Congress authorized the mobilization of 13,600 troops, and militia companies all across New England began to converge on Cambridge. One day after Concord, the soldiers of Smith and Percy hunkered down in their Boston barracks. The citizen-soldiers who were gathering in neighboring Cambridge were being prepared to lay siege to the mighty British army in Boston. On the great drama of the American Revolution, the curtain had risen. It would not descend for eight long years.

TAKEAWAY
Awaiting Leadership

Thanks to a well-developed network of colonial spies and couriers, many Massachusetts militia companies were prepared to fight the British soldiers who ventured out of Boston to seize Patriot arms at Concord. Lexington was a miserable Patriot defeat, but the Battle of Concord stunned the British, inflicting heavy casualties on them—yet, because the Patriot militia lacked overall leadership, the Americans failed to deliver a decisive blow.

Chapter 7

GREEN MOUNTAIN TRIUMPH
AND CANADIAN CATASTROPHE

Early Victories and an Early Disaster

O<small>N</small> F<small>EBRUARY</small> 20, 1775, <small>THE</small> H<small>OUSE OF</small> L<small>ORDS</small> received from Lord North—the very minister whose policies had helped propel the colonies into revolution—a plan for reconciliation with America. The Lords approved, and a week later, so did the House of Commons. One day after the battles of Lexington and Concord, the plan arrived in Boston. North proposed to allow the colonies to tax themselves to support civil government, the judiciary, and the common defense, but Parliament would still wield regulatory taxing authority. On July 31, 1775, the Second Continental Congress rejected the plan—not over issues of taxation, but because the plan authorized Parliament to deal with individual colonies only, which meant that the Crown would recognize neither a colonial union nor a Continental Congress. With Lexington and Concord behind them, it was clear that a majority of colonists now irrevocably regarded themselves as Americans, not as Virginians, New Yorkers, or citizens of any other individual colony. They had, most of them, moved beyond the half-measures North proposed.

CONSEQUENCES

IN HIS APRIL 22, 1775, REPORT to Lord William Barrington, secretary of state for war in the cabinet of George III, General Thomas Gage called Lexington and Concord nothing more than "an affair that happened here on the 19th." He was not deliberately minimizing the battles so much as he entirely failed to grasp their significance. By ten o'clock in the morning on April 19, moments after the first American fell at Lexington, Committee of Safety couriers were spurring horses north and south. Within hours, New York, Philadelphia, and most points between the two had word of the battles. Within days, Virginia and the rest of the South knew about them, too.

"An *affair*"? Lexington and Concord constituted a *national event*— that is, an event broadcast throughout the very nation that the event itself was helping to create.

A Bold Enterprise

No sooner did revolutionary leaders in Connecticut hear of Lexington and Concord than they sent Benedict Arnold, a wealthy New Haven merchant who served as captain of militia, to Massachusetts, where—just ten days after the battles—he persuaded Massachusetts authorities to promote him to colonel with command of a "bold enterprise": the capture of Fort Ticonderoga.

A portrait of Benedict Arnold, published in London on March 26, 1776, when he was a hero of the ill-fated Patriot invasion of Canada—well before he turned traitor in 1779.

REALITY CHECK
Revolution in Shades of Gray

That even the conservative Lord North proposed reconciliation suggests that virtually no one in England wanted an armed showdown with the colonies and even hardliners were willing to make substantial compromises to avoid a revolution. Many schoolbook histories of the American Revolution paint the era in deceptive contrasts of black and white—the Crown demanding absolute domination, the colonies demanding absolute liberty. Reality, however, was much more a matter of degree, and only after the fighting was well under way did a majority of colonists begin to favor outright independence from the mother country.

One of the key forts of the French and Indian War, Ticonderoga took its name from an Iroquois word meaning "between two waters." The stockade had in fact been built where Lake George drains into Lake Champlain in northeastern New York. This put it on the main route connecting Canada with the upper Hudson Valley. In effect, "Fort Ti" was the gateway to all Canada. And there was a bonus. It was also a principal repository of British artillery, which the Americans sorely needed. No wonder, then, that Massachusetts welcomed Arnold's proposal. And no wonder, too, that when Arnold returned to Connecticut, he learned that the Connecticut Assembly had already approved an almost identical plan to capture Fort Ticonderoga—but had given the assignment to one Ethan Allen.

Hungry to be a hero, Arnold showed up at the muster of Connecticut troops preparing to march to Fort Ti and presented them with his commission from the Massachusetts Committee of Safety. That did not impress the Connecticut troops, who, to a man, voiced their loyalty to Ethan Allen, many declaring that they would "march home rather than serve under any other leader."

What made him so popular? Born in the Connecticut village of Litchfield in 1738, Ethan Allen grew to the height of six feet, four inches, turned out for service in the French and Indian War (but saw no action), then went to work as an iron monger. In 1765, he sold his blast furnace and moved to Northampton, Massachusetts, where he blew the proceeds of the furnace sale on an orgy of what he himself described as "riotous living." During this period, he amused himself—and possibly others—by composing obscene jokes about the local clergy. In July 1767, the selectmen of Northampton had had enough and voted to kick Allen, his wife, and his child out of town.

Allen left his family in the care of his brother in Salisbury, Connecticut, and

Ethan Allen (pointing to the map) "in council" with some of his Green Mountain Boys. This wood engraving appeared in Harper's Monthly *in 1858.*

obtained a wilderness land grant in the New Hampshire Grants—an area that later became the state of Vermont. After settling in a mountain outpost called Bennington in 1769, he sent for his family and secured a commission as colonel of a local vigilante band, known as the Green Mountain Boys, which he helped raise in 1770. Its founding purpose was to confront a sheriff's posse sent by New York authorities to evict settlers who had received New Hampshire grants—the New York government had suddenly laid claim to the valuable territory, citing a 1664 charter to the Duke of York. Allen led the Boys in battle against the New Yorkers, wielding nothing more than birch rods, which they used to deal a sound thrashing to the posse. At times things got rather ugly. When Allen caught a New Yorker, one Charles Hutchinson, living in a cabin on New Hampshire land, he ordered the Boys to burn it down. When Hutchinson protested, Allen responded: "Complain to that damned scoundrel your governor! God damn your governor, your laws, your king, council and assembly!"

That's the kind of man Ethan Allen was, and to the Connecticut Assembly, he and his Green Mountain Boys seemed the obvious choice for the mission to Fort Ticonderoga. Yet he was not vainglorious and, in the end, agreed to share joint command with Benedict Arnold.

"Ever since I arrived to a state of manhood and acquainted myself with the general history of mankind, I have felt a sincere passion for liberty. . . . [T]he first systematical and bloody attempt at Lexington to enslave America thoroughly electrified my mind and fully determined me to take part with my country."

Ethan Allen, Narrative, 1779

THE TAKING OF FORT TI

In the predawn gloom of May 10, two or three hundred volunteers awaited the boats that would carry them to within a half-mile of the fort. After the sun had risen, they were still waiting. Finally, two boats showed up, and Allen and Arnold decided it was better to make do than to sacrifice the element of surprise by waiting for more transportation. Accordingly, the two commanders packed into the boats as many men as they dared—just 83, and themselves—then crossed two miles over Lake Champlain in a nasty squall. As elbows flailed in an effort to bail the overloaded and leaky craft, Allen, ever the optimist, pronounced the storm a lucky stroke. It muffled their noise and cloaked their arrival.

The crossing was a race between the water rising in the boats and the closing distance to the opposite shore. Allen, Arnold, and their men prevailed, disembarking neither drowned nor dry, then charging the fort full on. A startled sentry spied them, drew a bead with his musket, pulled the trigger—and the powder flashed in the pan, igniting without firing a round. Another sentry nicked one of Allen's officers with his bayonet, which seemed to do no more than earn the wrath of the six-foot-four Vermonter. He raised his sword, then turned it, striking the soldier with the flat of the blade, knocking him out of the way without doing him fatal harm.

Ethan Allen seized Fort Ticonderoga "In the name of the Great Jehovah and the Continental Congress," stunning a sleepy Lieutenant Feltham on May 10, 1775. This steel engraving was created in the nineteenth century, after a painting by the American artist Alonzo Chappel.

Allen entered the stockade and, with Arnold at his heels, bounded up a set of stairs. At the top was one Feltham, lieutenant of regulars, who, having hastily drawn on his breeches, held them up with one hand. "By what authority"— that's the way he put it—did Allen and his men "presume to trespass on His Majesty's property?"

It was a question tailor-made to the personality of Ethan Allen, who declaimed: "In the name of the Great Jehovah and the Continental Congress!"

With that, he brandished his sword above Lieutenant Feltham's head and demanded possession of the fort, together with "all the effects of George the Third."

These were not a mere lieutenant's to surrender, but the fort's commandant, Captain Delaplace, arrived on the scene and instantly capitulated. Fort Ticonderoga was now an American military installation. From the fort, Allen dispatched Seth Warner, third in command behind himself and Arnold, to capture another outpost nearby, at Crown Point. It also readily fell, and, together, the two places yielded up 78 cannon, six mortars, three howitzers, a pile of cannonballs, a cache of flints for firelock muskets, and other supplies. Just how the Patriots made use of these weapons will be seen in the next chapter.

Continental Congress and Continental Army

On the very day of victory at Fort Ti, delegates from a dozen colonies (as before, Georgia abstained) met for a second time in Philadelphia, on this occasion not at Carpenters' Hall, but a block away, at the State House, which was destined to be renamed Independence Hall.

Among the more colorful delegates were John Hancock, who had replaced Edmund Randolph as president of the congress, and Benjamin Franklin, nearly seventy years old, and probably the most famous American of his day. Franklin was author-publisher of the extraordinarily popular *Poor Richard's Almanack* series, a world-renowned scientist and inventor, and an agent representing the business interests of Pennsylvania in London. Also a delegate was Virginia's Thomas Jefferson. A lawyer by profession, he was, like Franklin, widely respected as a scientist (he was an amateur naturalist), but he was even more absorbed in another avocation, architecture, and would later design his own magnificent home, Monticello, as well as the neoclassical campus of the University of Virginia, of which he would become principal founder. Jefferson was among the most radical of the delegates and a bold and incisive political author.

REALITY CHECK
Derisory Defense

The taking of forts Ticonderoga and Crown Point were daring exploits, but hardly superhuman feats of American frontiersmen. Apparently, the British failed to appreciate as fully as the Americans did the strategic importance of Fort Ticonderoga. They defended the outpost with just 48 men, most of them sick or disabled soldiers assigned light duty. Confronted by nearly twice that number of able-bodied Americans, Captain Delaplace had little choice but to give up. Crown Point was defended even more feebly.

The sober but visionary John Adams was one of the driving forces behind the American Revolution. This nineteenth-century lithograph is also a reproduction of a Gilbert Stuart painting.

A nineteenth-century print reproduces Gilbert Stuart's great portrait of Thomas Jefferson— renaissance man, founding father, and author of the Declaration of Independence.

In contrast to these rather flashy figures was sober-sided John Adams of Massachusetts. Formal in manners, he had the slightly overstuffed bearing of a distinguished attorney (which he was) rather than the lean panache of a revolutionary. His words were always measured—and yet the sentiments behind them were in some ways the most visionary of any of the delegates. Although he was passionate about the cause of Massachusetts, he saw the Revolution in truly continental terms. So it is not surprising that it was he who proposed that the *Continental* Congress adopt the so-called Boston army, which had assembled just outside of Boston (see Chapter 8), and transform it into the *Continental* army. Even when an army acted locally, Adams believed it should do so as a national force. The Second Continental Congress agreed and, on June 14, 1775, passed a resolution creating the Continental army with personnel to be drawn from all of the colonies. On the same day, Adams proposed a commander in chief for the new army, a "gentleman from Virginia who is among us here, and who is George Washington of Virginia."

George Washington's appointment as commander in chief of the Continental army, 1775, as imagined by a Currier & Ives artist for a print of the event, published during the first centennial of the United States, 1876.

At forty-three, Washington was a well-connected and prosperous planter who had more than twenty years' experience (off and on) as a military commander. At age twenty-two, Washington led a small force that fought the very first battle of the French and Indian War, and next fought under General Edward Braddock in the catastrophic Battle of the Wilderness on July 9, 1755, in which 997 of 1,459 officers and men engaged had been killed. Prominent in the Virginia provincial congress of 1774, Washington had been one of seven Virginia delegates to the First Continental Congress as well as a member of the second. Experienced though he was, there were doubtless other men in the colonies with even more extensive military qualifications, but none whose character was held in higher esteem. Washington possessed dignity, modesty, courage, and a command presence that were universally respected. The congress approved him unanimously and then named his chief lieutenants: Artemas

Ward (already commanding the Boston army); Charles Lee, like Washington, a Virginian; Philip Schuyler, a wealthy New Yorker; Israel Putnam, a veteran officer of Connecticut; and Horatio Gates, who, like Washington and Putnam, had served in the French and Indian War. By the end of 1775, the Continental army would muster a total of 27,500 troops from all of the colonies.

"Mr. President, Tho' I am truly sensible of the high Honour done me in this Appointment, yet I feel great distress, from a consciousness that my abilities & Military experience may not be equal to the extensive & important Trust: However, as the Congress desire it I will enter upon the momentous duty, & exert every power I Possess In their service & for the Support of the glorious Cause."

Washington's remarks on accepting command of the Continental army, June 16, 1775

CONTINENTAL AMBITIONS: THE INVASION OF CANADA

TO THE CONTINENTAL CONGRESS, which had created a Continental army, the adjective *continental* became highly seductive. The delegates began to consider the following: Canada was a big part of the continent; therefore, the Canadians must be eager to join a continental revolution.

It was, in fact, a reasonable assumption. After all, Canada was mostly French, not British. It had no meaningful cultural or national connection with the nation that had conquered it. So, on June 1, 1775, the congress voted to authorize a commission to invite Canada to join the struggle for independence, and the delegates were shocked when the Canadians replied that they were simply not interested. The Quebec Act (see Chapter 5), which had so outraged the colonists of the lower thirteen colonies, had succeeded in winning the loyalty of most Canadians.

Rebuffed, the congress approved on June 27 a resolution to invade Canada, which had been endorsed by both Ethan Allen and Benedict Arnold. Indeed, Arnold had jumped the gun on May 17, just a week after the fall of Ticonderoga, by leading a lightning raid on St. John's, about twenty miles southeast of Montreal. There he captured a seventy-ton, sixteen-gun British sloop-of-war. He was rewarded on June 1 with command of American forces on Lake Champlain, then, two weeks later, was ordered to relinquish that command to a more senior officer. He responded by threatening to lead a mutiny, but soon relented—though not before Massachusetts authorities accused him of embezzlement of military funds—a charge on which he was later cleared.

The first weeks of revolution revealed Benedict Arnold as a man of daring, courage, and resourcefulness; yet it also showed him to be no George Washington. He was impulsive, self-centered, and arrogant—not to mention careless with money, both his own and that of the government. His lobbying the congress to invade Canada was motivated as much by his personal ambition as it was by a desire to further the emerging nation's continental ambition. Arnold believed that his only competition for leadership of this enterprise was Ethan Allen, and, most likely, Allen felt the same way with regard to him. But on June 27, the congress passed over both Allen and Arnold, naming Major General Philip Schuyler to lead the invasion.

The gallant Patriot general Richard Montgomery was killed on December 31, 1775, while storming Quebec during the doomed Patriot invasion of Canada.

Philip Schuyler, one of the four major generals of the Continental army, shouldered much of the blame for the failure of the invasion of Canada and for the loss of Fort Ticonderoga.

Putting this patrician New Yorker in charge was a logical choice, but not necessarily the best choice. He was a veteran of the French and Indian War, although he had served in the capacity of an administrator rather than as a battle commander. Moreover, he was not in the best of health. Yet he certainly exercised excellent judgment in his choice of a second in command, the dashing Richard Montgomery, who had fought as a British regular in the French and Indian War, married a wealthy young American, and settled in the colonies instead of returning with his regiment to England.

Authorized to march in June, Schuyler dithered and delayed until September. By this time, Montgomery discovered that, while Schuyler idled, the British were preparing to recapture Fort Ti and Crown Point. Montgomery therefore resolved to take matters into his own hands and dashed off to his commanding officer a polite note to the effect that, reluctant as he was to act without orders, he believed that "prevention of the enemy is of the utmost importance." With that, Montgomery, on his own initiative, advanced out of Fort Ticonderoga and headed for Canada with about twelve hundred men, including Ethan Allen and his Green Mountain Boys.

Spurred by Montgomery's message, Schuyler finally started marching—although by this time he had learned that General Washington had authorized the persistently persuasive Benedict Arnold to lead a parallel operation. While Schuyler attacked Montreal, Arnold's mission was to capture Quebec.

The Invasion Begins

Benedict Arnold had no monopoly on disappointment. After he captured Fort Ticonderoga, Ethan Allen returned to Bennington, expecting a hero's welcome. Instead, his Green Mountain Boys, who were getting ready to invade Canada, voted him out of his command and elected as their new colonel one Seth Warner. Apparently, many of the boys did not approve of Allen's lavishly blasphemous language and hard-drinking habits.

Unlike Benedict Arnold, Ethan Allen accepted the decision with perfect good grace, and when some of the Boys threatened to quit if he were no longer their colonel, Allen appealed to them to stay with the regiment and give their complete loyalty to Warner. Then he wrote to General Schuyler with a request that he be

POP CULTURE
A Matter of Ego
Vermonters have long cherished the story of what happened when Ethan Allen, back in Bennington after his triumph at Fort Ti, found himself sitting through a long-winded sermon by the Reverend Jedediah Dewey. After the cleric had spent two hours praising God for the gift of victory, Allen stood up and posed a question: "Parson Dewey, aren't you going to tell the Lord about me being there, too?"

permitted to join the Canadian expedition, not as an officer, but as a humble scout. Schuyler agreed.

Schuyler caught up with Montgomery on September 4, 1775, and, together, they led an assault on St. John's, the site Arnold had raided. It was now defended by about two hundred British regulars and a contingent of Indians. Hoping for the kind of instant results achieved at Fort Ti, the Americans instead found themselves up against a well-entrenched and highly determined enemy. After nearly two weeks of combat, Schuyler's precarious health took a turn for the worse, and he was evacuated to the rear, leaving Montgomery in command of what had become a protracted siege. Such operations are often as hard on the besiegers as on the besieged. About half of Montgomery's force was felled by sickness as autumn turned to an early winter. In the meantime, Canada's governor, General Carleton, reinforced St. John's to a strength of some seven hundred men.

While languishing at St. John's, Montgomery sent Ethan Allen and John Brown, a militia officer, on an expedition to recruit willing Canadians. Brown set off for the settlement of La Prairie, and Allen recruited along the Richelieu River. To his delight, he found more than a few Canadians willing to take up arms. This inspired Allen to take it upon himself to capture Montreal, which he discovered was feebly defended. No sooner did he make this decision, however, than his recruits, who had joined on the spur of the moment, began to drift away on the spur of the moment, before the assault on Montreal could be gotten under way. With the 110 recruits that remained with him, Allen turned back toward St. John's and linked up with Brown, who had some two hundred recruits in tow. That made a total of more than three hundred soldiers, which Allen and Brown decided was sufficient to take Montreal after all.

Their plan was to converge on the town from opposite directions: Allen would cross the St. Lawrence River with his 110 men below Montreal, and Brown would cross the river above the town. Allen made his crossing during the wee hours of September 25, but Brown failed to cross, leaving Allen exposed. He could not get all his men back across the river before General Carleton took him and twenty of his command captive.

MEDICAL ISSUES
Defiant to the End

Ethan Allen was a hard-drinking man with a fierce temper. Those familiar with his rages predicted he would not live long—and they were right. Felled by a stroke at age 51, he lingered before finally succumbing on February 12, 1789. His physician, seeking to soften the blow of a fatal prognosis, told his patient, "General, I fear the angels are waiting for you." Weak as he was, Ethan Allen fixed his eyes on the doctor: "Waiting, are they? Waiting, are they? Well, goddam 'em, let 'em wait!"

Ethan Allen was clapped in irons and sent to England to be tried for treason. Reasoning that hanging Allen would only give the American Revolution a martyr, British authorities shipped him back across the Atlantic to Halifax, Nova Scotia, in June 1776, and in October he was paroled in New York City. The abortive attempt to take Montreal had not just failed, it mobilized Canadian sentiment *against* the Revolution and even drove many Indians to side with the British.

Captured on September 25, 1775, during the Patriot invasion of Canada, Ethan Allen narrowly escaped execution in England as a traitor. An imprisoned Allen is shown in chains in this nineteenth-century colored engraving.

Cold Victories

Although Allen and Brown's bumbling assault on Montreal proved abortive, Montgomery's long-suffering troops enjoyed some success. They captured a British fort at Chambly on October 18 and used the supplies they found there to press the siege against St. John's, which was wearing down and finally surrendered on November 2, 1775. Yet this hardly came as a momentous triumph. The garrison Montgomery had defeated was better clothed and better fed than his own miserable men, who celebrated their triumph by begging to go back home. Worse, the siege had consumed two months, and Canada was really no closer to having been conquered.

Montgomery rallied his troops with a promise of warm clothes and hot food to be had in Montreal. Devoted to their commander, the ragtag force easily achieved what Allen and Brown had been unable to accomplish. They captured Montreal on November 13, which, it turned out, was now defended by no more than 150 British regulars and a handful of local militia. They also captured three British warships and some smaller vessels. Now there was nothing for Montgomery to do but wait for word from Benedict Arnold in Quebec.

Arnold's Agony

Benedict Arnold marched out of Cambridge, Massachusetts, with eleven hundred volunteers on September 12. They found Maine already frigid, and the *bateaux* (long, flat-bottomed boats used in the north country rivers) intended to carry them up the Kennebec River from Fort Western (present-day Augusta, Maine) had been thrown together so hastily that the green (uncured) wood fell apart in the icy water. Arnold and his men waded a total of 180 miles.

That was bad. Then the food ran out, and the men began to eat their soap. When the soap was gone, they boiled anything made of leather, including moccasins. Some men died, more deserted. By November 9, just six hundred reached the south bank of the St. Lawrence River. Arnold had estimated a journey of twenty days. It had taken forty-five.

Arnold knew that the fortress-town of Quebec was garrisoned by a handful of Royal Marines and regulars, in addition to about four hundred militiamen. He believed that his force, however depleted, could prevail against such numbers—provided he could attack right away. That's when a fierce wind swept across the St. Lawrence, keeping his men from crossing for two full nights. It was just enough time for the British to reinforce Quebec to a strength of twelve hundred men.

Although he observed the arrival of the reinforcements, Arnold, determined to make his mark on this American Revolution, refused to give up. Under cover of darkness during the early hours of November 14, his men crossed the river, advanced through the Plains of Abraham, and easily overwhelmed the militia there. Arnold then sent a detachment toward the town under a flag of truce, presumably hoping to solicit the surrender of the British. The artillery barrage the garrison let loose put an end to any hope for a speedy peace.

Patriot forces were too few and too far from sources of supply to succeed in their invasion of Canada in 1775. This nineteenth-century engraving depicts Benedict Arnold's expedition to capture Quebec.

As the artillery pinned the Americans in place, the British frigate *Lizard* sailed up the St. Lawrence, behind Arnold's position, cutting off his route of retreat. From within Quebec, eight hundred troops prepared to attack the invaders. Despite the presence of HMS *Lizard*, Arnold's troops were able to sneak away, withdrawing to Pointe-aux-Trembles, where, on December 2, they rendezvoused with Montgomery and his men. Combined, the forces of Montgomery and Arnold numbered about a thousand men. The two commanders decided to march back to Quebec for a second try.

THE BATTLE OF QUEBEC

No sooner were they within sight of the town than the commanders realized that, without artillery, a siege would take a very long time. Quebec's defenders were warm and dry. Arnold and Montgomery were out in the cold and had little hope of surviving a winter-long operation. A more immediate problem was that, at the end of the year—and the year was rapidly nearing its end—the terms of enlistment for all of Arnold's New Englanders would expire. Unless they were in the middle of a battle, they would be free to go home. And there was worse news. General Carleton continued to receive reinforcements. By the end of December, eighteen hundred British and Canadian soldiers were gathered in Quebec.

An engraving after the dramatic painting by John Trumbull depicts the death of Continental army general Richard Montgomery at the Battle of Quebec (December 31, 1775).

Vastly outnumbered now, how did Arnold and Montgomery respond? On December 31, the day before the enlistments would expire, they attacked—in the teeth of a full-force blizzard and against nearly twice their number (well-fed men fighting from fortified positions), they attacked. It was an enterprise at once gallant and tragic. Advancing from the left, Montgomery led his men, dragging siege ladders, through the snow. On the right, Arnold was at the head of six hundred troops, who leaned into an onslaught of blizzard and bullets, one of which caught Arnold in the leg. Unable to continue, he turned over command to Daniel Morgan, an extraordinary frontier commander from Virginia.

Against impossible odds, Morgan's men breached Quebec's "Lower Town" and there hunkered down to wait for Montgomery, who had entered the outer defenses of the fortress and whose men struggled over barricades and other obstacles, the object of which was not so much to stop an invading army, but to slow it, so that each man would become a better a target.

From within their stockade, the British defenders watched. When Montgomery and most of his officers were at pointblank range, they loosed a volley of musket fire and a round of grapeshot—

a cluster of small iron balls that, when fired from a cannon, sprayed in deadly fashion across the field of fire. The volley and the grape cut down Montgomery and most of his officers as if by some invisible scythe.

As he dealt death to Montgomery's assault, Carleton ordered reinforcements into the Lower Town, where Morgan's men began to surrender. Although he knew his situation to be hopeless, Morgan himself kept fighting until he glimpsed a priest among the roiling mass of Quebec's defenders.

"Are you a priest?" Morgan called out.

The startled man nodded.

"Then I give my sword to you. But not a scoundrel of these cowards shall take it out of my hands."

Falling Apart

By January 1776, the invasion forces of Allen, Brown, and Montgomery had been killed, wounded, captured, or deserted. Of Arnold's command, less than half remained. Forty-eight had been killed, thirty-four wounded—including Arnold himself—and 372 made captive. Others had deserted along the way. Still, Benedict Arnold refused to leave Canada. He lingered on the outskirts of Quebec from January to April 1776, in anticipation of reinforcements from the South.

While Carleton's force had grown to more than two thousand, General Washington struggled with the Second Continental Congress to fund a relief force for the Canadian invasion. This was organized by early spring. The congress sent a message to Arnold, informing him that he had been promoted to brigadier general and instructing him to go to Montreal on April 2, 1776, to take command of American forces there, freeing up Major General David Wooster to leave Montreal and assume command outside of Quebec. Wooster was joined there on May 1 by Major General John Thomas, who took over command of a combined force of twenty-five hundred. At least, that was what the roll sheets said. Disease, desertion, and the expiration of enlistment reduced this number to some six hundred men fit for duty. Neither Wooster nor Thomas was willing to attempt to storm Quebec with a force of that size. But on May 2, as the ice began to break up on the St. Lawrence

ALTERNATE TAKE

If Canada Joined the Patriots . . .

What if Canada had joined the American Revolution? Had that province done so voluntarily, the British would have been denied a key base of operations and a substantial number of loyal colonial troops. The Revolution might have been much briefer. However, had the Patriots taken Canada by force, the vast territory would probably have become a liability rather than an asset, the Americans finding themselves fighting a Canadian rebellion even as they themselves rebelled against the British.

The two infantry-men at the left and the mounted officer are British soldiers, and the two grenadiers at the right are Hessians—German merce-nary troops in the service of the British. This wood engraving is from the nine-teenth century.

River, rendering it navigable, Thomas received news that ships were carrying to Quebec thirteen thousand British (including forty-three hundred German mercenaries known as Hessians) under Major General John Burgoyne. Thomas took the hint. He tried to withdraw from the environs of Quebec, but, under fire from Royal Marines, his men panicked, turning the retreat into a headlong, chaotic flight. The army became a mob, and the mob, over a period of weeks, fell ill as smallpox swept its ranks, killing Thomas himself on June 2.

By the spring of 1776, the American army in Canada had come apart. On June 1, 1776, the Second Continental Congress received word from Brigadier General John Sullivan, whom it had sent with reinforcements into Canada in the hope of salvaging some part of the operation. "I have done every thing I possibly could in time to get information of the true state of affairs," Sullivan wrote, "and can in a word inform you that no one thing is right. Every thing is in the utmost confusion and almost every one frightened as they know not what."

Defeat at Three Rivers

Congress had ordered Sullivan to continue—or renew—the assault on Quebec. In an attempt to do this, he sent Brigadier General William Thompson with two thousand Continental

TRIVIA POINT
The Hessians Are Coming

The British employed some thirty thousand mercenaries to help fight the Americans. They were hired guns from various German states, but probably because their principal commanders all came from Hesse-Cassel and Hesse-Hanau, they were collectively called Hessians. They did not come cheap. The Duke of Brunswick *(Brunschweig),* the first German to agree to supply mercenaries in the American Revolution, received £7 per soldier furnished. The soldiers themselves were paid directly by the British Crown, at the same rate the empire's own troops were paid. In addition to the per-soldier fee, the duke was paid an annual subsidy of £11,517. British commanders initially thought the money was well spent. Hessians were very well trained and had a fierce reputation as combatants. Never-theless, they won not a single engagement against the Americans during the entire war.

army soldiers to a place called Trois-Rivières, on the north bank of the St. Lawrence River, halfway between Montreal and Quebec. Sullivan believed that Trois-Rivières was held by no more than eight hundred troops. Take it, he reasoned, and he would have an ideal base from which to launch a successful assault on Quebec, thereby snatching from the fire the whole misbegotten invasion.

What Sullivan did not know was that Burgoyne's regulars were on the march, and six thousand of them, under Brigadier General Simon Fraser, were already at Trois-Rivières.

Thompson moved his men by *bateaux* to a landing spot ten miles above Trois-Rivières during the night of June 6. He left 250 men to guard the boats, then set out for Trois-Rivières with his four regimental commanders, Arthur St. Clair, William Irvine, William Maxwell, and Anthony Wayne, leading a total of 1,750 men. Thompson relied on a French Canadian guide, who, either by accident or by design, took the force via a roundabout route, thoroughly exhausting the troops by the time they neared their objective.

Wayne was the first to make contact with the enemy. He glimpsed redcoats in a clearing and rallied his weary regiment to a surprise attack that utterly routed the numerically superior British. Thompson approached with more troops and gave chase to the fleeing British—until he and his men stumbled over the entrenchments occupied by the main body of Simon Fraser's soldiers. Even now, Thompson failed to realize just how badly outnumbered he was. Instead of withdrawing, he attacked—and was quickly repulsed. He worked feverishly to rally his scattering forces to form them up for a second attack, but he could not, and he called a general retreat.

An army is never more vulnerable than when it shows its back to the enemy—hard to shoot behind you—and Carleton could easily have cut off the American retreat and scooped up prisoners at will. But the Canadian wilderness was as hard on big armies as it was on small, and Carleton decided that he could not afford to shelter and feed some two thousand POWs. Instead of pursuing Thompson, he left the dispirited Americans to wander in the swampy wilderness, where they fell prey to Indians and Canadian militiamen. By June 11, just eleven hundred American soldiers staggered into the village of Sorel. The others were wounded, killed, captured, or just plain missing. Carleton's forces had suffered eight killed and nine wounded.

Admiral Benedict Arnold

The worst thing about the failed American invasion of Canada was that its abject failure prompted the British to prepare a counterinvasion from Canada down to the lower thirteen colonies. Both sides realized that the first step to such an invasion was mastery of Lake Champlain, the critical waterway straddling Canada and America. Battered as his forces were, Benedict Arnold took it upon himself to improvise a fleet to challenge the British on Lake Champlain. He put his haggard men to work felling enough trees to cobble together the ugliest, clumsiest craft ever to ply the lake waters. Four "galleys" emerged, christened the *Washington, Congress, Trumbull,* and *Gates.* These were supplemented by eight or nine smaller craft, called "gundalows," a word related to *gondola* and describing flat-bottomed, open boats, with pointed prows fore and aft.

In the meantime, the British dismantled an ocean-going warship, HMS *Inflexible*, and rebuilt it at St. John's for service on the comparatively shallow lake. They similarly modified two schooners and a large gundalow. In addition to these more-or-less conventional vessels, they built from scratch at St. John's a mammoth *radeau*—a giant scow with sails. Christened the *Thunderer,* it carried a crew of three hundred and mounted two massive howitzers, six 24-pounders, and another half-dozen 12-pounders.

Ninety-two feet long with a beam of thirty-three feet, *Thunderer* was impossible to maneuver and for that reason was never committed to battle. In addition to their large ships of war, the British also had at their disposal many smaller vessels, including longboats and gunboats.

Arnold set out with ten vessels from Crown Point on August 24, 1776. He dropped anchor off the inhospitably rocky Valcour Island and waited for more craft to be built. When the Battle of Valcour Island began, on October 11, Arnold commanded fifteen vessels. The enemy, however, had twenty gunboats, thirty long

NUMBERS
Galley and Gundalow Specs

The galleys Arnold built were awkward, but big. Assuming the *Washington* was typical, they measured 72 feet, 4 inches long with a beam (width) of 20 feet. Crewed by 80, they were essentially gun platforms, each mounting two 18-pound guns, two 12-pounders, two 9-pounders, four 4-pounders, a single 2-pounder, and eight swivel guns on the quarterdeck. The smaller gundalows carried 45 men and sported one 12-pounder in the bow and two 9-pounders amidships.

boats, and some larger craft, the sight of which inspired Arnold to weigh anchor and pull back. But it was too late to avoid battle. During October 11 and 12, the two improvised fleets slugged it out, the Americans by far getting the worst of the hammering. When October 13 dawned, Arnold was left with only two of his large craft, *Congress* and *Washington,* which he used to flee from the British, maintaining with his pursuers a running battle all the way to Buttonmould Bay on the Vermont shore of Lake Champlain. He unceremoniously beached what was left of the two hulks—doubtless there wasn't much—then burned them, leading his men overland to Crown Point. When he realized that there was no possibility of defending this position, he burned the buildings in the village to keep them out of British hands and fled all the way to Fort Ticonderoga—the rallying point from which the invasion had been launched two years earlier.

CANADIAN SUNSET

By the numbers, the Battle of Valcour Island must be judged the culminating disaster of the very bad idea that was the American invasion of Canada. Of the fifteen craft Arnold had built, eleven

Made on the spot by British officer C. Randle, this sketch shows the improvised "Continental squadron" at Valcour Island just before the Battle of Valcour Island, October 11, 1776. The schooner Royal Savage *is depicted in the center. From left to right are the schooner* Revenge, *the galley* Washington, *the gundalow* Philadelphia, *the galley* Congress, *the gundalow* Jersey, *the galley* Lee, *the gunadalows* Boston, Spitfire, New Haven, Providence, Connecticut, *and* New York, *the sloop* Enterprise, *and the galley* Trumbull.

were sunk. Of the 750 men engaged in the battle, eighty were killed or wounded. In contrast, not a single one of the seventeen to twenty British gunboats involved in the battle was so much as scratched. The two larger British vessels, the *Carleton* and the *Inflexible*, were damaged, but still serviceable. Casualties were very light.

Yet the numbers do not tell the whole story. By his audacity and resourcefulness, Benedict Arnold conjured from nothing a "Champlain Squadron" that kept Carleton occupied, thereby bleeding the momentum from the British advance. As winter approached, Carleton abandoned his grand plan of linking up with the British forces in the lower thirteen colonies under General Howe, thereby effecting what might have been an invasion sufficiently devastating to have put an end to the American Revolution in 1776. Benedict Arnold had surely lost the battle, but he may well have saved the Revolution.

TAKEAWAY

A Quixotic Quest Fails

After scoring a quick triumph at Fort Ticonderoga, New York, Ethan Allen and Benedict Arnold became key figures in an unrealistically ambitious scheme to conquer Canada in an effort to make the American Revolution truly a continental struggle.

Chapter 8

BOSTON VICTORY

*How the Patriots Drove the British Out of Boston—
and Fought the Misnamed Battle of Bunker Hill*

THERE HAS LONG BEEN A SCHOOL OF CYNICAL HISTORIANS who identify the authors of the American Revolution as a cadre of merchants—men like John Hancock—who were looking for a way around Britain's onerous taxes, duties, and trade regulations, especially the virtual monopoly the Tea Act gave to the East India Company. There can be no denying that American mercantile interests helped drive the Revolution. Unlike so many other revolutions before and after this one, the War for Independence was not a class struggle. Many of the most vocal movers and shakers were well off, thank you very much. But neither was the American Revolution a mere case of armed tax avoidance by greedy businessmen. It was, this Revolution, a force—analogous to a force of nature—which attracted to itself an extraordinary mix of individuals—people like the brilliant young physician Joseph Warren, the highly accomplished artisan Paul Revere, the brilliant attorney John Adams, the earnest demagogue Sam Adams, and the sublime orator

Patrick Henry, as well as such prosperous merchants as John Hancock and Benedict Arnold, plus colorful frontiersmen like Ethan Allen.

RIGHT MAN, RIGHT TIME

REMARKABLE AS ALL OF THESE FIGURES WERE, none was a professional soldier—and whatever else a revolution is, it involves armies fighting armies. The colonies had militiamen and militia officers, but precious few individuals who knew very much about leading troops into battle. That's where another extraordinary figure came in.

George Washington was master of a northern Virginia plantation called Mount Vernon, a place on the lordly Potomac that had come to him as an inheritance by way of his half-brother. A prosperous planter—thanks in no small measure to marriage with Martha Custis, a wealthy widow—Washington was no drawing-room dandy. As a twenty-two-year-old Virginia militia colonel, he had started the French and Indian War near a Pennsylvania place called Great Meadows when he opened fire on a party of French soldiers on May 27, 1754. Later, he survived the worst defeat the English suffered in that war, at the Battle of the Wilderness (near present-day Pittsburgh) on July 9, 1755.

Washington knew what it meant to fight, to win, and, even more important, to lose. Now he donned a colonel's uniform once again—this one American blue and buff instead of British red and white—to serve Virginia and the Revolution as chairman of a committee to "consider ways and means to supply these Colonies with ammunition and military stores."

On May 10, 1775, the very day that Ethan Allen and Benedict Arnold took Fort Ticonderoga, delegates from twelve colonies (as usual, Tory-dominated Georgia hung back) convened in the first meeting of the Second Continental Congress in Philadelphia. John Adams, a delegate from Massachusetts, proposed that Congress adopt the colonial force that was gathering outside of Boston, preparing to do battle with the British army holed up in Boston. The colonists were calling this force the Boston army, but Adams wanted to rename it the Continental army and transform it from a local military unit into a national legion. His fellow delegates liked the idea and not only called for a name change, but for the new army to be made up

NUMBERS
Britain's Worst Defeat

At the Battle of the Wilderness (also known as the Battle of Fort Duquesne, the Battle of the Monongahela, and Braddock's Defeat), British brigadier Edward Braddock lost 456 killed, 520 wounded, and about a dozen captured of the 1,373 men in his command. The first big battle of the French and Indian War, it was the most disastrous defeat the English suffered in that war—or any other fought on the North American continent, including during the Revolution. Braddock was among the slain.

This view of George Washington's beloved Mount Vernon was published in London in 1800, one year after his death. By that time, Washington was perhaps the most respected military and political leader in the world.

REALITY CHECK
Command Presence

The American Revolution is long over. Our side won. Yet the subject of Washington as a general remains one of intense controversy. Some say he was a great general. Others, pointing out that he lost many more battles than he won, rate him as a number of his contemporaries did: quite low. The truth lies somewhere between these extremes and takes in more than the issue of military competence. The British had many experienced generals—a few quite good, many pretty bad. Yet whether good or bad, British leadership was fragmented, whereas the Americans would mostly look to a single leader. It was not that Washington was a military genius—far from it—but he did possess a serviceable grasp of tactics and, as we will see, a remarkable understanding of strategy. Far more important, he was a man of great character and apparently limitless courage, who seemed naturally to command loyalty and evoke confidence.

of men drawn from all the colonies. But who would command such a force?

On June 14, John Adams rose to make a nomination. Fellow Bostonian John Hancock, president of the congress, cocked his ear, doubtless expecting to hear his own name. Instead, Adams spoke of a "gentleman from Virginia who is among us here, and who is George Washington of Virginia."

Washington protested. "I do not think myself equal to the command," he said, and while he may have been quite sincere, he also knew that no one else in the colonies was more equal to the command than he. After he accepted the commission, it was Congress that selected his lieutenants: Artemas Ward (already commanding the Boston army); Charles Lee, like Washington, a prominent Virginian; Philip Schuyler, a wealthy New Yorker; Israel Putnam, a Connecticut veteran of the French and Indian War; and Horatio Gates, also a combat veteran.

A broadside from about 1776 aimed at recruiting soldiers to serve in the Continental army. The poster featured a pictorial representation of the Manual of Arms, the complex series of steps necessary to prepare, load, aim, and fire the flintlocks of the period.

DAVID AND GOLIATH IN NORTH AMERICA

THE ARMY WASHINGTON WAS COMMISSIONED TO COMMAND consisted of the Boston army, plus riflemen recruited in Pennsylvania, Maryland, and Virginia—which, by the end of 1775, added up to 27,500 Continental soldiers. These troops were to be augmented with militia forces contributed by the individual colonies. Although it was a considerable achievement to raise an army of nearly 30,000 from nothing, the British had a standing army of 55,000 in 1775 and a navy of 28,000—sailors who manned the Royal Navy's 270 warships in 1775. In that same year, the colonies had just one naval vessel. Even more significant in judging the military potential of the colonies versus the mother country was sheer population. England had 8 million people in 1775, of whom 2,350,000 might be considered eligible for military service. The colonial population at that time was about 2,256,000 in 1775, excluding Native Americans and including 506,000 slaves. This yielded potential military manpower of just 175,000 men.

Were Washington and the rest of the revolutionaries deluded to believe they stood a chance in the coming struggle?

Not really. Numbers were one thing, but people quite another. Suppressing the American Revolution was not a popular cause in Britain. Lord Shelburne complained that whereas 300,000 Englishmen had entered the army during the French and Indian War (which, in Europe, was fought as the Seven Years War), no more than 30,000 troops could be raised to put down the rebellion—and this number included the so-called Hessians, who were paid German mercenaries.

Yet the Americans did have some important advantages. By no means were all of them agreed on the cause of independence, but those who did choose to fight fought for a cause in which they believed. The average British soldier, treated brutally, felt little enthusiasm for his government or his leaders. The Americans also fought in their own country, on mostly familiar ground, whereas the British and the Hessians were far from home. It is not the case that all American soldiers were frontiersmen; yet they were familiar with the American climate and terrain, neither of which lent themselves to standard European methods of warfare (see Chapter 6, "Long Odds—But Just How Long?").

British soldiers were generally better trained than American troops. In particular, the American armies lacked trained artillerists, military engineers, cavalrymen, and men with military administrative experience. Despite this, a number of colonial army officers were veterans of the French and Indian War and other Native American conflicts. They did not have formal military training, but they had more tactical experience fighting under frontier conditions than their British counterparts.

NUMBERS
The Bigger Budget

Even if Britain had trouble assembling an army to fight the rebellion, it certainly would have no problem outspending the colonies. The British government's so-called sinking fund—its pool of ready cash—amounted to about £3 million per year. The annual revenue of the American colonies amounted to £75,000.

Contrary to popular lore, few American soldiers in the Continental army or the various militias were frontiersmen skilled with firearms; however, those troops who did have such skill were generally excellent marksmen, which gave them a great advantage over British and Hessian soldiers. European troops were trained to load, fire, and reload as rapidly as possible; marksmanship was not considered important. In contrast, American riflemen were determined to make every expensive bullet count—so they learned to shoot and shoot well.

William Howe, replaced the inept Thomas Gage in 1775 and served until 1778. Howe achieved a number of important victories over Washington and the Patriots, but he failed to win the American Revolution. This print was made during his tenure as commander in chief.

Lieutenant General John Burgoyne was dubbed "Gentleman Johnny" by subordinates and colleagues alike. As interested in writing fashionable plays as he was in suppressing the American Revolution, he proved more successful in the former than in the latter pursuit.

The British Commanders Arrive

By the end of May 1775, about ten thousand colonial troops surrounded Boston, principal headquarters of the British army in America. But without a navy, the Americans could not stop waterborne traffic into and out of the city, and on May 25, HMS *Cerberus* sailed into Boston Harbor with three major generals sent to assist Thomas Gage in stamping out the rebellion.

William Howe was the senior of the three. He had served in the War of the Austrian Succession and in the French and Indian War, and this experience had taught him about the differences between European and American warfare. Unlike most of his colleagues, he was eager to modify British combat methods to suit the American environment.

John Burgoyne and Henry Clinton, junior to Howe, were of character and temperament very different from their commander. "Gentleman Johnny" Burgoyne was a member of Parliament, a playwright, a noted drawing-room wit, and an incorrigible lady's man. Dandy though he was, his troops loved him, because he was both courageous and, in contrast to most of his colleagues, humane.

Henry Clinton was no Burgoyne. Sour and humorless, he believed in the manual of arms and the received wisdom of those generals who had gone before him. He was hardly a dynamic leader of troops, but he was an able administrator and sound planner.

THE FIGHT THAT SHOULD HAVE BEEN THE BATTLE OF BUNKER HILL

FOR HIS PART, GAGE WAS PLEASED to have all three men in his command, varied as they were in talent and personality. To Howe he assigned the mission of crushing the American army in a single blow. In response, Howe proposed to make an amphibious landing at Dorchester Point, to the right of Cambridge, as Clinton landed at Willis Creek, on the left. The object of this assault was to capture the high ground at Charlestown—Bunker Hill—which overlooked Boston as well as the position of the besieging army. The beauty of this amphibious assault was that the British warships in Boston Harbor would provide formidable covering firepower. Once Bunker Hill had been secured, the plan was for Howe and Clinton to converge on Cambridge, the encampment of the colonial army, and destroy it.

The one thing the British had failed to consider was that spies in service to the local Committee of Safety had discovered their plan. General Artemas Ward, in command of the Boston army, quickly called a council of war. The Committee of Safety recommended occupying and fortifying Bunker Hill before the British could take it. Ward pointed out that his army had very little ammunition (no more than eleven barrels of powder) and, even worse, Bunker Hill, conspicuous on Charlestown Peninsula, was exposed to the guns of the British fleet. To make this situation even more dangerous, Ward pointed out that the only way off the hill was via Charlestown Neck, a narrow isthmus that flooded at high tide. Without an avenue of retreat there was every possibility that the army would be destroyed if the defense of Bunker Hill went badly.

To these perfectly reasonable objections, Major General Israel Putnam offered a strange answer: "Americans are not at all afraid of their heads, though very much afraid of their legs. If you cover

Second in command to General Howe, Sir Henry Clinton replaced him as commander in chief of British forces in North America after Howe retired in 1778. Resigning his own command in 1782, Clinton absorbed much of the blame for the defeat of Cornwallis at the decisive Battle of Yorktown in 1781. This portrait was printed in Paris around the time that he assumed command.

PLAN OF BUNKER HILL BATTLE

This simplified nineteenth-century map of the Battle of Bunker Hill clearly shows that the major action took place on Breed's Hill.

ALTERNATE TAKE
Breed's versus Bunker

Occupying Breed's Hill was a mistake. Bunker Hill was higher and steeper, as well as farther from the guns of the Royal Navy. The Americans could have fortified it such that it would have been virtually impregnable. Because it was lower and less steep, Breed's Hill was easier to fortify, but it was also more fully exposed and, therefore, much more vulnerable. Had the Americans held Bunker Hill, the British might well have been defeated.

these, they will fight forever." It was, in fact, so strange that he was given command of the occupation and defense of Bunker Hill.

A veteran of the French and Indian War, Putnam, at fifty-seven, was sufficiently aged to have earned the sobriquet "Old Put." His second in command, Colonel William Prescott, another French and Indian War veteran, argued with him that it was better to occupy Breed's Hill, which was closer to Boston than Bunker Hill. After some back and forth, Old Put agreed and decided to concentrate his twelve hundred men on Breed's Hill, leaving a small force to fortify Bunker Hill by way of covering a potential retreat.

Nearly twelve hundred Americans dug into Breed's Hill while Gage and Howe readied twenty-five hundred British redcoats for the attack. The assault would be backed by land-based artillery as well as by the cannon of the sixty-eight-gun ship of the line *Somerset*, two floating artillery batteries, the frigate *Glasgow*, the armed transport *Symmetry*, a pair of gunboats, and two sloops of war, *Falcon* and *Lively*.

At dawn on June 17, a Royal Marine aboard HMS *Lively* saw the Americans working on Breed's—not Bunker—Hill. He alerted his captain, and, soon *Lively* opened fire on Breed's Hill. Within minutes the entire British fleet followed suit. As is not uncommon among rival military branches, the navy had not bothered to consult the army, and these opening shots surprised Gage, Clinton, and Howe more than they did the Americans, who figured they would be fired on. The generals put their heads together to transform their broad plan of attack into immediate action. Clinton proposed immediately attacking across Charlestown Neck to assault the rebel rear, but Gage and Howe overrode him and proposed disembarking from the Mystic River side of the peninsula, then marching around to the American rear. The problem was that this meant awaiting a favorable tide, which gave the Americans six more hours to continue digging in.

On the other hand, it also gave the British six more hours to pour on the cannon fire. The first cannonball to find its mark took the head off one Asa Pollard. The sight unnerved the men around him. Seeing this, Prescott leaped to the parapet of the fortification and purposely exposed himself to fire, as if to proclaim Pollard to have been the victim of a lucky British shot.

Putnam commanded the action not from Breed's but from Bunker Hill. Twice he ventured out of the fortification and across Charlestown Neck to demand reinforcements from Artemas Ward, who at last released twelve hundred New Hampshiremen under the command of John Stark and James Reed. Stark marched these reinforcements four miles through a storm of incoming artillery fire. He did not rush, but advanced in perfect marching order at the measured military cadence of the day, as if on parade. When a subordinate officer urged him to increase the tempo double-time, Stark replied that "one fresh man in action is worth ten fatigued men" and maintained the beat.

At one o'clock, twenty-three hundred British solders disembarked at Moulton's Point, at the tip of Charlestown Peninsula. Only now, however, did Howe contemplate the difficulty of the objective he faced. Breed's Hill had been topped with sturdy fortifications. Moreover, when Howe saw that men were also occupying Bunker Hill, he assumed that the rebels had a substantial reserve—that *both* hills were completely occupied.

And there was worse news. Howe observed Stark's column of sharpshooters, marching with a stately beat to reinforce the rebel fortifications.

Howe took a breath and ordered his men to halt, pending the arrival of reinforcements. Once again, the British had given the Americans the gift of time. Colonel Prescott used it to dig deeper fortifications. At this point, Dr. Joseph Warren, a promising Boston physician and, with Samuel Adams, one of the most radical of Boston's revolutionaries, joined the defenders of Breed's Hill.

The twenty-five hundred redcoats were divided between Howe and Brigadier General Sir Robert Pigot, who was to attack the earthwork defenses at the top of the hill. Such an attack called for a preliminary artillery bombardment concentrated on the spot. Howe gave the order to commence firing, the guns spoke, and then the guns fell silent. Howe's artillerists had mistakenly supplied their six-pounder cannons with twelve-pound cannonballs. They wouldn't fit.

Awaiting fire, Pigot's troops were now raked by rifle fire from houses in Charlestown. Pigot called for the fleet to open fire on Charlestown. The British gunners used "hotshots"—cannonballs

DETAILS, DETAILS
Quotable

The Continental Congress had conferred on Dr. Warren a major general's commission, which meant that he outranked Colonel Prescott. But when the colonel offered to relinquish command, Warren replied: "I shall take no command here. I came as a volunteer with my musket to serve you." This was the essence of a democratic revolution.

The tough Patriot major general Israel Putnam, shown here in a 1778 German print, distinguished himself at the Battle of Bunker Hill but was badly defeated the following year when he commanded troops in Brooklyn at the Battle of Long Island.

heated red hot—and also fired hollowed-out cannonballs known as "carcasses." These were filled with flammable pitch, set ablaze, and fired. They shattered on impact, disgorging flame. Between these and the hotshots, all of Charlestown was soon ablaze.

Now the battle had a backdrop from hell itself. Howe deployed 350 of his finest light infantry along the Mystic River beach and ordered them to make a bayonet charge into the Yankee position fronting the Mystic. The British advanced gallantly. But the fire from Putnam's and Stark's men was withering. Three American volleys took the lives of ninety-six of the best soldiers in the Royal Army, also killing or wounding every member of Howe's personal staff. As for Howe, he led from the front and emerged unscathed yet in deep shock as he contemplated his dead. This was intensified by the news that Pigot had also been thrown back.

"Don't fire," he ordered, "until you see the whites of their eyes!"—adding: "Then, fire low."

General Israel Putnam in response to the British bayonet charge, perhaps the single-most famous command in American military history

A Taste of Victory

Seeing the British assault collapse and then withdraw, the defenders of Breed's Hill cheered.

Victory!

Prescott congratulated his men, but warned them that the battle was hardly over.

But it seemed over—over and won—and some men began to drift away. Nor could Putnam coax the reserves on Bunker Hill to move out to reinforce Breed's Hill, which, he knew, would soon fall under renewed attack.

Victory? All of the American commanders were keenly aware that their ammunition, scant to begin with, had dwindled.

A print from 1909 depicting the British assault on Breed's Hill. Three costly infantry charges were required to take the hill, which made this British victory seem like a Patriot triumph.

Howe shed his initial shock and, within fifteen minutes of the first assault, was ready to attack again. He decided not to divide his forces this time, but to join his troops to Pigot's and make a brute-force frontal assault on the fortification at the top of Breed's Hill while a small secondary force kept the Mystic flank occupied. The second human wave rolled—and, like the first, fell under withering fire.

For a second time, Pigot and Howe ordered retreat. But they must have seen signs that the Americans were themselves starting to weaken under the pressure of the assaults. Reinforcements were called up—but a distressing number of these Patriots avoided the front line by cowering in the shadow of Bunker Hill.

There was good reason to hide. The defenders possessed a sufficient amount of rifle bullets and musket balls to drive back a third assault—but they didn't have enough powder to drive all that lead. Commanders accordingly ordered their men to split the prepared paper powder cartridges that formed the charge that fired the ball. The powder was divided, which gave every man powder, but also reduced the range of each American rifle and musket by about one half.

Four hundred Royal Marines and Royal Army regulars mounted a third assault. The Americans returned fire, but this time the British pierced their lines. Combat became hand to hand. The British had bayonets. Most of the Americans did not. Prescott ordered his men to "club their muskets"—that is to swing the weapon by its barrel and use the stock as a club to "twitch" the enemy's bayonet-tipped guns away. But it was no use. More and more of the red-coated attackers clambered over the parapets.

Now it was Prescott's turn to order retreat. He made it, however, a fighting retreat, down Breed's Hill, across to Bunker Hill, traversing Charlestown Neck, then withdrawing onto the mainland. More British troops fell in the pursuit, but it is in retreat that any army is most vulnerable, and this was the phase of battle in which the Americans suffered their heaviest losses—some 450, including 140 dead, Joseph Warren among them, a physician, a major general, and, in this combat, an infantryman.

The Taste of Defeat

To the British, it could not have felt like victory. They held both Breed's Hill and Bunker Hill. But of the 2,400 men actually engaged in combat, 1,054 had been shot, of whom 226 were dead. A casualty rate of nearly 50 percent is catastrophic, but Howe understood that the catastrophe had been compounded by the nature of who had been killed and who had done the killing. Hurt or killed were the cream of his soldiery. They were the victims—of provincials, bumpkins led by farmers and merchants. The unemotional Henry Clinton confided to his diary: "A dear-bought victory, another such would have ruined us."

As for the Americans, they no longer held Bunker or Breed's Hill, yet they came away from battle feeling like anything but the losers. They had bloodied the army of the Crown.

UNDER SIEGE

IF THE AMERICANS DID NOT FEEL LIKE LOSERS, the British hardly felt like victors. The heavy casualties Gage had suffered discouraged him from using Bunker Hill to mount a counteroffensive against the army continuing to grow in neighboring Cambridge. Because he failed to attempt a breakout, he remained under the siege that had begun on April 19, 1775, when the British retreated from Lexington and Concord.

If the siege was hard on Gage's soldiers, it was much harder on the people of Boston, who suffered shortages of food, were exposed to bombardment from both sides, and were frequently victimized by British soldiers, who took whatever they wanted—typically without bothering to distinguish between Loyalist and rebel.

The Patriot siege force was headquartered at Cambridge—the center of the army—with the rest of the troops deployed in Roxbury, Dorchester, and Jamaica Plain. Until Washington arrived on July 2 to take over, the troops were under the nominal command of Artemas Ward; however, the conglomerate of colonial militias insisted on taking orders exclusively from their own officers. Washington's first task was to impose unified command, and he also had to deal with shortages of weapons, ammunition, and provisions. Most vexing was the fact that most of his men were enlisted for the short term—usually just three months—and different militia bands had different expiration dates. Thus Washington's available manpower continually and variably dwindled. Although the Continental army was supposed to stabilize the enlistment situation, it would prove to be a chronic problem throughout the Revolution.

"I found a mixed multitude of People here," Washington wrote to his brother John Augustine on July 27, 1775, "under very little discipline, order, or Government." Doubtless, many of these men were idealistic revolutionaries thoroughly committed to the goal of liberty, but many were rowdy, shiftless men, who joined the militia because they were out of work or out of luck. And while Washington looked for ways to bring order to them all, to supply them all, and to keep them from leaving the army at the expiration of their enlistments, he also had to deal with politicians back in Philadelphia—men who had been quick to authorize an army and to put him in charge of it, but who now proved exasperatingly slow to vote the funds for it. As galling as all this was, Washington was most aggravated by the torrent of wannabe majors and colonels, men without any military experience, who saw a command in the Continental army as their passport to future influence and personal advantage.

ALTERNATE TAKE
The Siege That Did Not Have to Be

If Howe had attempted a breakout, he would almost certainly have avoided the Siege of Boston. His troops were well equipped and highly disciplined, whereas most of the Boston army was a rabble. Although he did not have the sheer numbers to mount a frontal attack, he controlled the coastal waters and could have used the Royal Navy to outflank the Boston army by land and sea. Had he been a bolder and more innovative commander, willing to coordinate sea and land forces, he might have ended the rebellion in a single action. Certainly, he would have crippled it.

DETAILS, DETAILS
And the Entrée This Evening Is . . .

Timothy Newell, deacon of the Brattle Street Church, recorded in his journal an invitation from "two gentlemen to dine upon *rats*." Everyone was hungry in Boston.

This eighteenth-century British map of Boston and the surrounding area shows the lines, batteries, and encampments of redcoats and Patriots alike.

"Such a dearth of public spirit, and want of virtue, such stock-jobbing, and fertility in all the low arts to obtain advantages of one kind or another . . . I never saw before, and pray God I may never be witness to again. . . . Could I have foreseen what I have, and am likely to experience, no consideration upon earth should have induced me to accept this command."

George Washington, letter to
General Joseph Reed, November 28, 1775

Washington Resolves to Attack

The fluid, ill-supplied nature of the American forces was bad—and there was even worse. The besieged British garrison of Boston was about to be reinforced by sea. Washington therefore convened a council of war on January 16, 1776, and presented his case for ending the siege by attacking the British—*before* the arrival of reinforcements stacked the odds against the Americans. Accordingly, a call went out for thirteen militia regiments to serve during February and March. Word of the American failure in Quebec arrived on the seventeenth, prompting Congress to allocate three of the promised militia regiments for service in Canada; despite this, on February 16, Washington proposed a surprise attack against Boston over the ice of the frozen Charles River, using the sixteen thousand men then available. Washington's subordinate commanders countered with a less ambitious proposal to take a more modest objective in the hope of drawing the British out into open battle. Washington reluctantly accepted a plan to occupy Dorchester Heights.

Back in November 1775, Henry Knox—until recently a Boston bookstore owner, and now a Continental army colonel—had proposed to Washington a plan to transport the artillery captured at Fort Ticonderoga (see Chapter 7, "The Taking of Fort Ti") more than three hundred miles to Cambridge, where it could be used to bombard Boston in preparation for the attack on the British garrison. Such a journey with heavy artillery over nonexistent roads was an epic undertaking. Knox reached Fort Ti on December 5, 1775 and selected 50 or 60 cannon and mortars, then had his men build 42 sledges, which would be hitched to 80 yoke of oxen—a yoke being a working pair, making, therefore, a grand total of 160 animals. The artillery began arriving in Cambridge on January 24—approximately 59 pieces, including 14 mortars, 2 howitzers, and 43 cannon. The timely arrival of what Knox dubbed his "noble train of artillery" emboldened Washington.

In the Meantime . . .

While Washington prepared to attack Boston, and while General Gage did very little about it, the Royal Navy— the most powerful in the world—should have been making short work of the rebellion. In the eighteenth century, most of the colonial population lived along the Atlantic coast, whose cities and towns made perfect targets for naval warfare. By the end of the Revolution, the Royal Navy had committed about one hundred major warships to the

NUMBERS
Continental Army Enlistment

On January 14, 1776, only 8,212 men of the 20,370 authorized by Congress for the Continental army had been enlisted. Of this number, a mere 5,582 were present and fit for duty. Five thousand militiamen had arrived to replace the Connecticut militia, which left upon expiration of their enlistment on December 10. The replacements, however, were slated to leave on January 15, 1776. To make matters yet worse, of the men assembled, about two thousand lacked muskets and were therefore wholly unarmed. Those who did carry guns had at most ten rounds of ammunition each.

Former Boston bookstore owner Henry Knox served Washington as commander of the Continental army's artillery. In an epic trek, he brought captured British artillery from Fort Ticonderoga to Boston during December 1775–January 1776. The artillery was instrumental in the Patriot's triumphant siege of British-occupied Boston.

American theater of operations. Supplied with a contingent of marines, these should have made a decisive impact on the war.

Why didn't it? Impressive as the Royal Navy appeared on paper, it was bogged down in corruption and poor leadership. Had Admiral Samuel Graves, commander in charge of British operations in American waters, bombarded key American towns along the seaboard, he might have brought a quick end to the Revolution. Although the mighty Royal Navy supplied transport to land forces, it was never used in a coordinated and decisive manner.

NUMBERS
Big Guns

The total weight of the guns Knox transported three hundred miles from Fort Ticonderoga to Cambridge was 119,900 pounds (approximately sixty tons)—in addition to 2,300 pounds of lead—all hauled by a combination of animal and manpower.

THE UNFOUGHT BATTLE OF BOSTON

Properly displeased with Gage's performance, the British crown relieved him on October 10, 1775, and put William Howe in overall command. A short time later, on January 27, 1776, Howe's admiral brother, Richard, replaced Graves as commander of the fleet. By this time, too, the British Boston garrison had grown to about eight thousand men—just about half the number of the Americans gathered outside of the city.

The arrival of Knox's artillery prompted Washington to fortify Dorchester Heights in March and position the artillery within the fortifications. During the night of March 4, 1776, a labor detail of twelve hundred men covered by eight hundred of the Continental army's best troops, moved a train of 360 ox carts loaded with walls and other elements of fortification—which had been prefabricated in Cambridge—up Dorchester Heights. The work proceeded by the light of the moon while a thick ground fog shielded the activity from enemy eyes. By three o'clock on the morning of March 5, the heights had been fully fortified. It was a job so quick and thorough that Howe believed twelve thousand men had been involved, and one of his engineers estimated twenty thousand.

"The rebels have done more in one night than my whole army could do in months."

General William Howe, on the fortification of Dorchester Heights, 1776

Washington must have realized that his more conservative officers had been right after all. Occupying Dorchester Heights had been a very good idea. It overlooked Boston as well as the British fleet in Boston Harbor—yet was too high for British ground-based or shipboard guns to reach. Howe contemplated making an assault with twenty-two hundred men, but called off the attack at the last minute because of a storm. In the meantime, on March 9, Washington tried to add a portion of the Heights then called Nock's Hill to the ground he occupied—but was quickly driven off by the British.

That, Howe understood, was a minor and quite inconsequential victory. On sober reflection, he decided that an attack against Dorchester Heights would be a waste of blood. Yet as long as Dorchester Heights was occupied, Boston would be held under siege—until the rebels chose to storm and take it. Stymied, on March 7 he ordered the withdrawal of British forces from Boston. By nine in the morning on March 17, eleven thousand British soldiers and sailors were waiting to board ships of the royal fleet. To prevent its falling into rebel hands, the 64th Regiment planted explosive charges in and around their Boston headquarters, Castle William, then blew it up. That served as a signal for the British military personnel, accompanied by about a thousand civilian Loyalists, to board the ships for evacuation.

As for the Americans watching from the heights of Dorchester, their guns remained silent. By secret agreement, Washington had given the British permission to depart in safety—with the proviso that they leave Boston and its citizens unharmed. The only building to suffer destruction was Castle William.

The siege had lasted eight months. For all that time, a miscellany of colonial militia and then militia plus the Continental army, had held what Washington described as the "flower of British soldiers" utterly helpless. During this period, just twenty Patriot soldiers had been killed. The British had meant to bring Boston and all of Massachusetts—the very font of the rebellion—to their knees. Instead, the army of King George III was on its way to Halifax, Nova Scotia, where there was no talk of revolution.

TAKEAWAY
Failure to Act Decisively

Had they acted aggressively, the British could have crushed the American Revolution shortly after it had begun; however, their failure to break out of Boston or to use its navy effectively doomed the redcoats to a prolonged siege and an ignominious withdrawal from the cradle of the American Revolution.

Chapter 9

WE HOLD THESE TRUTHS

Thomas Paine's Common Sense *and
Thomas Jefferson's Declaration of Independence
Give the Revolution Purpose, Direction, and
Historical Meaning*

*M*OST HISTORIANS AGREE that the American Revolution began on April 19, 1775, with the battles of Lexington and Concord. No historian asserts that it began on July 4, 1776, the date on which the birth certificate of the United States—the Declaration of Independence—was approved by the Continental Congress. The difference between these two dates, separated by more than a year, is important, because the American Revolution was not always absolutely about winning independence from Britain. Even after the shooting had started—and the British army had been forced to leave Boston—there was no universal agreement on what the fighting was all about.

THE WAR OF WORDS

THE WAR OF BULLETS outran the war of words in the American Revolution. Thomas Hutchinson, who had served as royal governor of Massachusetts, once remarked that the fight for American independence had really begun back in 1765, with the protest against the Stamp Act; however, John Adams, surely among the principal advocates of independence, recalled years after independence had been won that, discontented as most

Americans were, virtually no one talked seriously of independence from Britain before 1775–76.

With the American Revolution in full swing, this British cartoon from September 3, 1778, comments on the struggle for control of America, which is pictured as a zebra of thirteen stripes—one for each colony. The Crown's Lord North tries to lead it by the reins, but George Washington has it by the tail.

Revolutionary Moderation

As mentioned in Chapter 5, the Maryland-born Philadelphia attorney and president of the Pennsylvania assembly Joseph Galloway brought before the First Continental Congress on September 28, 1774, a "Plan of Union." His plan was intended to give the colonies a dose of home rule without severing them from the Crown. It was defeated by a single vote, whereupon Galloway declined to serve in the Second Continental Congress and wrote another attempt at reconciliation, "A Candid Examination of the Mutual Claims of Great Britain and the Colonies: With a Plan of Accommodation on Constitutional Principles." No one much cared, and in 1776, Galloway left America for Britain, where he repeatedly floated schemes of reconciliation—even after the Revolution had ended in American independence.

If Galloway was stubbornly immoderate in his moderation, he was not the only revolutionary moderate with hopes for reconciliation. The Second Continental Congress, which convened in Philadelphia on May 10, 1775, rang with debate over the issue of separation versus reconciliation with England. One of the debaters was Maryland-born Pennsylvanian politician John Dickinson, whose *Letters from a Farmer in Pennsylvania to Inhabitants of the British Colonies* (1767–68) was a popular and influential condemnation of the

Townshend Acts. Now, Dickinson presented the Second Continental Congress with a document known as the "Olive Branch Petition." It respectfully reviewed the colonies' grievances against the Crown, but then professed attachment "to your Majesty's person, family, and government, with all devotion that principle and affection can inspire." The people of America, Dickinson wrote, were "connected with Great Britain by the strongest ties that can unite societies." The petition concluded by beseeching "your Majesty . . . to procure us relief from our afflicting fears and jealousies."

Against the protest of Adams and the other New Englanders, the members of the Second Continental Congress endorsed the Olive Branch Petition—although they did so specifically as individuals rather than on behalf of the congress. Richard Penn, a descendent of the illustrious founder of Pennsylvania, William Penn, carried the petition to London and King George—who refused so much as to receive the messenger. Instead, on August 23, 1775, while Penn cooled his heels, George III proclaimed "our Colonies and Plantations in North America, misled by dangerous and designing men," to be in a state of rebellion and ordered "all our Officers . . . and all our obedient and loyal subjects, to use their utmost endeavours to withstand and suppress such rebellion." While America's colonists may have wavered between reconciliation and independence, the British monarch apparently had no doubts. It was he who defined the colonies as rebellious.

Edmund Burke, a brilliant philosopher and politician, strove to be a voice of reason in the struggle between Britain and its colonies. He argued that the government's stubbornly legalistic assertion of imperial rights offended the sensibilities of those subject to it and thereby incited rather than suppressed revolution.

George's prime minister, Lord North, the very man whose policies had been instrumental in propelling the colonies to the brink of revolution, suddenly differed with his king and secured from Parliament—then (grudgingly) from the king—approval of a plan for reconciliation, which would have conceded much of the power of taxation to the colonies. On July 31, 1775, two days before adjourning, the Second Continental Congress rejected North's reconciliation plan.

But that wasn't the end of it. On November 16, 1775, the liberal British statesman Edmund Burke, who favored American independence, introduced before Parliament a bill to "Compose American Troubles," in which he audaciously asserted parliamentary supremacy over royal prerogative where the colonies were concerned. In effect, Burke had given up on trying to persuade George to reconcile with the colonies and hoped instead to secure for Parliament the direct authority to do so. The bill was defeated.

> *"Magnanimity in politics is not seldom the truest wisdom; and a great empire and little minds go ill together."*
>
> —
>
> *Edmund Burke, speech to the House of Commons, urging reconciliation with the colonies, March 22, 1775*

As for the colonies, even as hopes for reconciliation faded, some began to struggle desperately against independence. On November 4, 1775, the assembly of New Jersey tried simply denying independence out of existence by dismissing as "groundless" the many reports of colonists seeking independence. On November 9— the very day that Congress received news of George III's refusal to receive Penn and the Olive Branch Petition— the Pennsylvania Assembly issued instructions to its Continental Congress delegation to "dissent from and utterly reject any propositions . . . that may cause or lead to a separation from our mother country or a change of the form of this government."

Even as it digested the king's arrogant spurning of the Olive Branch Petition, the Second Continental Congress found itself unable to defy the king. Only after much bitter debate did Congress issue on December 6 a response to the rejection. It began by reaffirming allegiance to King George III, but denied the authority of Parliament, because the colonies were not (and could not be) represented in that body.

The Momentum of Independence

As some colonies sought to deny even the existence of an independence movement, others grew impatient with Congress and wrote new constitutions for themselves, each of these documents in effect a state declaration of independence. Before it wrote its constitution,

Born in England, Thomas Paine immigrated to the United States on the eve of the Revolution and became active in the cause of independence. His pamphlet, Common Sense, *was published on January 10, 1776, sold a staggering half-million copies in a matter of months, and instantly galvanized the independence movement.*

Massachusetts asked the Continental Congress to issue a model constitution for it and the other colonies. When Congress demurred, Massachusetts issued a modified version of its 1691 charter, replacing the royal governor of the original document with a twenty-eight-member elected council.

By early 1776, threecolonies —Massachusetts, New Hampshire, and South Carolina—had created constitutions without royal authority. Even so, none of these documents made an explicit and definitive break with the mother country. Soon, however, other colonies wrote bolder documents, and by the time the Declaration of Independence was adopted on July 4, 1776, seven colonies had made the transition to states by means of brand-new constitutions.

COMMON SENSE CREATES COMMON CAUSE

BY THE END OF 1775, there was no denying that a revolution was being fought. What Americans hoped to achieve by this revolution was, however, still an open question. As the most eminent physician in America, Benjamin Rush of Philadelphia thought unanswered questions were like undiagnosed pains. Accordingly, this delegate to the Continental Congress, already a firm believer in independence, called on Thomas Paine, who had moved from England to Philadelphia in November 1774, to write a pamphlet that would make the case for

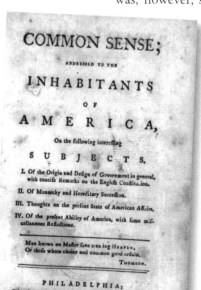

Title page of the first edition of Thomas Paine's Common Sense. *The pamphlet not only focused the American Revolution on achieving absolute independence from Britain, it sought to make the American cause both global and timeless: "The cause of America is in a great measure the cause of all mankind," Paine wrote.*

independence. Paine set to work immediately, and when Rush read it, he was pleased that it boiled everything down so persuasively and with so much common sense. In fact, it was Rush who slapped that title on the pamphlet.

Published on January 10, 1776, *Common Sense* ran to forty-seven printed pages and was offered for sale at two shillings a copy. In common, straightforward language it marshaled every conceivable argument for independence, and it did so more persuasively than any piece of political writing that had come before it. Understanding that most colonists didn't like Catholics, Paine compared King George III to the pope. Then he went on to blast the whole notion of the hereditary succession of kings as an absurdity. One by one, he demolished all arguments in favor of reconciling with England, then capped this by demonstrating the economic benefits of independence. Through it all, Paine wove two main themes—first, that a republican form of government was inherently superior to government by a hereditary monarch, and, second, that equality of rights was the common birthright of humanity, one that no just government could fail to defend.

But it was the way he ended *Common Sense* that revealed the persuasive genius of the pamphlet:

> O ye that love mankind! Ye that dare oppose, not only the tyranny, but the tyrant, stand forth! Every spot of the old world is overrun with oppression. Freedom hath been hunted round the globe. Asia, and Africa, have long expelled her. Europe regards her like a stranger, and England hath given her warning to depart. O! receive the fugitive, and prepare in time an asylum for mankind.

With this peroration, Paine instantly transformed what might otherwise have seemed a family squabble between colonies and mother country into an international event of enduring importance to all humankind. Everyone everywhere, Paine argued, had a stake in the outcome of the American struggle for independence. It was a revolution for all humanity.

DETAILS, DETAILS
Starting from Scratch

On October 18, 1775, New Hampshire repeated Massachusetts's request for a model constitution. Congress again declined, but advised New Hampshire to "establish such a government, as in their judgment will best produce the happiness of the people," and thus on January 5, 1776, New Hampshire became the first colony to write a state constitution entirely from scratch.

The Freshet

Within three months, 120,000 copies of *Common Sense* had flown from bookstore shelves. Those who lived in the northern colonies were familiar with the phenomenon of the spring freshet: a stream that is languid in summer and fall, freezes in winter, only to swell with the thaw of spring into a raging torrent. This was the effect of *Common Sense* on the independence movement.

> *"Every post and every day rolls in upon us Independence like a torrent."*
>
> John Adams, letter to James Warren,
> May 20, 1776

England's most celebrated man of letters, Samuel Johnson was an eloquent apologist for the Tory cause and was enlisted by the Crown to defend colonial policy with a 1775 pamphlet entitled Taxation No Tyranny, *in which (among other things) he pointed to the hypocrisy of slave-holding Virginians clamoring for "liberty."*

The Continental Congress shook off its lethargy. On February 18, it commissioned privateers, merchant ships officially authorized to raid and capture British vessels. On February 26, Congress embargoed exports to Britain and the British West Indies. On March 3, it sent Silas Deane to France to negotiate for aid. On March 14, it ordered that all Loyalists—those who continued to profess allegiance to the king—be disarmed. On April 6, Congress proclaimed all American ports open to the trade of every nation, *except* for Great Britain.

Now, too, colonies voted themselves independent states. Virginia's resolution of independence, promulgated on May 15, 1776, was the most famous of all: "Instead of redress of grievances," it declaimed, George III has given "increased insult, oppression and a vigorous attempt to effect our total destruction. . . . Our properties are subjected to confiscation, our people, when captivated, compelled to join in the murder and plunder of their relations and countrymen, and all former rapine and oppression of Americans declared legal and just." This being the case, the delegates of Virginia Assembly "declare the United Colonies free and independent states, absolved from allegiance to, or dependence upon, the crown or parliament of Great Britain."

On May 15, the Continental Congress officially recommended that states that had not yet established a "Government sufficient to the exigencies of their affairs" do so now. On June 7, Richard Henry Lee of Virginia proposed that Congress adopt another resolution, a declaration "That these United Colonies are, and of right ought to be, free and independent States . . . and that all political connection between them and the State of Great Britain is, and ought to be totally dissolved." His resolution included taking "the most effectual measures for forming foreign alliances" and preparing "a plan of confederation" among the colonies.

THE DEBATE

Sponsors of Lee's resolution decided to postpone debate on it for three weeks because, they felt, some of the colonies were "not yet ripe for bidding adieu to the British connection." During this interval, Delaware, Connecticut, New Hampshire, New Jersey, and Maryland instructed their congressional delegates to vote for independence. Then, on July 1, the great debate began.

Pennsylvania's Dickinson argued for delaying the debate further, but Adams and Lee urged immediate action. South Carolina and Pennsylvania obliged—by immediately voting against independence. The Delaware delegation was divided, and New York, in the midst of reshuffling its government, abstained. This left, as of the end of July 1, the vote at nine to four in favor of independence. Pretty good, but the radicals in the Delaware delegation wanted to drum up an overwhelming majority in favor of independence, so they sent Delaware representative Caesar Rodney on a Paul Revere–style midnight ride from Dover to Philadelphia. After his eighty-mile gallop, he arrived just in time to swing the Delaware vote to independence. This prompted South Carolina's delegation to switch to independence, which, in turn, moved Pennsylvania to vote likewise. New York continued to abstain, but the majority, on July 2, was overwhelming.

FORGOTTEN FACES
Samuel Johnson

The great lexicographer, essayist, literary critic, and general man of letters Samuel Johnson was one of the most famous men in eighteenth-century Britain, but he is rarely thought about in relation to the American Revolution. Yet a number of Johnson's essays were political in nature, and although he was a staunch Tory (his famous *Dictionary* gave a full definition of the word *Tory* but defined *Whig* in just two words, "A faction"), his conservatism was always thoughtful. Early in March 1775, he published at the request of the Crown the pamphlet *Taxation No Tyranny,* in which he responded provocatively to charges especially from Virginians—that the policies of Parliament and King George III had made slaves of the Americans: "If slavery thus be fatally contagious, how is it that we hear the loudest yelps for liberty among the drivers of Negroes?"

DETAILS, DETAILS

Four for Four

Roger Sherman has the distinction of being a "quadruple signer," the only man to sign all four major documents of independence: The Articles of Association (enacted by the First Continental Congress in 1774), the Declaration of Independence, the Articles of Confederation, and the Constitution.

THE DECLARATION

CONGRESS HAD NOT WAITED FOR THE CONCLUSION of the debate to get its paperwork started. During the three-week gap between the introduction of Lee's resolution of independence and the start of the debate, the members appointed a committee to draft a declaration of independence. On the roster were John Adams, Benjamin Franklin, Robert Livingston, Roger Sherman, and Thomas Jefferson.

Adams was seen as the senior member, since he had been a prime mover of the Revolution. At seventy, Franklin was not only the oldest member of the committee, he was the most renowned, having earned an international reputation as a scientist, inventor, writer, editor, and politician. The scion of a prosperous old New York family, Livingston brought a touch of conservatism to the committee. Sherman, from Connecticut, had been apprenticed as a cobbler but was always a voracious reader; self-educated, he became

Thomas Jefferson, Benjamin Franklin, and John Adams meet in Jefferson's Philadelphia lodgings, at the corner of Seventh and High Streets (present-day Market Street) to review Jefferson's draft of the Declaration of Independence. The scene was imagined by illustrator Jean Leon Gerome Ferris (ca. 1909).

a legislator and highly respected economic theorist, as well as the author-publisher of a series of popular almanacs based on his own astronomical calculations.

The fifth member of the committee was Thomas Jefferson. He had a fine education from the College of William and Mary and was a prominent Virginia attorney. Hardly electrifying on the podium, he had nevertheless earned a reputation as a bold writer, and John Adams deferred to him as the best writer on the committee. He asked Jefferson to draft the Declaration of Independence.

In 1825, many years after he wrote the declaration, Jefferson explained in a letter to Henry Lee what he had been about. He said that he was not trying to "find out new principles, or new arguments, never before thought of," but, rather "to justify ourselves in the independent stand we are compelled to take" and, finally, to "appeal to the tribunal of the world . . . for our justification." We have already pointed out that the American Revolution was unlike most revolutions in that it was not a movement of the economically downtrodden against the privileged classes; on the contrary, the leaders of the Revolution were mostly from the privileged classes. Congress, the drafting committee, and Jefferson made the Revolution even more unusual by asking the entire world to approve of it. Since the founding of the first American colonies in the seventeenth century, Americans had been accustomed to presenting their home as an example to the rest of the world. The Puritans spoke of their colony as a "city on a hill"—a beacon of righteousness—and a "new Jerusalem"; Pennsylvania was founded as a haven of religious and political toleration; Georgia started out as a utopia. So it was now, with the idea of American independence.

And it truly was a bold experiment in government. Never before had a people decided to invent themselves, to break with a king in order to create a nation without a king, a nation not founded on the basis of a royal claim or a tribal affiliation, but on the foundation of an idea. It was now up to Jefferson to express that idea. To do so, he neither aimed at originality of principle and sentiment nor did he copy from any specific model (for none existed). Instead, as he explained to Lee, he intended the declaration "to be an expression of the American mind," and to give to that expression the proper tone and spirit called for by the occasion. All its authority rests on the

REALITY CHECK
Just a Piece of Parchment

To be sure, being nominated to write the document was a vote of confidence—yet it was not so momentous an honor as it seems now in the eye of history. No one on the committee felt that the declaration had to be especially eloquent or profound—a document for the ages. They just wanted a piece of paper that would make a legally defensible argument for independence and that would stand up to the scrutiny of foreign powers, notably France.

REALITY CHECK
Don't Worry, Be Happy

Jefferson's use of the word *happiness* was radical in a political document—yet perhaps not quite as radical as it may strike us today. In the late eighteenth century, the word *happiness* had a connotation that it has long since lost. As today, it did describe an emotional state of pleasure, contentment, and well-being, but it also implied physical and financial well-being. To be happy, in Jefferson's day, was to enjoy physical security and a reasonably comfortable—adequate—living, so that, in effect, to pursue happiness was to seek an adequate place in society: a living, a home, a place to be. Less radical than our understanding of "happiness"? Maybe. But finding a satisfying and secure place for oneself was nevertheless a tall order in a world ruled by kings and tyrants who sat atop a social ladder from which they had removed quite a few of the rungs.

harmonizing sentiments of the day, whether expressed in conversation, in letters, printed essays, or in the elementary books of public right, as Aristotle, Cicero, Locke, Sidney, etc."

Of all these authors Jefferson named, it was to the seventeenth-century British philosopher John Locke to whom he owed the greatest debt. For Locke had enumerated the basic rights of human beings. According to him, there were three: the right to life, liberty, and property. "We hold these truths to be self-evident," Jefferson wrote, "that all men are created equal, that they are endowed by their Creator with certain unalienable Rights, that among these are Life, Liberty and—" and *what?* Jefferson veered away from Locke, substituting for "property" the phrase "the pursuit of happiness." Perhaps no phrase in any document of American government has drawn greater and more profound commentary than this. Historians and social critics have seen in it the truest "expression of the American mind," an acknowledgment of what later generations would call the "American dream." Jefferson seemed to be saying that America should by rights be a place for self-fulfillment—or, at least, a place in which people are free to pursue such self-fulfillment.

Jefferson's rough draft of the declaration included an angry condemnation of King George III for having "waged cruel war against human nature itself, violating its most sacred rights of life & liberty in the persons of a distant people who never offended him, captivating & carrying them into slavery in another hemisphere, or to incur miserable death in their transportation thither." This ringing indictment of slavery was strange, coming as it did from a Virginia planter who owned slaves. That it was more a condemnation of the slave trade—the abduction of Africans from Africa and their transportation for sale in America—than of slavery itself does not explain away the fact that Jefferson kept his slaves lifelong and never set a single one of them free. Parse the passage as we may, what it comes down to is that Jefferson, very much part of a slave-owning class of white Americans, tried to pin the blame for slavery on the king of England. In any case, it was medicine far too strong for Jefferson's fellow southern slaveholders—and for a good many northern Yankees as well. Southern planters needed slave labor to work their large plantations. Northern farmers, whose lands were typically smaller, had no need for slaves—but plenty of northern merchants thrived on slavery nevertheless. It was all part of what they called the triangular trade, a long-established pattern of colonial commerce in which New England merchants transported their simple manufactured goods to Africa in exchange for slaves (that was one leg of the triangle). The slaves thus purchased were transported to the West Indies (the second leg), where they were, in turn, traded for rum and molasses, which was sold back in New England (the closing leg of the triangle).

Along with a few other editorial changes, Congress struck from the declaration Jefferson's noble if hypocritical passage on slavery, so that the "unanimous Declaration of the thirteen united States of America"—these entities were no longer to be called colonies—announced the commencement of a fight for liberty and the inalienable rights of humankind by a nation that nevertheless intended to keep a portion of its population enslaved.

Celebration

Approved on July 4, the declaration was published on July 9, 1776—as John Adams wrote to one of the signers of the document, Samuel Chase—to the accompaniment of bells, which "rang all day and almost all night."

Adams was elated by the celebrations, but he remained soberly realistic. Politically and legally, the Declaration of Independence had resolved the object of the ongoing revolution. It would not be home rule and reconciliation, but outright and absolute independence. By the numbers, though, the prospects for anything other than catastrophe did not look good. Britain had far more people, money, and ships than the colonies. Yet Adams also knew that the ideas expressed in *Common Sense* and the Declaration of Independence were not about numbers and could not, in fact, be quantified. It was for these ideas that the people would fight, and it was for these they would prevail.

ALTERNATE TAKE
Antislavery Clause

What if Congress had not struck down Jefferson's condemnation of slavery? Some believe that the American Revolution would have been endowed with greater moral force and that the United States would have saved itself from a later civil war. More likely, however, none of the southern delegates would have approved the Declaration of Independence, and the antislavery clauses would not have survived ratification.

NUMBERS
A Nation in Thirds

In 1815, reflecting on the state of the newborn nation back in July 1776, John Adams wrote: "I should say that full one-third [of the American people] were averse to the revolution." Did that mean, therefore, that two-thirds were wholly dedicated to independence? No. Another third, Adams observed, "the yeomanry, the soundest part of the nation, always averse to war, were rather lukewarm" on the idea of a revolution.

The Declaration of Independence

In Congress, July 4, 1776
THE UNANIMOUS DECLARATION OF THE THIRTEEN UNITED STATES OF AMERICA

WHEN IN THE COURSE OF HUMAN EVENTS, it becomes necessary for one people to dissolve the political bands which have connected them with another, and to assume among the powers of the earth, the separate and equal station to which the laws of nature and of nature's God entitle them, a decent respect to the opinions of mankind requires that they should declare the causes which impel them to the separation.

We hold these truths to be self-evident:

That all men are created equal; that they are endowed by their Creator with certain unalienable rights; that among these are life, liberty, and the pursuit of happiness; that, to secure these rights, governments are instituted among men, deriving their just powers from the consent of the governed; that whenever any form of government becomes destructive of these ends, it is the right of the people to alter or to abolish it, and to institute new government, laying its foundation on such principles, and organizing its powers in such form, as to them shall seem most likely to effect their safety and happiness. Prudence, indeed, will dictate that governments long established should not be changed for light and transient causes; and accordingly all experience hath shown that mankind are more disposed to suffer, while evils are sufferable than to right themselves by abolishing the forms to which they are accustomed. But when a long train of abuses and usurpations, pursuing invariably the same object, evinces a design to reduce

The signing copy of the Declaration of Independence: First to sign was John Hancock. Durable legend has it that, after making his signature especially conspicuous, he remarked, "There, I guess King George will be able to read that." There is, however, no evidence that Hancock said anything of the kind about a document George III was neither intended nor expected to see.

them under absolute despotism, it is their right, it is their duty, to throw off such government, and to provide new guards for their future security. Such has been the patient sufferance of these colonies; and such is now the necessity which constrains them to alter their former systems of government. The history of the present King of Great Britain is a history of repeated injuries and usurpations, all having in direct object the establishment of an absolute tyranny over these states. To prove this, let facts be submitted to a candid world.

He has refused his assent to laws, the most wholesome and necessary for the public good.

He has forbidden his governors to pass laws of immediate and pressing importance, unless suspended in their operation till his assent should be obtained; and, when so suspended, he has utterly neglected to attend to them.

He has refused to pass other laws for the accommodation of large districts of people, unless those people would relinquish the right of representation in the legislature, a right inestimable to them, and formidable to tyrants only.

He has called together legislative bodies at places unusually uncomfortable, and distant from the depository of their public records, for the sole purpose of fatiguing them into compliance with his measures.

He has dissolved representative houses repeatedly, for opposing, with manly firmness, his invasions on the rights of the people.

He has refused for a long time, after such dissolutions, to cause others to be elected; whereby the legislative powers, incapable of annihilation, have returned to the people at large for their exercise; the state remaining, in the mean time, exposed to all the dangers of invasions from without and convulsions within.

He has endeavored to prevent the population of these states; for that purpose obstructing the laws for naturalization of foreigners; refusing to pass others to encourage their migration hither, and raising the conditions of new appropriations of lands.

He has obstructed the administration of justice, by refusing his assent to laws for establishing judiciary powers.

He has made judges dependent on his will alone, for the tenure of their offices, and the amount and payment of their salaries.

He has erected a multitude of new offices, and sent hither swarms of officers to harass our people and eat out their substance.

He has kept among us, in times of peace, standing armies, without the consent of our legislatures.

He has affected to render the military independent of, and superior to, the civil power.

He has combined with others to subject us to a jurisdiction foreign to our Constitution and unacknowledged by our laws, giving his assent to their acts of pretended legislation:

For quartering large bodies of armed troops among us;

For protecting them, by a mock trial, from punishment for any murders which they should commit on the inhabitants of these states;

For cutting off our trade with all parts of the world;

For imposing taxes on us without our consent;

For depriving us, in many cases, of the benefits of trial by jury;

For transporting us beyond seas, to be tried for pretended offenses;

For abolishing the free system of English laws in a neighboring province, establishing therein an arbitrary government, and enlarging its boundaries, so as to render it at once an example and fit instrument for introducing the same absolute rule into these colonies;

For taking away our charters, abolishing our most valuable laws, and altering fundamentally the forms of our governments;

For suspending our own legislatures, and declaring themselves invested with power to legislate for us in all cases whatsoever.

He has abdicated government here, by declaring us out of his protection and waging war against us.

He has plundered our seas, ravaged our coasts, burned our towns, and destroyed the lives of our people.

He is at this time transporting large armies of foreign mercenaries to complete the works of death, desolation, and tyranny already begun with circumstances of cruelty and perfidy scarcely paralleled in the most barbarous ages, and totally unworthy the head of a civilized nation.

He has constrained our fellow-citizens, taken captive on the high seas, to bear arms against their country, to become the executioners of their friends and brethren, or to fall themselves by their hands.

He has excited domestic insurrection among us, and has endeavored to bring on the inhabitants of our frontiers the merciless Indian savages, whose known rule of warfare is an undistinguished destruction of all ages, sexes, and conditions.

In every stage of these oppressions we have petitioned for redress in the most humble terms; our repeated petitions have been answered only by repeated injury. A prince, whose character is thus marked by every act which may define a tyrant, is unfit to be the ruler of a free people.

Nor have we been wanting in our attentions to our British brethren. We have warned them, from time to time, of attempts by their legislature to extend an unwarrantable jurisdiction over us. We have reminded them of the circumstances of our emigration and settlement here. We have appealed to their native justice and magnanimity; and we have conjured them, by the ties of our common kindred, to disavow these usurpations which would inevitably interrupt our connections and correspondence. They too, have been deaf to the voice of justice and of consanguinity. We must, therefore, acquiesce in the necessity which denounces our separation, and

hold them as we hold the rest of mankind, enemies in war, in peace friends.

We, therefore, the representatives of the United States of America, in General Congress assembled, appealing to the Supreme Judge of the world for the rectitude of our intentions, do, in the name and by the authority of the good people of these colonies solemnly publish and declare, That these United Colonies are, and of right ought to be, **FREE AND INDEPENDENT STATES;** that they are absolved from all allegiance to the British crown and that all political connection between them and the state of Great Britain is, and ought to be, totally dissolved; and that, as free and independent states, they have full power to levy war, conclude peace, contract alliances, establish commerce, and do all other acts and things which independent states may of right do. And for the support of this declaration, with a firm reliance on the protection of Divine Providence, we mutually pledge to each other our lives, our fortunes, and our sacred honor.

[Signed by]

John Hancock

[President]

New Hampshire
JOSIAH BARTLETT,
WM. WHIPPLE, MATTHEW THORNTON.

Massachusetts Bay
SAML. ADAMS,
JOHN ADAMS,
ROBT. TREAT PAINE,
ELBRIDGE GERRY.

Rhode Island
STEP. HOPKINS,
WILLIAM ELLERY.

Connecticut
ROGER SHERMAN,
SAM'EL HUNTINGTON,
WM. WILLIAMS,
OLIVER WOLCOTT.

New York
WM. FLOYD,
PHIL. LIVINGSTON,
FRANS. LEWIS,
LEWIS MORRIS.

New Jersey
RICHD. STOCKTON,
JNO. WITHERSPOON,
FRAS. HOPKINSON,
JOHN HART,
ABRA. CLARK.

Pennsylvania
ROBT. MORRIS,
BENJAMIN RUSH,
BENJA. FRANKLIN,
JOHN MORTON,
GEO. CLYMER,
JAS. SMITH,
GEO. TAYLOR,
JAMES WILSON,
GEO. ROSS.

Delaware
CAESAR RODNEY,
GEO. READ,
THO. M'KEAN.

Maryland
SAMUEL CHASE,
WM. PACA,
THOS. STONE,
CHARLES CARROLL of
  Carrollton.

Virginia
GEORGE WYTHE,
RICHARD HENRY LEE,
TH. JEFFERSON,
BENJA. HARRISON,
THS. NELSON, JR.,
FRANCIS LIGHTFOOT LEE,
CARTER BRAXTON.

North Carolina
WM. HOOPER,
JOSEPH HEWES,
JOHN PENN.

South Carolina
EDWARD RUTLEDGE,
THOS. HAYWARD, JUNR.,
THOMAS LYNCH, JUNR.,
ARTHUR MIDDLETON.

Georgia
BUTTON GWINNETT,
LYMAN HALL,
GEO. WALTON.

This scene of the signing of the Declaration of Independence was always one of the most popular of Currier & Ives's many prints. The original print was published between 1835 and 1856.

PART THREE

The Times That Tried Men's Souls

Chapter 10

WASHINGTON THE LOSER

George Washington Loses Long Island and Manhattan but Not the War

BRITISH MILITARY COMMAND HAD SENT TROOPS to Boston because that was the hotbed of the rebellion. It was a sensible thing to do. But after the redcoats' defeat in Boston, the commanders took a new tack. As the source of the rebellion, Boston (and the rest of Massachusetts) was also the fortress of rebellion, the place where the rebels were strongest. The new plan was to attack the Revolution where it was the weakest. There were at least two places where Loyalists—Tories, as they were called—substantially outnumbered the Patriots: South Carolina and New York. We'll focus here on New York, then cover the southern campaign in Chapter 18.

TARGET: NEW YORK

IN 1776, PHILADELPHIA WAS THE BIGGEST CITY in the colonies, and Boston was the trendsetter. New York City came in third, but it was nevertheless a strategically important prize—with a splendid harbor (perfect anchorage for the British fleet) and control over the mouth of the Hudson River, which was not only a principal avenue into the American interior, but also a point of demarcation between New England and the rest of the colonies. Seize

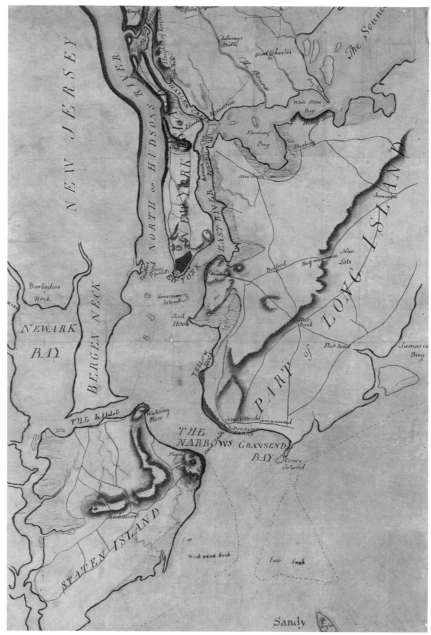

This map of New York and Staten Island, with parts of Long Island and New Jersey, was published at roughly the time of the American Revolution. The dark area at the tip of Manhattan represents the full extent of New York City at the time. Everything to the north was hilly countryside traversed by many streams and springs. Only as New York City expanded northward during the nineteenth century was Manhattan transformed into its present-day flat topography.

the Hudson, and New England—the brain of the Revolution—would be severed from the rest of the American body. It would be a decapitating blow.

This was the plan: General Howe, having withdrawn from Boston all the way to Halifax, Nova Scotia, would take on reinforcements and descend south to capture and occupy New York City. Using New York as a base, Howe would advance up the Hudson River, control it, take Albany, and thereby cut off New England from the other colonies. Once Howe had reached Albany, General Guy Carleton would join him there, and the two would operate in concert and essentially at will to mop up the remnants of the rebellion. It was hardly an innovative strategy. Divide and conquer had been around at least since the days of Caesar, and the British themselves had much experience with it, having employed it extensively in wars of colonial conquest elsewhere in the empire.

To Defend New York

Charles Lee had a reputation as a "colorful" officer. Born and raised in England, he entered his father's British regiment as an ensign in 1747 and served with Brigadier General Edward Braddock in the French and Indian War. But whereas Braddock and most other British officers were conservative and conventional to a fault, Lee, during the French and Indian War, raised eyebrows by accepting adoption into the Mohawk tribe and getting "married" to the daughter of a Seneca chief. After that war ended, Lee offered his services as a soldier of fortune and fought as a freelance officer attached to the Polish army. He immigrated to America in 1773 and rushed to join the most radical of the revolutionaries. He was among the very first to urge his fellow Patriots to raise an army—presumably on the assumption that he would command it.

During the often tedious days of siege duty around Boston, Lee added to his "colorful" reputation by earning widespread notoriety for the obscenity of his speech and for personal behavior one contemporary described only as being compounded of "dirty habits." It was this officer that Washington transferred from the siege of Boston in January 1776 to attend to the defense of New York, which Washington well knew, would sooner or later be targeted. Urgent though the transfer was, Lee did not arrive in Manhattan until

This contemporary engraving (published between 1776 and 1790) of Continental army major general Charles Lee on a prancing horse with sword aloft, goes a long way in suggesting Lee's haughty and supercilious manner.

February 4 on account of an acute attack of the gout—doubtless a symptom of his lifestyle.

Whether it was the lingering effects of gout or an attack of acute realism, Lee was not sanguine about his ability to defend New York. He wrote on February 19: "What to do with the city puzzles me. It is so encircled with deep navigable waters that whoever commands the sea must command the town." Clearly, the possessor of the Royal Navy commanded the sea. Nevertheless, Lee proposed deploying four to five thousand troops on Long Island, especially at a fortified position on Brooklyn Heights, which overlooked lower Manhattan. Farther uptown, he would station soldiers to defend Kings Bridge, which connected Manhattan with the Bronx on the mainland. To try to hold Manhattan against a sea attack was futile, Lee believed, and he would not try. On the contrary, he would allow the British to invade Manhattan, which (he also believed) would be "a most advantageous field of battle." Surely—if they wanted it badly enough—Manhattan would fall to the British, but, Lee reasoned, he could make the battle so costly that Parliament would think twice about continuing the war.

As it turned out—and this was typical of Lee—there was a vast gulf separating his bold plan from his will and capacity to implement it. Pleased that Lee had a plan, Washington did not arrive in New York to establish his headquarters until April 13, 1776. When he arrived, Washington was appalled to find that Lee had not even begun to build the fortifications he spoke of. Nor would Washington have the satisfaction of reprimanding Lee personally; supposedly having seen to the fortification of New York, he was now in Charleston, South Carolina, charged with planning the fortification of that city. Never one to fume idly, Washington set the Continental army to work digging up the island to erect earthen trenches and walls.

Washington had reason to be alarmed at the waste of so much time, but, fortunately for him, the British outdid Lee in lassitude. As it turned out, the nineteen thousand Continentals and militiamen who assembled to defend New York had a full five months to prepare their fortifications. It would be September before the British attacked.

THE REDCOATS ARE COMING—SLOWLY

Just how slowly did William Howe move? His first three ships landed off Sandy Hook, a spit of land projecting from New Jersey into

---

DETAILS, DETAILS
Dubious Pension

Lee's radical affiliations did not prevent his collecting half-pay from the British army. He'd been drawing this officer's pension since 1765 (when the French and Indian War ended) and saw no reason to stop now, even after Congress appointed him major general, subordinate only to Washington and Artemas Ward. Members of the Continental Congress were put off by the idea of the third highest-ranking commander in the cause of revolution being in the pay of the enemy and bought Lee off by promising to compensate him for any of his property the British might confiscate. On the strength of that promise, Lee wrote to the British paymaster requesting the discontinuance of his half pay.

Raritan Bay, opposite Staten Island, on June 25. One hundred twenty-seven more ships, carrying ninety-three hundred soldiers, followed on the twenty-ninth, making a display so impressive that Daniel McCurtin, an American sentinel, described them as "a fleet of pine trees trimmed . . . I thought all London was afloat."

And this was only the beginning. On July 12, Admiral Lord Richard Howe, William's brother, arrived with 150 more ships and reinforcements from England. These were followed by more British troops in addition to German mercenary forces—the dreaded "Hessians." Still, there was no movement to attack. At last, on August 12, even more soldiers arrived, having been shipped north after the first British expedition against Charleston, South Carolina, failed (see Chapter 18). By the end of August, therefore, Howe mustered 31,625 troops. Assembled at Sandy Hook was the largest force the British would ever muster in the American Revolution and, according to most historians, it was the greatest expeditionary force the British had ever sent overseas including during the French and Indian War.

Washington's Weakness

Washington was outnumbered and outgunned, although he did have the advantage of fighting from prepared fortifications. He had deployed 6,500 troops on Long Island, many of them gathered atop fortified Brooklyn Heights under the redoubtable Israel Putnam. In the woods and farmlands to the southeast and south of the fortified Heights—in the modern Brooklyn neighborhoods of Sunset Park, Parkville, and Flatbush—New Jersey militia general William Alexander and Continental general John Sullivan were stationed with contingents of about 1,600 and 1,500 men, respectively. Yet another unit occupied Governor's Island in New York Harbor, off the lower tip of Manhattan. Continental soldiers and militiamen were deployed in and around New York City, among these a brigade of 2,400 troops commanded by Thomas Mifflin, a prominent Philadelphia Quaker turned general, who occupied Fort Washington, overlooking the Hudson near the north end of Manhattan (close to the present location of 180th Street). Directly east of this, on the Harlem River, 1,800 of General George Clinton's men defended Kings Bridge, the link to the mainland.

In total, Washington had about 19,000 troops in and around New York City. This represented the bulk of America's organized,

---

REALITY CHECK

Staying in the Fight

Lee's strategy anticipated the thinking of George Washington himself. Like Lee, Washington had no illusions about the ability of the Continental army and the all but nonexistent Continental navy to defeat the British army and navy. But, like Lee, Washington believed that he could make every fight so costly that the British people and government—hardly unanimous in their opposition to American independence—would lose their stomach for continuing the war. For Washington, the Revolution was never about winning, but about not losing—staying in the war so long that the British, though undefeated, would simply give up.

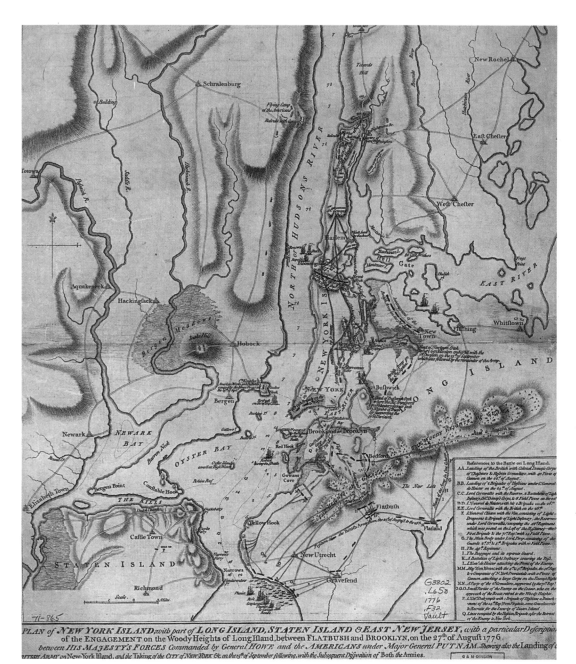

Published in 1776 by one William Faden of London, this map was intended to illustrate "the engagement on the woody heights of Long Island, between Flatbush and Brooklyn, on the 27th of August 1776 between His Majesty's forces commanded by General Howe and the Americans under Major General Putnam," as well as the "landing of the British Army on New-York Island, and the taking of the city of New-York &c. on the 15th of September following."

mobilized military strength—and Washington set them all in the jaws of a trap by dividing his forces between Manhattan and Long Island, with the East River and Long Island Sound separating them while also exposing them to the British fleet. Those ships could bombard the troops at will and deposit invaders anywhere along Manhattan and Long Island.

Although Washington was sometimes deficient as a tactician, he usually had a sound grasp of the bigger picture, of strategy. However, in the case of New York even this may have failed him. The Continental Congress pressed Washington to hold New York City, but it did not order him to do so. Ultimately, the decision was a military, not a political, one, and Washington could have asserted himself by choosing the strategically more viable course of withdrawing northward onto the mainland and away from the water, into the wilds of Westchester County, where the British fleet could not follow. Depriving Howe of the support of naval gunfire would have evened the odds. Moreover, it would have required Howe to seek and pursue Washington's men—a kind of warfare to which the conventional British army was notably unsuited. Washington chose, however, to make his stand on Long Island and in Manhattan.

ONSLAUGHT

ON THE NIGHT OF AUGUST 26, 1776, the 17th Light Dragoons, the 33rd West Ridings, the 71st Highlanders, the Guards, and a dozen more regiments took positions in the area of southeast Brooklyn then called—and still called today—the Flatlands. Their commanders were highly motivated. Henry Clinton was still stunned by the cost of the Battle of Bunker Hill. Charles Cornwallis arrived fresh from his defeat at Charleston. Lord Hugh Percy had witnessed the humiliation of the redcoats on the long march back from Lexington and Concord to Boston.

Not only did these field commanders thirst for revenge, they seem to have been inspired to a rare degree of imagination in their attack. Under cover of darkness, they

REALITY CHECK
Lack of Tactical Experience

Historians—especially military historians—have made something of a sport criticizing George Washington as a military commander. All are agreed that he was a courageous leader who usually inspired great loyalty. Yet many point out that he was often an inept tactician. Certainly such criticism is justified in the case of the Battle of New York. But, given Washington's background, his lack of skill in deploying his men is not surprising. He had experience leading relatively small groups into combat during the French and Indian War. He had no experience commanding a force as large as 19,000 men.

A panoramic view of the Battle of Long Island published in London in 1776. The perspective is from Brooklyn (on Long Island), with New York City visible at the right.

led their combined forces of ten thousand men in a broad arc to the northeast, which put them in position, on the morning of the twenty-seventh, to attack Sullivan's left flank—which was exactly the opposite side from which the attack had been expected. Surprise was total. Worse for the Americans, as Clinton, Cornwallis, and Percy attacked from the northeast, five thousand Hessians bore in from the Flatlands, heading due north, and seven thousand Highlanders swooped in from the west. Thus twenty-two thousand attacked from three sides, overwhelming the thirty-one hundred Americans deployed in front of the Brooklyn Heights fortifications. The American plan had been to use riflemen—who were dead-on shots—to thin out the British ranks. The trouble was that, with so many attackers closing in on three sides, the rifles could not be reloaded fast enough.

Given the overwhelming force of the attack, the performance of the American officers and troops was often remarkable. New Jersey's Alexander—popularly called Lord Stirling, because he had inherited that Scottish title—managed to hold off the attackers long enough to cause significant casualties among the Highlanders. He was not routed, but retreated with his force intact. Of course, even an orderly retreat does not win a battle, and by noon, the opening phase of the combat was over. The survivors fell back on the Brooklyn Heights fortifications.

The initial onslaught, so well planned, so overwhelming in its execution, achieved remarkably little. The portion of the American army deployed on Long Island was still mostly intact and had withdrawn into heavily fortified Brooklyn Heights, from which it would not be easy to dislodge them. Unluckily for the British, the winds were against the fleet, which meant that Admiral Howe could not mount an attack from the water. Doubtless recalling the high price of attacking fortified Breed's Hill outside of Boston, General Howe decided to bide his time and to dig in, so that, when he decided to make the assault on Brooklyn Heights, he could do so from prepared positions at the very closest range. It was a conservative tactic, typical of the British commander. It lacked boldness, it sapped momentum, and it gave the Americans time to think and regroup.

The Genius of Washington

Washington had faltered as a tactician and a strategist. His army was threatened with annihilation in a single battle. This moment was the first of many in the American Revolution, a dark moment when all seemed lost. It was at such moments that Washington revealed his true genius for war.

His mere presence inspired courage in others, and that was crucial; however, Washington himself was so confident that he could hold Brooklyn that he brought some of his Manhattan units into the fortifications at Brooklyn Heights. Having done this, he almost instantly realized it was a bad mistake. By August 28, it was clear to him that Brooklyn Heights would fall. He needed to save his army, which meant evacuating his troops.

A retreating army is a vulnerable army. The moment Howe realized that Brooklyn Heights was being evacuated, he would launch an all-out attack that very likely would wipe out most of the American force. Refusing to panic—and refusing to allow his officers and men to panic—Washington commenced the stealthy silent retreat of thousands of troops, moving them from Brooklyn Heights, to the bank of the East River, and across that river into Manhattan. He used the storm and dense fog of the night of August 29 through the early morning of the thirtieth to cover these movements. The secrecy was so thorough, and the evacuation managed so skillfully, that, as a Hessian major reported to his patron in Europe: "We had no knowledge of this [evacuation] until four o'clock in the morning. . . . The entire American army has fled to New England, evacuating also New York." He, and the British, were entirely unaware that the Americans had merely sneaked across the river into Manhattan.

"Rejoice, my friends, that we have given the Rebels a [damned] crush . . . It was a glorious achievement, my friend, and will immortalize us and crush the rebel colonies."

A British officer, September 3, 1776

The Turtle

David Bushnell was still a student at Yale College (1771–75) when he demonstrated to his doubting professors that gunpowder could be detonated underwater.

COME THE REVOLUTION, HE BELIEVED HE HAD FOUND a practical use for this discovery: what he called a "water machine." A pear-shaped vessel made of oak and reinforced with iron bands, it was, in fact, the world's first working (sort of) submarine. Those who saw it did not think of a pear, but a turtle, and so it was named. Bushnell's *Turtle* measured about seven and a half feet long by six feet wide and was operated by one man, who controlled two hand-driven screws for propulsion in four directions. The *Turtle* operator could submerge the vessel by pulling a hand-spring valve that flooded a compartment in the hull, and then could make the machine surface again by operating a foot pump. Bushnell equipped the vessel with an explosive mine on a projecting boom. The *Turtle* would approach a vessel, attach the mine to its hull below the water line, then pull back. The explosive charge was timed to detonate after the *Turtle* had retreated to safety.

On September 6, 1776, in New York Harbor, Sergeant Ezra Lee, whom Bushnell had instructed, sailed the submerged *Turtle* up to the HMS *Eagle*. He could not attach the mine, however, and was forced to withdraw as the explosive detonated harmlessly in the East River. The *Turtle* was tried a few more times, but proved unsuccessful on each occasion. What if it had worked? The British were especially complacent in their control of major American harbors. Had enough submarines been built quickly enough, perhaps the fleet would have been terrorized sufficiently to keep the British army on the defensive even where it was the strongest. This might have shortened the war.

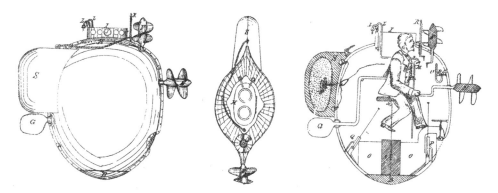

This profile, head-on view, and cutaway cross-section of Bushnell's Turtle *was published in 1881. The innovative vessel is generally considered the world's first military submarine—although it failed to sink a single British ship.*

Peace Feelers

Considering the enormous advantages he possessed, Howe moved with a remarkable lack of aggression, allowing August to dissolve into September before he took up more advantageous positions along the west shore of Long Island, deploying his troops in the neighborhoods today called Long Island City and Astoria in Queens.

Not that Howe or his admiral brother sat totally idle as summer drew to a close. Continental general John Sullivan, captured at the Battle of Long Island on August 27, was a frequent guest of the Howe brothers, and he gathered the impression that they had substantial authority to treat for peace. Sullivan accordingly talked the Howes into paroling him on a mission to Congress seeking peace. Congress responded by sending a committee—Benjamin Franklin, John Adams, and South Carolina congressman Edward Rutledge—to meet with the Howes. The committee's preliminary objective was to find out just how much negotiating authority the brothers actually possessed.

The meeting took place on September 11, on Staten Island, just opposite Amboy, New Jersey. The atmosphere of expectation soon gave way to disappointment. General Howe left his brother to deal with the committee on his own. He assured the Americans that he and his brother possessed great authority, although, of course, anything agreed to would have to be endorsed by London. That was enough to send the committee packing. There would be no negotiated peace.

A Matter of Time

The leisurely pace with which the Howes went about the conquest of New York suggests that they believed that time was on their side. Modern military historians freely criticize both General and Admiral Howe for their failure to campaign aggressively, and it is true that time is rarely on the side of any large expeditionary force, which is expensive to maintain in the field. But perhaps they also realized that time was very much against George Washington. He faced the chronic problem of expiring militia enlistments—which always threatened to diminish his ranks at most inopportune moments—and he faced a critical crisis of morale, which was aggravated by bad weather and inadequate supplies. By late August, probably one-fourth of the defenders of New York were sufficiently ill as to be unfit for duty, victims of smallpox and other diseases endemic to large military encampments, especially dysentery.

REALITY CHECK
A Fragile War
That Congress was willing to talk peace suggests just how tenuously it supported the war after Washington's defeat on Long Island. Moreover, peace talks collapsed not because Congress was unwilling to negotiate, but because the Howes proved to have little or no authority to negotiate meaningfully. Imagine Washington's feelings at this time, knowing how little confidence his government had in him.

Surveying the sorry situation in Manhattan, General Nathanael Greene counseled Washington to burn and abandon the city. The general referred the matter to Congress, which, on September 3, passed a resolution against the deliberate burning of the city. Congress did not demand that Washington hold New York, but reasoned that if it were lost, it could always be recaptured—provided it was left intact. Washington therefore resolved to do his best to defend Manhattan, and, on September 7, he began deploying his troops on the island. He stationed Knox and Putnam downtown with a large contingent, then dispatched nine thousand men to defend the ground between Harlem and Kings Bridge. Greene was assigned a unit of militiamen to repel landings along the East River.

Yet again, Washington revealed his weakness as a tactician. He spread his troops very thinly over sixteen miles of Manhattan, leaving the middle of the island with the weakest defense and deploying his least reliable troops—the militia—as his first line of defense against an invasion via the East River shore. On September 12, his own chief lieutenants belatedly argued him into consolidating his strength uptown by evacuating everything below Fort Washington and making a stand where fortifications were strongest. At length, Washington agreed. But time had run out.

INVASION AT KIP'S BAY

ON SEPTEMBER 15, 1776, ADMIRAL HOWE'S INVASION FLEET, finding calm weather and favorable winds at last, sailed up the Hudson on Manhattan's West Side, and up the East River on the city's opposite side. Transport barges had accompanied the warships up the East River, and, covered by the menacingly open gun ports of the East River flotilla, they disembarked soldiers at Kip's Bay, where 34th Street today ends at FDR Drive. The operation commenced with a brief bombardment at eleven o'clock in the morning, followed by the troops landing in eighty-five flatboats. The militiamen Washington had deployed as East River sentries, dissolved, running in panic and sowing their panic among the other troops, militia and Continental army alike. Alarmed by the sound of the initial British cannonade, Washington rode down from his Harlem headquarters to inspect. When he saw his frontline in chaos, he rode into the knots of fleeing men, lashing out with his riding crop at officers as well as men. It was a combined display of frustration and personal leadership—both qualities that made Washington oblivious to the surrounding danger. Fortunately for the American cause, an aide grabbed the bridle of Washington's horse and led both him and his rider away, barely steps ahead of the Hessians.

The British Settle In

As the British landed, the Americans—except for Knox and Putnam's downtowners—rushed northward to the high ground of Harlem Heights and Fort Washington north of present-day 125th Street. Howe did not give chase, but marched inland and uptown only as far as modern 42nd Street. He and his two subordinate commanders, Clinton and Cornwallis, appropriated as their temporary headquarters the Murray house, on the estate owned by the wealthy merchant Robert Murray (today the Manhattan neighborhood known as Murray Hill).

Recreating the legend of Mrs. Murray and General Howe, this early twentieth-century print, from a painting by E. Percy Moran, is titled Mrs. Murray's Strategy.

The plan was to use the headquarters to coordinate forays to the north, and General Clinton was particularly insistent in urging Howe to mobilize quickly against Kings Bridge, in upper Manhattan. This, he pointed out, would put the invading force in a position to defeat Washington's forces in detail before they were fully consolidated. Never one for bold action, Howe countered that a vigorous assault on the city would wreck too many houses—houses needed for winter quarters. Clearly, Howe anticipated a long campaign. No, he would continue landing his troops at Kip's Bay, allow his forces to accumulate, and then advance to the north. Washington, who had left his army vulnerable through poor tactics, was reprieved by the lethargic conservatism of the British commander.

MANHATTAN BATTLEGROUND

ANYONE CAN APPRECIATE THAT THE MANHATTAN OF 1776 was a different place from today's city, but it takes an exercise of imagination to visualize just how different it was. To be sure, it was smaller, with fewer than twenty thousand inhabitants, most of them living at the southern tip of the island, below Wall Street. To the north of this lay Greenwich Village, a rural place dotted with the summer estates of the city's wealthiest residents. Beyond this was a landscape of hills and streams. Manhattan's landscape was one of hill and dale, before decades of intensive real estate development flattened the topography below 125th Street to the level expanse from which skyscrapers rise today. From Harlem Heights, the American defenders commanded a magnificent view of the undulating island landscape. What they saw on September 15 was a line of bright scarlet advancing at a stately pace along the eastern road, inching toward the American position. Simultaneously, the Americans saw, advancing more rapidly along the western road, the columns of Knox and Putnam, led by one of Washington's staff officers—young Aaron Burr of New Jersey—whom Washington had belatedly but urgently sent downtown to order the advance so that these troops would not be cut off.

This ca. 1776 drawing of New York City shows what looks more like a provincial town than what would one day be a city of more than eight million people. Trinity Church, the tallest building at the time, can be seen to the right of center; Rutgers House, a Lower East Side mansion owned by Patriot colonel Henry Rutgers, is in the foreground, on the left.

The simultaneous advance of opposing forces, one on the east side of Manhattan Island, the other on the west, was visible to Washington and the other men on the Heights of Harlem, but not to any of the British or American troops on the march. A hilly, forested spine ran down the center of Manhattan, blocking the view from east to west and west to east—until one reached a kind of notch in this spine called McGowan's (or McGown's) Pass (the remains of which may be discerned today in the northeastern corner of Central Park). If any of the British troops were sent to scout the pass, the advancing American column would be discovered and, surely, cut off.

The tension among Washington and the other observers of this northerly progression must have been nearly unbearable. But, true to form, nothing disturbed the leisurely pace of Howe's advancing troops, and apparently no one on the British side thought it necessary to send scouts. As a result, the men of Putnam and Knox scaled the Harlem Heights without having been detected by the British. Now, at least the bulk of Washington's Manhattan force was consolidated in a defensible position.

The Attack—At Last

By sunset of September 15, Howe had set up forward positions from McGowan's Pass west and slightly south to the Hudson River (at about the present location of 105th Street). The night passed quietly. Then, just before dawn on September 16, Thomas Knowlton, a tall, handsome Connecticut lieutenant colonel, led a hundred special troops—Connecticut Rangers—down a steep defile called the Hollow Way, which ran sharply down from the Heights to the Hudson. Encountering elite soldiers of the famed Black Watch Highlanders, he engaged them, but promptly withdrew as more Highlanders approached. Howe mistook this withdrawal as the start of an American rout, and ordered a general attack.

In a stroke of leadership genius, Washington, who had compounded his several tactical blunders by entrusting the East River shore to mere militiamen, used these very same soldiers—those who had cut and run at Kip's Bay—against the British now. He offered them an opportunity to redeem themselves, and they seized it. Charging through a buckwheat field fronting the Hudson on the site of modern Barnard College, they ran head on into the Highlanders, who now recoiled in retreat.

THE DIFFERENCE BETWEEN HOWE AND WASHINGTON
The military experience of George Washington was limited, but within its limits, it was rich in defeat, beginning with combat in the French and Indian War and culminating, at this point, in the retreat from Long Island. Washington knew how to lose, to be defeated without being beaten, to hold an army together even when victory was denied it. Wars, of course, are not won by losing battles, but they can be lost by losing battles. Washington's genius lay in his ability to lose battles without losing the war.

In contrast was General William Howe. The defeat of the Highlanders at the buckwheat field—a minor action that involved a mere fraction of the vast force he had with him on Manhattan—disheartened him out of all proportion. With thousands of troops at the ready supported by a magnificent naval fleet, he could easily have shaken off this encounter and attacked Washington on the flanks or the rear. Even fighting from the fortified Heights, it was highly improbable that Washington could have withstood a well-coordinated attack. Apparently stunned, however, Howe did nothing.

Nathan Hale

Certain names were carried over from the Revolution into American popular culture. Even people who don't know the Battle of Trenton from the Battle of Bunker Hill know the name of Benedict Arnold—a synonym for traitor—and the name Nathan Hale: the man who had but one life to lose for his country.

HALE WAS AN EAGER twenty-one-year-old Connecticut schoolmaster, who took command of an elite company of rangers. When Washington asked for a ranger to volunteer as a spy behind the enemy lines, shortly before the Battle of Harlem Heights, Hale stepped up.

Spies were numerous in the American Revolution, but it was universally regarded as a trade without honor—so much so that a friend tried to talk Hale out of volunteering. Hale responded: "I wish to be useful, and every kind of service, necessary to the public good, becomes honorable by being necessary."

One story goes that Hale's Tory cousin, Samuel Hale, betrayed the young spy, and that may have been. But the fact is that, Nathan Hale lacked the one quality all successful spies possess: the ability to blend in. He was tall yet plump, with a head of flaming red hair. He also walked about Manhattan conspicuously taking notes. There are various versions of how he was caught. One holds that, on September 21, 1776, somebody got curious enough to search him. His notes were found, he admitted his assignment, and he was hanged the next day. More likely, he was captured not in Manhattan but on Long Island—some say by a Loyalist major Robert Rogers. Perhaps. But there is no official record of this. The Connecticut Society of the Sons of the American Revolution believes Hale was arrested on the shore of Long Island, signaling to what he thought was the boat that was supposed to take him to Norwalk, Connecticut, but which turned out to be a British frigate.

Again, there is no official account. In fact, the only official record of his capture is a note General William Howe made in his diary on September 22: "A spy from the enemy by his own full confession, apprehended last night, was executed [this] day at 11 o'clock in front of the Artillery Park."

Hale was given no trial, but he was given the opportunity to speak before he swung, and apparently, he gave quite a speech. Unfortunately, no one recorded it. However, John Montresor, a British soldier who had witnessed the hanging, told an American officer, William Hull, that Hale had died with great dignity and with the words, "I only regret that I have but one life to lose for my country." If Hale did say this, he was probably not being spontaneous. Any schoolmaster would be familiar with a speech from the British playwright Joseph Addison's successful 1713 play *Cato:*

How beautiful is death, when earn'd by virtue! Who would not be that youth? What pity is it That we can die but once to serve our country.

A ninetheeth-century illustration depicting Hale's execution.

Fire

Four days went by, and Howe stood still. Then, sometime in the early dark hours of September 21, a fire broke out in a house near Whitehall Slip, at the southern tip of Manhattan. The inferno rapidly spread north and west, razing 493 houses before British troops got it under control. Howe believed the Americans had deliberately started the blaze, while the Americans accused the British of the same thing. Whatever the cause, putting the fire out occupied Howe's troops—he was very concerned about housing his army—and almost certainly compounded the effect of the buckwheat field defeat, contributing to the delay in attacking Fort Washington (on the Hudson) and adjacent Harlem Heights.

MANHATTAN FORFEIT

SEPTEMBER BECAME OCTOBER, and by the middle of that month, Howe had yet to make his move against Fort Washington and Harlem Heights. For his part, Washington was in no position to counterattack, and while he may have marveled at Howe's lack of gumption, he did observe the movement of barges, which suggested to him that Howe, at long last, was looking for landing places in Westchester County, above his own position. That is, Howe was preparing to surround Washington. Accordingly, on October 16, 1776, the American commander decided that he must evacuate Manhattan altogether.

Leaving behind garrisons at Fort Washington and (across the Hudson in New Jersey) Fort Lee, Washington moved the bulk of his forces north, to the village of White Plains in Westchester County. He moved quietly and slowly, so as not to attract attention. Yet Howe managed to advance even more slowly and was several times raided by small hit-and-run American forces, which cost him casualties.

Defeat at White Plains

When Washington reached White Plains—well ahead of Howe—he deployed his troops on three hills, yet, once again, committed a serious tactical mistake. He failed to fortify the highest of these hills—

Before dawn on September 21, 1776, fire broke out near Whitehall Slip, at the southern tip of Manhattan, destroying 493 houses before British troops got it under control. This hand-colored print, published in Paris about 1778, shows slaves looting some of the buildings and soldiers beating citizens. Despite their blue coats, the troops are British; perhaps the artist intended to depict British artillerymen, who, unlike red-coated infantry troops, wore blue coats with red facings.

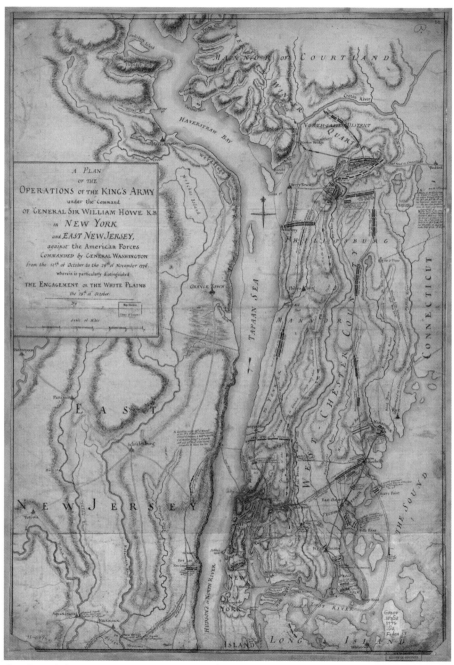

"A plan of the operations of the King's army ... in New York and east New Jersey, against the American forces . . . from the 12th of October to the 28th of November 1776, wherein is particularly distinguished the engagement on the White Plains the 28th of October." This map was published in London, probably in 1776.

Chatterton's—which commanded the other two, as well as the rest of the surrounding landscape, and was therefore the key military prize in the area. He entrusted Chatterton's defense to just sixteen hundred militiamen under Alexander McDougall of New York.

Perhaps it was Howe's own weaknesses as a commander that endowed him—at least on this single occasion—with an eye for weakness in others. With uncharacteristic alacrity, he directed his principal attack against Chatterton's Hill. An artillery barrage was followed by an inept infantry assault and then a skillful and bold cavalry charge. The very first combat employment of cavalry in the American Revolution, this had a devastating effect on the American militiamen. They panicked. Fortunately, the more seasoned soldiers of Maryland and Delaware behind the militiamen did put up a fight, but were also finally forced into retreat—although intact and in good order.

HOWE'S HALF VICTORY

Howe won. But he didn't win much. He took Chatterton's Hill, and, having taken it, seemed satisfied. That, of course, was precisely the problem. Instead of resting, he should have been pursuing. Had he done so, he might have destroyed Washington's army before it could withdraw farther north. Instead, he allowed Washington to slip away, where, at North Castle, he took on supplies from New England. Fed and furnished with fresh ammunition, Washington and his army did not feel like defeated men. They had lost Long Island, Manhattan, and now White Plains. Yet, in this last battle, they had inflicted more casualties than they had suffered: approximately 150 killed and wounded versus British losses of 214 killed and wounded in addition to 99 casualties among the Hessians.

DISASTER

WASHINGTON WAS NOT USUALLY GIVEN either to complacency or delusion, and the strangely good feeling created by White Plains did not last long. Early in November, he saw that Howe had suddenly halted his northerly advance and now turned back toward Manhattan. What did this mean? Washington convened a hasty counsel of war with his officers and reached the conclusion that Howe intended to invade New Jersey.

REALITY CHECK
All the King's Horses

Just as popular mythology depicts the American revolutionary soldier as a frontiersman practically born with a gun in his hands, so it assumes the typical Yankee had a way with horses. In fact, cavalry was all but unknown in the Continental army and even less familiar among the colonial militia, which were infantry forces. Confronted by an unfamiliar weapon—the horse—fiercely employed, militiamen typically broke ranks.

ALTERNATE TAKE
The Last Battle?

White Plains was yet another American defeat—yet it was also another example of William Howe's inability to exploit victory. Had he pursued Washington's retreating army, he might have brought the Revolution close to the end.

Prison Hulks

At the corner of Myrtle Avenue and Cumberland Street in Brooklyn's Fort Greene Park stands the Prison Ship Martyrs' Monument. Designed by architect Stanford White and dedicated in 1908, it commemorates Patriots who languished and died on British prison hulks—decommissioned and decaying ships at anchor off American shores— in Wallabout Bay during the Revolutionary War.

SOME PRISONERS CAPTURED IN LAND BATTLES were incarcerated in these ships, but most American prisoners were American merchant sailors captured by the British at sea. Aboard such hulks, the most infamous of which was the HMS *Jersey*, POWs succumbed to starvation and epidemic diseases, having been weakened by flogging and other abuses.

By 1780, the British had anchored a dozen prison hulks in Brooklyn's Wallabout Bay. It is believed that between 11,500 and 12,500 men died on the hulks, and were either rowed to shore for burial in anonymous shallow graves or simply heaved overboard. On the Jersey alone 1,100 men were jammed together below decks. The daily death rate on this vessel was approximately twelve men. With the end of the war in 1783, a mere 1,400 survivors were released from the entire prison flotilla. All were sick and in a semistarved condition. Philip Freneau, the New York–born poet often known as the "Poet of the American Revolution," wrote an epic poem entitled "The British Prison-Ship" (1781) about his experiences as a prisoner on one of the ships; it is excerpted here below:

The British Prison-Ship

Conveyed to York we found, at length, too late,
That Death was better than the prisoner's fate
There doomed to famine, shackles, and despair,
Condemned to breathe a foul, infected air,
In sickly hulks, devoted while we lay,—
Successive funerals gloomed each dismal day

The various horrors of these hulks to tell—
These prison ships where Pain and Penance dwell,
Where Death in ten-fold vengeance holds his reign,
And injured ghosts, yet unavenged, complain:
This be my task—ungenerous Britons, you
Conspire to murder whom you can't subdue. . . .

When two long months in these dark hulks we lay,
Barred down by night, and fainting all the day,
In the fierce fervors of the solar beam
Cooled by no breeze on Hudson's mountain
      stream,
That not unsung these threescore days shall fall
To black oblivion that would cover all. . . .

Three hundred wretches here, denied all light,
In crowded quarters pass the infernal night. . . .
Meagre and wan, and scorched with heat below,
We looked like ghosts ere death had made us so:
How could we else, where heat and hunger joined
Thus to debase the body and the mind?

The British used decrepit hulks moored off-shore to confine Patriot prisoners of war. The most infamous of these was the HMS Jersey, *anchored off Brooklyn.*

It was not an unreasonable conclusion, but it was quite wrong nevertheless. Washington should have appreciated the value of the prize he had left on Manhattan's Hudson shore. Fort Washington had been garrisoned by two thousand men when Washington evacuated the island. Freshly reinforced, it was now held by nearly three thousand soldiers, most of them Continental troops. On the night of November 14 through the morning of the fifteenth, thirty flat-boats landed a British assault force against Fort Washington. The British demanded surrender of the fort on the fifteenth. The Americans refused, and, on November 16, the British attacked from three directions.

Word reached Washington, who galloped to Fort Lee, New Jersey, which was directly across the Hudson from Fort Washington. Exhibiting his customary personal courage, Washington rowed across the river with generals Putnam, Greene, and Hugh Mercer. They made a stealthy reconnaissance and concluded that Fort Washington was a lost cause. It surrendered at three that very afternoon, November 16. Fifty-three Americans were killed in the Battle of Fort Washington. British and Hessian losses were much heavier—458 killed and wounded—but 2,818 American officers and enlisted soldiers were captured.

The loss of a strategic fort together with so many American soldiers (and their scarce equipment) was a disaster compounded by the surrender of Fort Lee four days later. Now all of Manhattan and much of the Jersey bank of the Hudson belonged to the Royal Army. That was bad enough, but there was worse. Howe's victories may not have destroyed Washington's army, but they did split it up, leaving Charles Lee in command of units in North Castle, in Westchester County; William Heath controlling troops at Peekskill, up the Hudson from Manhattan; and Washington, commanding the main body of troops, which he led in a long, dreary retreat across a New Jersey landscape churned to mud by the bleak rain of a cold November.

TAKEAWAY
Defeats, but Not the End

Washington suffered a series of major defeats in and around New York City in 1776, yet the British commander, William Howe, repeatedly failed to exploit his victories. Had he done so, the Revolution would have been ended. Failing to do so, Howe not only prolonged the war, he gave Washington a chance to recover.

Chapter 11

WASHINGTON THE WINNER

Pennsylvania, Then Crosses the Delaware to Counterattack at Trenton and Princeton with Spectacular Results

GEORGE WASHINGTON WAS DEFEATED. The mistake the British war leaders made was assuming this meant he was beaten. An imperfect man of arms, his tactical sense often deeply flawed, Washington was nevertheless a great general because he refused to be beaten, no matter how badly or how often he was defeated. This was a quality of character, to be sure, but it was also a product of Washington's insight into the nature of the war he was fighting. He understood that victory would not be—could not be—the military triumph over the most powerful nation on the planet. He saw that the British army and navy could capture any number of American cities, but that the war would not end until one or the other side stopped fighting. As long as he had an army, he would not stop fighting. He believed that the same was not true of the British, who would stop—if the war proved costly enough. Losing was bad, but fighting was everything, and by fighting he could prevail.

To Keep the Army Alive

BUT TO KEEP FIGHTING, Washington needed to keep his army alive and keep his army together. Do this, and each passing day would make the war more costly for the British, whose soldiers and seamen, no matter how capable, were far from home and could not be maintained abroad forever.

To preserve the army from annihilation by the British, Washington withdrew to New Jersey. But how to preserve it from dissolution by the parsimony of Congress, the poverty of the United States, and the expiration of enlistments? Before the battles of Long Island, New York, and White Plains, he had some 19,000 soldiers. After these encounters, he was left with 16,400. These were divided: 4,400 with Washington at Newark, New Jersey; 1,000 under William Alexander ("Lord Stirling") at the New Jersey towns of New Brunswick and Rahway; 4,000 at Peekskill, New York, under General William Heath; and 7,000 with Charles Henry Lee still in the White Plains area. Washington needed Lord Stirling's troops to remain where they were to intercept any attempted British amphibious operations, and he also wanted Heath to keep his 4,000 troops in readiness to defend the Hudson highlands, lest the British succeed in severing New England from the Mid-Atlantic region. It was now critical, however, to consolidate Lee's large contingent—which included some of the best soldiers in the Continental army—with his own Newark-based troops, and Washington called on Lee to march.

When Lee delayed, Washington pressed him. Lee replied lamely to Washington's chief aide, Adjutant General Joseph Reed, that he could not cross the Hudson at Dobbs Ferry in time to help Washington; Washington therefore ordered Heath to send 2,000 of his men by way of Kings Ferry.

Crisis of Command

What was going on? The "colorful" Lee clearly had his own agenda, which presumably included acting on his intense hunger for Washington's office as commander in chief. Lee believed himself far more qualified than the man on whom Congress had conferred command, and he intended to engineer the defeat of those troops directly under Washington's personal command. With this, the way would be opened for his own ascension. The last thing George Washington and the beleaguered Continental army needed at this low point was a crisis of command. Whereas Washington's forces were divided and dispirited, with many troops anticipating the expiration of their enlistments (and hardly likely to re-up), Howe's men, basking in victory, had plenty to eat and had no choice about when to leave the army. They were in until someone in charge said it was over.

There were many ways Howe might deliver a killing blow. Two of the most obvious were moving against Heath up the Hudson, thereby clearing a path for more troops to invade from Canada, even as he might march into New England; or marching directly to the capital of the rebellion, Philadelphia, which he could capture while picking away at Washington's retreating army in the process. Fortunately for Washington and the American cause, Howe took neither of these courses.

It was an old story. Had Howe taken action, he could have dealt the American Revolution a potentially fatal blow. Instead of seeing opportunity, Howe saw only the change in season. Fall was giving way to winter, and winter warfare was hard. Why do it if you didn't absolutely have to? So, instead of finishing Washington off and bringing the American Revolution to a quick conclusion, Howe bedded down himself and his army for the winter at Amboy, New Brunswick, and Princeton on his eastern front, and in Bordentown and at Trenton—the main British post—along the Delaware River, on his western front. Howe believed that there would be plenty of time to engage Washington in the spring.

THE BROTHERS HOWE

Traditionally, American historians have ascribed Howe's lack of aggression to a conservative personal character and an adherence to British military convention. There is doubtless much truth in this perception. It also true, however, that neither of the Howe brothers shared General Gage's contemptuous dislike of the Americans; quite the contrary, they respected the colonials and continued to hope for reconciliation between the colonies and the Crown. By stretching out the war through a long, cold winter, they may have believed that the rebels would fall into misery deep enough to prompt their coming to their senses and seeking forgiveness and an end to the war. This interpretation of the Howes' military restraint is supported by their November 30 offer of a complete and absolute pardon to all persons who signed a declaration of allegiance within sixty days. Pointedly, the brothers avoided approaching Congress with the offer, but instead appealed directly to the people—and when a substantial number of New Jerseyans responded favorably, Washington countered with a proclamation of his own, inviting any and all who had accepted the amnesty to renounce it and swear allegiance to the cause of independence. There was a reverse side to this proclamation: those who failed to renounce the amnesty and sought a British pardon he advised to move behind the British lines—for their own protection.

Running Naked

While he set up his various winter quarters, Howe ordered Henry Clinton to march out of New York with about six thousand men to occupy Newport, Rhode Island, which would put him in position to mount a spring campaign in New England. He also dispatched Charles Cornwallis to chase Washington beyond New Brunswick, New Jersey, thereby securing the main British force plenty of room for a peaceful winter's nap.

Much as Lee considered himself a better commander than Washington, so Cornwallis deemed himself Howe's superior where tactics and strategy were concerned. Assigned to chase Washington out of the way, he instead boasted that he would bag the general and his army as a hunter bags a fox. If Howe moved with a deliberation that bordered on lethargy, Cornwallis drove his army unsparingly, so that, by November 29, he was closing in fast on Newark. That was sufficient to send Washington and his four thousand men in flight to New Brunswick, barely ahead of Cornwallis's Hessian shock troops.

The Patriots lost more battles than they won, and after British victories at the battles of Long Island and White Plains, and with George Washington in retreat across New Jersey, many in England predicted the end of the American Revolution. This cartoon, "News from America, or the Patriots in the Dumps," was published in London in November 1776 and shows Lord North holding a letter announcing British victory. Note the varied responses of North's listeners, especially that of the disconsolate woman with the Liberty Cap.

His men, Washington lamented, were practically naked, a naked army on the run. Yet even in their ill-clothed, ill-equipped, ill-fed condition, Washington's troops managed to outmaneuver and outrun the pursuing enemy. Unlike their Hessian and British counterparts, the Americans were not weighed down with sixty-pound packs.

> "The Cry of want of Provisions comes to me from every Quarter."
>
> George Washington, winter, 1776–77

Leaving Alexander at Princeton to harass and delay the British advance, he and his four-thousand-man contingent arrived at Trenton on December 3. He had hoped that Lee would meet him there, but Lee was several days away. On December 7, therefore, George Washington evacuated New Jersey by crossing the Delaware into Pennsylvania. He spread out his troops across some twenty-five miles of Pennsylvania riverfront, and to ensure that the British would not easily pursue him, he sent soldiers to locate and destroy every boat of any size for seventy-five miles up and down the lower Delaware.

Determined as he had been to bag Washington, Cornwallis was exhausted.

The New, Comprehensive and Complete History of England was published in London about 1783, the year Britain lost America. Yet this illustration from the book highlights a very minor British triumph in the American Revolution, the capture of Major General Charles Lee in 1776—no great loss to the Continental army.

Washington hadn't outfought him, but he had outrun him, and Cornwallis secured Howe's permission to halt on the Jersey side of the Delaware. Like Howe, he now believed it was best to wait until spring before dealing Washington and the Revolution a death blow.

The End of Lee

Charles Lee and his army finally arrived in New Jersey in November, but as they trudged toward Washington, Lee wrote to General Heath that he doubted the commander in chief could make good use of his force on the Delaware. He revealed an agenda of his own: to personally "reconquer . . . the Jerseys." And so he made little enough haste to reach the Delaware, encamping his troops a few miles below Morristown while he established himself three miles away in Basking Ridge in the tavern of one Widow White. On November 13, he began a letter to General Horatio Gates, who, he knew, had perhaps even less regard for Washington as a commander than he did. "Entre nous," he wrote, "a certain great man is most damnably deficient." He continued: "Tories are in my front, rear and on my flanks. The mass of the people is strangely contaminated. In short unless something which I do not expect turns up we are lost."

Just as Lee was finishing this letter, a unit of British dragoons burst through the Widow White's door and took the discontented Continental general prisoner. His capture was doubtless a boon to the Patriot cause. Without him, Lee's army continued the march to join Washington on the Delaware. Lee narrowly escaped trial in London as a British deserter and was instead held as a POW in New York. There, on March 29, 1777, he offered the British a plan (he said) that would "unhinge the organization of the American resistance" by regaining control of Maryland, Pennsylvania, and Virginia. His captors saw no value in the proposal and released Lee in April 1778 as part of a prisoner exchange. His brother officers embraced him at Valley Forge, and his attempted treason went undetected for some seven decades.

DETAILS, DETAILS
Annus Horribilis

For Charles Lee, things went from bad to worse. He performed so poorly in the Battle of Monmouth Courthouse (June 28, 1778) that he was suspended from command for a year. During his enforced idleness, he nearly fought a duel with Friedrich von Steuben, the gallant German officer who had lent his services to the Continental army as its inspector general, and he did fight a duel with Lieutenant Colonel John Laurens. Laurens wounded Lee seriously enough to prevent his accepting a challenge from General "Mad Anthony" Wayne a bit later. At the end of his suspension, Lee responded to a rumor that Congress intended to dismiss him with a letter so offensive that it succeeded in provoking his dismissal on January 10, 1780. He died in Philadelphia two years later.

TRIUMPH AT TRENTON

ENCAMPED WITH WASHINGTON'S ARMY, Thomas Paine pulled up a drumhead to use as a desk and, by the light of a campfire, wrote the first of the papers collected in 1783 as *The American Crisis*. Published on

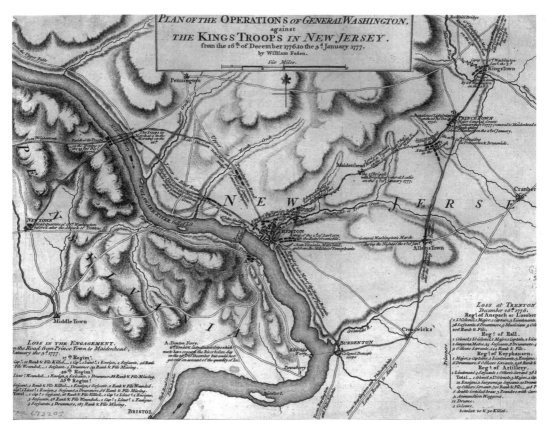

"Plan of the operations of General Washington, against the Kings troops in New Jersey, from the 26th, of December, 1776, to the 3d. January 1777." Published in London in 1777, this map shows Washington's victories at Trenton and Princeton.

December 19, 1776, the first "Crisis" essay began: "These are the times that try men's souls. The summer soldier and sunshine patriot will, in this crisis, shrink from the service of his country; but he that stands it now, deserves the love and thanks of man and woman. Tyranny, like hell, is not easily conquered." As Paine's *Common Sense* had earlier galvanized the cause of independence, so this essay shamed the "summer soldiers" and reinvigorated the retreating Revolution. New recruits began reinforcing the Continental army and the militias. Nevertheless, by Christmastime, Washington commanded no more than six thousand troops fit for duty. He could wait for more, but, if he did, those enlistments set to expire on New Year's Eve would reduce the forces on the Delaware to just fourteen hundred men, even with the arrival of new soldiers. Moreover, a hard freeze of the river would enable the British—who, thanks to Washington's foresight in diligently appropriating everything that floated, could find no boats—to march into Pennsylvania, where he and his army had taken refuge.

For their part, the British were in no hurry to cross. They believed that Washington's hungry, ill-clothed army would likely disintegrate before the winter had even ended. As the British and their Hessian hirelings saw it, the people of New Jersey— militiamen both organized and unorganized—were a greater menace than Washington. They continually harassed and sniped at soldiers.

In fact, the British assessment of the situation was, if anything, too conservative. Washington's army was both smaller and hungrier than they thought. The last thing any formally trained veteran commander would think of doing with such an army would be to lead it in a counteroffensive, which would likely fail. Yet, Washington reasoned, inaction and dissolution were worse than the failure of a positive move. Besides, there was some encouraging news reaching him about popular resistance throughout New Jersey. In addition, at this very moment, Pennsylvania militiamen had taken it upon themselves to conduct quite effective hit-and-run raids against British installations along the Delaware. These had drawn a large contingent of Hessians away from Trenton area and down to Mount Holly, New Jersey, to oppose the militia.

On December 22, 1776, as Washington pondered the feasibility of taking the field, he received a message from his adjutant, Colonel Joseph Reed: "We can either give [the Mount Holly militia] a strong reinforcement—or make a separate attack—the latter bids fairest for producing the greatest and best effects." Reed expressed the consensus of Washington's officers:

> We are all of the opinion my dear general that some-thing must be attempted to revive our expiring credit, give our Cause some degree of reputation & prevent total depreciation of the Continental money which is coming very fast. . . . Even a Failure cannot be more fatal than to remain in our present situation. In short some enterprize must be undertaken in our present Circumstances or we must give up the cause.

His recommendation was to attack Trenton. "Delay is now equal to a total defeat."

The commander in chief wasted no time. Reed's dispatch in hand, he called his commanders to a council of war and presented the adjutant's proposal for crossing the Delaware and attacking one of the enemy's New Jersey outposts. There was no debate. All agreed on the operation. Now Washington turned to Colonel John Glover, commander of a regiment of tough Marblehead (Massachusetts) fishermen. An old hand when it came to small boats, Glover assured Washington that he should not "be troubled" about the crossing. His "boys" would "manage it." Washington wrote the orders that evening and issued them in the morning.

REALITY CHECK
Ye Merry Gentlemen

Legend portrays the Hessians as fat and happy in Trenton, having enjoyed a drinking party on Christmas day (and night), which put them in no condition to fight off Washington's attack on the morning of December 26. In fact, there was no party— and the Hessians were anything but happy. The people of Trenton had largely deserted the town, and Colonel Johann Gottlieb Rall and his men expected an attack—not from Washington, but from rebel guerrillas. Sleepless with vigilance for more than a week, the Hessian garrison was relieved by the Christmas-night storm. Rall reasoned that no one would try to cross the Delaware in a winter storm, let alone launch an attack in one. This—and not overindulgence in Christmas cheer— prompted Rall and his officers to let down their guard.

This Currier & Ives print from the centennial year of American independence, 1876, is one of many depictions of Washington crossing the Delaware en route to victory against the Hessians at Trenton, New Jersey. The battle was not the turning point of the American Revolution, for much more hardship and defeat lay ahead. But it certainly rescued the struggle for independence from immediate collapse.

Trenton was garrisoned not by the British, but by the Hessians, some of the best and most ruthless soldiers in all Europe. Yet Washington's most immediate problem was not the Hessians, but the condition of the Delaware River. It had frozen, then, under warm rains, melted, only to refreeze—but not solid. On the night of December 25, the Delaware roiled in a swift current that sent great sheets of broken ice crashing and whirling. It was on this night that Washington loaded twenty-four hundred soldiers and eighteen cannon into the Durham boats he had hoarded, to keep them out of British hands. These sturdy vessels were used locally for ferrying freight across the river. Now they would carry an army. They crossed at McKonkey's Ferry (the modern Pennsylvania town of Washington's Crossing), nine miles above Trenton. At the same time, approximately a thousand militiamen, under General James Ewing, prepared to cross at Trenton Ferry, in order to block the possible retreat of Hessians from Trenton. Washington had also ordered Colonel John Cadwalader to lead a diversionary crossing at Bordentown.

It was a very good plan—tactically far superior to anything Washington had done so far in this war. But plans are one thing, and execution another. Ewing could not manage to get across the treacherous river, and Cadwalader suffered so many delays that he was of no use. As for Washington, his intention to disembark on the Jersey bank by midnight, so that he could advance to Trenton under cover of darkness, did not come to pass. The miserable weather delayed everything, and the treacherous crossing was not completed until about three o'clock in the morning on the twenty-sixth. His men were not on the march until four, which meant that the assault on Trenton would have to come well after daybreak.

Washington considered aborting the mission, but (as he later wrote), "As I was certain there was no making a Retreat without being discovered, and harassed on repassing the River, I determined to push on at all Events."

What must it have been like to march nine miles from the Jersey bank through the frigid, stormy predawn gloom that morning after Christmas? Anxious to preserve whatever surprise he could, Washington had ordered complete silence, so there was none of the customary soldier's talk to ease the fatigue and the fear. No lights were to be struck, either, so the comfort of a friendly pipe was likewise denied. Snow and freezing rain made it impossible to fire muskets reliably. Washington therefore ordered his men to fix bayonets. If they could not fire, they would thrust.

This print by E. Percy Moran (ca. 1914) shows Washington inspecting the colors captured from the Hessians during the brief and brilliant Battle of Trenton.

When they reached the Hessian encampment at Trenton, Washington's men knew instantly that they had been detected. They heard the German sentry's frantic cry: *"Der Feind! Heraus! Heraus!"* ("The enemy! Get up! Get up!").

Rall rallied his men as best he could, but was soon mortally wounded, shot through the chest. Some reports give the duration of the battle as two hours; others, no more than a half hour. Either way, when it was over, 106 of the 1,200 Hessians engaged were dead or wounded. The rest were prisoners of war. Remarkably, Washington suffered no more than four wounded.

The Revolution Saved

Washington wanted to continue the counteroffensive with immediate attacks on Princeton and New Brunswick, but because his other commanders had failed to cross the river, he, too, had to withdraw back across the Delaware to the Pennsylvania camp. It hardly mattered. A starving, defeated army had beaten the best soldiers in Europe. The Revolution would continue.

The triumph at Trenton reinvigorated the Continental army. Generals Henry Knox and Thomas Mifflin, who had pleaded with their men to extend their enlistments—slated to end on December 31—succeeded in winning six more weeks of service from them. Washington made similar pleas throughout the army and was gratified by the response. "To a man," he wrote Congress, the regiments had extended their enlistments by six weeks.

PRINCETON

WASHINGTON DID NOT INTEND to waste that time. Once again, he crossed his army into New Jersey and took up positions at Trenton. Cornwallis marched out of Princeton with almost eight thousand fresh troops, who reached Trenton on January 2. It had been a slow

The victories of Washington, though few and far between, were a favorite subject of America's premier nineteenth-century image-maker, Currier & Ives. This print of the general at the Battle of Princeton was published in 1846.

advance, delayed by Patriot resistance and miserable weather. Washington used the time to dig earthworks along the Assunpink Creek south of Trenton. Leaving a skeleton force of four hundred there with orders to make noise and keep the fires lighted—to deceive Cornwallis into thinking he was about to bag his fox after all—Washington pulled the main body of his army back. But this was no retreat to Pennsylvania. While Cornwallis and his army bedded down, planning to attack at daylight what they believed to be Washington's entire army at Trenton, Washington silently withdrew his main force at one o'clock in the morning on January 3, 1777, and began marching toward Princeton, New Jersey.

When he advanced on Trenton, Cornwallis left twelve hundred troops under Lieutenant Colonel Charles Mahwood as a rear guard. At first light on January 3, Mahwood was on the march to join the main British force at Trenton. Suddenly, through the mists, there was the glint of bayonets.

Hessians, Mahwood thought.

No, *Americans!*

Mahwood believed that he had arrived too late. He thought that these were Washington's troops retreating from Trenton and defeat at the hands of Cornwallis. Actually, they were a detachment under General Hugh Mercer, whom Washington had sent to destroy Stony Brook Bridge, which the British relied on to reach the Trenton road. The clash between Mahwood's men and Mercer's—at William Clark's orchard near a Quaker meetinghouse, within view of Washington's main body of troops—was the start of the Battle of Princeton.

Thomas Gainsborough, the preeminent British portraitist of the eighteenth century, painted this likeness of Charles Cornwallis in 1783—two years after his surrender at the Battle of Yorktown.

At first, the American militia, stunned, recoiled in panic, unable to load and reload faster than Mahwood's men could use their bayonets. Seeing this, Washington spurred his horse to the scene, riding through a continual volley of musket balls as if they were no more than a hailstorm. In the presence of the commander in chief, the panic hardened into courage. The militia held long enough for Henry Knox to commence an artillery barrage, and for Daniel Hitchcock's brigade of Rhode Islanders and Massachusetts men, along with Pennsylvanians under Edward Hand, to reinforce Mercer. Now it was Mahwood and his men, overwhelmed, who turned about and ran in panic down the Trenton road—but not before Hugh Mercer, Washington's close comrade, a veteran in his native Scotland of the Battle of Culloden and, in America, of the French and Indian War, fell mortally wounded in William Clark's wintry orchard.

Washington resisted the impulse to pursue the fleeing attackers, for he knew they would lead him straight to Cornwallis, who had a much bigger army. Instead, he advanced into Princeton, engaged the few British soldiers remaining there, and took the town.

Victory Diluted

Princeton belonged to Washington—but he could not afford to occupy it. He knew that Cornwallis would soon counterattack with his superior numbers. Even more disappointing, he realized that he was in no position to carry out his earlier plan to attack New Brunswick, which was a prize far more valuable than Princeton. Washington knew that the British had stockpiled a large amount of supplies there and, even more important, had deposited a Royal Army paymaster's war chest with some £70,000. But he did not have the men to take the town.

WINTER QUARTERS

Swallowing his disappointment, Washington decided that the time had come to end his counteroffensive on a double note of triumph: Trenton and Princeton. He would retire to winter quarters—not, however, in Pennsylvania, but in New Jersey, at Morristown, on a plateau whose steep sides made the encampment highly defensible. Washington had, after all, learned something of tactics.

The recent victories helped Continental army recruiters attract new soldiers, but they could not outpace the expiration of the six-week extensions of enlistment. It was a good thing that Howe, Cornwallis, and Baron Wilhelm von Knyphausen, commander in chief of the Hessians, were so disheartened by defeat at the hands of so meager an army that they, too, retired to winter quarters in the tiny corner of New Jersey they still held. The American Revolution was as frozen as the creeks and streams of the countryside, even the broad, fateful Delaware.

Chapter 12

ENGLAND'S BEST-LAID PLANS

How the Patriots Defeated "Gentleman Johnny" Burgoyne's Bold Invasion from Out of Canada

TRENTON AND PRINCETON WERE MIRACLES. They *saved* the American Revolution. But, Washington well knew as he camped with his men in frigid Morristown, they had by no means *won* the war. Despite these victories, prospects loomed as bleakly as the New Jersey winter. The army was all but naked and lived on the most meager of provisions. Through the crowded encampment smallpox raged, whittling down the army man by man.

FORT NONSENSE, SPRING, 1777

WASHINGTON DID HIS BEST to keep the army alive and together. He pleaded with Congress for funds, and he kept the men busy with drills and with building a hilltop fort overlooking Morristown. It was christened Fort Nonsense—no one knows by whom—but the name suggests its purpose, which was not to accomplish some profound tactical end, but simply to keep cold, hungry men busy.

The army shivered, went hungry, even sickened, but it survived, and with the arrival of spring came an infusion of fresh troops. For newcomers and veterans alike, army life also improved. Benjamin Franklin and Silas Deane, whom Congress had sent as emissaries to France, had made progress in winning the French to the American cause.

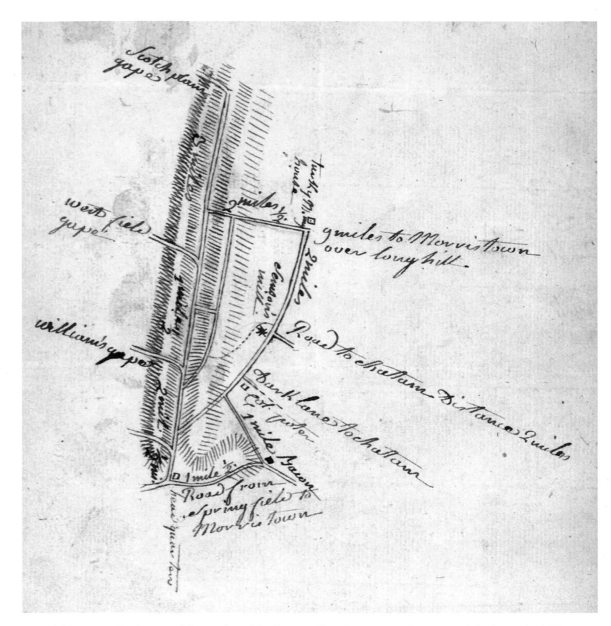

This pen-and-ink map of the roads to Morristown, New Jersey, was almost certainly drawn in 1778, when Washington was headquartered here. The site of the commander's HQ is indicated at the lower left, where the road to Scotch Plains intersects with the road from Springfield to Morristown.

Louis XVI was always happy for an opportunity to do injury to the English, and although he was not quite ready to conclude a full military alliance with the United States, he was pleased to allow private firms to furnish muskets, munitions, clothing, and other much-needed supplies. More than thirty French cargo vessels sailed to America that spring.

In June, Marie Joseph Paul Yves Roch Gilbert du Motier, Marquis de Lafayette, arrived with a party of other young European idealists—among them the German Johann de Kalb— eager to fight for liberty. They came armed not only with a fighting spirit, but with European military experience and know-how, which they were quite willing to share with the officers and men of the Continental army.

An E. Percy Moran illustration titled Lafayette's Baptism of Fire *(ca. 1909), depicts a victorious Lafayette with a slain redcoat to his right and a plucky little drummer boy to his left.*

GENTLEMAN JOHNNY'S PLAN

YET IF SPRING BROUGHT A RENEWAL OF HOPE to the Americans, it also ushered in a fresh resolve for the British. "Gentleman Johnny" Burgoyne, a flamboyant officer who had grown weary of William Howe's halting timidity, had spent the winter in London, where he occupied his time by revising a plan General Guy Carleton had tried and failed to execute in 1776. It was an operation to divide New York along the Hudson, cut off New England from the rest of the colonies, and essentially decapitate the Revolution. He drew up his revision in a document titled "Thoughts for Conducting the War from the Side of Canada," which he submitted to Lord Germain, secretary of state for the American colonies, on February 28, 1777. Burgoyne's proposal was for a three-pronged attack on New York:

1. The main army would march south along Lake Champlain and the upper Hudson.

2. Simultaneously, a smaller force would stage raids throughout the New York frontier country, from Oswego through the Mohawk Valley.

MEDICAL MATTERS
Smallpox

While in Barbados with his half-brother Lawrence in 1751, nineteen-year-old Washington contracted smallpox. On the European continent, where smallpox had been endemic, many of the British soldiers had also been previously exposed as children. For a military man, this was a valuable thing, since it conferred lifelong immunity from a disease that routinely plagued encampments. In an age when inoculation with a small amount of live smallpox virus was a subject of intense controversy, Washington, at first skeptical of inoculation, advocated the inoculation of all Continental army recruits; however, inoculation never became mandatory for enlistment.

3. Howe would send an army up the Hudson to meet Burgoyne's main force at Albany, creating a great pincers movement that would neatly amputate New England from the rest of the colonies.

It was a very good plan. King George greeted it warmly, noting in the margin of Burgoyne's manuscript, "the force from Canada must join [Howe] at Albany." If the king was happy, Lord Germain was happy, and he authorized Burgoyne to carry it out. But it was one thing to please the king and quite another to direct a successful war. Germain had failed to consult or even consider Burgoyne's place in the military pecking order. Giving Burgoyne command of the expedition was a slap in the face of Guy Carleton, who not only outranked Burgoyne, but who had originally formulated the plan Burgoyne had embroidered upon. Even worse, the plan meant that William Howe, commander in chief of British forces in America, had to subordinate his actions to those of Burgoyne.

Carleton may or may not have entered into any of Germain's thoughts, but the secretary did take pains to avoid offending Howe. No sooner did he approve Burgoyne's plan on March 3, than he also approved a plan Howe had submitted for attacking Philadelphia. He did this without bothering to consider that if Howe was busy taking Philadelphia, he would have neither the time nor the men to meet Burgoyne in Albany. In effect, Germain had authorized two mutually exclusive courses of action. Moreover, he did not bother to tell Burgoyne about it.

That was bad enough, but there was even worse. It is known that, before he left Canada, Burgoyne saw a letter from Howe to Carleton informing Carleton that he had no intention of helping Burgoyne. Despite this, Burgoyne decided to carry on with his operation, presumably hoping that, when all was finally said and done, Howe would have a change of heart or otherwise find the time to join him in Albany. The British commanders clearly moved in mysterious ways.

Burgoyne Begins

On June 17, 1777, Burgoyne marched out of St. John's, Newfoundland, bound for Lake Champlain. At his back were seven thousand infantrymen—British redcoats and Hessian mercenaries—in addition to a small force of English and German artillery specialists (he had 138 assorted cannon), four hundred Native Americans, and a handful of Canadian and Tory thrill seekers.

As if 138 cannon were not capable of delivering a sufficient barrage, Burgoyne let loose on June 23 with a proclamation in which he accused the leaders of the "unnatural Rebellion" of perpetrating "Arbitrary Imprisonments, Confiscation of Property, Persecution and Torture . . . without Distinction of Age or Sex, for the sole Crime . . . of having adhered in Principle to the Government under which they were born." He then concluded with a threat, that if the "Phrenzy and Hostility should remain, I trust I shall stand acquitted in the Eyes of God and Men in denouncing and executing the Vengeance of the State against the wilful Outcast." The Patriots were unimpressed.

WITHOUT A FIGHT

The Patriot press could be as free with grandiose statements as the pompous Burgoyne, as when the papers took to calling Fort Ticonderoga, captured by the Patriots in May 1775, the "Gibraltar of America." Perched on the western shore of Lake Champlain, it did command fleet movements on the lake, and Washington directed the Connecticut painter John Trumbull to design improvements to the fortifications, which he did under the guidance of Tadeusz Kosciuszko, a Polish officer and military engineer who had joined the American cause in August 1776. But no amount of fortification could substitute for manpower, and General Arthur St. Clair, in command of the Lake Champlain sector, could spare only about one-fifth of the strength necessary to defend Fort Ticonderoga adequately.

POP CULTURE
National Lampoon

A writer who signed himself "A New Jerseyman" (historians think he was Francis Hopkinson, an able political satirist who was also a signer of the Declaration of Independence) published a verse lampoon of the proclamation in the *New York Journal* of September 8, 1777:

. . . I will let loose the dogs of Hell,
Ten thousand Indians, who shall yell
And foam and tear, and grin and roar,
And drench their moccasins in gore;
To these I'll give full scope and play
From Ticonderog to Florida;
They'll scalp your heads, and kick your shins,
And rip your — and flay your skins,
And of your ears be nimble croppers,
And make your thumbs tobacco-stoppers.
If after all these loving warnings,
My wishes and my bowels' yearnings,
You shall remain as deaf as adder,
Or grow with hostile rage the madder,
I swear by George and by St. Paul
I will exterminate you all.

This 1777 watercolor sketch of Ticonderoga (as seen from a point on the north shore of Lake Champlain), was made by James Hunter, a member of General Burgoyne's expedition to retake the fort.

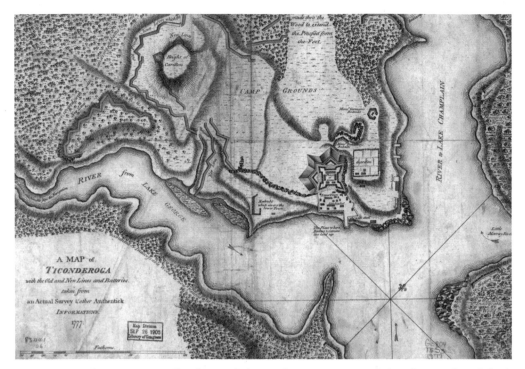

A 1777 map of Fort Ticonderoga and environs shows the traditional bastion plan of the fort, each of its four corner projections providing covered crossfire intended to defeat any approach, and its strategic location on Lake Champlain and very near Lake George.

Gentleman Johnnie Burgoyne wanted that fort, and on July 1, 1777, he divided his forces at Lake Champlain, sending the British contingent down the west side of the lake, while the Hessians under Baron Friedrich von Riedesel, took the east. Riedesel's assignment was to occupy Mount Independence, just across the lake from the fort. Getting there, however, was not easy. The Hessians were classic European soldiers, accustomed to and equipped for combat on open battlefields. Their heavy packs and thick woolen uniforms were not made for trekking through a swampy forest, in the heat of July.

While the Germans inched their way toward their objective, the Britons, on the more open west shore, advanced rapidly, clearing the forest to make way for the artillery with which they would bombard Fort Ticonderoga. Burgoyne planned a conventional, by-the-book siege—but then a young lieutenant of the Royal Engineers, Twiss by name, spied Mount Defiance, an eight-hundred-foot hill just to the southwest of the fort, which, short of men as he was, St. Clair had left completely undefended. Twiss brought Mount Defiance to the attention of Major General William Phillips, the chief artillery officer. High and steep, the hill looked to be nearly inaccessible, but Phillips turned to Twiss and declared: "Where a goat can go a man can go and where a man can go he can drag a gun." And so the British did, setting up an artillery position that looked directly down on Fort Ti.

Arthur St. Clair must have seen it all. And it was enough to prompt him to evacuate Fort Ticonderoga—"Gibraltar" or not— on July 6 without firing a shot. If it ever became necessary to evacuate Fort Ticonderoga, the American plan called for falling back to Mount Independence, opposite the fort across Lake Champlain. St. Clair did withdraw to Mount Independence, but he decided not to hold it, either, and instead withdrew all the way to Skenesboro, at the south end of Lake Champlain. In other words, he saw the British coming, and he ran away.

If you're going to run, it's best to make a good job of it. But St. Clair did not. Panicked, he neglected to order the destruction of a boat bridge across Lake Champlain. This gave the British Advance Corps a ready means of pursuit—although chasing through the rugged, thickly wooded terrain in this area was no easy matter. For one thing, Riedesel's Germans were still bogged down and could not meet up with Simon Fraser's Advance Corps. Fraser was also stumbling along when, on July 7, he stumbled into a New Hampshire regiment, which quickly surrendered.

Yet the fight wasn't over. The rear guard of St. Clair's main force, commanded by Colonel Seth Warner, made a surprising rally, turned, and attacked Fraser. Unlike the New Hampshire militiamen, Warner's troops—perhaps ashamed at having been compelled to relinquish Fort Ti without so much as firing a shot— fought with a competent ferocity, methodically firing into Fraser's lines with deadly accuracy. As his force dwindled, Fraser was about to withdraw when, suddenly, the belated Baron von Riedesel arrived with his Germans.

Deep in the American woods, they attacked in high European style. Moving to the measure of martial music—yes, the regimental band had lugged its instruments (mostly fifes and drums) through swamp and forest—Riedesel's men flanked the rear guard, then thrust with a devastating bayonet attack. The Hessians were greatly feared for their skill with the bayonet—a weapon American soldiers never liked to use.

St. Clair heard the sounds of struggle and ordered one of his militia units to the rescue. Those men refused the order.

Seeing that he and his men were alone in this fight, the gallant Seth Warner ordered his troops to scatter—every man to save himself. Of the thousand soldiers who had constituted the rear guard, only six hundred eventually straggled in to rejoin St. Clair's main column, which had taken refuge in a decrepit Hudson River outpost called Fort Edward. Three hundred men had been captured, fifty killed, and the rest went missing.

THE BRITS DECLARE VICTORY

Back in 1775, when the Americans had taken Fort Ticonderoga and declared themselves in possession of the continent's Gibraltar, the British downplayed the loss. Now that the fort was back in British hands, King George III, hearing the news, ran into his wife's dressing room, shouting "I have beat them! I have beat all of the Americans!"

He had done no such thing. True, Washington and Congress were so appalled by St. Clair's action—or inaction—at Fort Ti that they court-martialed the general. He was acquitted, however, and probably should have been. For although he lost the fort, he had kept most of his army intact, thereby foiling one of Burgoyne's main missions, which had been to destroy that army.

Not that Burgoyne perceived any failure. He was, after all, now within just twenty miles of his first big objective, Albany, where he hoped to meet up with General Howe and General Barry St. Leger. Recall, however, that Howe had no intention of breaking off his Philadelphia campaign. Didn't Burgoyne know that he was headed to a rendezvous that wasn't going to happen? But, then, clinging to delusion was not the only peculiar thing Burgoyne did. He decided to advance those final twenty miles to Albany not by the simple expedient of floating men and equipment over Lakes Champlain and George and then the Hudson—this is what his own plan called for—but instead set them to work hacking out a road through the wilderness. Those who knew Gentleman Johnny's character were less puzzled by this than most. They believed he had made a bargain with Colonel Philip Skene, the prominent Tory proprietor of Skenesboro, to build a road between his settlement and Albany. That would certainly do wonders for business in Skenesboro.

If General Burgoyne showed little concern for his reputation where the Skenesboro road was concerned, he was soon about to face a far more serious threat to it.

When he had issued his pompous proclamation concerning the righteous punishment that was about to befall the rebels, Burgoyne also included an admonition to Britain's Indian allies to attack no white men except rebel soldiers. Throughout the colonial wars—but especially beginning with the French and Indian War—white armies used Indian allies as scouts, as additional soldiers, and as instruments of terror. Native Americans had a well-deserved reputation for fighting in ways that conventional white armies did not. Burgoyne pledged that "his" Indians would not be employed to commit atrocity, and he even issued "certificates of protection" to all Loyalists (Tories) who asked for them. Show this piece of paper to an attacking Indian and he would put down his hatchet.

Or so the promise went.

On July 27, 1777, Jane McCrea, a Tory girl who lived with her brother on the Hudson, between Saratoga and Fort Edward, was captured by "Burgoyne's" Indians as she was making her way to Fort Edwards to see her fiancé, a Tory in Burgoyne's service. With her and a Mrs. McNeil (an American cousin of General Simon Fraser) in tow, the Indians started back to Fort Ann, where Burgoyne was headquartered; however, when they arrived, they had only Mrs. McNeil—and the scalp of Jane McCrea. Her fiancé identified it.

The massacre of Jane McCrea by British-allied Indians was a public relations nightmare for the English and Loyalists and became an enduring episode in the lore of the American Revolution. This graphic Currier & Ives print of the murder was published ca. 1846.

Gentleman Johnny, who wanted to bask in his victory, found himself instead in a pickle. The Tory—Loyalist—community, on whom he depended for support and cooperation, was outraged over the Jane McCrea atrocity. But when her killer was identified as a Wyandot named Panther, Burgoyne decided not to punish him, lest he alienate his Native American allies. This prompted an indignant letter from General Horatio Gates, who commanded American forces at Bennington, Vermont:

POP CULTURE
The Tale of Jane McCrea

Jane McCrea's murder quickly became both the subject of anti-British propaganda and grist for the folklore mill, as an abundance of ballads and poems suddenly appeared in colonial newspapers telling her sad tale. Some historians believe she had been unintentionally shot during an argument among her drunken captors over who should guard her. Others think she was accidentally shot by a member of an American rescue party. In verse, however, she was always depicted as the victim of an Indian hatchet. Frontier martyrdom was a horrible fate, to be sure, but in the case of McCrea, it appears to have done wonders for her image. Before her death, she was described by those who knew her as "a country girl... without either beauty or accomplishment," but she was portrayed in popular narratives of her death as a pretty girl with "clustering curls of soft blonde hair" or as a real stunner, with tresses "of extraordinary length and beauty...darker than a raven's wing."

That the famous Lieutenant General Burgoyne, in whom the fine Gentleman is united with the Soldier and Scholar, should hire the savage of America to scalp Europeans and the descendants of Europeans, nay more, that he should pay a price for each scalp so barbarously taken, is more than will be believed in Europe, untill authenticated facts shall, in every Gazette, convince mankind of the truth of the horrid fate... The miserable fate of Miss McCrea was particularly aggravated by her being dressed to receive her promised husband, but met her murderer employed by you.

Burgoyne had more than jeers and insults to worry about. Although she was a Tory, Jane McCrea was nevertheless a young white woman, and her murder stirred patriotism among the farmers of Bennington, who flocked to join the army of Horatio Gates.

Despite the McCrea incident, Burgoyne doubtless took some satisfaction in completing, on July 29, the Skenesboro road, complete with some forty bridges. The month consumed in building it, however, had given the American forces in the vicinity ample time to regroup and resupply. Burgoyne's officers recognized this and urged their commander to make haste for Albany. Instead, Burgoyne set up camp outside of Fort Edward, where he intended to await the arrival of all of his forces, so that he could enter Albany at full strength. This should impress Howe.

Howe?

On August 3, Burgoyne received a dispatch from that commander, warmly congratulating him on the capture of Fort Ticonderoga, then going on to inform him—quite matter of factly—that his "intention is for Pennsylvania, where I expect to meet Washington, but if he goes to the northward...be assured I shall soon be after him to relieve you."

This should hardly have surprised Burgoyne, but it surely dashed his delusions—although he softened the blow with the knowledge that at least General Barry St. Leger would meet him and that, united, they could still inflict ample punishment on the rebels. In the meantime, he kept Howe's letter to himself—for the sake of morale.

TOWARD BLOODY ORISKANY

BARRY ST. LEGER WAS INDEED ON THE MARCH. On June 18, 1777, one his colonels, Daniel Claus, sent a dozen Iroquois braves, mostly Cayugas, to scout the American stronghold at Fort Stanwix and to take prisoners for interrogation. These prisoners reported that Fort Stanwix was garrisoned by a large American force—and St. Leger, gullible enough to believe them, delayed his attack on the fort. The fact was that Fort Stanwix, long neglected, was falling apart. Its commandant, twenty-nine-year-old Colonel Peter Gansevoort, put his 750-man garrison to work patching and plugging the fortifications in the full knowledge that his attackers, well armed, would greatly outnumber him.

Barry St. Leger fought militia general Nicolas Herkimer at the bloody Battle of Oriskany (August 6, 1777). Although St. Leger won a tactical victory, he suffered a strategic defeat, which contributed to the collapse of the British campaign in the North.

War on the frontier was never exclusively about armies laying siege to other armies in forts. It was a dirty business that relied on a strong stomach for bloody work and a willingness to practice guile. Patriot militia general Nicholas Herkimer invited Joseph Brant, the most charismatic and talented pro-British Native American leader, to parley at the wilderness village of Unadilla, about sixty miles south of Fort Stanwix. What Herkimer really intended was to assassinate Brant. Four of his men concealed pistols beneath their cloaks and were assigned to gun him down when they were within range. But it is one thing to kill a man in the heat of battle and quite another to shoot him at close range and in cold blood. When the time came, just one of the four drew his weapon and was so nervous that the clumsy flintlock piece became entangled in the folds of his garment. The Indians accompanying Brant saw the pistol, let out a war whoop, then leveled their own weapons. Freezing for several minutes in a standoff, both sides departed the field without firing a shot.

This portrait of the brilliant Mohawk war chief Joseph Brant (Thayendanegea) was engraved for the London Magazine *in 1776. Brant, who held a brigadier's commission in the British army, was a highly effective ally of the redcoats.*

Gansevoort also had a few tricks up his sleeve—or in his powder horn. He sent Ahnyero, a prominent Oneida warrior known to the Americans as Thomas Spencer, out of Fort Stanwix to infiltrate a great Native American council convening at Oswego toward the end of July. There Ahnyero obtained the details of St. Leger's plan to attack the fort, and he was able to give Gansevoort details concerning troop strength.

But by this time, St. Leger had received some intelligence of his own. He had sent thirty riflemen (under a Lieutenant Harleigh Bird) and two-hundred Iroquois (led by Chief Hare) to ambush a supply party en route to Fort Stanwix. The attackers missed the party, which reached the fort and delivered its supplies. The British and Indian force attacked the supply party on its return from the fort, managing to kill just one man. But the mission hadn't been a total loss. Bird got a good look at Fort Stanwix and reported to St. Leger that it was actually quite weakly held.

Thus encouraged, St. Leger began marching toward Fort Stanwix on August 3. Because the fort was an important objective, he advanced with full military pomp—band playing, colors flying—in the hope of intimidating the garrison into a bloodless surrender in the manner of Arthur St. Clair. Coming to a halt just out of range of the fort's artillery, St. Leger demanded Gansevoort's surrender. Ganesvoort replied defiantly, and so, on August 4, St. Leger commenced artillery bombardment.

> *"I have only to say that it is my determined resolution, with the forces under my command, to defend this fort, at every hazard, to the last extremity, in behalf of the United States, who have placed me here to defend it against all their enemies."*
>
> *Peter Gansevoort, in response to a British demand that he surrender Fort Stanwix, August 3, 1777*

St. Leger's barrage made a lot of noise and smoke, but managed to kill only one man. Indian snipers, however, managed to pick off one garrison solder after another, even as the men worked feverishly to cover the fort's interior roofs and parapets with sod.

The Battle Joined

On August 6, three messengers from General Herkimer penetrated the Indian lines surrounding Fort Stanwix and delivered to Gansevoort a message from the general. It explained that he was at the Native American town of Oriskany, ten miles southwest of Fort Stanwix, with eight hundred militiamen. Herkimer proposed that Gansevoort coordinate with him an attack on St.

Although mortally wounded, Patriot general Nicholas Herkimer continued to direct the chaotic Battle of Oriskany. Herkimer is pictured on the far left, seated on his saddle, which is on the ground. The image appeared in the May 1857 edition of Ballou's Pictorial, an illustrated newspaper from Boston.

Leger's lines. Eager for some alternative to waiting for the full force of St. Leger's assault, Gansevoort fired three cannon shots to signal Herkimer that he had received the message and would comply. Immediately, he dispatched two hundred men under Lieutenant Colonel Marinus Willett to link up with Herkimer. These men fell upon one of St. Leger's encampments, attacked, and killed fifteen or twenty British. It was a nice little triumph, but it alerted St. Leger to Willett's presence. Now Willett would never be able to break through to Herkimer.

As for Herkimer, he decided to exercise prudence and wait for a successful sortie from out of Fort Stanwix before he launched his attack. Discipline was always a problem among militiamen. They were eager for a fight and accused Herkimer of cowardice. Some said he had Loyalist sympathies. That was not the case, but Herkimer would be hard pressed to prove it, since one of his brothers was fighting for St. Leger. For soldiers, especially inexperienced soldiers, waiting is harder than fighting. Herkimer scented mutiny and, much as he wanted to wait, he decided it was better to attack now—while he still had an army.

Thanks to his Indian scouts, St. Leger was ready for him. He sent Joseph Brant with four hundred Indians and four hundred Loyalist troops—the Tory Rangers (under John Butler) and the Royal Greens (commanded by John Johnson)—to surprise Herkimer's force. This they did six miles outside of Fort Stanwix, where a wide ravine was crossed by a log causeway. The battle began at ten o'clock in the morning on August 6.

It looked to be precisely the disaster Herkimer had hoped to avoid. Within the opening minutes of the Battle of Oriskany, most of Herkimer's officers—the men who had taunted him to attack—were killed. When a musket ball shattered Herkimer's leg, he propped himself against a saddle, took out a pipe and tobacco, lit it, and, even as he bled to death, did his best to direct the panic and mayhem that passed for a battle.

An entire American regiment broke and ran. But the others—all the others—rallied, engaging the enemy hand-to-hand. Their ferocity stunned Tories and Indians alike, and soon the Tories and Indians were suffering casualties as numerous as those of the Americans.

At length, a sudden and furious thunderstorm brought an intermission to the combat. Both forces disengaged, withdrew, and regrouped. When the storm passed, the wily John Butler ordered his Rangers, whose uniforms were green, to turn their coats inside out, exposing a lining that looked like the American uniforms. Thus transformed, his men advanced into the American lines—but the ruse did not long endure, and the sneak attack was beaten off. With that, discouraged by heavy losses, the Indians deserted the British, whereupon both Butler and Johnson ordered their men to withdraw. Standard battle doctrine calls for giving chase to a withdrawing enemy, but the Americans were in no condition to do that. Half their number had been killed, wounded, or captured, and Herkimer was mortally wounded. As for the British, 33 had been killed, 41 wounded. Indian losses included 17 Senecas killed, including their ablest warriors, and 16 wounded; as many as 80 Indians from other tribes were also killed or wounded. Worst of all, 23 war chiefs had been slain or severely wounded.

Oriskany was hardly a victory for either side, but the British did manage to check Herkimer's attempt to reinforce Fort Stanwix. Realizing this, St. Leger once again demanded Gansevoort's surrender, sending two officers to warn him that "If the terms are rejected, the Indians, who are numerous and much exasperated and mortified from their losses in the action against General Herkimer, cannot be restrained from plundering property and probably destroying the lives of the greater part of the garrison."

DETAILS, DETAILS . . . And a Bottle of Rum

The British were disappointed in the poor performance of the Indians at Oriskany. And it was true: none of the warriors had fought as well as they could have. Did the British officers consider that this might have been due to the vast quantities of rum they had given the Indians in an effort to hone them for battle?

Willett made no attempt to disguise his indignation: "Do I understand you, Sir, . . . that you come from a British colonel, to the commandant of this garrison, to tell him, that if he does not deliver up the garrison into the hands of your Colonel, he will send his Indians to murder our women and children[?]"

Willett again refused to surrender. In the meantime, General Philip Schuyler, fifty miles from Fort Stanwix, sent a Massachusetts brigade under Ebenezer Learned to relieve the fort. He followed this up with the First New York Regiment under Benedict Arnold. Arnold's men intercepted Major Walter Butler (the brother of Tory Ranger commander John Butler) and Hon Yost Schuyler, a prominent Tory, taking both captive. Arnold personally interrogated the prisoners, promising a full pardon to Hon Yost Schuyler—together with restoration of his property—provided that he return to St. Leger's camp and tell the Indians that Walter Butler, Joseph Brant's close friend and confidant, had been captured and would be hanged. Hon Yost Schuyler eagerly agreed. Not only did he carry the news, he also wildly exaggerated his report of the strength of Arnold's force. The result was remarkable; instantly, six hundred Indian warriors melted away, and St. Leger himself took alarm at the report of Arnold's strength. Like his American counterpart, St. Clair, he fled, lifting the siege of Fort Stanwix on August 22, and, not wishing his withdrawal to be encumbered by heavy baggage, abandoned a large store of equipment and artillery. This in itself was bad enough, but the effect it had on the Indians was even worse. Was this the way Englishmen fought a war? Then they would have no more of it. Soon virtually all of Britain's Native American allies had deserted the cause.

Patriot commander John Stark leads his men at the Battle of Bennington, August 16, 1777. The figures at the left who wear blue coats with red trim are captured Hessians; however, the nineteenth-century artist has attired them in Napoleonic rather than earlier eighteenth-century uniforms, and none of the Hessians in America wore bearskin "busby" headgear.

VICTORY AT BENNINGTON

THE AMERICAN REVOLUTION was not simply a war of red-coated Britons against blue-coated Americans. The British had the aid of local Loyalists, or Tories, some of whom made excellent frontier

NUMBERS
Hessian Fate

When the American Revolution ended in 1783, 17,313 Hessians— out of a total of 29,839—returned to Germany. Of the rest, some 7,700 had died, including about 1,200 killed in action and at least 6,354 who were victims of illness or accident. Many Hessians deserted at the Battle of Bennington; the deserters were never rounded up, and few returned to their regiments voluntarily. About 5,000 Hessians in all decided to settle in North America, either in the United States or Canada. In most cases, this was a voluntary choice, but it is also true that a significant number of Hessians were "dumped" in America by commanders who judged them to be criminals or otherwise unfit (usually because of illness) to return to Germany. There are no accurate estimates of how many current residents of the United States and Canada are descended from Hessians.

soldiers, but many of whom were unreliable. They also had the services of about thirty thousand fierce Hessian mercenaries.

By the summer of 1777, Burgoyne was facing a problem that was rife on both sides: desertion. Soldiers did not desert because they were frightened or unwilling to fight. They deserted when they became hungry, and, Burgoyne noted, as his supplies dwindled, the rate of desertion rose. To stop his army from melting away, he decided to appropriate provisions with a quick raid on Bennington, Vermont, where there was known to be a substantial store of Patriot goods.

Burgoyne began by sending some of the few Indians who remained with him on a mission to steal horses, which were needed for the raid. When the Indians returned with the purloined mounts, Burgoyne tried to whittle down their price. Instead of bargaining, the Indians responded by cutting the animals' hamstring muscles, rendering them useless. The raid was off to a most unpromising start; however, Lieutenant Colonel Frederick Baum, the German mercenary commander Burgoyne had assigned to lead the raid, believed he had little to worry about. As far as he knew, Bennington was garrisoned by a handful of militiamen. An initial engagement at Cambridge, New York, on August 12, confirmed Baum in his confidence. His Hessians routed fifty Americans with ease.

Unknown to Baum, General John Stark, Patriot veteran of Bunker Hill, had been accepting enlistments, many motivated by the Jane McCrea outrage. He had built up a sizable force by the time news reached him that Baum's Indian auxiliaries were looting the countryside. Stark sent two hundred militiamen to drive them off. On the way, however, they stumbled on Baum's main Hessian column and quickly withdrew. Fortunately for the Americans, a bad thunderstorm on the fifteenth discouraged Baum from giving chase. The weather provided Stark time enough to take on an additional four hundred reinforcements in the form of the Vermont militia, led by the redoubtable Seth Warner. Thwarted by the rain, Baum seems to have abandoned raiding tactics and instead dug his men into defensive positions.

On August 16, Stark and Warner skillfully deployed their combined forces, enveloping Baum on the front, rear, and flanks. Baum did see two of the detachments sent to outflank him, but because they wore civilian clothes, he mistook them for the local Tories

Colonel Philip Skene had promised would come to his aid. Thus, the Americans were able to position themselves under the very eyes of the enemy.

The attack, when it came, came from all sides. Indians, Tories, and Canadians unceremoniously broke and ran. The Hessians and the British regulars held their ground in hilltop defensive positions. Stark and Warner pressed the attack for two merciless hours. Now it was the turn of the Hessians to break. Except for his faithful regiment of dragoons, they drifted away.

With ammunition dwindling and desertion thinning his ranks, Baum ordered his men to draw sabers and charge into the enveloping Americans. The charge was quickly crushed. When Baum sustained a fatal wound, his men surrendered.

While this action was under way, Hessian reinforcements under Lieutenant Colonel Heinrich von Breymann arrived outside of Bennington. Here Stark's poorly organized troops met them and fumbled in a fight until more of Warner's Vermont militiamen reached Bennington from Manchester. Stark regrouped, combined with the Vermonters, and counterattacked Breymann with a vengeance.

> *"We'll beat them before night, or Molly Stark will be a widow."*
>
> *General John Stark, at Bennington*

When it was over, 207 men from the combined British and German forces lay dead. Some seven hundred had been taken prisoner. The cost to the Americans was thirty dead and about forty wounded. A fine victory, it lifted American morale even as it kept out of Burgoyne's hands the supplies he so badly needed.

In London, it had seemed such a good plan—this idea of sweeping the Revolution away in one grand march from the north. The king loved it. But now it was the redcoats' turn to experience what had been a familiar companion of the Continental army: want of ammunition, want of proper clothing, and, most of all, want of food. To Burgoyne's hungry, tired soldiers, great plans were of no account, no matter what the king had thought of them.

TAKEAWAY
A Plan Fails Again

British general Burgoyne was a bold strategist, but a mediocre leader, who had no understanding of the realities of frontier combat. This exposed his army to defeat in northern New York and ruined the British grand strategy to sever rebellious New England from the rest of the country.

Chapter 13

PHILADELPHIA FIASCO AND SARATOGA TRIUMPH

Washington Loses at Brandywine, Philadelphia, and Germantown as Subordinates Triumph at the Battles of Saratoga

To SAY THAT GEORGE WASHINGTON had a lot of war to fight with very few resources is certainly a historical cliché. It comes as news to no one. But less appreciated is the fact that the British had much the same problem, as was evident from the failure of Burgoyne's grand plan to divide and conquer the rebellious colonies. He didn't have enough men to do the job, and General Howe was unwilling to spare him any. Why? Howe thought it more important to capture Philadelphia, capital of the revolutionary government. In truth, both Burgoyne and Howe had good ideas. The problem was not only that there were insufficient resources to carry both out simultaneously, but that nobody seems to have recognized this fact.

PHILADELPHIA CALLS

FOR ALL HIS EXCESS OF CAUTION, William Howe was an experienced commander who had earned his rank through combat experience, especially in the French and Indian War, where he compiled perhaps the most brilliant record of any British officer. Moreover, in contrast to many other senior commanders, he was a relatively young and vigorous man, having been promoted to major general in 1772, when he was just forty-three. When, on October 10, 1775, the Crown replaced Thomas Gage with William Howe, it had every reason to expect that he would do a splendid job and make quick work of the American rebels. Imagine the consternation in the British corridors of power when Howe repeatedly proved just as stodgy and unimaginative in fighting the American Revolution as Gage had been.

Howe was disappointed as well. He needed a major victory, a meaningful victory, and he needed it soon. Clearly, he did not think that effectively subordinating himself to Gentleman Johnny Burgoyne was the path to that victory. So while Burgoyne fought in the wilderness of New York and Vermont, he would strike at the very heart of American civilization—such as it was—by taking Philadelphia, the chief metropolis of the continent.

On the face of it, Philadelphia really did seem a no brainer. It was a nexus of wealth and culture, and it was the rebel capital, the very place at which the Declaration of Independence had been signed. Yet, paradoxically, in contrast to Boston, Philadelphia was no hotbed of revolutionary passion. Host city to the Continental Congress, Philadelphia was also a bastion of loyalty to the Crown. Whether in the twenty-first century or the eighteenth, centers of wealth—old, established wealth—tend to be centers of political and social conservatism, and such was the case with Philadelphia even at the height of the American Revolution.

Howe turned his back on Burgoyne, but he didn't quite forget him altogether. He rationalized his decision to take Philadelphia rather than rendezvous with Gentleman Johnny by listing three points. Point one: Philadelphia (and all Pennsylvania) had a substantial Loyalist population, which would rally to the Crown; therefore, Philadelphia would fall easily, allowing Howe to release some men to Burgoyne. Point two: Taking Philadelphia would decapitate the Revolution, which would surely help Burgoyne. Point three: Attacking Philadelphia would draw Washington's forces away from Burgoyne.

This third point even now sounds like quite a stretch, but Howe seems sincerely to have believed it. He believed that Washington, who had shown himself capable of any number of tactical blunders, would swallow the Philadelphia gambit, moving everything he had south to defend Philadelphia rather than making the less obvious but more effective move to the north, where, by joining forces with Horatio Gates, he could pose a real threat to Burgoyne.

As it turned out, Howe would be proved right about Washington. He took the bait, throwing all that he had into the defense of Philadelphia. Yet Howe repeated the error British commanders made over and over again. He underestimated the effectiveness of the Continental army and other colonial forces. Washington's defense of Philadelphia would be costly to the British. Worse, the colonials in New York and Vermont would defeat Burgoyne even without the help of George Washington's army.

Howe Moves (Even More Slowly Than Usual)

By the summer of 1777, Washington's Continental army had moved from its encampment in Morristown, New Jersey, to the banks of the Neshaminy Creek in Pennsylvania. There the commander and his officers waited in speculation as to what the British would do next. By late August, the speculation ended. The British fleet under William Howe's admiral brother, Richard, arrived at the head of Chesapeake Bay. Certainly, the fleet was carrying troops who would land, then march to Philadelphia.

The original plan Howe had presented to Secretary of State Lord Germain called for marching overland to Philadelphia. Going most of the way by sea instead should have hastened the operation, but, in the hands of William Howe, it actually slowed things down. He had begun readying the expedition to leave New York City in April, but it wasn't until July 23 that the fleet, loaded with fifteen thousand troops, actually embarked.

"The army is not yet in motion, though preparing to move. . . . We may venture to think that, by the blessing of Providence, this ungrateful rebellion will be crushed in the course of the present campaign [against Philadelphia]."

Ambrose Serle, civilian secretary to William Howe, writing to the Earl of Dartmouth, May 20, 1777

Once he finally did get under way, Howe unerringly found a way to create even more delay. Instead of taking the direct water route between New York and Philadelphia via the Delaware River, he chose the much longer route around Cape Charles and then up the Chesapeake. Was this the result of his characteristic caution? He may have imagined that the Delaware was hazardous to navigate (it was not) or that it was very well defended (it was not). Howe compounded his misjudgment by failing to put in at Delaware Bay, where he could have disembarked at the fine port of New Castle, Delaware, which was just thirty-three miles from Philadelphia. Instead, he sailed up Chesapeake Bay and disembarked his men at Head of Elk, Maryland, nearly sixty miles from Philadelphia. Worse, more than a month's sailing—from July 23 to August 25—with fifteen thousand men packed into troop transports under the sun of summer, had transformed healthy fighting men into feverish invalids by the time they got off the boats. Howe would need time to get his troops rested and recovered. He also had to take the time and trouble to scare up cavalry mounts to replace all the horses that had died during the voyage. Horses, it seems, tolerated the unnecessarily long voyage even less well than men.

For Washington, Howe's ineptitude was a gift. He had plenty of time to assemble and move his army. On August 24, he led his Continentals— at the time, some eleven thousand men—in a grand parade through the streets of Phila-delphia, then south to engage Howe and his principal subordinates, Cornwallis and Baron Wilhelm von Knyp-hausen, the new commander in chief of the Hessians.

Genl. Knyphausen's trick of buttering his bread with his thumb; according to Philadelphia tradition of the British occupation of 1777.

POP CULTURE
Butter Fingers

Most histories of the American Revolution remark on how much the Americans—military men and civilians alike—feared the Hessians, who were not only regarded as Europe's best soldiers, but who also had a reputation for brutality. This was true in the early part of the war, but after two or three years, their combat record in America proved so consistently poor that they were less feared by the Patriots than scorned. Knyphausen in particular was made the universal butt of a slander that originated in a satirical American cartoon, which depicted the general spreading the butter on his bread with his thumb. Americans made much of the German's table manners—or lack of them.

The Hessians—Britain's mercenary troops—were widely hated and feared by Patriot civilians and soldiers alike. Tradition holds that the Hessian commander Baron Wilhelm von Knyphausen was so ill mannered that he used his thumb to butter his bread, as demonstrated in this satirical cartoon engraving.

Washington Stumbles

With plenty of time to prepare—and enough time left over for a parade—Washington nevertheless fell victim to surprise. Early on the morning of September 11, four little girls were playing "close by Polly Buckwalter's Lane," near the road to Kennett Square, Pennsylvania, south of Philadelphia near the border with Delaware. They looked up to see a band of horsemen.

"Girls," one the riders called out, "you'd better go home!"

"Why?"

"Because the British regiments are coming up the road."

All of the girls ran home, and one reported seeing redcoats "in great numbers." In fact, all they saw was a small diversionary force, but Washington took the assessment of these young eyewitnesses at face value.

He should have known better. He transferred the bulk of his forces to intercept what he believed was Howe's main force, in the process leaving many of the fords across Brandywine Creek in southeastern Pennsylvania completely undefended. It was across these fords that the British now splashed. That put Howe in position to surprise the Americans from the right rear. It was the Battle of Long Island all over again, as Washington found himself facing the enemy from precisely the opposite direction he had anticipated.

Defeat on the Brandywine

First to be hit were the New Hampshire soldiers, under John Sullivan. They were untested troops and Sullivan an uninspired commander. Beginning with them, the thin blue line crumbled along the Brandywine.

Howe sent Knyphausen's Hessians against the American center at Chadd's Ford, Pennsylvania, while he and Cornwallis crossed the Brandywine at two more unguarded fords, successfully outflanking the bulk of Washington's army, catching it in the jaws of a vise.

Sullivan struggled to limit the damage by sending General Adam Stephen and General William Alexander (New Jersey's redoubtable "Lord Stirling") to counter at least some of the British advance. It was a move that further revealed Sullivan's limitations as a tactician. Removing Stephen's and Alexander's men from the

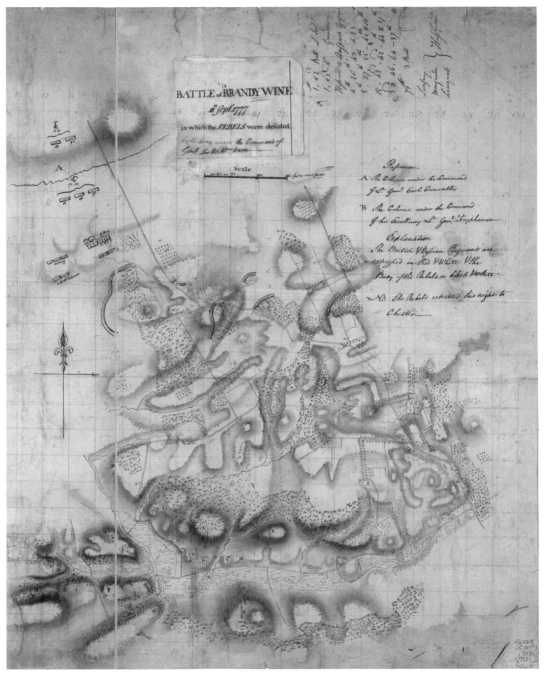

A manuscript map titled "Battle of Brandywine, 11th Septr. 1777, in which the rebels were defeated by the Army under the command of Genl. Sir Willm. Howe"—the 1777 sketch is unfinished, but it does show the local topography and the general deployment of troops.

The artist who created this nineteenth-century wood engraving did his best to make the Patriots look good at the Battle of Brandywine, but General Washington badly mishandled this engagement, which led to the British capture of Philadelphia, the "rebel" capital.

line created a gap in that line, which Howe was quick to detect. At about four o'clock in the afternoon, he ordered a bayonet charge through it. Learning of this, Washington sent General Nathanael Greene to repair the breach. But it was too late. A bayonet attack was intended to create panic, and it did just that. Although the Americans fought fiercely, they did so with little coordination as the bayonet-wielding British deeply penetrated their lines.

Bad as the situation was, it got much worse. As Howe and Cornwallis crossed the Brandywine, Knyphausen's Hessians smashed through the American center. Seemingly oblivious of the Americans' close-range fire—such was the fabled Hessian discipline—they advanced through the line and captured the Continental artillery. This Knyphausen turned against the retreating Americans, blasting them with their own powder and shot.

WE SHALL DO BETTER ANOTHER TIME

If Delaware captain Enoch Anderson's recollection is accurate, the Americans were bloodied but unbowed by their defeat. As they fell back on Chester, there was "not a despairing look, nor . . . a despairing word. We had solacing words always ready for each other— 'Come, boys, we shall do better another time.'"

Washington rested his men at Chester for the night, then withdrew closer to Philadelphia. Close behind, Howe occupied Chester, just fifteen miles from the nation's capital.

If Washington's army was still game for a fight, the Continental Congress seemed dazed. Alexander Hamilton was at pains to persuade the delegates to evacuate the capital, lest

Eyewitness

Joseph Clark, a young New Jerseyan fighting in the American ranks, recorded in his diary that, as "night was spreading its dusky shade through the gloomy valley . . . our army was something broke."

By nightfall, the Battle of Brandywine was all over. Washington's army made a limping retreat to Chester, Pennsylvania, which still put it in position between Howe and Philadelphia. Yet that army had been battered. Of the eleven thousand or so American soldiers engaged, some thirteen hundred had been killed, wounded, or made prisoner. The Continental army also gave up eleven irreplaceable artillery pieces. On Howe's side, 577 out of 12,500 men were killed or wounded.

the government itself be captured. On September 18, Congress left, pausing first at Lancaster, Pennsylvania, and then settling in the village of York.

While Congress was preparing to move, Washington, on September 16, briefly tangled with Howe at the White Horse Tavern and at Malvern Hill, both west of Philadelphia. The Polish Patriot Casimir Pulaski had begun putting together a small cavalry force for the Continental army, and these men now did their best against the Hessians, holding them until a larger infantry force arrived under General Anthony (later known as "Mad Anthony") Wayne and General William Maxwell. A sudden cloudburst, however, put an end to the combat, as the Americans were forced to withdraw—despite outnumbering the Hessians. The Patriot powder and cartridges had been stored in homemade boxes and were soaked, useless. Wayne and Maxwell made haste for Reading Furnace (in Chester County, Pennsylvania), where they could get fresh ammunition.

MASSACRE

THE RUINED GUNPOWDER was an omen of ill tidings. On September 18, Hessians fell upon Valley Forge and, finding it unguarded, captured it, appropriating a large quantity of flour, horseshoes, tools, and other Patriot supplies. Howe set up an outpost here.

In the meantime, Washington sent Wayne from Reading Furnace with fifteen hundred men and four cannon to Warren's Tavern, near the town of Paoli. His mission was to harass the British rear guard. Wayne was one of the Patriots' best commanders,

"Mad Anthony" Wayne was one of America's most capable early military commanders, during the American Revolution and after. This etching was made in 1782, the year Wayne was sent to Georgia to drive out the remaining British forces there.

Although physically unhurt, Sullivan became another casualty of the battle. The Continental Congress tried to suspend him from command, accusing him of misconduct at the battle. It would have been easy for Washington to allow Sullivan to take the fall, but his character would not permit his doing so. The commander in chief defended Sullivan, refused to sanction him, and officially acquitted him of any wrongdoing. Washington knew that Sullivan was a man of limited military talent, but he was a gallant officer, and, most of all, Washington realized that the fault in this defeat lay not with his subordinate but with himself. He had failed to give Sullivan adequate, clear, and timely orders. He had exposed Sullivan to surprise attack. General Washington understood this much: If any single man lost the Battle of Brandywine, it was himself.

but, on this occasion, he made the mistake of failing to note the activity of local Tories. They reported Wayne's movements to Howe, who sent Major General Charles Grey to surprise Wayne's camp during the early dark hours of September 21.

Grey ordered his men not to load their muskets and, if they were already loaded, to remove the flints from the locks, so that they could not fire. There would be no gunfire in this attack. The bayonet was to be used exclusively. It was a bold and brutal tactic. For this nighttime attack, Grey wanted his men to move swiftly and silently, visiting upon the unsuspecting rebels maximum terror. This meant that he wanted his men moving and slashing, not standing and shooting.

They did just that. Only after the terrible battle was near its end did Grey order his men to load and fire—because the panic-stricken survivors of the initial attack ran about in front of their campfires, presenting targets in vivid silhouette.

By the British tally, five hundred men had been killed. Wayne counted 150—but they were 150 men hacked and bloodied so thoroughly that local residents who beheld the aftermath of the carnage dubbed the encounter the Paoli Massacre. Bad as it was, it could have been worse. Wayne never succumbed to panic. He did not abandon his cannon, and he did manage to lead most of his men to safety.

PHILADELPHIA FALLS

WASHINGTON WAS ACCUSTOMED to the bloody cost of battle, but the Paoli Massacre shook even him. He consolidated his troops at Pott's Grove (modern Pottstown), Pennsylvania, a move that prompted Howe to change the direction of his advance. He now started his main body of troops across the Schuylkill River. On September 26 , Cornwallis led four British and two Hessian regiments into Philadelphia. Washington remained at Pott's Grove and made no further attempt to resist the taking of the capital. The Continental army parade through the capital must now have seemed to many Patriots a bitter memory. As for Cornwallis, he camped his invaders in Germantown—today a Philadelphia neighborhood, but in 1777 a village just north of the city.

The Liberty Bell

In 1751, the Pennsylvania Assembly ordered from the Whitechapel Foundry in England a bell to commemorate the fifty-year anniversary of William Penn's Charter of Privileges, the colony's original constitution. The bell bore a quotation appropriate to the occasion, from Leviticus 25:10, "Proclaim Liberty throughout all the land unto all the inhabitants thereof."

THE BELL WAS NOT HUNG in the Philadelphia's Pennsylvania State House until March 10, 1753. When it was test rung that very first day, it cracked. The bell was taken down and given to a pair of Philadelphia foundry workers, John Pass and John Stow, who melted it down and recast it, adding copper to the metal to make it less brittle. Rehung on March 29, the bell was rung—the sound so feeble that it became a joke throughout Philadelphia. Pass and Stow remelted and recast the bell, and yet again, the test ring was disappointing. State House officials ordered a new bell from the original foundry, Whitechapel. When it arrived, this bell also produced a sound no one liked. With that, the Pennsylvanians gave up. The Pass and Stow bell remained in the State House steeple, and the Whitechapel bell was put in a cupola on the State House roof, where, attached to a clock, it rang the hours.

The Pass and Stow bell was used ceremonially and to summon people for special events. In 1772, a petition was submitted to the assembly complaining that people in the neighborhood were "incommoded and distressed" by the constant ringing of the bell.

Tradition has it that the bell was rung for the First Continental Congress in 1774, the Battle of Lexington and Concord in 1775, and, on July 8, 1776, to summon the locals to hear a reading of the newly adopted Declaration of Independence. Most historians believe that, by 1776, the State House steeple was in such disrepair that the bell could not have been rung. It is true, however, that the bell was removed and hidden before the British occupied Philadelphia

in October 1777. But that was true of all large bells in the city. The Americans feared that the British would melt them down to cast as cannon. Returned to the repaired State House steeple after the war, the bell was used for ceremonial purposes from 1790 to 1800, when Philadelphia was the nation's capital.

The bell did not become the "Liberty Bell" until 1837, when it appeared as a frontispiece in an antislavery publication entitled *Liberty.* No one knows just when the bell was cracked, but the fissure does appear in the 1837 illustration, making it an apt metaphor for a nation whose idea of liberty was flawed by slavery. From this point on, the Liberty Bell became one of the symbols of the abolitionist movement; however, in 1847, the American novelist George Lippard wrote a fictional short story published in *The Saturday Currier,* which portrayed the aged bellman of Pennsylvania State House anxiously awaiting word that Congress had declared independence. The old man suddenly hears his grandson— who had put his ear to the State House chamber door—cry out "Ring, Grandfather! Ring!" The story created a nationwide sensation, and the association of the Liberty Bell with American independence was born.

The name "Liberty Bell" was bestowed on the Pennsylvania State House bell in 1837 when it was used as the frontispiece to an abolitionist publication titled Liberty.

Counterstrike

The loss of Philadelphia, left undefended, was a hard blow, and a number of officers began to question Washington's fitness for command. Yet the impact of the loss was of more psychological than strategic importance. Congress, after all, continued to govern from York, Pennsylvania, the Continental army remained intact, and the whole process of moving from New York to capture Philadelphia had taken so much time that Howe was never able to reinforce Burgoyne up north. The net result was that British possession of Philadelphia failed to end the American Revolution.

As had happened in the past, defeat, which disheartened most men, seemed to come as a tonic to George Washington. He was determined to recover from the chain of disasters—Brandywine, Paoli, Philadelphia—by counterattacking, and he proposed to do so not where the British were weakest, but where they were strongest: Germantown.

At daybreak on October 4, Washington encountered Howe's advance units just outside of Germantown. At this time, some nine thousand British soldiers were camped in the village.

Washington's forces—eight thousand Continentals plus three thousand militiamen—outnumbered them and the advance troops. The British 40th Regiment quickly withdrew from Washington's men, falling back on the large house of Benjamin Chew. Constructed of stout local stone, the house was as good as a fortress, and, from it, the 40th poured fire on Sullivan's troops.

The focal point of the Battle of Germantown was Washington's attempt to capture the Benjamin Chew House, in which the British had taken refuge. This 1898 painting is by Howard Pyle.

Always the pragmatist, Washington wanted simply to bypass the Chew house and proceed into Philadelphia, but his artillery chief, Henry Knox, talked him into pausing to bombard the house. It was a bad idea. American gunpowder was notoriously uneven in quality—something that would not be corrected until the beginning of the nineteenth century, with the arrival from France of E. I. du Pont, master powder chemist—and Knox's cannonballs bounced off Chew's walls. The cost to Washington was an hour's delay in which casualties mounted. Worse, hearing the artillery and assuming the attack was proceeding at full tilt, General Adam Stephen quick-timed his men into combat, but, caught in the morning fog, first fired on and then collided with the rear of "Mad Anthony" Wayne's column. Few things are worse in war than accidents of friendly fire, and Wayne's men responded to the bewildering attack with panic followed by paralysis. Making a bad situation even worse, Nathanael Greene's advance slowed, ending all possibility of a coordinated attack on the British encampment. Fearing the loss of his army, Washington ordered a withdrawal.

TRIUMPHANT DEFEAT

Militarily, the Battle of Germantown was the crowning disaster of the train of catastrophes that had begun at Brandywine. Washington lost 152 men killed and 521 wounded. At least 400 were captured. Howe's casualties were also heavy—535 killed and wounded—but he still held Philadelphia.

Yet while Germantown was a tactical defeat for the Americans, it turned out to be a surprising strategic victory. French observers accompanying the Continental army thought little of the defeat but were mightily impressed by Washington's audacious decision, after having lost Philadelphia, to attack. They were persuaded that Washington was a great leader and that he and the Continental army were committed to seeing the struggle through to victory. Their report to the imperial French government pulled King Louis XVI closer to a formal, full-scale military alliance with the United States.

DETAILS, DETAILS
Germantown

Today, Germantown is a working-class Philadelphia neighborhood. At the time of the Revolution it was the seat of large English-style houses like the Chew residence, which bore the dignified name Cliveden. (Built in 1763, it still stands at 6401 Germantown Avenue, where it is now a museum.) Germantown occupied higher ground than Philadelphia proper and for that reason was thought to offer protection from the yellow fever epidemics that periodically plagued the city. The village was fashionable enough that George Washington would live there (in the Deshler-Morris House at 5442 Germantown Avenue) during part of his presidency.

Eyewitness

Strangely enough, most British officers were as frustrated by the Battle of Germantown as Washington. Lieutenant Sir Martin Hunter recorded in his diary that this battle was "the first time we had retreated from the Americans." He wrote that General Howe had ridden up personally, exclaiming, "For shame, Light Infantry! I never saw you retreat before. Form! Form! It's only a scouting party."

BACK TO BURGOYNE

GENTLEMAN JOHNNY BURGOYNE was already in a very disagreeable situation. He had learned what he certainly should have known—that Howe was not going to meet him in Albany. He also received word of the Hessian defeats at Bennington, and then he found out that Barry St. Leger had failed to take Fort Stanwix. Obviously, the grand plan for crushing the Revolution was not going well, and Burgoyne considered withdrawing to the safety of Fort Edward or to Fort Ticonderoga. In his 1854 "The Charge of the Light Brigade," Lord Alfred Tennyson, nailed the attitude of the British soldier: "Theirs not to reason why,/ Theirs but to do and die." Flamboyant and flashy as he was, Burgoyne was at bottom a good British soldier. His orders from London, as he understood them, did not include the option of falling back; therefore, the failure of others notwithstanding, he had no choice but to "force a junction with Sir William Howe"—even if Howe was busy some 250 miles to the south. So he marched into Albany, calling to his troops as they crossed the Hudson on September 13, "Britons never retreat!" And, as if to ensure that these would be no mere empty words, he ordered the boat-borne bridge spanning the river dismantled.

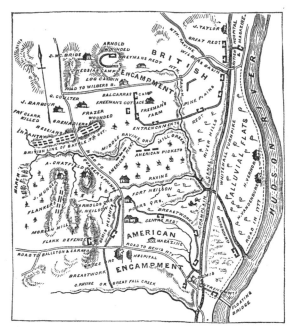

This map shows the battles of Freeman's Farm and Bemis Heights during the Saratoga campaign, on September 19 and October 7, 1777. The battles pitted Burgoyne's conventional European tactics against Arnold and Morgan's more innovative approaches. Note the highly regimented disposition of the "British line of battle" versus the American deployment, which takes advantage of the terrain.

The Fight at Freeman's Farm

Locals did not make Burgoyne's march to Albany easy. They had busied themselves wrecking the many small bridges that spanned countless streams, and because Burgoyne had a lot of guns and carts, he had to rebuild each ruined bridge. The march was typically at the rate of a mile a day, sometimes less.

Slowed by Patriot sabotage, Burgoyne was also blinded by the desertion of most of his Native American allies, who left in disgust after the Battle of Bennington and the retreat from Fort Stanwix. Thus, on

September 16, Burgoyne did not see the rebel army, but he did hear the distant roll of reveille drums somewhere to the south. He sent a reconnaissance party, which reported wagon tracks leading to an abandoned farm.

Freeman's Farm, it was called, although in its forlorn state, unharvested wheat undulating in the breeze, it didn't look like much of a farm. To Burgoyne, however, it was a welcome sight. The British army, like other European armies, was trained to fight on a field of battle, but the heavily forested eastern American landscape offered few open fields. Here, at last, was one.

The thing to do, therefore, was to lure the Americans out into it. His heart quickened by the prospect of advantageous combat, Burgoyne made a beginner's blunder. Although he did not yet see the Americans, he believed he was (as the military jargon of the time put it) "in the face of the enemy." One of the prime rules of engagement is never to divide your forces in the face of the enemy. Burgoyne divided his into three.

On September 19, he assigned General Simon Fraser to lead twenty-two hundred men along a path to Freeman's western fields. Burgoyne decided to take eleven hundred men south and then west to meet up with Fraser on the farm itself. To the east, the third column, eleven hundred Hessians in three Brunswick regiments under Baron von Reidesel, was tasked with advancing south, down the river road. The plan was for all three columns to envelope the Americans on the open field. But there was a tricky part. The three columns would be out of sight of one another as they moved toward their objective, so Burgoyne planned to coordinate their movements by means of signal guns.

Apparently, there was no limit to Gentleman Johnny's capacity for hope. He must have known that there was no reliable means of coordinating movement through the broken terrain around Freeman's Farm, no matter how many signal guns he used. By dividing his forces, Burgoyne invited defeat in detail—the chipping away of each small force—should they fail to reunite.

Whereas Burgoyne was blind, the Americans saw everything. Opportunity was indeed ripe—if only Horatio Gates had not been nearly as cautious as Howe himself. Instead of moving out to exploit Burgoyne's blunder, he just waited and watched as his subordinate, the

DETAILS, DETAILS
Wild Turkey

Daniel Morgan was a guerrilla at heart. He disdained the martial bugle, which would alert the enemy as well as his own men, and instead relied on his ability to mimic the call of the wild turkey. His men's ears were perfectly attuned to this signal, whereas the enemy thought nothing of it.

dashing Benedict Arnold, pleaded with him to act. Finally, Gates yielded, ordering skilled riflemen under the frontier-savvy Daniel Morgan and light infantry led by Henry Dearborn to engage the enemy.

The British and German troops had started out before dawn, but the terrain was so rough and the going so slow that it was nearly one in the afternoon before Burgoyne's center column broke through to Freeman's field. Now they were out in the open, exposed. Suddenly, from the woods on the south edge of the field, shots rang out. Every British officer in the front line fell, victims of Morgan's sharpshooters.

Amazed by their success, Morgan's riflemen did exactly what Burgoyne hoped they would. They came out of the woods and into the field to pursue the men of the British front line. Of course, Burgoyne hadn't counted on his troops stampeding to the rear in panic, but neither had Morgan figured on colliding with the main body of the British center column.

In this early nineteenth-century engraving of the Battle of Bemis Heights during the Saratoga campaign, the Patriots are shown, from ambush cover, delivering devastating fire into the neatly regimented British lines.

Stunned, the American riflemen fled in disarray back into the woods. At first, it looked to Morgan as if he had been badly mauled, but then he sounded his trademark turkey call, and his men, in obedience, instantly re-formed their ranks.

The British were not nearly so responsive. Shaken by the attack from the woods, their officers dead, the survivors ran back toward the main body. The men of that force confused them with Morgan's troops and fired indiscriminately, mowing down many of their own. Burgoyne looked on. He decided that he could not afford to wait for the signal gun from Fraser's column. Instead, he fired his own and moved his main force onto Freeman's Farm, forming his lines along the northern edge of the field.

What happened next no one knows for sure. The strongest evidence suggests, however, that Benedict Arnold boldly assumed command. Now that Burgoyne's ranks were neatly formed up, out in the open, in good European style, Morgan and Dearborn took positions along the southern edge of the clearing while seven more American regiments were sent down from Bemis Heights, just south of the farm.

For the next three or four hours, a firefight ensued, pitting the tactics of the American frontier against those of Europe. Firing from cover, the Americans cut through the ranks of the three British regiments that stood shoulder to shoulder. Despite these terrible losses, the British troops maintained their discipline as Burgoyne's artillery returned fire with devastating results. Each time the Americans attempted to charge out of the woods to force the battle to a conclusion, the artillery drove them back.

In any battle, time can be an enemy or an ally. Both sides wanted to make it their ally. Burgoyne knew that if he could hold out, Reidesel and Fraser would reinforce him. The Americans knew that they needed to destroy Burgoyne's center before time ran out and the fresh troops arrived.

Reidesel was the first to arrive, breaking through from the east and opening up with his artillery. Arnold had ridden back to Bemis Heights to fetch more troops, so he was absent from the field when the Germans arrived. Without him, the Americans managed to hold their ground for a while, but were forced to fall back as darkness settled over Freeman's Farm. Fraser did not reach the battlefield until the action was about finished. His men traded fire with an American brigade, but had little effect on the battle.

By nightfall, Burgoyne tallied his losses: some 600 men in all. Of the 800 troops in the three regiments that absorbed the brunt of the combat, 350 were killed, wounded, or captured—a catastrophic 44 percent casualty rate. (American losses totaled 319, including 65 killed, 208 wounded, and 36 missing.) Yet Burgoyne claimed victory, because, as the smoke cleared, he possessed Freeman's Farm.

In fact, had he resumed the battle over the next day or two, he might well have crushed Gates, who had failed, really, to lead the battle. Gates had had more than enough men at Bemis Heights—four thousand versus nine hundred—to annihilate the men Reidesel had left to guard Burgoyne's supplies. Take away his supplies, and Burgoyne would have been faced with the choice of surrender or starvation. Benedict Arnold understood this and argued bitterly with Gates to launch a raid on the guards, to no avail. A small-minded man, Gates retaliated by leaving Arnold entirely out of his report to Congress on the battle. Arnold responded by asking Gates for a "pass to Philadelphia . . . where I propose to join General Washington, and

Modern military historians consider Patriot commander Daniel Morgan the only bonafide military genius to fight on either side during the American Revolution. Untutored in the military art, he nevertheless had an innate grasp of tactics and was an inspiring leader of men. Eschewing a traditional uniform, he wore the kind of frontier gear shown in this nineteenth-century colored engraving.

REALITY CHECK

The Diva

Some historians have argued that Benedict Arnold was a fine officer driven to become a traitor by the jealousy of other officers. It was not that simple. Arnold was a brave man, but he was also a prima donna, far more concerned with his own advancement than with the cause he supposedly served. To get what he wanted, he typically threatened to resign. After his tireless performance at Valcour Island (see Chapter 7) in October 1776, he returned a popular hero, but his insufferable arrogance had alienated several brother officers. When, in February 1777, Congress created five new major generalships, Arnold was pointedly passed over in favor of his juniors. Washington personally intervened to prevent him from resigning.

may possibly have it in my power to serve my country, tho I am thought of no consequence to this Department." Gates unceremoniously relieved Arnold of command and barred him from entering his headquarters. The other officers persuaded Arnold to stay on, and Gates acquiesced, but refused to reinstate him officially.

WHEN BENEDICT ARNOLD WAS AN AMERICAN HERO

LUCKY FOR AMERICA that Benedict Arnold was talked out of leaving. The fight at Freeman's Farm was the first phase of what historians call the Battle of Saratoga. The second phase, at Bemis Heights, would give Arnold a chance to be a hero.

Burgoyne was licking the wounds that resulted from his "victory" at Freeman's Farm. He had finally given up on Howe, but he received word from Sir Henry Clinton, whom Howe had put in charge of New York City when he left for Philadelphia, that he was sending three thousand troops to the upper Hudson. It was a stingy number—Clinton could have spared seven thousand—but it was better than nothing.

Or so Burgoyne thought. Clinton did not start the reinforcements on their way until October 3, by which time Burgoyne's situation was probably beyond hope of salvation. Indeed, the contingent Clinton sent took time out to capture Forts Montgomery, Clinton, and Constitution along the Hudson. Then Clinton sent Burgoyne a message in reply to his urgent request for reinforcements, asking him also if he should proceed to Albany or retreat. Burgoyne had pointed out that he could not stay where he was beyond October 12. Clinton's reply was of little help: "In answer to your letter of the 28th of September by C.C. I shall only say, I cannot presume to order, or even advise, for reasons obvious. I heartily wish you success." In any case, the reply never reached Burgoyne. Continental army surgeon Dr. James Thatcher explained why in a diary entry of October 14, 1777.

> We have been trembling alive to [the] menacing prospect [of the arrival of Clinton's forces in Albany], but our fears are in a measure allayed by the following singular incident. After the capture of Fort Montgomery, Sir Henry Clinton despatched a messenger by the name of Daniel Taylor to Burgoyne with the intelligence [that he was

not rushing to Albany]; fortunately [Taylor] was taken away as a spy, and finding himself in danger, he was seen to turn aside and take something from his pocket and swallow it. General George Clinton [the Patriot commander], into whose hands he had fallen, ordered a severe dose of emetic tartar to be administered. This produced the happiest effect as respects the prescriber, but it proved fatal to the patient. He discharged a small silver bullet, which being unscrewed, was found to enclose a letter from Sir Henry Clinton to Burgoyne. "Out of thine own mouth thou shalt be condemned." The spy was tried, convicted and executed.

In fact, by the time the message was intercepted, Burgoyne had already begun surrender negotiations with General Gates at Saratoga, but that gets us ahead of the Battle of Bemis Heights. Soon after sending the intercepted "silver-bullet" message, Clinton received a request from Howe for reinforcements. Howe outranked Burgoyne, so Clinton promptly turned tail, abandoned the three forts he had captured, quick-marched south, and left Gentleman Johnny to manage—on his own—as best he could.

In the two weeks since the Battle of Freeman's Farm, Burgoyne had scratched out elaborate entrenchments and redoubts on Bemis Heights. The passage of those two weeks also brought reinforcements to Gates, troops commanded by General Benjamin Lincoln. Once Lincoln arrived, he set to work harassing Burgoyne's rear positions. Burgoyne suspected he was in trouble, but he had no idea how deep that trouble was. The arrival of Lincoln's contingent meant that he was now outnumbered, eleven thousand to five thousand.

On October 7, Burgoyne made a decision. He could either hole up, waiting to be nibbled away, or he could take action. He decided to send out a reconnaissance-in-force of 1,650 men to determine just what it was that he faced.

The answer came quickly. Gates sent Morgan to hit the right flank of the reconnaissance force while General Enoch Poor attacked the left. Benedict Arnold, with neither orders nor

This 1851 print depicts the John Neilson House at Bemis Heights, New York. The house served as a brigade-level headquarters for the Continental army during the Saratoga campaign, in 1777. It was owned by farmer John Neilson, who donated its use during his tour of duty in the 13th Albany County Militia Regiment. Generals Enoch Poor and Benedict Arnold quartered here.

authorization, assembled a detachment to attack the breastworks behind which some of Burgoyne's men had taken cover. This accomplished, he galloped—directly across the line of British fire—to an advancing column of Continental troops under General Ebenezer Learned. They were marching toward the British right. Arnold took command, leading them away from the right and instead into a frontal assault against "Breymann's redoubt," a position occupied by Hessians. It was a much better move to neutralize these soldiers, but Arnold did not escape unscathed. His horse was shot from under him, and then he took a bullet in the leg. He had to be carried from the field.

Burgoyne Gives Up

The British fared much worse. The officer corps was decimated, and one of Britain's best commanders, the dashing Simon Fraser, was among the fallen. Nevertheless, with Arnold out of the action, the American charge against Breymann's redoubt petered out. Yet it— and the other elements of the American attack—had done a great deal of damage. Burgoyne suffered six hundred killed or wounded, whereas the Americans had lost fewer than 150. The British general retreated with the survivors to the village of Saratoga. Gates gave chase and, on October 12, maneuvered around Burgoyne, cutting him off from the Hudson. As Burgoyne had said: Britons never retreat. Now they could not.

Burgoyne asked Gates for surrender terms on October 13. Gates replied with a demand for unconditional surrender. Although he was outnumbered more than two to one and hopelessly cut off from retreat or supply, Burgoyne refused the demand. Gates must have known that he held all the cards. Incredibly, however, he met with Burgoyne on October 16 to draw up the Saratoga Convention, by which Burgoyne and his men would not be made prisoners of war, but would return to England "on condition of not serving again in North America during the present contest."

On October 17, the British formally relinquished their fortifications and Burgoyne officially surrendered his army to Gates, after which the two commanders dined together. Burgoyne offered a toast to General Washington, and Gates responded with a toast to King George III.

Chapter 19

THE FRENCH CONNECTION

*How the United States Earned Its
Most Important Ally*

THOMAS PAINE'S *Common Sense* and Thomas Jefferson's Declaration of Independence were both documents aimed at elevating a local revolution into a world event—a struggle that was not only politically and historically justified, but in which all humankind had a stake. If this sounds like a hard sell, it really wasn't. Most of the nations of Europe were willing to see the American Revolution—this collection of mostly small-scale battles mostly fought on the edge of a New World wilderness—as a phase or theater of a great world war, which had begun in the seventeenth century and, but for brief truces, engulfed much of the eighteenth century, too. The Seven Years War, of which the French and Indian War was the American phase, had been fought in the 1750s and early 1760s, yielded to an uneasy peace, and now—as most Europe saw it—had erupted again in 1775. France and England were typically the principal antagonists in this sporadic world war. The revolutionaries in America now asked themselves, would they square off again?

THE WAGES OF ALLIANCE

THE ARCHITECTS OF THE AMERICAN REVOLUTION were eager to exploit the traditional enmity between France and England. For America, the benefits of a Franco-American alliance were obvious. If any nation on earth was richer and more powerful than Britain, it was France, and the infant United States of America—without industry, without credit, without (really) much of a government—could use all the help it could get. Likewise, the benefits to France were self-evident. The latest war had resulted in France losing its New World possessions. Here was an opportunity to put Britain on the losing end for a change. Besides, any opportunity to weaken a rival was a good opportunity, and fighting the rebellion in America was certainly a drain of British resources. Louis XVI had absolutely no objection to kicking his enemy when he was down.

Destined to fall victim to the French Revolution, Louis XVI allied France with the American Revolution— not from any desire to promote liberty or undermine a fellow monarch, but to diminish a rival empire. This hand-colored engraving was made during his lifetime.

Yet an alliance with America was hardly a no-brainer for the French. To begin with, France was a monarchy, in which the first grumblings of revolution were already being heard. Was it a good idea for an absolute monarch to contribute to a revolution against the government of another monarch? Second, there was the apparent one-sidedness of the struggle in America. Here was a loosely federated group of rather feeble colonies daring to rise up against a great power. Who was more likely to prevail? By all means, hitch your wagon to a star—but avoid those seemingly destined to fall.

To their credit, the members of the Continental Congress were sufficiently worldly wise to understand the delicacy of the French situation. Accordingly, they courted an alliance that began by seeking aid just short of outright war.

Courting an Ally

But it was the French who made the first move. Charles Gravier, comte de Vergennes, was foreign minister to Emperor Louis XVI. As early as 1775, Vergennes was persuaded that the Americans were serious about winning their independence. He had plenty of reservations about entering into a full-scale alliance with the rebels, but he burned with a hatred of the English and desire to avenge the defeat of France in the Seven Years War. In September 1775, therefore, Vergennes sent a secret agent, one Achard de Bonvouloir, to poke around America and report back on the colonial situation. In November 1775, Congress created a five-man Committee of Correspondence, chaired by Benjamin Franklin, to make contact with "our friends abroad." They began with Achard de Bonvouloir, who responded so favorably that Congress, in April 1776, decided to send Silas Deane, Congressman from Connecticut, to Paris for the purpose of purchasing—on the cuff, naturally—uniforms and equipment for twenty-five thousand men, as well as artillery and munitions. In addition, he was instructed to send out feelers about establishing an alliance.

Charles Gravier, comte de Vergennes, France's foreign minister, took the first steps in creating a Franco-American alliance. The noted French engraver Edme Bovinet created this portrait in 1785, two years before Vergennes's death.

Enter the Figaro Man

No sooner did Deane begin making inquiries in Paris, than Vergennes, in May 1776, resolved to help the Americans. It is unclear if Deane influenced this decision or if Vergennes had simply, by this time, decided on his own. Still unwilling to commit to an open and outright alliance, Vergennes approached a young Parisian who had already become famous as the creator of a delightfully scheming barber/valet named Figaro. Pierre Augustin Caron de Beaumarchais's comic play *Le Barbier de Séville* premiered to great acclaim in 1775 and earned its author both renown and a small fortune.

In April 1776, the Continental Congress sent Silas Deane of Connecticut to France with instructions to negotiate aid and, if possible, a full-scale alliance. This engraving is based on a drawing from life by the American Revolution–era portrait artist Pierre Eugene du Simitiere.

Pierre de Beaumarchais earned enduring fame as the playwright who created the character Figaro, the wily and hilarious hero of both Le Barbier de Séville *and* Le Mariage de Figaro. *In real life, Beaumarchais was even wilier than Figaro; he was the financier who put together an elaborate shell company that allowed the government of France to secretly finance much of the American Revolution.*

Doubtless, Beaumarchais was a literary genius. But he started out his professional life as a mechanical genius. His father had been a watchmaker, and the son learned enough about the watchmaker's art to invent a new kind of escapement mechanism, the component of a watch on which its accuracy depends. Instead of rewarding him with a fortune, the invention buried Beaumarchais in a cascade of lawsuits. It was his legal troubles that prompted his first literary work, a series of brilliant legal and moral defenses, *Mémoires,* which made a splash among discriminating readers, but failed to blow away his myriad legal problems. Eager to escape the consequences of some less-than-successful litigation, Beaumarchais, in 1773, accepted a royal assignment to conduct secret diplomatic missions to England and Germany. This is how he came to the attention of Vergennes.

The foreign minister reasoned that, in Beaumarchais, he had a young man with a spy's discretion, a diplomat's savvy, and a writer's ready wit for invention. He therefore asked the creator of Figaro to put together a new fiction. He was to invent a company—a front—for the purpose of laundering money that the French Crown, in cooperation with another enemy of England, Spain, intended to send to America. Beaumarchais obliged by creating Roderigue Hortalez & Cie. The beauty of this brand-new firm was that it functioned, in part, as a genuine trading company, even as it passed through funds to the American Revolution—right under British noses. Eager to do harm to the English, but not yet ready to provoke a war with them, Louis XVI was prepared to funnel one million livres through Hortalez and into the Revolution's coffers. Spain had a like amount ready to go.

And there was more. Not content to use Hortalez as a mere funnel, Vergennes instructed Beaumarchais to use the company to raise another million livres from private investors. Using its funds—furnished by France and Spain as well as private investors—Hortalez & Cie. would obtain military supplies from French stocks, for which the Americans would pay not with cash (which they didn't have), but with rice, tobacco, and other commodities. In turn, Hortalez would replenish its funds—and reward its investors—by importing these commodities and selling them in France.

A GOOD SCHEME—WHILE IT LASTED

In June 1776, the French Crown paid Beaumarchais a million livres, to which, by August, he added a million collected from Spain, then raised funds from investors. Beaumarchais already had an American friend, Arthur Lee (youngest son of the prominent Virginia family that produced several revolutionary leaders and would later give the southern Confederacy its greatest general, Robert E. Lee), with whom he discussed the Hortalez scheme. Through Lee, Beaumarchais contacted Silas Deane in July, and the supply pipeline from France to America was complete.

Viewed from one angle, the Hortalez scheme was a fabulous success. Historians estimate that the victories at Trenton and Princeton were made possible by French supplies. As much as ninety percent of the weapons and ammunition used in the two battles at Saratoga—Freeman's Farm and Bemis Heights—had come via the Beaumarchais scheme. In all, millions in military aid was funneled to the American Revolution well before King Louis XVI made an official alliance. Yet Hortalez was also a fiasco, plagued by enough intrigue to have furnished Beaumarchais with another play or two—had he chosen to write it all up. There was interference by certain British agents, to be sure, but this wasn't as troublesome as the interference of various French officials, who were either jealous of the cozy relations between Beaumarchais and Vergennes or who were just plain uncooperative.

Based on his own ledger books, the Continental Congress, as of 1781, owed Beaumarchais 3,600,000 livres. It was a staggering sum, which he never collected, and such a loss would have ruined a lesser man. But Beaumarchais proved to be a business as well as mechanical and literary genius. In the course of supplying America's war needs, Beaumarchais brought his ships back from America via the West Indies, where he picked up cargoes of sugar and other commodities, which he sold in Europe at great profit. In this way, he more than offset his losses and, indeed, cleared a tidy little fortune.

THE CHARMING FRANKLIN

THE AMERICAN REVOLUTION would make many reputations, but for those who had already made theirs, the conflict represented a grave risk. Benjamin Franklin, almost seventy years old when the war

POP CULTURE
Figaro, Figaro

The sequel to *Le Barbier de Séville, Le Mariage de Figaro,* did not follow the original until 1784, but it would prove even more successful. Although both plays are still read today, they are best known in the form of the operas based on them, Gioacchino Rossini's *The Barber of Seville* and Wolfgang Amadeus Mozart's *The Marriage of Figaro.*

REALITY CHECK
Silas and Scandal

Silas Deane worked tirelessly on behalf of the cause—you would think that he would have received thanks from Congress. Instead, Arthur Lee charged Deane with embezzling funds Congress entrusted to him to pay for supplies. When the French gave the goods to America gratis, Lee charged, Deane simply pocketed the cash. Deane was neither prosecuted nor officially cleared, and, in 1780, he stormed off to France, where he passed the time writing vengeful letters to his old American friends, assailing the French alliance, and urging reconciliation with England. In 1781, The Royal Gazette, a Loyalist New York–based newspaper, obtained the letters and published them. Deane was widely denounced as a traitor. He went into self-imposed exile, first in Belgium and then in London, where in 1784 he published his defense in "An Address to the Free and Independent Citizens of the United States". In 1789, Deane felt comfortable enough to return to America, but he died aboard ship under mysterious circumstances. He was posthumously exonerated by Congress in 1842.

began, was already internationally renowned as a scientist, inventor, author, editor, and entrepreneur, not to mention a charmer of the fair sex. He staked all he had on the struggle for independence.

A man of abundant wit, innate charm, and easy-going sophistication, Benjamin Franklin was a favorite of Paris high society and the court of Louis XVI. More than any other American figure, he was responsible for forging the Franco-American alliance that was critical to the success of the Revolution. This chromolithograph from about 1882 is a delightful depiction of Franklin's welcome in France in 1776.

Congress understood that Franklin was nowhere more famous and more revered than in France, which he had visited in his capacity as business agent for Pennsylvania in 1767 and 1769. Wisely, the Committee of Correspondence recommended that Franklin be sent to join Arthur Lee and Silas Deane as commissioners to negotiate, once and for all, a full and formal treaty of alliance with the emperor.

> *"We must all hang together, or assuredly we shall all hang separately."*
>
> *Benjamin Franklin, at the signing of the Declaration of Independence*

Franklin arrived in Paris on December 4, 1776. Lee—who was, on a good day, sour and irascible (but whom some historians have described as psychotic)—was immune to Franklin's reputation and charm. He snubbed him. Deane, however, welcomed his company and worked productively with him to open negotiations with the Crown.

The Gallant Lafayette

There was much negotiation to be done; however, the American commissioners were hardly starting out cold. Hortalez was steaming along, and, already, some young Frenchmen were eagerly discussing direct military involvement in what they saw as an epochal event in world history. The most famous of this group was the Marquis de Lafayette. He had been born to a noble family, then orphaned at thirteen, which left him with a fabulous fortune by the time he married, in 1774, the daughter of the wealthy and powerful duc d'Ayen. The marriage gave him entrée into the inner circle of Louis XVI's court. Lafayette could have lived in comfort and pleasure; these, however, were hardly adequate to quench his restlessly idealist spirit. But it took a chance remark to determine the course of the young man's life. On August 8, 1775, Lafayette was a guest at a dinner during which the Duke of Gloucester proclaimed his sympathy for the cause of American liberty. That did it. Lafayette knew what he must do. He decided to sail for America.

Lafayette was not so impulsive as to leave without preparation. First, one of his friends, the comte de Broglie, told him about Johann Kalb, a Bavarian-born Frenchman serving with de Broglie's military unit. Kalb, de Broglie said, also talked of fighting in America and intended to speak to Silas Deane about it. The comte de Broglie introduced Lafayette to Kalb, and the pair called on Deane together. Impressed, Deane drew up agreements with both men and promised them commissions as major generals in the Continental army.

Despite Deane's enthusiastic recommendation, the Continental Congress gave Lafayette a cool welcome. He seemed too good to be true. A volunteer? An aristocrat, come all the way from Paris, and offering to serve at his own expense? What was his game? But Lafayette persisted, and, on July 31, 1777, Congress handed him his major general's commission. August 1, he was presented to George Washington. When Congress chose him to lead the Continental army, Washington had replied modestly that he feared he was not equal to the task. Yet he knew what it meant to burn with dreams of martial glory. On the eve of the French and Indian War, at the age of twenty-one, he eagerly accepted a lieutenant colonelcy in the Virginia militia. So he well understood how the gallant young Frenchman would want to very much to volunteer even in the service of another country. Washington formed an instant bond with the marquis, although he also recognized two problems.

DETAILS, DETAILS
The Ex Saves His Neck

Beaumarchais was smart, and he was lucky. With the onset of the French Revolution, he was arrested in 1792—not because he was a nobleman (he was not), but because he was rich (indeed he was). He won release and was spared a date with the guillotine through the intervention of a well-connected former mistress, whose heart (apparently) was as generous as her purse was ample.

REALITY CHECK
Lord of . . . Nothing

Kalb is customarily referred to as the Baron de Kalb. In fact, he had no such title. Understanding that Americans were impressed by hereditary titles—never mind that they were fighting to become an independent *republic*—Kalb decided to fatten up his résumé by styling himself a baron and adding the ennobling particle de. No one seems to have questioned him on this.

He was only twenty years old, and he spoke almost no English. Nevertheless, he was a European-trained military officer with an intense desire to fight the English in the cause of American liberty.

Despite Lafayette's shortcomings, Washington committed him to battle—at Brandywine under Nathanael Greene (see Chapter 13, "Defeat on the Brandywine"), where the young man displayed conspicuous gallantry and sustained a severe wound in the thigh. He did not recover in time to participate in the Battle of Germantown, but, on November 25, he did lead a small force to victory against some Hessians in a skirmish at Gloucester, New Jersey. This encouraged Washington to ask that Congress grant Lafayette "a command equal to his rank." He was accordingly assigned, on December 1, 1777, command of a division of Virginia light infantry.

ALLIES AT LAST

WHILE BEAUMARCHAIS WAS SUPPLYING the Revolution under the table and Lafayette and Kalb were boldly fighting for it, the French emperor was moving steadily toward a full-scale alliance. Victory at Saratoga and Washington's boldness at Germantown—despite his defeat there—tipped the balance. On December 17, 1777, French authorities informed Franklin and his fellow envoys in Paris that the emperor was now pleased to recognize the independence of the United States of America. It was the first nation to do so. A few weeks later, on January 8, 1778, Vergennes told the envoys that the government was now ready to conclude a formal alliance.

Two treaties were quickly hammered out. The Treaty of Amity and Commerce made French recognition of American independence official, and the Treaty of Alliance pledged a military alliance. The Continental Congress ratified the two Franco-American treaties on May 4. The French ambassador to Britain announced the treaties on May 13. The British Crown immediately recalled its ambassador from Paris. Spain's offer of mediation was rebuffed by both nations and, on June 20, following a brief naval battle, Britain declared war on France. The United States and the empire of Louis XVI were now allies. This would change the course of the war—but not nearly as fast as the Americans hoped.

Chapter 15

DEFEAT AND DESPAIR

The Patriots Lose the Critical Delaware River Forts, Washington Is Plotted Against, and the Continental Army Starves and Freezes in the Valley Forge Winter

IT HAD SEEMED LIKE SUCH A GOOD IDEA. Capture Philadelphia, the capital of the rebellion, and, surely, the rebellion would have to come to an end. But no such thing happened. Worse, taking Philadelphia had cost the British a defeat at Saratoga, and now that Howe owned the city, he had to defend it. He could not afford to let Philadelphia become another Boston, the focus of a siege. As Howe saw it, the threat came from two major Delaware River forts: Fort Mifflin on the Pennsylvania side of the river, and Fort Mercer on the Jersey bank. Between these, the Americans had stretched spiked barricades—*chevaux de frise,* they were called—across the river. They were a kind of trip wire intended to prevent the passage of ships.

BATTLE OF FORT MERCER

WILLIAM HOWE WAS DETERMINED to neutralize the Delaware River forts. No American officer knew much about the art of fortification, but French military engineers were masters of it, and Washington had the services of one of the best, the Chevalier de Mauduit du Plessis, who arrived in October of 1777 to help Colonel Christopher Greene, commandant of Fort Mercer, plan an effective defense of this installation. The Americans could spare no more than

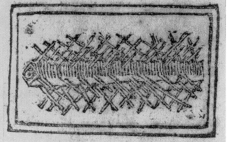

CHEVEAUX-DE-FRIZE, large joints or beams, ftuck full of wooden pins, armed with iron, to ftop breaches, or to fecure a paffage of a camp againft the enemy's cavalry.

Largely untutored in the military art, the officers of the Continental army nevertheless had access to any number of books on the subject, including Thomas Simes's A New Military, Historical, and Explanatory Dictionary, *which was published in Philadelphia in 1776. Its definition of* cheveaux de frise *(which the dictionary spelled* frize*)—"large joints or beams, stuck full of wooden pins, armed with iron, to stop breaches, or to secure a passage of a camp against the enemy's cavalry"—was accompanied by a helpful illustration.*

the four hundred Rhode Islanders to garrison the fort. Instead of complaining that he had too few men to work with, Mauduit du Plessis concluded that there was simply too much fort for the men he had. To correct this, he ordered a new interior wall to be built, which cut off the northern wing of the fort. To the Americans, this must have seemed an odd thing to do, but it was a stroke of engineering know-how that spelled the difference between victory and defeat.

On October 21, 1777, Howe sent two thousand Hessians under Colonel Carl Emil Kurt von Donop to capture Fort Mercer. The Hessians were the best, and Donop had selected the best of the best, an elite *jäger* corps—"hunters," troops specializing in advance-guard and reconnaissance tactics. In addition, he had the fine Regiment von Mirbach, plus two cannon. At half past four in the afternoon of October 22, Donop sent an officer to Greene, demanding the immediate surrender of the fort and warning that he would give "no quarter."

Greene refused to surrender, whereupon Donop methodically arrayed his forces for attack, moving deliberately under Greene's eyes, as if to express a profound contempt of the colonials. At about nine in the evening he attacked in two columns, two battalions of grenadiers and the Regiment von Mirbach from the north; the others from the west.

"Vittoria!"—*Victory!*—shouted the northern column as it stormed over the breastworks. It was a very fine battle cry, except that, in this case, it proved premature. The Hessians found themselves not in the middle of the American fort, but trapped in an empty compound and facing du Plessis's interior wall.

At the same time, Donop personally led the western column through the *abatis*—felled trees, sharpened at one end, the pointed ends aimed against would-be attackers—then advanced across the ditch that surrounded the fort. But now he and his men came up short against the berm, the ledge that had been mounded between the ditch and the parapet of the fort. Somehow, Donop had neglected to bring along scaling ladders.

Each second that a force storming a fort is stalled is a second in which people are likely to die. Without firing a shot, Greene had been watching the approach and frustration of the northern and western columns of Hessians. Now it was time for the order—and a hail of grapeshot (cannon-fired cluster ammunition intended to kill as many people as possible) and musket fire poured down on the massed and jostling ranks of the Hessians. Donop was one of the first to be shot. Grapeshot or a musket ball tore through his leg, inflicting a wound that would quickly prove fatal.

Under intense fire, the Hessians withdrew. They re-formed their ranks and decided to attempt the south wall of Fort Mercer. These were brave soldiers, but, apparently, their commanders had little regard for their lives. If the north and east approaches had been impossible to breach, the south was even more formidable because it exposed the attackers not only to fire from the fort, but also from rowing galleys—shallow-draft gunboats—stationed on the river.

The Americans had won the day. Then came the next day— October 23. This time, the sixty-four-gun British frigate *Augusta* and the forty-four-gun *Roebuck*, accompanied by the *Merlin* (eighteen guns), sailed up to the *chevaux de frise* and opened fire on the rowing galleys and "floating batteries" (additional obstructions placed to block river passage). Instead of meekly submitting, the galleys, along with guns of Fort Mifflin, returned fire until, at noon, HMS *Augusta* exploded. By three, *Merlin* had been run aground. It, too, burst into flame and exploded. *Roebuck* prudently withdrew. Another day belonged to the Americans.

BATTLE OF FORT MIFFLIN

THE HAVOC THE GUNNERS OF FORT MERCER had wreaked made Howe all that more determined to take its companion, Fort Mifflin. Four-hundred-fifty men garrisoned the fort, but it was neither as well engineered nor as advantageously sited as Fort Mercer. The inland side was particularly exposed and vulnerable.

On November 10, the British opened fire from five floating batteries in the river. Major André-Arsène de Rosset, Vicomte de Fleury, the French engineer assigned to assist Lieutenant Colonel Samuel Smith to defend Fort Mifflin, feverishly directed efforts to repair the damage wrought by the relentless bombardment. The fort

DETAILS, DETAILS
Spiky Barrier

A *chevaux de frise* is a defense consisting of obstacles from which spikes or barbed stakes protrude. The French phrase means "horses of Frieseland" and refers to the location in the Netherlands where the defense was first used against cavalry in the sixteenth century.

NUMBERS
Fort Mercer: Casualties

Of the 1,200 Hessians who stormed Fort Mercer, 400 fell dead or were wounded. American casualties were 14 killed and 23 wounded.

endured five days of pummeling. On November 14, Smith, badly wounded, was evacuated and command was given to Major Simeon Thayer. He refused to surrender. But, by this time, repair and resistance were out of the question. When the sun set on the fourteenth, Fort Mifflin was a heap of rubble. Thayer and the survivors of his garrison—just 200 out of 450 men—evacuated the ruin on November 15 and holed up in Fort Mercer. The British began bombarding it during November 20–21, ultimately forcing its abandonment as well, and thus both Fort Mifflin and Fort Mercer were lost. As for the Americans' rowed galleys, these were deliberately put to the torch to keep them out of British hands.

During January 1778, David Bushnell—the young man who had invented the Turtle submarine (see Chapter 10, "The Turtle")—turned his creative talents to creating something the British (against whom they were used) dubbed "infernals." These were clusters of kegs packed with gunpowder and sent floating down the Delaware River. Actually, they were rudimentary marine mines. Rigged with special triggering devices, they exploded on contact with an object, such as a British ship. Initially, the infernals created great alarm among the British—not because they might explode, but because many soldiers and sailors believed the kegs were the equivalent of Trojan horses, filled with soldiers, ready to spring into action. After they figured out that the kegs were explosive devices, British crewmen made it a practice simply to fire at any object seen floating in the river. This caused the waste of a great deal of ammunition, but it also safely detonated many infernals.

A MATTER OF TIME

As with the loss of Philadelphia, the destruction of the Delaware forts was a blow to the Americans, yet it gave the British little reason to celebrate. Casualties had been high, but, even more important, the British had paid a heavy price in time lost. Clearing the forts took two months—two more months during which Burgoyne, up north, was left without reinforcement. Howe took a city and leveled two forts, but it cost him an army.

"Infernals" were kegs bound together, packed with gunpowder, and floated down the Delaware River as primitive marine mines. They were designed to explode on contact with a ship's hull. Revived and somewhat improved during the Civil War (1861–1865) as "infernal machines," they were deployed in rivers by the Confederates. The Civil War infernal pictured here was discovered in the Potomac River. Photographed in 1861 by James F. Gibson, it was subsequently sketched by A. R. Waud, a Civil War field artist for the New York Illustrated News *and other journals of the period.*

WASHINGTON UNDER SIEGE

TAKING PHILADELPHIA AND THE RIVER FORTS was one thing, but the British may not have realized that they had scored a victory far more important than the possession of a town or the destruction of some guns. Brandywine, Germantown, the Delaware forts—all were American losses, and all were under the command of George Washington. At the same time, the Saratoga battles had ended in the capitulation of an entire British army—for which Horatio Gates was eager to take full credit; Washington had had nothing to do with it. Whatever else he accomplished, Howe had succeeded in making a number of important people begin to doubt the competence of General George Washington.

On the political front, Samuel Adams, Richard Henry Lee, Thomas Mifflin, and Dr. Benjamin Rush saw discontent over Washington's military leadership as an opportunity to regain for New England the political leadership of the Revolution. They regarded Benjamin Franklin and Silas Deane, who had control over American affairs in Europe, as members of Washington's clique, and they feared that this group was selling America to France, entangling it in an ultimately dangerous foreign alliance. They began a whispering campaign questioning the wisdom of allowing Washington to continue in charge.

With political opposition to Washington simmering, certain military opportunists decided that the time was ripe to make a move against the commander in chief. What happened next would be labeled the "Conway Cabal," named after Thomas Conway, one of that select group of European idealists who came to America to fight in the cause of liberty. He had been born an Irish Catholic in 1733, but was raised in France from age six and joined the French army in 1747. His commanders gave him permission to go to America, and he arrived in Morristown on May 8, 1777. Washington asked Congress to make him a brigadier general, but, as the junior-

POP CULTURE
The Battle of the Kegs

In 1777, Francis Hopkinson, one of the wittier signers of the Declaration of Independence, wrote "The Battle of the Kegs," excerpted below. It was wildly popular with the American army:

"Arise! Arise!" Sir Erskine cries.
"The rebels—more's the pity—
Without a boat are all afloat
And ranged before the city.

"The Motley crew, in vessels new,
With Satan for their guide, sir,
Packed up in bags, or wooden kegs,
Come driving down the tide, sir.

"Therefore prepare for bloody war;
These kegs must all be routed.
Or surely we despised shall be,
And British courage doubted. . . .

"From morn till night, these men of might
Displayed amazing courage;
And when the sun was fairly down,
Retired to sup their porridge. . . .

"Such feats did they perform that day
Against those wicked kegs, sir,
That years to come, if they get home,
They'll make their boasts and brags, sir."

FORGOTTEN FACES
James Wilkinson

Wilkinson settled on the Kentucky frontier after the war. In 1787 he secretly took an oath of allegiance to Spain, was dubbed code name "Number Thirteen," and turned traitor in an effort to bring western Kentucky under Spanish rule. However, Wilkinson was also working against the Spanish, and the scheme collapsed. He emerged with his skirts so clean that, in 1791, he was made a lieutenant colonel, and, after the Louisiana Purchase, was appointed governor of the Louisiana Territory above the thirty-third parallel. He then hatched a plan to conquer Spain's Mexican provinces, drawing Aaron Burr into the plot—only to betray Burr to President Thomas Jefferson. With Jefferson's authority, Wilkinson arrested Burr, who was tried and acquitted of treason. By now, many suspected Wilkinson of treachery, but he had covered his traces so thoroughly that nothing could be proved. Amazingly, he was promoted to major general in 1813. Wilkinson made such a mess of the Montreal campaign during the War of 1812, however, that he was finally decommissioned.

most of twenty-four Continental army brigadiers at the time, Conway was impatient for advancement. He peppered Congress with pleas, remarking in one letter that Washington was doubtless a noble fellow, but "his talents for the command of an Army . . . were miserable indeed." And he also wrote to Horatio Gates, flattering him with the judgment that "Heaven has been determined to save your country; or a weak General and bad Councilors would have ruined it."

On October 28, 1777, Horatio Gates's adjutant general James Wilkinson—another notorious military opportunist—having heard about this letter, mentioned it to Major William McWilliams, aide-de-camp to General William Alexander ("Lord Stirling"). McWilliams passed the gossip on to his boss, Alexander, who loyally reported it to General Washington. Not one to suffer fools, Washington confronted Conway, who tap-danced, denying that he had used the phrase "weak General," but admitting that he had written to congratulate Gates on his victory. Having made his denials, Conway abruptly resigned his commission on November 14.

The voluntary resignation of a disgruntled officer should have ended it, but Thomas Mifflin, loudest among Washington's critics in the Continental Congress, became president of the congressional Board of War at just this time. He personally promoted Conway not merely to major general, but to the post of inspector general of the Continental army, a position that effectively put him outside of the normal chain of command, giving him extraordinary authority to monitor and report on the efficiency of the army and its officers.

James Wilkinson, adjutant general under Horatio Gates, sought to exploit the Conway Cabal to his advantage. Perhaps the most colorfully corrupt officer in American military history, Wilkinson went on after the American Revolution to conspire with Aaron Burr in a scheme to found a personal empire in the American West. The historian Frederick Jackson Turner called Wilkinson "the most consummate artist in treason that the nation ever possessed," while author Robert Leckie put the emphasis on his uncanny ability to avoid successful prosecution, calling him a "general who never won a battle or lost a court-martial." This painting is by the celebrated Colonial-era portrait artist Charles Willson Peale.

Washington seethed—and was especially concerned about how this promotion over the heads of twenty-three other brigadiers would affect morale. However, concerned to avoid contributing to a crisis, he told Conway that he intended to respect the decisions of Congress. Conway took this—or claimed to take this—as an attempt to undermine him as inspector general. Washington protested the accusation to Congress.

By this time, Congress and the public were hearing rumors of an ongoing "secret correspondence" between Conway and Gates. Sensing that congressional as well as public opinion was turning against him, Gates told Washington that he believed Alexander Hamilton—at the time Washington's aide—had secretly copied some of his correspondence, including Conway's letters to him. His implication was that Hamilton was trying to stir up trouble. Washington calmly replied that he had learned of the contents of Conway's letter to Gates through Gates's very own aide, James Wilkinson! But whereas Gates had spoken to Washington privately, Washington made his reply very publicly, through the Continental Congress.

It was a brilliant maneuver. Drawn out into the light of day, Washington's challengers looked like what they were: little men attempting to tear down a giant. Washington's congressional detractors pulled in their horns, and Washington's many loyal supporters came to the fore with a vote of confidence.

Washington made no attempt at vengeance against Gates. He judged him to be an unspectacular yet solid commander and decided, therefore, to let bygones be bygones. The two worked together cordially for the rest of the war. That was the kind of man Washington was. As for Conway, the commander in chief left him to Congress. Conway again tendered his resignation, and, this time, Congress quickly accepted.

"What Is to Become of the Army This Winter?"

With the hindsight of more than two centuries, we all agree that Washington's victory over the "Conway Cabal" was a very good thing for America. Yet, at the time, faith in Washington was hardly a foregone conclusion. As the summer of 1777 turned to fall, there was good reason not only to question his leadership, but the viability of the Revolution itself. True, an entire British army had surrendered at

DETAILS, DETAILS
Choose Your Weapons

On July 4, 1778, John Cadwalader, a Pennsylvania militia general loyal to Washington, challenged Conway to a duel. The two met on the field of honor, and Conway was wounded—with a high degree of symbolic irony—in the mouth.

The winter of 1777 at the Continental army's Valley Forge encampment was by no means the coldest period of the Revolution, but because of a shortage of funds and the inefficiency of the Continental Congress, the troops were inadequately clothed, sheltered, and fed. Despite privation and suffering, however, Washington made use of the Valley Forge winter to train his army, which emerged in the spring a more effective fighting force.

Saratoga, but the capital was in enemy hands and, even worse, the Continental army was about to face the prospect of another winter ill clothed, ill fed, and ill housed.

Washington chose Valley Forge, Pennsylvania, on the west side of Schuylkill River, as his army's winter quarters. Situated between Philadelphia, where the enemy was located, and York, to which Congress had evacuated, it was centrally positioned. It also offered terrain that was readily defended, with good drainage, and it was close enough to the woods to ensure an ample supply of wood for fuel and for building shelters. Yet the site was exposed to the winter winds and was distant from the hospitality of any local village. The worse problem was that, because the Philadelphia campaign had kept Washington's army in the field well into the winter—until December 11—the troops retired to winter quarters late in the season. They were exhausted and low on supplies.

For six months, from December 1777 to June 1778, ten thousand men huddled miserably in makeshift huts. About four thousand of them had so few clothes on their backs that they almost never ventured outside of their shelters. Some twenty-five hundred men did not survive the winter. Washington spent much of his time pleading with Congress. His letter of December 23, 1777 was typical: "What then is to become of the Army this Winter? and if we are as often without Provisions now, as with it, what is to become of us in the Spring?" As John Brooks, a Massachusetts colonel wrote to a friend, "Nothing but virtue has kept our army together."

THE FORGE

DOUBTLESS, THE ONE THING Washington did *not* think of when he chose to house his army at Valley Forge was the name of the place. But it is worth thinking about. A forge is where iron and steel are hammered into strong and useful shapes. For those who survived,

REALITY CHECK
Late to Shelter

Contrary to historical myth, the winter of 1777–78 was not especially harsh. The reason it took such a toll on soldiers was that Washington had gone into winter quarters late and had to race against the elements to build adequate huts. Worse, the state of supply was poorer than ever, with many soldiers half naked and shoeless. Starvation was a real possibility. Although no men starved to death, many of the army's horses did.

this place and that winter were just such a forge. The Continental army entered the winter encampment a collection of young farmers and tradesmen. It emerged a forged weapon.

With Washington and his men at Valley Forge were Lafayette and Kalb, as well as a Prussian officer named Friedrich Wilhelm Augustus von Steuben. He had been born in a fortress, at Magdeburg, where his father was a military engineer. An officer by seventeen, Steuben fought in the Seven Years War and served on the staff of Frederick the Great. The work of the staff officer was to ensure that the orders of high command were executed by those in the field. A strong staff was one of the secrets of the success of Frederick's army—the French and British paid little attention to the staff level—and Steuben's experience would prove invaluable to the American army.

Why he left the Prussian army in 1763 is not fully known, but Steuben found work as chamberlain in the court of a smalltime prince of Hohenzollern-Hechingen. Like many aristocrats great or small, Steuben's prince eventually ran out of money, and in 1775 Steuben sought employment in the armies of France, Austria, and Baden. Finding nothing suitable, he encountered a friend of Benjamin Franklin, who recommended the American service. Franklin wrote a letter commending Steuben to Washington, Hortalez & Cie. ponied up travel expenses, and Steuben arrived in Portsmouth, New Hampshire, on December 1, 1777. He reported to Valley Forge on February 23, 1778, and instantly drew up a training program for the Continental army. He then chose one hundred promising men, whom he trained intensively and personally. Each of these first hundred in turn trained a group of shivering, hungry soldiers at Valley Forge. They, in turn, trained more. And so it went that winter. The Continental army received a viral infusion of Prussian discipline.

More Foreign Aid

It was the freedom-loving, democratic Americans who called Johann Kalb "Baron de Kalb." He was, in fact, the son of Bavarian peasants, who had become a lieutenant in a German regiment of the French infantry in 1743. In 1768, the French Crown sent him on

REALITY CHECK
While the Army Froze . . .

Many historians attribute the acute shortage of supplies during the Valley Forge winter to the simple fact that Congress, lacking the authority to tax, had little money to spend on its army. It is true that funds were always short, yet it was also the case that many in the government who were responsible for supplying the forces were incompetent or corrupt. Even worse, the local farmers, who could have done so much to help, preferred to sell their produce to the British, who had plenty of cash.

Friedrich Wilhelm Augustus von Steuben was a Prussian officer who served on the staff of no less than Frederick the Great. He introduced himself to Benjamin Franklin in Paris and found his way to America, where he greatly improved the training and discipline of the Continental army. This etching is based on a contemporary portrait by Pierre Eugene du Simitiere.

FORGOTTEN FACES
Tadeusz Kosciuszko

After the American Revolution, Congress voted Kosciuszko the right of U.S. citizenship and commissioned him a brigadier general in the U.S. Army. He chose to return to Poland, however, as a freedom fighter. After victories in several important battles, he was defeated by Russian forces in 1794, wounded, and held prisoner for two years. In 1797, he returned to America, where Philadelphians greeted him with wild enthusiasm. Before leaving for France in 1798 to promote Polish freedom there, Kosciuszko freed his slaves and set aside a portion of his estate to be used to pay for their well-being and education. When Napoleon refused to commit himself to establishing an independent Poland, Kosciuszko withdrew from public life until after the French emperor's downfall. He then attempted, unsuccessfully, to work with Czar Alexander I to create a new Polish government. Nevertheless, as he had done in America, Kosciuszko set free all of the serfs on his family's Polish holdings.

a secret expedition to the North American colonies to assess their true allegiance to Great Britain. Doubtless, he got an eyeful and an earful, but, most of all, he discovered that he liked America, and when the Revolution got under way, he and Lafayette took up arms for the new nation.

Kalb assisted in training during the Valley Forge winter, but his first major combat assignment came in April 1780, when he was sent to lead the relief of Charleston, South Carolina. Unfortunately, that city fell to the British before he reached it. Kalb subsequently fell, mortally wounded, in the Battle of Camden (Chapter 21, "Disgrace at Camden").

In addition to soldiers of French and German nationality, two dashing Poles came to the aid of American liberty. Tadeusz Kosciuszko was a Polish nobleman, thoroughly trained in the military art in the academy at Warsaw. He studied military and civil architecture in Paris—along with painting, for good measure—and when he returned to Poland in 1774, he taught drawing and mathematics to the daughters of a general, Józef Sosnowski. Kosciuszko fell in love with one of the girls, tried elopement, was caught, and, desperate to escape the wrath of her father, dashed off to France again. There he heard talk of the glorious American Revolution, which he joined in 1776.

Tadeusz Kosciuszko, a young Polish nobleman, possessed both a passion for liberty and training as a military engineer. He brought his expertise in fortification to the American cause. This dramatic nineteenth-century lithograph shows Kosciuszko consulting maps in the heat of battle.

In August, Kosciuszko was hired by the Pennsylvania Committee of Defense in Philadelphia to help plan fortifications to defend the residence of the Continental Congress against the British. In spring 1777, he joined Horatio Gates as an engineer, directing construction of fortifications that helped prevent Burgoyne from retreating at Saratoga and therefore contributed to the victory in those battles.

From Saratoga, Kosciuszko went to West Point, New York, to strengthen the fortifications there. In March 1780, he was named chief of the Continental army's engineering corps and served in the southern theater under Nathanael Greene.

The Revolution's other Polish freedom fighter was Casimir Pulaski, who had fought to free Poland from the domination of Russia and Prussia. A wanted man in Poland, he fled first to Saxony and then France, where he was living on a shoestring in December 1776, when he met Benjamin Franklin. Ever on the lookout for promising European military talent, Franklin persuaded Pulaski to join the American cause and wrote the usual letter of recommendation to Washington.

Pulaski was a stubborn man who was frequently hard to get along with, but he was a superb cavalry officer—and if the Continental army was deficient in experienced military engineers, it was even more destitute of cavalrymen. Pulaski created and trained the Pulaski Legion in 1778—the first significant cavalry unit the Americans possessed. In May 1779, he fought in the defense of Charleston, and on October 9, 1779, he was mortally wounded in a spectacularly gallant cavalry charge at the Battle of Savannah.

THE WORLD'S WAR

THE WORK OF A SMALL LEGION of European officers and the formal alliance with France made good on the claim of *Common Sense* and the Declaration of Independence—that the American Revolution was a revolution for the world. Emperor Louis XVI had his own political agenda, of course. He was not interested in American liberty, but in British defeat. Yet many who fought under the French flag—like those who came from German states or from Poland—took little interest in politics but had an overwhelming passion for the spirit of liberty. They did not risk—or even sacrifice—their lives to foil England or even to liberate America, but, rather, to free humankind by proving that a revolution against tyranny, a struggle to create a new kind of nation with a government of the people, was more than a philosophical proposition. It could become an accomplished fact and new epoch in world history.

TAKEAWAY

Washington Stumbles, Regroups

The loss of the Delaware forts was a blow to the Americans and, along with the defeats at Brandywine and Germantown, led some to lose confidence in Washington as a military leader. This crisis of confidence was compounded by the ordeal of the Valley Forge winter, which did, however, provide an opportunity for Steuben and other European volunteer officers to train the Continental army to standards approaching those of the best European forces.

Kosciuszko's countryman Casimir Pulaski was an exceptional cavalry officer and almost single-handedly organized and trained the Continental army's small cavalry contingent. On October 9, 1779, while leading a cavalry charge at the Battle of Savannah, Pulaski fell mortally wounded. He is depicted in this nineteenth-century engraving here as the dashing hero that he doubtless was.

Chapter 16

SPRING AND HOPE

The Franco-American Alliance and the Developing Skill of the Continental Army Give the Cause of Independence a Second Wind

THE FRENCH, TOGETHER WITH THE TRAINING provided by experienced foreign officers, were instrumental in the survival of the Continental army during the Valley Forge winter of 1777–78—instrumental not only in its physical survival, but in retaining the wholeness of morale. For an army is more than a group of armed men. It is a kind of organism that thrives on discipline, shared values, a fighting spirit, and hope. Thanks to the training, the Continental army emerged from Valley Forge a better fighting force. Thanks to the new alliance with France, it had hope that it could now present a more effective threat to the British and Hessian armies.

THE FRANCO-AMERICAN ALLIANCE: A MIXED BAG

AS WE SAW IN THE LAST CHAPTER, there was a faction in the Continental Congress that thought Ben Franklin and Silas Deane wielded too much power and that they were conceding too much of America's future to the French. France was a powerful nation now willing to help the United States achieve independence. So why look such a gift horse in the mouth?

The wary delegates to Congress had legitimate concerns. They understood that the American and French war aims were not identical. Whereas the Americans wanted to secure independence, the French wanted to defeat Britain. Well, suppose they did. What would happen next? Some feared that, having driven the British out of the thirteen colonies, France would move next to reestablish its own North American empire, which might well present a far greater threat to American liberty than the rule of King George III.

There could be no denying, though, that, even if Americans were not universally pleased with the alliance, its impact on the British was immediate and dramatic. In February 1778, a dispirited William Howe asked to be relieved as commander in chief of British forces in America. On March 7, Britain's secretary of state for the North American colonies, Lord Germain, chose Sir Henry Clinton to replace Howe. Clinton was less than thrilled with the assignment. Gone was the early arrogance of the British commanders, who spoke of simply crushing the rebellion. They now understood that the Americans were willing to do whatever it took, not so much to achieve decisive military victories, but to stay the course, to outlast the increasingly weary redcoats.

Clinton believed the situation to be bad. On March 21, when he received a new set of orders from Lord Germain, he had reason to believe that things were even worse than he had thought. The simple fact was this: The alliance between America and France shifted the focus of the war from the rebellious Americans to the French. Germain ordered Clinton to send five thousand men to the island of St. Lucia in the West Indies, and another three thousand to reinforce St. Augustine and Pensacola, Florida. These were places immediately threatened by the French fleet and the landings of French soldiers. Less eight thousand men, how were New York and Philadelphia to be held? Lord Germain had an answer. Those British troops still occupying Philadelphia were to be withdrawn to augment occupation forces in New York City.

If 1778 was a tough year for the Patriots, it was yet another bitterly disappointing year for Tory politicians in England. Why couldn't the Royal Navy and British army crush the colonial rebellion? This cartoon from 1778, entitled "An extraordinary, gazette, or the, disappointed politicians," depicts Tory politicians reading the latest dispatch ("gazette") from General Henry Clinton, perhaps reporting on the British evacuation of Philadelphia in June 1778. On the wall are maps of Britain's North American possessions: a large map on the left, showing the nation's colonial holdings in 1762, and a smaller map in the center, crawling with snakes and showing greatly contracted holdings in 1778. On the far right is a picture captioned "The mountain in labor," apparently giving birth to a mouse.

It is difficult to imagine Clinton's consternation. Philadelphia, the rebel capital, won at the cost of many casualties—won, indeed, at the cost of Burgoyne's entire army, stranded up north—was to be given back to those rebels, surrendered without a fight.

BATTLE AT MONMOUTH

TO ATTACK IS TO RISK MUCH, but to retreat is often to risk even more. An army is at its most vulnerable when it makes an exit. Before dawn on June 16, 1778, George Washington observed Clinton starting to move artillery out of the redoubts (strong points) around Philadelphia. Washington could only reasonably assume that Clinton was preparing for some operation. He speculated that it would be a sweep through New Jersey—long a thorn in the British side. Accordingly, Washington called a council of war on June 17. George Washington was never an impulsive commander, and while he never shrank from accepting responsibility for his decisions, he rarely made them without seeking the advice of his officer. In this case, he let Charles Lee persuade him to hold his troops in quarters at Valley Forge until there was a more certain indication of the enemy's intention.

As it turned out, Washington didn't have long to wait. Henry Clinton was no William Howe, and he moved with a speed that was quite astounding for any British commander. By June 18—just one day after Washington's council of war—he had marched ten thou-

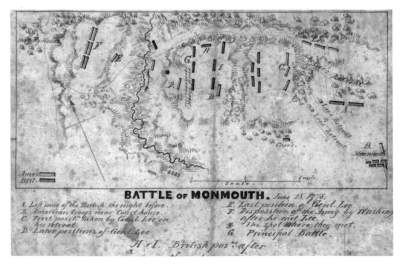

This manuscript map of the Battle of Monmouth Courthouse, June 28, 1778, presents the sequence of events by which Continental army general Charles Lee squandered an opportunity for victory by scattering his troops. Contrast the cohesiveness of the British deployment (the dark rectangles) with the dispersion of the Americans (the light rectangles).

sand regulars and three thousand local Tories out of Philadelphia and had set them marching toward Haddonfield, New Jersey. Washington roused his men, but fell to disputing with the prickly Lee over who should command the striking force aimed directly at Clinton's column. Washington believed that the eager and energetic Lafayette was the best man for the job, Lee, second only to Washington in seniority, demanded command. In an eighteenth-century army governed as much by gentlemanly propriety as by military necessity, Washington realized he had no choice but to bow to Lee.

Washington soon had reason to regret his capitulation to polite convention. On June 28, the advance guard of a New Jersey militia force found itself tangling with some of Clinton's best regiments. That it was in great peril and desperately needed assistance was obvious, yet Lee made no move. Stunned, Washington ordered him to attack at once. Lee acted, but bungled the attack, scattering his troops. Panicking as he watched his army being defeated in detail, Lee ordered a retreat—acting so hastily that one unit, under Mad Anthony Wayne, was left stranded and exposed. Fortunately, Wayne was as able as Lee was feeble, and acted quickly to extricate his men and himself.

Like Wayne, George Washington was at his best when on the verge of disaster. Washington galloped directly into the retreating mass of Charles Lee's army. Lafayette looked on and later admiringly described how the commander in chief unceremoniously relieved Lee of command, then immediately assumed command himself. Lafayette reported that Washington "stopped the retreat" by his mere presence, which broadcast "calm courage." This was the greatness of George Washington.

It is, however, one thing to avert disaster and another to convert disaster into triumph. Not even the courage of Washington could pull that off. Lee's bumbling had cost the Americans the initiative, the momentum of combat. The two sides proceeded to slog it out near Monmouth Court House, fighting in a midsummer heat that killed some thirty-seven Americans and sixty British, victims of sunstroke. There was neither victory nor defeat, just mutual exhaustion, as both the Americans and the British withdrew. The

One of the most famous names to emerge from the American Revolution never actually belonged to anyone. "Molly Pitcher" was a nickname bestowed on a woman who may have fought in the Revolution— or who may have been a fiction. Some historians believe that Molly was one Margaret Corbin or perhaps Mary Hayes McCauley (also known as Mary Ludwig Hays), who was, perhaps, the wife of William Hays, a Patriot artilleryman at the Battle of Monmouth. After Hays fell, Mary took his position at the cannon. Legend holds that, after the battle, Washington issued Mary a warrant as a noncommissioned officer. None of this explains the origin of the nickname, however, which some believe originated in what soldiers called women who carried pitchers of water to men on the battlefield to cool and swab the cannons. Molly Pitcher could also have been a composite of any number of women who volunteered to help on the battlefield.

REALITY CHECK
Monmouth Victory?

Most historians call the Battle of Monmouth Court House indecisive. Technically, however, the Americans could have claimed victory in that they held the field after the battle was over. Washington was too realistic to claim such a thing, however. He understood what his army—the army he had foolishly entrusted to Lee—had failed to do: destroy the enemy. The British withdrew, but they did so with their army intact. They had, in fact, accomplished what they set out to do: evacuate Philadelphia. Perhaps there was one respect in which Monmouth Court House might be judged a clear American victory. It resulted in the court martial of the incompetent, but all too highly placed, Charles Lee, who was removed from service.

indecisive encounter had cost 356 American casualties—killed, wounded, or missing—and 358 British killed or wounded. (Some historians believe that British losses were significantly higher.)

TESTING THE ALLIANCE

THE MERE FACT of the Franco-American alliance was sufficient to shake British high command, but the actual combat effectiveness of the alliance had yet to be tested. Washington was determined to make use of his French comrades at arms as soon as possible. After the disappointing Battle of Monmouth Court House, he gave chase to Clinton's withdrawing army, hoping to trap him. Since a trap requires a *pair* of jaws—not just one—Washington planned to close in on Clinton from the north as well as the south. For this purpose, he decided to launch a Franco-American amphibious operation in the north, so that Clinton would be caught between his enemies.

The French naval force was commanded by Admiral Charles Hector Théodot, comte d'Estaing. He was not highly regarded by the high command of the French navy, a fact that makes one wonder just how committed the French were to the alliance. Of course, giving a major assignment to a figure of dubious ability sometimes motivates surprisingly effective performance. But not this time.

To begin with, d'Estaing sailed from Toulon on April 13, 1778, and somehow stretched what should have been a month's crossing into eighty-seven days. He was, therefore, too late to carry out the mission he had been assigned: to bottle up the British fleet in the Chesapeake. Instead, d'Estaing decided to proceed directly to New York City to engage the British there. On the face of it, this was a good Plan B, but the French admiral had failed to gain intelligence about New York Bay. When he arrived on July 11, he discovered something called Sandy Hook bar, a natural obstruction across New York Bay. He suddenly feared that his great men o' war would draw too much water to clear the bar and would run aground. For the next eleven days, he loitered with his fleet off the bar, debating with himself whether or not he should try to cross.

The quandary unresolved, a Plan C emerged. On July 29, D'Estaing left New York Bay and sailed north, to Newport, Rhode Island, where he would land the four thousand troops he carried—doubtless, they were by now heartily sick of the sea and in poor condition for a fight—to engage in an ambitious joint operation with about ten thousand Americans under John Sullivan and his subordinate commanders, Nathanael Greene and Lafayette. This time, however, it was the Americans who failed to make good speed. By the time New England militia reinforcements made the rendezvous with Sullivan, Clinton had reinforced General Robert Pigot, who commanded the Newport defenses.

There was still ample opportunity for a successful attack, however, but, between them, Sullivan and d'Estaing managed to sacrifice that as well. To begin with, the two allied commanders had no faith in one another, and the bad blood between them tended to create further delays. By the time d'Estaing had landed and had begun disembarking his troops, a reinforced British fleet hove into view. The smart thing to do would have been to off-load the troops as quickly as possible, then sail out to confront the fleet. Instead, against Sullivan's anguished protests, d'Estaing reloaded those troops he had already landed and put out to sea to meet the enemy, ruining the land operation and uselessly risking his troops in a naval battle.

At least they would have been at risk had the battle actually been fought. A bad storm on the night of August 11 scattered both the British and French fleets, battering them beyond fitness for combat. Admiral Richard Howe was able to slip away to New York (he never worried about Sandy Hook bar), effect repairs, and then sail off to the West Indies, to which his fleet had been ordered. For his part, d'Estaing limped off to Boston to refit his storm-battered fleet. He carried with him four thousand French troops, idle and seasick, leaving General Sullivan stranded and unreinforced, facing the British—who had been reinforced.

Battle of Newport

Sullivan was saved by an African-American unit commanded by a white Rhode Island militia officer named Christopher Greene. His men fought so fiercely that Sullivan was able to disengage his outnumbered main force from Pigot and thereby save his army—albeit at a cost. The operation in Newport had been billed as an opportunity to deal a massive blow to the British—not as a chance to barely escape alive. After the battle, five thousand disgusted militiamen left the American service as soon as their enlistments had expired.

REALITY CHECK
When You're a Stranger . . .

Americans had more than political reservations about the French. Like England, America was overwhelmingly Protestant. There was little love in America for the French and their Catholicism. French culture, French language, and French religion—all seemed as alien to any American as they seemed to any Englishman.

ALTERNATE TAKE
Missing the Boat

Had Admiral d'Estaing arrived at Chesapeake Bay on time, he could have landed enough soldiers to cut Clinton off from the seaborne sources of supply and transport on which the British depended. This would have been a disastrous blow to Clinton and might of itself have prompted the commencement of treaty negotiations. But the opportunity was missed, and the plan to sever the British army from the Royal Navy was consigned to the dustbin of might-have-been.

VICTORY AT STONY POINT

NEITHER WASHINGTON NOR SULLIVAN could have been very happy with America's French allies after this initial foray, but their presence had ended any hope Clinton had of mounting a new invasion from Canada. By orders of London, much of his army had been sent to the West Indies, where the French posed a great threat. Clinton decided that the most effective use he could make of the forces left to him was to stage a limited offensive from New York City. On May 30, 1779, he moved about six thousand troops in seventy ships and 150 flat-bottom boats up the Hudson River. His plan

Jean Baptiste de Verger, a French officer serving in America, sketched these two American soldiers: a black trooper of the light infantry and a musketman. Free blacks were extensively recruited for service in the Continental army.

was to capture West Point, a fortress that commanded the lower Hudson. Seize this, Clinton reasoned, and he could cut off the ready flow of men and materiel to and from New England.

Clinton's troops easily captured Stony Point, on the west bank of the Hudson, about thirty-five miles north of New York City. At the same time, they secured Verplanck's Point, on the opposite bank, then set about fortifying both these positions.

Washington was determined to prevent the British from controlling the Hudson. He needed to get a spy into Stony Point to scout out the fortifications and look for weaknesses. The dangerous job fell to militia captain Allen McLane, who, on July 2, disguised himself as a local farmer and escorted a Mrs. Smith into the fortress to "see her sons," who were supposedly Tories serving with the British. The ruse worked, McLane got a good look, and he reported to Washington that the works were unfinished and vulnerable.

On July 15–16, Washington sent Mad Anthony Wayne with a force of 1,350 handpicked men to make a surprise attack. He proposed to do precisely what "No Flint" Grey had done to him at Paoli (see Chapter 13, "Massacre")—use bayonets exclusively so that the attack would be stealthy. Except for a single battalion, all muskets were left unloaded.

Wayne made his move at midnight. The British were surprised, all right, but they rallied sufficiently to open fire on the attackers with muskets as well as cannon. Wayne's troops did not pause to return a single shot, but, oblivious of the British fire, continued to advance, overrunning and capturing the fort in a fierce bayonet assault that killed 63 redcoats and wounded 70 more. Even more spectacularly, 543 were taken prisoner, and all artillery and equipment confiscated. Wayne lost 15 killed and 80 wounded.

Having driven the British out of Stony Point, which Washington once called the "key to the continent," he decided that he could not spare the men to hold it. He therefore ordered Wayne to dismantle the works and withdraw. Although Washington gained little strategic advantage through Wayne's daring feat, the Battle of Stony Point was a triumph of morale that was the precious fuel needed to keep the Revolution alive.

Another Lee

One of Wayne's subordinates at Stony Point was Major Henry "Light-Horse Harry" Lee, who drew inspiration from the exhilarating attack. He eagerly volunteered to lead a raid on Paulus Hook, a lonely (and therefore vulnerable) British outpost on the site of present-day Jersey City, New Jersey, just across the Hudson River from Manhattan.

Light-Horse Harry Lee was not related to the incompetent Charles Lee, but was, rather, one of the Lees of Virginia, the family that was to produce a half dozen significant American warriors, the most celebrated of whom would be Light-Horse Harry's son, the Civil War's Robert E. Lee. Henry Lee led a unit of light dragoons, lightly armed elite mounted infantry—infantry soldiers who increased their mobility by riding into battle, but who fought dismounted, as infantrymen. Another Stony Point alumnus, the intrepid Allen McLane, scouted Paulus Hook in advance of Light-Horse Harry's attack and estimated that the British garrison numbered no more than two hundred. The place was ripe for the plucking.

On August 18, 1779, McLane guided Lee with four hundred dragoons through the difficult and complicated approach to the fort. It had to be approached at low tide, because a moat protected the only route in or out, and at high tide, that moat was impassable.

REALITY CHECK
Win Some, Lose Some

Taking an objective only to relinquish it was typical of the fighting in the Revolution. Neither side had sufficient manpower to defend the prizes they claimed. Clinton did later reoccupy Stony Point, but, by the time he did, it had lost most of its strategic value.

NUMBERS
The Troops: Black Soldiers

Black soldiers fought on both sides during the American Revolution, but because the British actively recruited the slaves of Patriot masters, more blacks fought for the British than for the Americans. It is estimated that about ten thousand blacks fought for the British and five thousand for the Americans.

The plan was to attack at half past midnight on the nineteenth, when the opportunity for surprise would be at its highest and the tide at its lowest.

The plan was a good one, but leading four hundred armed men quietly through the night is not easy, and McLane made a few errors of navigation that put Lee behind schedule. By the time Lee had mustered all of his soldiers at the edge of a salt marsh just five hundred yards from the fort, he found that half of the Virginia contingent, about a hundred men, had been lost—or had deserted. That left him with three hundred men, whom Lee was determined to use. He ordered his men not to prime their muskets. And just in case they didn't get the point about ensuring silent stealth, he passed the word that any one who fired without orders would be shot. This would be a bayonets-only operation, just like Stony Point.

The Battle of Paulus Hook was over in less than thirty minutes. During that brief span, fifty British soldiers had been "put to the bayonet"—and 158 fell prisoner to Light-Horse and his men, who suffered just two killed and three wounded. Surprise was total—but it didn't last forever. Alarm guns roused the British on the New York side of the Hudson. Lee scooped up his prisoners and withdrew from Paulus Hook at top speed.

Henry "Light-Horse Harry" Lee, one of the heroes of Stony Point, was a brilliant and fearless officer of dragoons—troops who rode into battle, but fought dismounted, as infantrymen. He is shown, appropriately, on his horse, in a nineteenth-century colored engraving.

TARGET: SPRINGFIELD

THANKS TO PROFESSIONAL TRAINING by the likes of Steuben and the growing experience of his officers—and himself—Washington commanded a much-improved Continental army. Yet, good as it had become, it was small, and Washington rarely had the resources to conduct major campaigns. He had to content himself with conducting hit-and-run raids. The British warded off the blows as they came, but did not attempt anything like a major counterthrust until June 1780, when the Hessian commander, Baron Knyphausen—assigned temporary command of New York City while Clinton campaigned in the South (see Chapter 18)—decided that enough was enough.

Knyphausen had heard that the Continental army was on the verge of mutiny and that the civilian residents in and around

Springfield, New Jersey (in present-day Union County) were so dissatisfied with the course of the Revolution that they were prepared to rally to the Loyalist cause. The facts were that the seldom-paid, poorly fed, ill-clothed, and indifferently supplied Continental army always had reason to grumble, and some of that grumbling might well have sounded like the prelude to mutiny. As for the citizens of Springfield, New Jersey, Loyalists mingled with Patriots, and, depending on who was loudest at a given moment, it was easy to conclude that a change—one way or the other—was in the air. In any case, Knyphausen felt that he had enough information to make his move, and, on June 7, 1780, with six thousand men, he crossed from Staten Island to Elizabethtown (present-day Elizabeth, New Jersey), then marched to the small village of Connecticut Farms (present-day Union, about two and a half miles southeast of Springfield). His purpose was to raise local support for an attack on Washington's encampment at Morristown.

Support was not what he met with at Connecticut Farms. The New Jersey militia fired on him and was soon reinforced by Continental troops. Doubtless more than a little put out, Knyphausen made an impromptu reprisal on the locals by burning a church and some other buildings—killing in the process the wife of Reverend James Caldwell; this was apparently collateral damage: an accident. His spleen vented, Knyphausen beat a retreat to Elizabethtown, where he regrouped.

On June 23, having caught his breath, Knyphausen launched a new raid, this time against Springfield itself. Nathanael Greene had no more than a thousand troops with which to oppose Knyphausen's six thousand. The Hessians easily took Springfield, but then—astoundingly—were fought to a standstill. Knyphausen responded to the resistance as he had at Connecticut Farms, only on a larger scale. He put to the torch all but four of Springfield's fifty houses before marching back to Staten Island.

If, by burning down Springfield, Knyphausen had thought to sap the will to fight from the New Jersey locals, he was badly mistaken. His terrorism galvanized the populace into renewed opposition to the British and Hessian invaders, who were completely swept from the state.

DETAILS, DETAILS
Light-Horse Rides Free

Congress gave Lee a gold medal for the raid on Paulus Hook, but some of Lee's own officers, consumed with envy, demanded the court-martial of their commander, charging that he had committed any number of blunders, including arrogantly asserting his precedence over senior officers. The trial vindicated Light-Horse Harry, who found himself on the receiving end of even more plaudits—both from the public and from George Washington.

TAKEAWAY

Alliance: Off to a Rocky Start

The entry of France into the American Revolution forced the British to divert many of their resources to the Caribbean (West Indies), which was a great boon to the Patriot cause; however, the early Franco-American military operations in the United States were disappointing failures.

PEACE OVERTURE

WITH THE FRENCH IN THE FIGHT—and, as the British saw it, creating the greatest threat in the West Indies, where the sugar and slave trade meant big profits—King George III gave serious thought to negotiating an end to the quarrel with his colonies. Early in the spring of 1778, he appointed Frederick Howard, 5th Earl of Carlisle, to chair a new peace commission, authorized to deal directly with the Continental Congress and even, if necessary, to suspend any act of Parliament passed since 1763.

In politics and diplomacy, timing is of the essence, and the Crown chose a most inopportune moment to authorize the Carlisle Commission. With the British trundling out of Philadelphia, Congress saw no need to negotiate anything short of total British withdrawal and the Crown's recognition of colonial independence. On April 22, therefore, the Continental Congress defiantly resolved that any individual or group that pretended to come to terms with the Crown's new peace commission was to be deemed an enemy of the United States.

Undaunted, the commission took a new tack, offering bribes to various congressional delegates. None, however, was even tempted to such corruption, and the bribery scheme succeeded in tainting the peace feelers by making the Crown appear both underhanded and desperate. The commissioners announced a new offer, including blanket amnesty and an agreement that the colonies would be given an unprecedented measure of independence and autonomy. Carlisle also tried to chip away at the Franco-American alliance by suggesting that France would soon turn on the Americans. No less a figure than Lafayette challenged Carlisle to a duel for thus defaming the honor of his country. Carlisle never responded to the challenge.

Finally, on November 27, 1778, the Carlisle Commission stopped trying. Clearly, the Americans had invested too much in the idea of independence to accept less now. They were determined that the war would be fought to its necessary end: the triumph of independence, absolute and without condition.

In the spring of 1778, George III authorized a commission to attempt to negotiate terms of peace with the Continental Congress. Led by the Earl of Carlisle, the "Carlisle Commission" was viewed with contempt by Congress—and as this cartoon, published in London on April 1, 1778, suggests, by many in England as well. Nothing came of this feeble peace feeler.

Chapter 17

FIRES IN THE WILDERNESS

The Story of the Least Understood Yet Perhaps Most Important Theater of the American Revolution: The Frontier of New York and Pennsylvania

THE AMERICAN REVOLUTION was a long war, spanning eight years from 1775 to 1783, yet whereas the four-year-long American Civil War (1861–65) consisted of 76 great battles (plus 310 "minor" ones, 6,337 skirmishes, and about 3,200 sieges and raids), the truly major battles of the Revolution were but few: Lexington and Concord, Bunker Hill, Ticonderoga, the Boston Siege, Valcour Island, Brandywine, Germantown, Long Island, Trenton, Princeton, Oriskany, Saratoga (Freeman's Farm and Bemis Heights), Monmouth Court House, Charleston, Cowpens, Camden, and Yorktown. A few of these contests lasted a day or more, but most were over within hours.

Was the rest of the war a time of peace? Hardly.

Most of the American Revolution was not fought in what military historians call "set battles," contests between formally formed armies or parts of armies, but was an extension of the general frontier violence between whites and Indians, which had begun in the New World virtually as soon as Columbus made contact with the native peoples. That is, most of the American Revolution was a frontier war in which both sides employed Indian allies

During the French and Indian War, Sir William Johnson forged a key alliance between the English and the Mohawks, even unofficially adopting Joseph Brant, who became the most important Loyalist Native American leader in the American Revolution. This engraving was created in 1756, in the aftermath of the French and Indian War.

in an effort to prevail, and in which the Indians sought to use the conflict between the white men to stave off the ongoing invasion of their lands. What took place in this frontier war was not a series of formal battles, but an ongoing round of raids and counterraids. It was, really, murder rather than war.

TAKING SIDES

AFTER THE FRENCH AND INDIAN WAR, in which the French had many more Indian allies than the British did, the Crown set up an Indian Department to try to create better relations with the Indians. In 1775, almost immediately after the first shots of the American Revolution were fired, the Continental Congress imitated the British example by creating an Indian Department of its own. However, the Americans were at a disadvantage. Many Indian leaders decided to try to remain neutral in the war between the whites, but many others decided that they had a stake in a British victory. The Crown, they reasoned, had authority to limit the spread of white settlement. Get rid of the king, and the Americans would run wild, rushing across the mountains and into the Indian homeland. Accordingly, some of the most thoughtful and influential Indian leaders urged alliances with the British.

The single most important Anglo-Indian alliance was forged well before the outbreak of the Revolution, between William Johnson and Thayendanegea, a Mohawk known to the English as Joseph Brant. Johnson had emigrated from Ireland when he was fifteen and settled in the Mohawk Valley northwest of Albany. He established a close commercial and personal relationship with the Mohawks, and when his first wife died, he married Degonwadonti—whose English name was Molly Brant—the daughter of his friend Nichus Brant and Nichus's Indian wife, Owandah. Molly, a quarter century Johnson's junior, had a younger brother: Joseph Brant. Johnson informally adopted him, and he had ample reason to be proud of his "son." Joseph Brant fought on the side of the British during the French and Indian War, acquitting himself with such skill and courage that he rose in prestige among Mohawks and colonists alike. After Johnson died in 1774, Brant continued a friendship with Johnson's son Guy. It was this relationship that would serve as the nucleus of an important Anglo-Indian alliance through the early phases of the Revolution.

The Mohawks were good allies to have. They had a reputation as fierce warriors and were the most important of the six tribes of the powerful and numerous Iroquois Confederacy. Mohawk leaders managed to talk three other Iroquois tribes, the Senecas, Cayugas, and Onondagas, into siding with the British.

Indeed, the Revolution split the Iroquois Confederacy, since the Oneidas and the Tuscaroras sided with the Americans. Much as the Mohawk-English alliance was the product of a personal relationship, so the Oneida-American alliance was largely the work of Samuel Kirkland, a teacher and Presbyterian minister who worked among the tribe and had earned the friendship of tribal leaders. The Oneidas brought along members of the Mahicans—also called the Stockbridges—who had once been numerous and powerful, but were now greatly diminished by ruinous warfare with the Mohawks. Another individual, James Dean, an agent for the Continental Congress's Indian Department, rallied the Tuscaroras to the American cause. These alliances were valuable, but they hardly offset the more numerous and powerful Indian alliances the British had made.

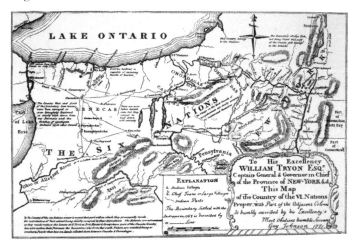

William Johnson's son Guy drew this map of the territory of the six Iroquois nations in 1771. The Iroquois, especially the Mohawks, often fought alongside the British and Loyalists during the American Revolution.

Panic on the Frontier

Throughout the Revolution, Indian warriors sometimes acted in concert with white troops and officers, and sometimes they acted on their own—albeit with encouragement from their white allies.

REALITY CHECK
A Means of Terror

Both the Americans and the British—but especially the British—deliberately used Indian allies as instruments of terror. For instance, William Tryon, the Tory governor of New York, urged British military commanders to "loose the savages against the miserable Rebels in order to impose a reign of terror on the frontiers." In London, Prime Minister Lord Chatham repudiated such action as "unconstitutional, inhuman, and unchristian," but he took no steps to curb the routine practice of terror.

By September 1776, the frontier of Virginia, Pennsylvania, and New York had been driven to panic by chronic Indian raiding. The raids became so common that, in New York's Mohawk Valley, many Tories, who had been forced out of their homes and lands by Patriots, disguised themselves as Indians in order to raid the usurping settlers.

Massacre in the Valleys

As 1777 drew to a close, a predictable and lethal pattern of raid and reprisal reigned throughout the New York and Pennsylvania frontier, especially in the Cherry, Mohawk, and Wyoming valleys. Against this background, in April 1778, Loyalists accumulated a substantial force of Tories and Indians along the upper Susquehanna. Their object was to break the raid-and-reprisal cycle by launching a decisive action. At the Indian town of Tioga, Pennsylvania, the Tory colonel John Butler gathered four hundred Tory Rangers and militiamen along with nine hundred Senecas and Cayugas. Most Indian raids were hit-and-run affairs involving relatively small numbers. This action, however, would be massive.

The objective was the Wyoming Valley of northern Pennsylvania. Butler and some of his Indian allies started building boats for the trip down the Susquehanna while the Seneca chief Gucinge led four hundred warriors to make initial assaults on settlements along the river's west branch. While this was going on, Joseph Brant mustered 450 Indians and Tories for an attack on New York's Cherry Valley, which was at the headwaters of the Susquehanna.

Although Cherry Valley had been a target of raids since 1776, the settlers there did remarkably little to defend themselves. Colonel Samuel Campbell took the desperate action of padding his small militia by dressing twenty-six boys in pointy hats made of paper and giving them wooden rifles to brandish. Strangely enough, this was sufficient to deceive Brant—albeit briefly—and send him to attack nearby Cobleskill instead of Cherry Valley. Cobleskill consisted of twenty houses, defended by Captain Christian Brown's twenty militiamen augmented by thirty-seven Continental soldiers from Colonel Ichabod Alden's 7th Massachusetts Regiment. They were overwhelmed by Brant's 450 men. Thirty-one Americans were killed and six wounded. The village was razed.

The Wyoming Valley had what appeared to be a more formidable system of defense—so-called forts, which were actually nothing more than somewhat fortified houses. These included Wintermoot's (or Wintermot's), Forty Fort, Jenkins' Fort, Wilkes-Barre Fort, and Pittston Fort. Most of them fell quickly. The troops at Wintermoot's were Tory sympathizers and gave up without firing a shot. Jenkins' Fort fell on July 2. Forty Fort, however, was garrisoned by 450 Continental troops and militiamen under Continental colonel Zebulon Butler (no relation to John Butler) and militia colonel Nathan Denison. When they refused to surrender, John Butler burned down Wintermoot's Fort on July 3 to make the commanders of Forty Fort believe they had withdrawn. Denison and his militiamen swallowed the bait and decided to pursue John Butler's retreating forces. The more experienced Zebulon Butler protested that he smelled a trap, but Denison prevailed, taking the entire 450-man garrison out of Forty Fort, and was immediately enveloped in an ambush. Three hundred Americans were killed or wounded.

With Forty Fort destroyed, the Wyoming Valley was defenseless. John Butler burned it to the ground even as Joseph Brant finally resolved to end the reprieve of the Cherry Valley. On July 18, he raided Andrustown, seven miles west of Cherry Valley, capturing fourteen settlers, killing eleven, then burning the town. After staging more raids in the region, he attacked the Mohawk River settlement of German Flats (present-day Herkimer) on September 12. The town was largely deserted—its residents having fled to nearby forts—but this didn't stop Brant from burning the empty buildings.

Devastating though these raids were, they did not have the decisive effect Butler and Brant had hoped for. In fact, they galvanized local Patriot militias to retaliate against Indian villages. No one was spared: old men, women, and children were killed, and their villages razed. Seeing the devastation visited on his people, Brant returned to Cherry Valley in November 1778. By this time 250 Continental soldiers of the 7th Massachusetts Regiment under Lieutenant Colonel Ichabod Alden had been sent to defend the valley.

During 1777 and 1778, the backcountry of New York and Pennsylvania was swept by raids and reprisals involving Indians allied either with the Americans or the British. On November 11, 1778, eight hundred Tories and Indians raided and obliterated Cherry Valley, New York. This 1856 engraving by Alonzo Chappel depicts a young patriot woman, Jane Wells, pleading for mercy during the massacre.

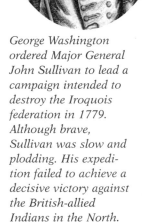

George Washington ordered Major General John Sullivan to lead a campaign intended to destroy the Iroquois federation in 1779. Although brave, Sullivan was slow and plodding. His expedition failed to achieve a decisive victory against the British-allied Indians in the North.

They were overwhelmed on November 11 by eight hundred Tories and Indians, who not only killed the defenders, but scalped, mutilated, and even cannibalized them. By two that afternoon, Cherry Valley had been essentially wiped from the earth.

THE SULLIVAN EXPEDITION

GENERAL WASHINGTON usually let the far frontier take care of itself, but this was too much. He did not merely send a force to try to salvage Cherry Valley, he authorized a campaign of extermination, an expedition intended to destroy the Iroquois Confederacy. Although Washington authorized the campaign at the start of 1779, it was June 18 before General John Sullivan—competent but cautious to a fault—marched his twenty-five hundred Continentals from Easton, Pennsylvania, to the Susquehanna. While Sullivan planned to burn a swath through the Susquehanna Valley, moving up to the southern border of New York, General James Clinton, with fifteen hundred soldiers, was to advance through the Mohawk Valley to Lake Otsego, then travel down the Susquehanna. In coordination with these two movements, Colonel Daniel Brodhead would lead six hundred men from Fort Pitt up the Allegheny. They would all destroy every Iroquois and every Iroquois village they could find. Sullivan and Clinton then planned to rendezvous at Tioga and, together, march north to Niagara, meeting Brodhead at Genesee. United, they would continue their sweep of absolute destruction.

Impatient with Sullivan, Clinton launched a six-day raid from his base of operations at Canajoharie on the Mohawk River beginning on April 21. It was a destructive raid: twelve Onondagas were killed and thirty-four captured; fifty houses were destroyed. Sullivan's column had yet to make its rendezvous with Clinton before Joseph Brant attacked Minisink in the Mohawk Valley. The town was destroyed and, of 170 Patriot militiamen, at least 140 were killed.

General Sullivan's campaign against the Iroquois killed and captured very few Indians, but it did prove highly destructive against abandoned Iroquois settlements. The Indians' crops and food reserves were badly depleted. This engraving is from 1778.

At last, on August 9, Sullivan reached Newtychanning. It had been an important Seneca village, but was now deserted. Nevertheless, Sullivan ordered its twenty-eight buildings burned. Arriving next at Tioga and making his rendezvous with Clinton, he posted General Orders, which called for the total destruction of the Indians. And that is just what Sullivan tried to do. During all of August and September 1779, his men laid waste the Indian settlements throughout the region. Yet few Indians were present in those villages. They were still campaigning and raiding. Doubtless, the destruction of the villages was devastating, but it was not decisive. The warrior enemy remained at large.

Eyewitness

"I flatter myself that the orders with which I was entrusted are fully executed, as we have not left a single settlement or field of corn in the country of the [Iroquois], nor is there even the appearance of an Indian on this side of the Niagara," Sullivan wrote to the Continental Congress in September 1779. But as Continental army major Jeremiah Fogg observed in his journal on September 30: "The question will naturally arise, what have you to show for your exploits? Where are your prisoners? To which I reply that the rags and emaciated bodies of our soldiers must speak for our fatigue; and when the querist will point out a mode to tame a partridge, or the expedience of hunting wild turkey with light horse, I will show them our prisoners. The nests are destroyed, but the birds are still on the wing."

COMBAT IN THE OLD NORTHWEST

NEW YORK AND PENNSYLVANIA were America's "near" frontier in the late eighteenth century. The "Old Northwest"—the region north of the Ohio River and east of the Mississippi—and Kentucky constituted the "far" frontier. Its distance from the centers of American civilization did not give this country immunity from the war.

On or about July 2, 1775, the leaders of the five Shawnee septs (bands) met at Chillicothe on the Little Miami River, in what is today the state of Ohio, to talk about how they should respond to a white invasion of Kentucky. One of the main Shawnee leaders,

REALITY CHECK
A Headquarters Destroyed

As destructive as Clinton's raid was, the most devastating blow was the destruction of one building in particular: the Iroquois longhouse, the headquarters in which representatives of the Iroquois Confederacy traditionally met. For the Iroquois, the longhouse was as much a symbolic presence as a physical building. It embodied the great Iroquois Confederacy, which was pictured as a "longhouse" stretching across what is now upper New York State. The worst aspect of its burning was that American-allied Oneidas—an Iroquois tribe—helped set the fire. Whatever else the American Revolution did, it undermined the integrity of this most powerful Native American political alliance.

Chief Cornstalk, advocated neutrality in the ongoing fight among the whites. Despite Cornstalk's counsel, Shawnees raided the new Kentucky settlements during the fall of 1775. Despite this, the whites kept coming, and in June 1776, the frontier commander George Rogers Clark traveled to Williamsburg to ask Virginia authorities (Virginia had jurisdiction over frontier Kentucky) to send troops to help resist the Indian raids.

While Clark was on his errand to the Virginia capital, Pluck-kemeh-notee, a Shawnee subchief known to the whites as Pluggy, made new and more devastating raids in Kentucky. En route to attack Harrodsburg, Pluggy was killed, his death moving Chief Black Fish to rally two hundred warriors in a major sweep intended to kill every white settler in Kentucky. On or about July 4, 1776, at a new council among the Shawnees, Iroquois, Delawares, Ottawas, Cherokees, Wyandots, and Mingos, Cornstalk suddenly abandoned his neutral stance and vowed to aid the British.

"It is better for the red men to die like warriors than to diminish away by inches. Now is the time to begin. If we fight like men, we may hope to enlarge our bounds."

Chief Cornstalk, July 1776

In the meantime, by the end of January 1777, Black Fish had driven most whites out of Kentucky. On April 24, he attacked Boonesboro, laying it under a four-day siege in which one settler was killed and seven wounded, including Daniel Boone, who had founded the settlement. Boonesboro held out, and Black Fish withdrew, returning periodically to jab at other settlements. However, by this time, Clark had secured a Virginia commission to raise a Kentucky militia. He planned to lead his new command against the British outposts at Kaskaskia, Cahokia, and Vincennes (in modern Illinois and Indiana). Then he would capture the most important British fort in the Old Northwest: Detroit. Untutored in the military art, Clark was nevertheless a natural strategist. He was aware that the British outposts he had targeted were far from Kentucky, yet he also understood that they were the means by which the

British supplied and armed the Indians who raided Kentucky. Destroy these forts, and the raids would stop.

Before Clark could get under way, however, Shawnee warriors, together with Wyandots, Mingos, and Cherokees, raided the area of Wheeling (in present-day West Virginia) during midsummer 1777. This prompted the Continental Congress to send General Edward Hand to recruit Pennsylvanians, Virginians, and Kentuckians for an assault on a British Indian supply depot on the Cuyahoga River, near present-day Cleveland. Unwisely, Chief Cornstalk, under a flag of truce, entered Fort Randolph (at the confluence of the Ohio and the Kanawha rivers) to deliver a warning: if Hand attacked, all the Shawnee and allied nations would retaliate. The commandant of the fort, Captain Matthew Arbuckle, ignored the warning as well as the white flag, and took Cornstalk, his son Silverheels, and another warrior prisoner. His intention was to hold them hostage to ensure the good behavior of the Shawnees; however, on November 10, 1777, a party of local white hunters, having heard that the chief was being held under light guard, broke into the fort and killed the Indians, afterward mutilating their bodies. Predictably, the Shawnees retaliated, overwhelming Hand's efforts to contain them.

Enter Daniel Boone

On February 8, 1778, during the Shawnees' campaign of vengeance, Chief Blue Jacket, with 102 warriors, captured a twenty-seven-man salt-making party at Blue Licks, Kentucky. Among the captives was Daniel Boone (see Chapter 3, "Pop Culture: American Frontiersman"). He had been born in 1734 of a lapsed Quaker in southern Pennsylvania and moved with his family to Yadkin County, North Carolina, when he was nineteen. While serving in the French and Indian War, he heard about Kentucky, a paradise (it was said) rich in game, and when the war was over, he left his Yadkin home to wander there, hunting for months, sometimes years, at a stretch. He then led settlers into the land and founded Boonesboro. When Blue Jacket captured him, the wily frontiersman pretended to turn traitor, accepted adoption into the Shawnee tribe, and offered to cooperate with one Henry Hamilton, the Crown's ruthlessly efficient liaison with the Indians. Because he paid bounties for American scalps, the Indians called Hamilton "Hair Buyer."

By pretending his cooperation, Boone managed to delay a British attack on American-held Fort Pitt (at the location of present-day Pittsburgh) and also secured intelligence about the ongoing assault on Boonesboro. Once he felt that he had heard enough, Boone made his escape, arriving at Boonesboro in time to lead the resistance there and to alert Fort Pitt. Boone's wit and courage helped save the far frontier for the American cause.

Daniel Boone

After the Revolution, Boone's fame developed in a manner that would become standard for many a legend of the American frontier. His exploits made him a celebrity. He was portrayed as a hero in the popular literature read primarily by easterners.

JAMES FENIMORE COOPER even used him as the model for Natty Bumppo (a/k/a Hawkeye, Deerslayer, Pathfinder) in his celebrated "Leatherstocking" novels (*The Last of the Mohicans,* etc.). His "press agent" was a Pennsylvania schoolteacher turned land promoter named John Filson, who traveled to Kentucky in 1782 and wrote *The Discovery, Settlement, and Present State of Kentucke,* which included a section subtitled "The Adventures of Col. Daniel Boone," a purported autobiography. However, by the time Filson's book was published, Boone had suffered one calamity after another. His passion for probing the frontier, pushing settlement ever westward, partook deeply of the "American dream," yet the fruits of that dream consistently eluded him. Swindled out of what should have been enormous profits on frontier real estate, Boone in 1799 followed his son to present-day Missouri, which was then foreign soil. He laid claim to 850 acres (but title to even that modest tract was invalidated with the Louisiana Purchase of 1803). His son Israel died in an Indian ambush during the last major frontier conflict of the Revolution. In 1780, Boone headed for Virginia with $50,000—most of it belonging to his friends—to buy the land warrants necessary to preempt eastern speculators from gobbling up Kentucky; the money was stolen along the way. It was all too typical of Boone's later years. Although he had become a successful surveyor, trader, and landowner, Daniel Boone lost everything through his own carelessness and the legal chicanery of land speculators. In the 1790s, he packed up his belongings and his family and moved to Missouri, where he died, a poor man, little noticed, in 1820.

Even in his own lifetime, Daniel Boone was a celebrated frontiersman. He saw service in the French and Indian War as well as in the American Revolution.

CLARK GETS MOVING

DURING MUCH OF 1778, the Shawnee chief Black Fish led Shawnees as well as Wyandots, Mingos, Delawares, Miamis, and Kickapoos in raids throughout the far frontier. Against this violent background, George Rogers Clark struggled to recruit an army. By the end of May 1778, he had no more than 175 men to lead against Kaskaskia and Cahokia, the first phase in his planned assault on British-held Detroit. He embarked with this small force on June 26, 1778, in flatboats, reaching the mouth of the Tennessee River in four days. He made a stealthy attack on Kaskaskia, which he took without firing a shot. Establishing his base of operations here, he advanced to Cahokia, which also surrendered peacefully.

His next objective, the fort at Vincennes, he knew would not fall so easily. After all, the "Hair Buyer" was based there and commanded forces far larger than the small band Clark had been able to muster. The only chance, Clark decided, was to make up in speed what he lacked in numbers. Therefore, on February 5, 1779, he commenced the 150-mile march to Vincennes through a hostile wilderness and in the depths of winter. Reaching the little village on February 23, he quietly took a few prisoners, who revealed that the British fort, Fort Sackville, was defended by only a few hundred men. The odds were better than Clark had thought, but he nevertheless understood that a "few hundred" was still more than 150. If he laid siege to Fort Sackville, the Hair Buyer would simply await British reinforcements. Without a better option, he resorted to pure bluff.

Clark sent one of his prisoners back into the village of Vincennes with a letter that proclaimed his intention to capture the place. The letter warned those loyal to the king to take refuge in the fort, because he intended to give them no quarter. To make things official—and to give the impression of great numbers—Clark signed the letter with the names of many officers, none of whom were present, of course. Then, as the townsfolk digested the letter and doubtless shared it with the Hair Buyer, Clark equipped some men with sticks on which were tied cloths painted to look like regimental banners. The idea was to suggest a multiplicity of forces.

Satisfied that he had made an impression, Clark attacked—and, almost instantly, the Indians deserted the British. Even more, a group of Kickapoo and Piankashaw Indians came forward to volunteer their

George Rogers Clark was the leading Patriot commander on the frontier. This nineteenth-century engraving shows him leading his men in a 150-mile march to seize Vincennes (in present-day Indiana), a British-held outpost on the far frontier.

services to Clark. With his Indian allies gone, the Hair Buyer surrendered Vincennes and Fort Sackville.

No Respite

Clark had hoped that taking the forts of the Old Northwest would bring an end to the raids. Indeed, some Indians sought peace—but many continued to fight, and raiding became so widespread in 1780 that Clark had to abandon his plan to attack Detroit in order to take direct action against the local Shawnees and Tories. Much of the raiding was led by the relentless Joseph Brant.

THE NEAR FRONTIER: LATE PHASE

CLARK FOUGHT BRILLIANTLY in the far frontier, but even he could not bring an end to the Indian wars there. Leading a much larger army than Clark, General Sullivan made even less headway against the Indians of northwestern New York. If anything, his campaign of destruction had served only to enflame the diehards, and on May 21, 1780, the Tory leader Sir John Johnson led a massive mixed Indian-Loyalist raid on the Patriot forts of the Mohawk Valley. His four hundred Tories and two hundred Indians burned Johnstown, New York, on May 23. Later, during the summer, Brant razed Caughnawaga and Canajoharie, then moved along the Ohio into Pennsylvania, intercepting a one-hundred-man Pennsylvania militia force under Archibald Lochry. Five officers and thirty-five enlisted troops were killed; the rest became prisoners.

This victory achieved, Brant and his men returned to New York, linked up with Johnson's Tories and a Seneca chief named Cornplanter, and—now eighteen hundred strong—swooped down upon the Scoharie Valley on October 15, then marched up the Mohawk, putting to the torch all that they found. In just five days, Johnson and Brant had destroyed as much as Sullivan had in a month of marching. Wounded while raiding with Johnson, Brant did not return to action until early 1781, however, when he hit the

DETAILS, DETAILS

Treaty of Greenville

Warfare in the Old Northwest did not end with the Treaty of Paris that ended the Revolution in 1783. It was not until 1795, when Mad Anthony Wayne prevailed against Blue Jacket, Tecumseh, and Little Turtle in the conflict known as Little Turtle's War, that relative peace came to the region. His victory at the Battle of Fallen Timbers (August 20, 1795) occasioned the Treaty of Greenville, by which the Indians ceded the disputed territory. War with the Indians did not resume until the outbreak of the War of 1812.

Mohawk and Cherry valleys. Washington had scant forces with which to oppose him. He sent Colonel Marianus Willett with 130 Continental troops and a handful of militiamen to do the best they could and, thanks to Willett's skill, the raids were suppressed for the rest of the summer. When they resumed in October, Willett responded vigorously and was fortunate enough to kill Walter Butler, the most important Tory leader in the region. This had the effect of dispersing the raiders.

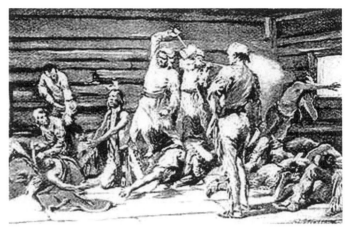

Gnadenhutten, in present-day Ohio, was the scene of a horrific atrocity of war in which Patriot forces captured, bound, and killed nearly ninety friendly Native Americans in misguided reprisal for raids carried out by hostile Mohawks and Delawares.

Massacre at Gnadenhutten

Joseph Brant stepped in to fill the leadership vacuum. He met with Chief Abraham, leader of the so-called Moravian Indians, Delawares who had been christianized by Moravian missionaries. Try as he might, Brant was unable to recruit the Moravian Indians to fight the Americans, whereupon British authorities ordered their removal from Pennsylvania westward to the Ohio country. Obediently, they set out for the banks of the Sandusky River, but their trek was interrupted early in 1782 by a terrible winter famine. They secured permission to move back temporarily to their western Pennsylvania mission towns on the Tuscarawas River.

They arrived at precisely the wrong time. Mohawks and Delawares had just finished an especially horrific series of raids, and Colonel Brodhead, who now commanded the Continental army in the area, sent Colonel David Williamson with a contingent of men to conduct reprisals. Williamson encountered Abraham and his Moravian Indians at the mission town of Gnadenhutten (in present-day Ohio). He told Abraham and the forty-eight men, women, and boys who were with him that they were to follow him to Fort Pitt, where they would find shelter and protection from all harm. Williamson asked Abraham to send runners to Salem, a nearby missionary-Indian town, and bring the Indians from there to Gnadenhutten. All would be taken to the safety of Fort Pitt.

It was a cruel deception. As soon as the Salem Indians arrived, Williamson sent his troops to bind the wrists of every Indian. There were now about ninety in all. They were allowed to pass the night thus bound, and, in the morning, Williamson announced that, as punishment for the Delaware raids, they would all be put to death. At the end of the day, each was struck with a single mallet blow to the back of the head. Somehow, two boys evaded death and lived to tell the tale.

The American authorities condemned the Gnadenhutten massacre, but Williamson was not punished. Predictably, the atrocity unleashed a massive Indian retaliation, all the way into Kentucky, very nearly forcing the abandonment of the Kentucky frontier until, in November 1782, George Rogers Clark had cobbled together a large enough militia force to intervene.

No End to It

Clark chased the raiders away and burned the Shawnee "capital" of Chillicothe (in modern Ohio) along with many other Shawnee towns. Worst of all, he destroyed perhaps ten thousand bushels of corn—the ration on which the Indians relied to survive the winter. This, rather than a direct military victory, brought a long pause in the raiding.

In the preliminary articles of peace the United States and Britain signed on November 30, 1782, the Crown agreed to cede the Old Northwest to the new nation. This did not end Indian-white warfare in the area, but it did bring a temporary peace in a theater of war without such famous names as Saratoga or Yorktown, but where the fighting was longer, harder, and crueler than anywhere else in the struggle for independence.

Chapter 18

GONE SOUTH

*The British Strategy in the South and
Why It Almost Crushed the Revolution*

WHEN THE BRITISH WERE BEATEN in Boston early in the war, the top command decided that it had been a mistake to attack the rebellion where it was the strongest. The decision was made to identify the places where support for the Revolution was soft and stage offensives there.

LOOKING FOR LOYALISTS

ONE OF THE REGIONS IN WHICH REVOLUTIONARY SENTIMENT was perceived as weakest was the deep South. In fact, the lower South had the second greatest concentration of Loyalists, just behind New York. This region stood in stark contrast to the upper South—that is, Virginia—and New England, which, together, harbored the fewest Loyalists. Many historians explain this by pointing out that New England and Virginia were the oldest of the English colonies and therefore had evolved a high degree of self-government. In short, they had more time to drift further from the Crown. The lower South also had a numerous and powerful class of wealthy merchants and large landowners, all people who tended to resist change. This was in contrast to tradespeople, small farmers, seamen, fishing folk, and frontier settlers, whose chronically precarious economic and social status made them eager to embrace change and, therefore, to favor the

NUMBERS

Patriots versus Loyalists

Pro-Revolution Patriots who honestly surveyed the situation concluded that about one-third of the American population was Loyalist. The Loyalists themselves saw this fraction as greater; they believed that more than half of the country still remained loyal to the king. Since no one took a formal poll, the only measure that approaches an objective estimate is the number of people who decided to leave America during and after the Revolution. Eighty thousand left for Canada or England—one of every thirty white American families.

Perhaps as many as one in three Americans was a Loyalist during the Revolution. In some places, Loyalists outnumbered Patriots and were actively recruited for service in Loyalist militia regiments. This broadside dates from 1777.

Firſt Battalion of PENNSYLVANIA LOYALISTS, commanded by His Excellency Sir WILLIAM HOWE, K. B.

ALL INTREPID ABLE-BODIED

HEROES,

WHO are willing to ſerve His MAJESTY KING GEORGE the Third, in Defence of their Country, Laws and Conſtitution, againſt the arbitrary Uſurpations of a tyrannical Congreſs, have now not only an Opportunity of manifeſting their Spirit, by aſſiſting in reducing to Obedience their too-long deluded Countrymen, but alſo of acquiring the polite Accompliſhments of a Soldier, by ſerving only two Years, or during the preſent Rebellion in America.

Such ſpirited Fellows, who are willing to engage, will be rewarded at the End of the War, beſides their Laurels, with 50 Acres of Land, where every gallant Hero may retire. . . . . Each Volunteer will receive, as a Bounty, FIVE DOLLARS, beſides Arms, Cloathing and Accoutrements, and every other Requiſite proper to accommodate a Gentleman Soldier, by applying to Lieutenant Colonel ALLEN, or at Captain KEARNY's Rendezvous, at PATRICK TONRY's, three Doors above Market-ſtreet, in Second-ſtreet.

Revolution. It was precisely these classes of people who most thickly populated New England.

But now we must pause. For in Virginia, a hotbed of revolution, there were a great many well-established large planters, including George Washington himself. Moreover, while tradespeople and small farmers did abound in New England, many of the most radical revolutionaries were prosperous New England merchants, such as John Hancock. Why were these people so willing to risk rocking their comfortable boats by embarking on the turbulent waters of rebellion?

Whereas the merchants and large landowners in New York and the lower South may have feared rebellion as a risk to the status quo and their immediate wealth, those in New England and Virginia saw that an economy unrestrained by burdensome taxes, duties, and trade restrictions would lead to greater prosperity in the long term. The nation as a whole would prosper, they felt, if it were independent from Britain, which it had proven itself to be a source of tyranny. It was not just that the present king was a tyrant or that the current Parliament was uncaring, but that, because Americans could never be adequately represented in Parliament, any taxation and regulation of commerce imposed by the mother country would always be, by definition, tyrannical. In short, the differences in attitude between the regions of the continent were differences not so much of class and economics, let alone geography, as they were of vision. In some places, the emphasis was on short-term risk and hardship, whereas, in others, it was on the future.

The British had no trouble finding Loyalists, but not every Loyalist was willing or able to fight. Historians estimate that, during the course of the war, about thirty thousand Tories served as combat troops directly under the command of British officers. Indeed, in the lower South, most of the fighting was done by Loyalists rather than British regulars. Some of them made very good soldiers. Unlike the British regulars and the Hessians, they felt that they were defending their homes, which made them well motivated—much as the Patriots were. On the other hand, they were mostly untrained, and regular officers complained that they were unreliable.

If, as soldiers, the Tories were a mixed bag, they were uniformly hated by the Patriots. Their presence in the war continually threatened to transform a revolution fought on lofty principles into a bitter civil war that pitted brother against brother. Oftentimes, British regulars and American soldiers treated one another with a certain degree of mutual respect. Loyalists received nothing of the kind from Patriot soldiers and officers. They were, in fact, given no quarter in combat on the grounds that they were traitors. This attitude intimidated some into refraining from fighting; others it motivated to ruthlessness and a determination to win at all costs.

THE SOUTHERN ROOTS OF WAR

THE BIG EVENTS AT THE BEGINNING of the American Revolution took place in New England, as we saw in the early chapters of this book, but there was also action, early on, in the South. It is now time to take a look at it.

Lord Dunmore was the hard-line, old-school royal governor of Virginia. Come 1775, he was not about to let his colony go the way of unruly Massachusetts, and when various coastal towns and plantations began making rebellious noises, he went on the march against them. The Virginia Council of Safety—a Southern version of the New England Committees of Public Safety—recruited a thousand militiamen and planted them at Great Bridge, a causeway that spanned a marshy stretch of the Elizabeth River about ten miles from Norfolk. Dunmore, personally leading two hundred British regulars, a band of Tories, a handful of Royal Marines, and unit that called itself the Loyal Ethiopians—runaway black slaves—started to cross the bridge. Their object was to seize control of Norfolk, which was seething with rebellion. The Patriot militia attacked, however, killing sixty of Dunmore's troops and sending the governor into retreat. He ushered as many Tories as he could onto British vessels riding at anchor in the harbor, then turned his back on Norfolk, relinquishing it to the rebels.

When the Patriot citizens of Norfolk, Virginia, defied the royal governor's demand for recruits and provisions, he set fire to the town on January 1, 1776. A nineteenth-century engraving depicts residents fleeing their burning homes.

Or not quite.

As he fumed aboard ship just off the coast, Dunmore sent word indignantly demanding that the citizens of Norfolk furnish his men with provisions. He was refused, of course, whereupon, on January 1, 1776, he ordered the ships' cannon to open up on the town. This done, he sent out landing parties with *flambeaux* (torches) to set houses and warehouses on fire. The Patriots had no artillery with which to attack the ships, so they contented themselves with retaliating by setting fire to the homes of prominent Norfolk Tories. Dunmore sailed off. Norfolk, rebel and Tory, burned.

> "They have destroyed one of the first towns in America . . . . They have done their worst, and . . . to no other purpose than to give the world specimens of British cruelty and American fortitude, unless it be to force us to lay aside that childish fondness for Britain, and that foolish, tame dependence on her. . . . How sunk is Britain!"
>
> Virginia Gazette, *January 2, 1776*

Battle of Moore's Creek Bridge

Among the more conservative groups in the South were the Scottish immigrants. In February 1776, a band of Highlanders who had settled in the North Carolina backcountry organized themselves into a Loyalist militia. Fifteen hundred marched out of the hills and down toward the coast, intending to rendezvous with British regulars and advance with them to intercept a rebel force reported to be on the move.

Patriot colonels Richard Caswell and John Alexander Lillington knew the backcountry well, and they knew the sentiments of the Highlanders. Anticipating that they would march to the aid of the Crown, the colonels sent about a thousand Patriot militiamen to dig shallow trenches across the line of march and to prepare an ambush. They set about the work with a passion—and only when it was nearly finished did someone realize that the trenches had been dug parallel to Moore's Creek, with the creek at their backs. Unwilling to leave themselves without a means of retreat, the prudent militiamen got into a better position, wielded the shovels again, and settled in. They did not bother to fill in the abandoned trenches.

It was those trenches that greeted the Scots just before dawn on February 28. Seeing them, they could assume only one thing: the Patriots had decamped. The place was defenseless. Carefree and bold, the Highlanders marched across the bridge—and were promptly cut down by rebel fire from the new trenches. Those who survived—about 850 Highlanders—were made prisoners of war. It was a fine victory, and although it was not a great battle by European standards, to the people of the South it was momentous. All through the Carolinas and up into Virginia, the Tories thought twice about tangling with the rebels. The British cause had suffered a serious blow to morale.

Assault on Charleston

The Battle of Moore's Creek Bridge shook many backcountry Loyalists, but it did not dissuade British military commanders from turning next to the urban South in an effort to exploit Loyalist sentiment in Charleston, South Carolina. Choosing to take a hopeful view, the British noted that South Carolina had yet to commit any overtly hostile action in the Revolution. True, South Carolinians had not rallied to the Crown, either, but the English generals chose to interpret the absence of aggression as a sign of Loyalist sentiment waiting to be awakened. Accordingly, on June 4, 1776, ten British warships and thirty troop transports dropped anchor off Charleston Bar.

Did General Henry Clinton, who had sailed with the fleet, note the absence of a welcoming party? We don't know. Certainly, he should have made careful observation of the forts that had been hastily erected on Sullivan's Island and James Island, which controlled the approaches to the inner harbor and to the city. He might have looked even closer. The waterfront warehouses had been pulled down. There was only one reason for such a thing: it made for a clear

DETAILS, DETAILS
Scottish Treasure
The Highlanders had foolishly carried their entire war chest with them, so the Patriots snatched some £15,000 in gold, along with 13 wagons, 1,500 rifles, 350 muskets, and 150 swords.

Charleston, South Carolina, successfully resisted invasion in 1776. British sailors marveled at how their cannonballs bounced harmlessly off the palmetto-wood walls of Fort Moultrie.

field of fire against any waterborne invasion. The fact was that—quietly—South Carolina had been preparing to "welcome" the British for quite some time. Two regiments had been raised and armed to garrison the new island forts. One regiment was commanded by Charles Cotesworth Pinckney, the other by William Moultrie. Moultrie's second in command was a remarkable officer from the Low Country named Francis Marion, who would earn the name Swamp Fox, and a reputation to match (see Chapter 21, "Swamp Fox"). Also present was a handful of North Carolina infantry and, down from Cambridge, Massachusetts, General Charles Lee, whom the Continental Congress had sent to supervise defenses.

Eyewitness

It is a compelling testament to the impressive appearance of the militiamen that Charles Lee, by nature a most arrogant and condescending officer, had nothing but praise for the regiments: "The behaviour of the garrison, both men and officers, with Colonel Moultrie at their head I confess astonished me. It was brave to the last degree. I had no idea that so much coolness and intrepidity could be displayed by a collection of raw recruits."

General Clinton planned to bring the warships close to Sullivan's Island and commence bombardment of the fort there. While the cannons roared against the fort, the transports would land their troops on Long Island, just a short distance from Sullivan's Island. Once assembled, the infantry would advance onto Sullivan's Island and take the battered fort. With this accomplished, invading Charleston should be a straightforward operation.

It was a reasonable plan, but it was based on faulty intelligence. The British had badly misread the sentiment of the Charlestonians. True, the prosperous city had a sizable Tory population, but most residents favored the Revolution and were determined to prevent the invasion of their city. The second error was a misjudgment of geography. The body of water separating Long Island from Sullivan's Island looked inconsequential—from a distance—but once the troops actually approached it, it proved to be unfordable. Clinton was able to land his men on Long Island, but as they struggled to cross to Sullivan's Island, the redcoats were picked off one by one.

The naval phase of the amphibious assault did not go well, either. Sullivan's Island was surrounded by treacherous shallows, on which the British ships, one after the other, ran aground. Even worse, their cannon fire was strangely ineffective against the walls of the fort. It was not that the cannonballs bounced off them, but that the wood seemed merely to absorb each projectile. Clinton was wholly unfamiliar with the material from which the forts were built: palmetto logs. This small palm tree, with broad, fan-shaped leaves, was abundant in the Carolina Low Country and had a dense structure that was virtually indestructible.

While the British cannon were ineffectual against the American fort, the South Carolinians' return fire was punishing. The British ships could barely maneuver in the shallow water and were therefore sitting ducks. Admiral Peter Parker had to abandon one of his frigates after it ran hopelessly aground. He then withdrew his remaining ships, all of which were seriously damaged. It must have been unspeakably frustrating to him. Collectively, his vessels mounted one hundred guns, whereas the fort had only twenty-one. Eighteenth-century naval combat was all about firepower. Everyone knew that the side with the most guns won. But not in this case. Sixty-four Royal Navy sailors were killed, and 131 were wounded. Losses among the Americans were seventeen dead and twenty wounded. Charleston was saved.

POPULAR CULTURE
Stately Tree

Ever since the defense of the Charleston forts, South Carolinians have been grateful for their palmetto trees. In company with a crescent moon, a palmetto graces South Carolina's state flag, which commemorates Charleston's successful resistance to the first British attempt at invasion. However, this is not the flag that was flown over Fort Sullivan; that flag did bear a crescent moon, but it floated above the word *LIBERTY* rather than beside a palmetto.

"No slaughterhouse could present so bad a sight with blood and entrails lying about, as did our ship."

Royal Navy officer serving in the failed invasion of Charleston

The Fall of Savannah

The defeat at Charleston, strangely enough, did not discourage the British, but made them even more determined to neutralize the South. A new target was chosen: the port town of Savannah, Georgia. Lieutenant Colonel Archibald Campbell was given thirty-five hundred soldiers and a naval escort and sailed from Sandy Hook, New Jersey, on November 27, 1778. He dropped anchor on December 23 off Tybee Island at the mouth of the Savannah River.

Facing Campbell and his 3,500 invaders were just 900 Continentals and about 150 militiamen under the command of General Robert Howe (no relation to the British Howe brothers). This made for lopsided odds; and they got even worse. British general Augustine Prevost was on the march from Florida with reinforcements for Campbell. Campbell, however, believed his position to be so favorable that he did not wait for the arrival of Prevost. On December 29, he landed his men at Girardeau's Plantation, about two miles south of Savannah. Dug into defensive positions just a half mile south of town were 700 of the Continentals, plus all 150 militiamen. Campbell rolled right over them.

SAVANNAH—FROM BAD TO WORSE

Campbell marched into Savannah and occupied the city. In the early autumn of 1779, French admiral d'Estaing, having failed in the first Franco-American amphibious operation against Newport, Rhode Island (see Chapter 16, "Testing the Alliance"), and having withdrawn to the French West Indies, took it upon himself to do something about this. Doubtless, he was anxious to redeem himself for his earlier failures, never mind that General Washington desperately wanted him to coordinate with operations in the North.

Heedless of his ally's desires, d'Estaing led a fleet of thirty-three warships, mounting two thousand guns, and escorting transports carrying more than four thousand troops to the Georgia coast. The French admiral achieved surprise and rapidly captured two British warships and two stores (cargo) ships, one of which carried a £30,000 payroll intended for the British garrison at Savannah.

D'Estaing instantly withdrew after this operation, then, on September 9, reappeared to land troops on Tybee Island. On September 16, after American units had joined the French troops, d'Estaing demanded the surrender of British-held Savannah. General Prevost requested a twenty-four-hour truce to ponder this demand. Doubtless fancying himself a gallant gentleman dealing with another gentleman, d'Estaing foolishly agreed. For his part, Prevost used the time to prepare a defense employing some thirty-two hundred troops. So much for the advantage gained by surprise. At the end of the twenty-four-hour truce, Prevost informed d'Estaing that he would not surrender, thank you very much, but intended to fight.

The battle, however, did not begin until October 9, when combined French and American forces numbering fewer than five thousand attacked. The Franco-American army had the advantage of numbers, but Prevost was defending from a fortification—and that gave him the decisive edge. Not only did he hold, he launched a counterattack that killed or wounded eight hundred, including 650 French troops. Prevost lost no more than a hundred killed or wounded.

Continental general Benjamin Lincoln, who had command of the American troops, pleaded with d'Estaing to make another assault, but the French admiral would have none of it. He was afraid of being trapped by bad weather or ambushed by the enemy fleet. He also worried about an outbreak of scurvy among his men. He needed to refit his ships, d'Estaing protested, and, once again, after another Franco-American failure, he withdrew to Martinique. Savannah would remain in British hands until July 1782.

Retargeting Charleston

Having taken and held Savannah, General Prevost set his sights on Charleston, which had previously proven an elusive target. In the spring of 1779, he was able to drive Moultrie's American forces back into the town. Yet when he reached the outskirts of Charleston, he found himself stymied. The inland defenses appeared most formidable. Prevost halted his advance and pondered his options. As he did this, South Carolina's Patriot governor, Edward Rutledge, suddenly made a startling offer. He was willing to declare his state neutral.

DETAILS, DETAILS
Casimir Pulaski Falls

Among those killed in the attempt to retake Savannah was young Casimir Pulaski, the bold Polish officer who had virtually created the Continental army's cavalry.

The brilliant Polish cavalry officer Casimir Pulaski died in service to the Patriot cause leading a cavalry charge in defense of Savannah, Georgia, on October 9, 1779. This nineteenth-century colored engraving recreates the moment of his mortal wounding in the battle.

This was a very different attitude from that of 1776. What had changed? Whatever it was, Prevost took the offer as a sign of serious weakness. However, news that General Lincoln was approaching with a large American force persuaded Prevost to hold off attacking Charleston. Instead, he retreated to Savannah, giving his men leave to loot and pillage all the way back.

As usual, the British moved slowly, and it was not until the end of 1779 that Henry Clinton assembled a new force to attack Charleston. He recalled to New York City 3,000 soldiers who had been sent to Newport, Rhode Island. To these he added 3,500 more troops, British, Hessian, and Tory. Royal Navy sailors made up an additional 5,000 men, and so, with a force of 11,500, Clinton embarked from New York on December 26, 1779. Winter storms scattered the fleet, and it was February 11, 1780, before the reassembled convoy sailed into Edisto Inlet. Clinton landed his forces on Johns Island, thirty miles south of Charleston.

Prevost's speculation that Charleston had grown weak since 1776 was correct. The city's burghers had sat out most of the war, becoming rich in the process. Thanks to the war, the city was now a center of privateering—state-sanctioned piracy—as the Continental Congress commissioned private ship masters to prey upon British shipping. Whatever they managed to appropriate from captured ships was theirs for the keeping. Yet the privateers were profiteers, not patriots, and with the fading of patriotism came a decay in the state of the city's defenses. The Sullivan's Island and James Island forts were now abandoned, idle. Only along the Neck, a narrow isthmus connecting Charleston with the mainland, were fortifications still maintained. The makeshift forts that had been hastily thrown up along the Cooper and Ashley rivers, which flanked the town, were insubstantial and weakly manned.

As he contemplated his target, Clinton moved more slowly and with greater deliberation than was customary even for him. He built up a siege force, little by little. Delay was frequently a strategic factor in this war. In the case of Charleston, it gave the Americans time to patch up the city's decayed defenses.

By the third week in March, Clinton was poised just outside of Charleston, waiting for additional troops. On March 20, American commodore Abraham Whipple realized that the flotilla he com-

REALITY CHECK
Clinton's Crawl

Clinton moved slowly by habit and inclination. This time, however, he was probably also playing out the clock. Heartily sick of America and the war in America, he had submitted his resignation to London and now hoped that he could soon turn over command to Cornwallis—and let him struggle with Charleston. Only after London rejected his resignation did Clinton begin seriously to move against Charleston.

manded was vastly outgunned by the British men-o'-war just off shore. Not wishing to lose his ships in a futile struggle, he withdrew from Charleston, sailing up the Cooper River. On this very day, British admiral Marriot Arbuthnot completed the treacherous crossing of Charleston Bar and was now in position to support the British land assault on the city.

During the night of March 28, Clinton ordered his men across the Ashley River. They took up positions across the Neck, thereby sealing the American garrison within Charleston. On April 1, Clinton directed his engineers to start digging a series of trenches to provide cover for a prolonged siege. True, 750 Virginia Continentals had managed to slip past surrounding British troops on April 6 to reinforce the Charleston garrison, but the situation was nevertheless becoming desperate. Even reinforced, the garrison could do nothing more than look on as Clinton painstakingly engineered his careful siege.

By April 10, most of Clinton's siege works had been completed. From these formidable positions, Clinton sent word to General Lincoln, demanding his surrender. When the American refused, Clinton ordered a naval bombardment of the city. He had the cannon loaded with heated ammunition and with carcasses—hollowed out cannonballs stuffed with blazing combustible materials—so that wherever a shot landed a fire would follow. The incendiary bombardment commenced on April 13. Large sections of Charleston burst into flame. Still, Lincoln held out. It was not from stubbornness, but from hope. He knew that General Isaac Huger was nearby, with a regiment or two of militiamen and three to five hundred Continentals. Huger might somehow provide a means of effective resistance or, at least, escape.

On April 14, Banastre Tarleton—a British officer who possessed a remarkable talent for wilderness warfare—and Major Patrick "Bulldog" Ferguson led British and Tory forces against Huger's encampment at Moncks Corner, South Carolina. Surprise was total, and American losses were heavy, with Huger barely escaping with his life. The defeat of Huger meant that Lincoln's Charleston garrison had no way out of the city—and Clinton's siege trenches were steadily closing in.

Banastre Tarleton marshaled Southern Loyalist and Native American forces with a combination of brilliance and utter ruthlessness.

On April 19, Lincoln convened a council of war, observing that the garrison was in a hopeless position and that the surrender of Charleston was the only alternative to the destruction of both the garrison and the city. Present at the council was Christopher Gadsden, lieutenant governor of North Carolina. He rejected even the mention of surrender, telling Lincoln that if he capitulated, civil insurrection would follow. He would not only have to fight the British, but the Carolinians as well. Lincoln decided that, of the two, the British were the more formidable and, on April 21, he proposed surrender terms to General Clinton. The British commander responded with a demand for unconditional surrender. Lincoln stalled, then, two nights later, sent a unit to jab at the British. If he could breach the British siege line, Lincoln might still save his army. But the probing attack was easily repulsed.

Clinton bided his time. Then, on May 8, he sent another surrender demand. Determined to extract better terms, Lincoln refused. Clinton's next reply came on the night of May 9. It was in the form of an artillery barrage so spectacular that the very citizens of Charleston petitioned Lincoln to give up. He did just that, on May 12, 1780, turning over in the process five thousand American soldiers, four hundred irreplaceable cannon, and six thousand muskets.

The loss of so many men, combined with the loss of the key Southern port of Charleston, was the worst American defeat in the Revolution—the losses of New York City and Philadelphia not excepted. Charleston was the doorway to the entire South. Whoever possessed it had a means of supply and communication that could sustain any army in the region. It looked now as if Britain's Southern strategy had paid off. The American Revolution was in as much jeopardy as it would ever be.

TAKEAWAY
British Target South—And Succeed

Loyalists were plentiful in the lower South (especially in South Carolina). For this reason, the British campaigned to gain complete control of the South, capturing Savannah in 1778 and Charleston in 1780.

Chapter 19

TREASON AND MUTINY

Benedict Arnold's Treason and Other Crises in the Patriot Ranks

FEW REVOLUTIONS PRODUCE truly satisfactory results. Most start out with an abundance of lofty idealism and even loftier speeches, full of brotherhood, self-sacrifice, liberty, and equality, only to end up as bloodier than necessary and dominated by a few individuals hungry for power. That this was not the case with the American Revolution is due in great measure to the character of the people who fought and led the struggle. John Adams, Benjamin Franklin, Thomas Jefferson, George Washington—these were men of enormous wisdom and ethical purpose. And they are only the best known of a whole group of similarly distinguished individuals. We have a right to expect one or two such men in any given generation, but to have been blessed with so many at just the right time, such was the fortunate soul of our Revolution.

Even so, it was not perfect. As we saw in the case of the Conway Cabal (see Chapter 15, "Washington under Siege"), the Revolution also had a generous helping of greed, dissension, selfishness, arrogance, and stupidity. It was, after all, a human event. Side by side with the idealists and the heroes were some turncoats—we'll look at just one—and profiteers.

THE HERO AND HIS WIVES

WASHINGTON NEEDED MEN like Benedict Arnold. Bold and skilled at arms, he had played a major role in the capture of Fort Ticonderoga, and he had performed with extraordinary valor and endurance in the invasion of Canada. The delaying action he improvised at Valcour Island ended in defeat but nevertheless saved the Revolution. And at the Saratoga battles, he did far more to win a glorious victory than the stodgy Horatio Gates, who was given the official credit. Yet with Arnold's courage and indomitable will came a most difficult temperament. His ambition was boundless, and so was his capacity for contempt, especially when he had to deal with people he judged to be far less capable than he. And he judged almost everyone that way.

A native of Norwich, Connecticut, born in 1741, Benedict Arnold was apprenticed by his father to a druggist. He bolted from his apprenticeship in 1758, during the French and Indian War, to enlist in a New York militia company. Bridling under the tedious discipline of part-time soldiering, he deserted his company after serving a bit more than a year and had to turn to his mother, doting and prosperous as she was, to bail him out of the trouble into which his rash action had immersed him. To make matters up, he reenlisted in March 1760, only to desert again. Now he came full circle. Making his way back to Norwich via the unmarked wilderness, he sought out his master and actually completed his pharmacy apprenticeship.

Arnold decided to make his way in the world. By the time he turned twenty-one, his parents had died, and he came into his inheritance. He sold the family property and used the proceeds to move with his sister to New Haven, where he opened up a pharmacy and bookstore. He discovered that he had a head for business. His store prospered, and he even began operating his own trading vessels, which sailed to Canada and the West Indies. By 1767, Arnold felt himself sufficiently well-off to take a wife. He married Margaret Mansfield, made his way in the world, then in 1775—eager to loose the economically oppressive grip of the mother country—he arrived in Cambridge at the head of a Connecticut militia company.

This was the start of his wartime career, and he was full of great expectations. Following his epic wilderness march to Quebec and his return from the disastrous American assault on that city at the end of 1775, Arnold was promoted to brigadier general. After Valcour Island, he was generally hailed as a hero—generally, but not universally. Some of the officers closest to Washington found Arnold insufferable. They distrusted his impatience and impetuosity. Most of all, they resented his arrogance. Thus, in February 1777, when Congress created five new major generalships, Arnold was not only passed over, he was snubbed in favor of his juniors.

Arnold tendered his resignation, and it took a great deal of verbal massaging from no less than George Washington to get him to change his mind. Washington assured him that his time would come, and, in fact, just two months later, after he fended off a British assault on Danbury, Connecticut, Arnold was promoted to major general. Yet even as Congress gave him what he wanted, it managed to insult him as well. The promotion list still positioned him junior to the five men who had been made major generals before him. Arnold's original complaint was not so much that he had not been promoted as that the others, junior to him, had been promoted ahead of him. Now Congress, while giving him the title of major general, deliberately failed to address his principal grievance. Yet again, he presented his letter of resignation.

Benedict Arnold was not just a traitor; he was a hero turned traitor. He is pictured here resting on his horse after being wounded when he led an attack on the Hessian redoubt during the Saratoga campaign in 1777.

What stopped him from following through this time were the demands of war. Burgoyne had begun his advance into upper New York, and in July Arnold joined General Horatio Gates's command in an effort to block the British general. This, as we saw in Chapter 13, resulted in the battles at Saratoga—and Arnold's defiance of his commander.

Horatio Gates, as we also saw, made every effort to suppress reports of Benedict Arnold's gallantry at Saratoga, but Congress learned of it and responded by officially conferring on him the seniority he merited.

The Good Life

Convalescing from a bad leg wound sustained at Bemis Heights, Arnold was given light duty in June 1778, commanding the Philadelphia garrison after the British withdrawal from that city. During his Canadian adventure, Arnold had proven himself capable of enduring the utmost wilderness hardship. Now that he was ensconced in North America's leading city, however, he immediately embraced the good life of Philadelphia's most prosperous and elegant social stratum: the Tories. There was, however, a price to pay. The Tory lifestyle cost plenty—a lot more than what Benedict Arnold had in his coffers. He was soon deeply in debt.

That General Arnold was living in a style well beyond the capacity of his known income did not escape the attention of local Patriot officials. In February 1779, Joseph Reed, president of the Pennsylvania Council and of the state, delivered to the Continental Congress eight charges of official misconduct against Arnold, including allegations of embezzlement in the form of appropriating government funds to purchase goods for personal use. Later historians would look into the matter and conclude that Arnold was guilty as sin but, in 1779, Congress was in no mood to smear a gallant Continental officer. It decided to consider only four of the eight charges preferred, and then found the general guilty of only two of the least serious charges. Washington issued nothing more consequential than a reprimand.

A narrow escape for Benedict Arnold? Not as he saw it. It is a measure of the man's arrogance that he declared that his honor would permit him to accept nothing less than a full acquittal. And there the matter stood while Benedict Arnold found something else to occupy his time. After bearing Arnold three sons in five years of marriage, Margaret Mansfield died, leaving the socially well-connected major general one of the most eligible bachelors in Philadelphia. This time, Arnold aimed high in the choice of a wife, courting Peggy (Margaret) Shippen, the nineteen-year-old daughter of one of Philadelphia's very best Tory families. The courtship wasn't cheap, of course, but it was successful. The couple married on April 8, 1779, then entered into a very costly life together. If Arnold had lived beyond his means with Margaret, he was far more extravagant as the middle-aged husband of a pretty, pert, spoiled

DETAILS, DETAILS
Party Animals

The extravagance of the Philadelphia Tories was legendary. On May 18, 1778, John André (who would become Benedict Arnold's liaison to Sir Henry Clinton), threw a party in honor of General Howe. It featured a mock tournament, called a *Meschianza* (a made-up word loosely based on the Italian word mescolanza, or "mix"), which included, among other things, a sumptuous dinner of twelve hundred dishes. Everyone was aware that the American army, nearly naked and close to starvation after a hard winter, was camped just outside of the city. Even to some Tories, the party seemed in very bad taste. Peggy Shippen, destined to become Benedict Arnold's second wife, begged her Tory father to let her attend. As a matter of principle, he refused.

young lady accustomed to wealth as a birthright. The financial tap dance that had gotten him into trouble in the first place became increasingly frenetic. Both civilian and military authorities began asking a lot of questions, to which Arnold's answers grew increasingly evasive and arrogant—yet, in eighteenth-century American society, as in British society, to question the honor of a "gentleman" was to hint at the darkest of accusations. Thus the questioning went only so far and no further, as Arnold's fellow officers and superior officers entered into a state of denial, forcing themselves to believe that a Continental army officer could be married to a Tory and could freely consort with Tories yet maintain his absolute loyalty to the cause of American independence.

Turning Traitor

By 1779, General Clinton's aide, Major John André, reported receiving letters that hinted at the willingness of a certain senior American officer to render "his services to the commander-in-chief of the British forces in any way that would most effectually restore the former government and destroy the then-usurped authority of Congress, whether by immediately joining the British army or cooperating on some concealed plan." Acting on Clinton's instructions, André began an enciphered correspondence with the officer. He soon discovered that the fancy rhetoric about the "usurped authority of Congress" notwithstanding, the disaffected officer was not moved by a passion of loyalty to the Crown, but was none other than Benedict Arnold, a man known to be moved by a single passion only: his desperate desire for cash.

General Sir Henry Clinton was willing to oblige, but what he proposed to Arnold was hardly imaginative. Communicating through André, Clinton asked Arnold to lead an American army into an ambush. With an accountant's mentality, Clinton offered two guineas a head for each soldier who surrendered. Arnold responded by demanding an additional £10,000, upfront and

REALITY CHECK
Fraternizing with Foes
Did Arnold's fellow officers frown on his familiarity with the enemy? Certainly they did, and, doubtless, their disapproval was part of the appeal for Arnold, who loved nothing more than to tweak the noses of his always-jealous colleagues.

Benedict Arnold turned traitor partly because neither General Washington nor the Continental Congress gave him the recognition and advancement he believed he deserved and partly because the British were willing to pay him. Married to the beautiful Philadelphia Tory Margaret (Peggy) Shippen, Arnold felt obliged to maintain an elegant way of life well beyond his means. He was chronically short of cash. The Arnolds' daughter, Sophia Matilda Arnold, is shown here with Peggy Shippen, in a wood engraving after a portrait by Daniel Gardner, ca. 1783.

ALTERNATE TAKE
West Point Domino Effect

For Arnold, assignment to West Point meant an opportunity to become rich. For the Revolution, the stakes were far greater. If West Point fell to the enemy, control of the Hudson would instantly go to the British, and the other Hudson River fortifications would also fall: Stony Point and Verplanck's Point, in addition to some smaller outposts and an infantry-cavalry force stationed at North Castle. The entire Hudson was imperiled. Its loss would delay, perhaps spoil entirely, execution of the Yorktown campaign, because Washington would be obliged to rush everything he had to retaking the Hudson. It is quite possible that the loss of West Point would have set into motion the loss of the entire Revolution. This, certainly, was how Clinton saw it. With unusual excitement, he wrote to Lord Germain on October 11, 1780, that very great things would come from "a plan," he wrote "of such infinite effect."

non-returnable, as a retainer, whereupon Clinton broke off negotiations. Arnold sought to reopen them in May 1780. Claiming that he had more than ever to offer Clinton, he explained that he was in line for command of the Hudson River fortress at West Point. Clinton was interested, but no deal was made. Then, on June 15, Arnold wrote to Clinton that the command assignment was imminent, and he turned to how he might arrange for the surrender of this important outpost. Nor did he leave it at that. He was adamant about his price: £10,000, regardless of outcome, and double that sum "if I point out a plan of cooperation by which Sir Henry shall possess himself of West Point, the garrison, etc., etc."

Clinton was as slow in his reply as he was in moving soldiers. He *would* pay—and £20,000, too—but only if West Point actually fell. Now, although he would not fork over the £10,000 retainer regardless of outcome, he pointedly assured the general that, whatever happened, he would not be "left a victim." Arnold took that to mean that he would be protected, presumably offered a British command. Increasingly pressed by his creditors and seeking to please his needy bride, Arnold agreed to the terms. Moreover, just to prove that he could deliver, he started giving Clinton a taste. Using his wife as a courier—no one questioned her moving in Tory circles—he transmitted tidbits relating to battle plans for the Yorktown campaign (see Chapter 22), which Washington was working on with the French general, the comte de Rochambeau. Mrs. Arnold never spoke with Clinton directly, but always through intermediaries, including Major André.

ARNOLD MANEUVERS

With financial relief within his grasp, Benedict Arnold was troubled by only one thing. General Washington, who thought highly of him as a combat commander, wanted him to head up a wing of the army in the forthcoming Yorktown campaign. It was a major assignment with plenty of opportunity for glory, so Washington was surprised when Arnold protested. He complained that his wound—now three years old—prevented the degree of exertion a major campaign required. He asked Washington to assign him garrison duty. West Point would do nicely. And on August 3, 1780, that was the post to which he was assigned.

HIGH TREASON

IMMEDIATELY UPON TAKING COMMAND of West Point, Arnold began preparing the fort to clear the way for the British assault. He diluted the garrison by sending two hundred men on a wood-cutting expedition. His subordinates urgently informed him that the chain stretched across the Hudson to block the passage of ships was in disrepair and needed attention immediately. Arnold made certain that no one touched the chain.

The commander also began creating a network of spies, working through one Joshua Hett Smith, the Tory brother of the former royal chief justice of New York. Arnold made no secret of his friendship with Smith, and, to be sure, the more cautious among the Continental officers objected to a highly placed American commander having regular contact with the enemy, but others pointed out that Arnold was, after all, married to a Tory, so it was only natural that his friends would be Tories as well, and no one made so bold as to raise the specter of outright treason. As for Arnold, his boundless arrogance, combined with his urgent need for money, prompted him not only to communicate cautiously through intermediaries, but to write boldly to Clinton himself. He continued to badger the general to reconsider that unconditional payment of £10,000.

Although Arnold was remarkably careless in his correspondence, both he and Clinton agreed that the actual espionage operation had to be carried out more carefully. It was arranged that a Colonel Beverly Robinson, local leader of the Tories, would openly request a meeting with Arnold for the purpose of discussing the disposition of Loyalist household property along the Hudson. Robinson would be accompanied by Major André, dressed in the

The Patriot fort at West Point occupied a strategic position above the Hudson River, a major artery of communication and supply. In command of West Point, Benedict Arnold offered the British plans that were the very keys to the fort. This nineteenth-century engraving depicts West Point on the western shore of the Hudson as it appeared in 1780.

civilian garb of a local landowner and using the name John Anderson. When the time was right, Arnold could present to André his plans for the surrender of West Point. Joshua Hett Smith was also chosen as a messenger.

At the meeting, Arnold and André set a suitable time for an extended planning session, and on September 21, the British sloop *Vulture*, a familiar sight on the Hudson, carried André to a remote hideout deep in the woods. There he and Arnold plotted until after four in the morning. It was too late for André to reboard the *Vulture*, so he left the hideout to spend the night at Smith's house between the Hudson River villages of Haverstraw and Stony Point, intending to board the *Vulture* on the twenty-third. As fate would have it, just before dawn of that day, Colonel James Livingston, commander of local American forces, launched an attack on the *Vulture*. Shooting at it from the bank of the river, Livingston did not sink the sloop, but he damaged it badly enough that it was forced to turn back. André had lost his ride, and he would now have to make his escape overland.

Vulture or no *Vulture,* Arnold was not about to give up £20,000. He persuaded André to remain in civilian clothing as John Anderson and to deliver to Clinton a packet of papers, including a full description of the defenses in and around West Point. André tucked the documents between his calf and his stocking, then pulled on his boot. Arnold wrote out passes for André and for Smith, who would guide him back to the British lines. Arnold assured them that the passes, signed by a major general, would easily get them past the American guards. And so André and Smith set off on the long walk to British-held White Plains.

André's Doom

As it turned out, this was a bad time for a spy to be wandering the countryside. Major General Benjamin Tallmadge, Washington's chief of intelligence, was personally leading patrols in Westchester and Fairfield counties to prepare for a strategy meeting between Washington and Rochambeau. Tallmadge wanted to be very sure that the commander in chief would not fall prey to some Tory or British force. But he had more on his mind than Washington's security. Others might not be terribly bothered by Benedict Arnold's behavior—which had become increasingly peculiar of late—but Tallmadge was. He had been making inquiries but had nailed down nothing definitive. Then he learned that Arnold had written a letter on behalf of someone named John Anderson, authorizing his safe conduct through American lines from West Point to Manhattan. To Tallmadge, it seemed a singular request. Manhattan was the principal British stronghold in America. West Point was a major Continental army outpost. What possible reason could Benedict Arnold have for wanting to get this John Anderson—whom no one had ever heard of—from the one place to the other?

Benedict Arnold gives Major John André the plans of West Point, telling him to deliver them hidden in his boot. Surely, no clandestine courier has ever found a more obvious hiding place.

Tallmadge did not have long to ponder this question. Returning from patrol, he received word that militiamen had intercepted a suspicious-looking fellow in Westchester. His name was John Anderson—he said—and although he had a pass signed by General Arnold himself, the militiamen decided to send him to Tallmadge's headquarters. In Tallmadge's absence, Lieutenant Colonel John Jameson ordered Anderson to be searched—and searched thoroughly. Off came boots and stockings, and there it was: detailed plans of West Point, along with précis of various confidential orders issued by General Washington. Jameson, who had puzzled with Tallmadge over Arnold's letters, was struck by the handwriting in these documents. It was that of Benedict Arnold.

Jameson explained to Tallmadge his decision not to await the major general's return, but to seize the documents and bundle them off immediately to General Washington.

But where was this John Anderson?

Jameson explained that he had sent Anderson on his way back to Benedict Arnold, accompanied by a messenger bearing a letter describing the papers that had been found on him. Apparently, it never occurred to Jameson that Benedict Arnold—an odd sort, but a hero, after all—had *given* Anderson the documents. They must have been stolen. This, Jameson judged, was a matter for Arnold to resolve, so he sent Anderson packing.

We can only imagine how Tallmadge received this news. If he upbraided Jameson, he did not waste much time doing so. Instead, he gave orders to intercept Anderson. This was done, and the man revealed himself as Major John André of His Majesty's army.

This mid-nineteenth-century depiction of the capture of Major André is charming in its naïveté. In real life, the consequences of André's espionage were anything but charming. With the full approval of George Washington, John André was hanged as a spy.

On September 29, 1780, Tallmadge convened a board to examine the major. It consisted of Nathanael Greene, William Alexander ("Lord Stirling"), the Marquis de Lafayette, Friedrich Wilhelm Augustus von Steuben, Arthur St. Clair, and Robert Howe, in addition to some more junior general officers. André spilled it all, perhaps hoping that this would save him from the gallows. It did not. Having secured a full confession, the board unanimously recommended André's execution as a spy. Washington received the recommendation and issued the order personally.

Arnold's Arrogance

Perhaps in his haste to intercept "Anderson," Tallmadge had given no orders regarding the messenger Jameson had sent along with André. The messenger delivered the letter to Benedict Arnold, who received and read it even before Washington had received the incriminating documents seized from André. In this way, Arnold learned that the game was up. He made a quick farewell to his wife and clambered onto a barge, which rowed him down the Hudson to the repaired *Vulture.* Clinton had promised him that, whatever happened, he would not be a victim. HMS *Vulture* carried Benedict Arnold to New York and into service as an officer of His Majesty's army.

If Benedict Arnold felt any shame, he hid it completely. Now ensconced in the British service, he received word of the death sentence pronounced upon André. This prompted him to put pen to paper in a letter to the commander in chief he had betrayed:

> If after this just and candid representation of Major André's case the board of general officers adhere to their former opinion, I shall suppose it dictated by passion and resentment. And if that gentleman should suffer the severity of their sentence, I shall think myself bound by every tie of duty and honour to retaliate on such unhappy persons of your army as may fall within my power— that the respect due to flags and to the law of nations may be better understood and observed. . . .
>
> But if this warning should be disregarded, and he should suffer, I call heaven and earth to witness that

your Excellency will be justly answerable for the torrent of blood that may be spilt in consequence.

Washington made no response, and on October 2, 1780, John André was hanged.

Eyewitness

Sentenced to hang as a spy, André, on the eve of his execution, wrote the following appeal to George Washington, requesting a soldier's death (by firing squad) rather than a spy's (hanging):

Buoyed above the terror of death by the consciousness of a life devoted to honourable pursuits, and stained with no action that can give me remorse, I trust that the request I make to your Excellency at this serious period, and which is to soften my last moments, will not be rejected.

Sympathy towards a soldier will surely induce your Excellency and a military tribunal to adopt a mode of my death to the feelings of a man of honour.

Let me hope, Sir, that if aught in my character impresses you with esteem towards me, if aught in my misfortunes marks me as the victim of policy and not of resentment, I shall experience the operation of these feelings in your breast, by being informed that I am not to die on a gibbet.

Washington made no answer.

Benedict Arnold may have slipped through his fingers, but Washington was determined that West Point would not. The commander in chief ordered the fort and its surroundings to be reinforced immediately. Then he continued making plans for the Yorktown campaign, which would effectively bring the American Revolution to a triumphant conclusion.

MUTINY

THE YEAR 1780, WHICH BROUGHT THE TREASON of Benedict Arnold, also brought the mutiny of the Continental army. It should have come as no surprise. Continental troops routinely went unpaid and even unfed. Congress had created the force, then treated it like an orphan. This was not entirely due to the parsimony of the congressional delegates. One problem was that the Continental Congress, under the Articles of Confederation, had no authority to levy direct taxes. It relied on the individual states to fund the Continental army

DETAILS, DETAILS

Jerseymen Mutiny

The mutiny of the Pennsylvania Line ended peacefully, but, a short time later, three New Jersey regiments mutinied. Washington took a more forceful approach than Reed. He issued orders to suppress the mutiny by force of arms. Those identified as ringleaders were tried, and they were hanged.

The plates for the first Continental currency were engraved by none other than Boston's Paul Revere. To increase its durability and convey a sense of value, the bills were printed on very thick paper, prompting the British to deride it as "the pasteboard currency of the rebels." So much paper money—"Continental currency"—was printed up that its worthlessness became a byword for, well, worthlessness. The expression "not worth a Continental" entered into the English language, where it still lurks.

voluntarily. Whenever those funds came up short—and they always came up short—pay, uniforms, and supplies would go unpurchased and unprovided. To compound this basic problem was the incompetence and corruption of those in Congress and in the Continental army responsible for administering logistics. Too often, what little was available never reached the soldiers. Indeed, most of the time, all that kept the Continental army together was the charismatic will of George Washington.

Nevertheless and despite Washington's leadership, there had been rumblings. At Morristown in May 1780, two Connecticut regiments of the Continental army refused to obey orders until they received their back pay. Washington responded by dispatching Pennsylvania troops to disarm them. But then, in January 1781, these very troops—the so-called "Pennsylvania Line"—staged a much larger mutiny of their own. They complained that they had not been paid in many months, that they had rags rather than uniforms to wear, and that they subsisted on a ration of bread and water. To make matters worse, they believed that they had been duped in the terms of their enlistment. The Pennsylvania soldiers had enlisted for "three years or the duration of the war." Recruiters had apparently told them that their actual term of service would be the shorter—not the longer—of these two alternatives. When three years had passed and the war continued, they demanded to be released.

The grievances were as powder packed into the keg. The spark that touched off the inevitable explosion came on the night of January 1, 1781, when recruiting agents appeared in the Pennsylvania camp offering the gold equivalent of twenty-five Spanish dollars (a common currency in colonial North America)—for *new* recruits. The half-naked, half-starved veterans were stunned, then outraged. Twenty-four hundred of them mutinied, moving to Princeton on January 3, setting up camp there, and sending a representative to plead their case to the Continental Congress.

Joseph Reed, revolutionary president of Pennsylvania, understood that the most immediate danger of a mutiny was that it would communicate weakness to the British and therefore invite attack. The quickest way to squash the mutiny, Reed decided, was to grant the mutineers' demands. He did just this—but not before word of the mutiny reached Sir Henry Clinton. The British commander did not order an attack, but he did send a pair of agents to provoke further defections. In this, however, he made the latest in a long string of British failures to understand what the American Revolution was all about. The mutiny of the Pennsylvania Line had nothing at all to do with patriotism or politics. The issue was not ideology, but shabby treatment. As soon as the promise of just treatment was forthcoming, the mutiny melted away. The men of the Pennsylvania Line turned on Clinton's hapless agents, seized them and delivered them to their commanders, who saw to it that they were quickly hanged as spies.

PROFITEERING

TREASON AND MUTINY POSED GRAVE THREATS to the Revolution, but even more serious was profiteering. The unpaid, unfed Continental army was ripe for corruption. Compounding the perpetual shortages was the inefficiency of the Continental army's quartermaster corps—its logistics department—and the legion of speculators who deliberately created shortages by cornering the market for certain goods. Congress had no authority to tax, but it could print up all the paper money it wanted. This provided temporary relief, but paper money that is not backed up by "specie"—gold or silver— soon becomes as valueless as, well, paper. Inflation became nearly catastrophic in America before the war was over.

One alternative remained: the "impressment of goods"—that is, the seizure of supplies, food, and transportation. Congress did not have the power to do this, but individual commanders could; however, they impressed goods at their peril. Taking something without paying for it seemed to be nothing less than precisely what the American Revolution was being fought to end: government tyranny.

If Congress could not levy direct taxes, it could solicit foreign loans. In the end, these staved off bankruptcy—though they hardly kept the American war chest full. What, finally, sustained the American Revolution? The fact is that treason, mutiny, and unbridled greed were part and parcel of the fight for independence, but, much as they hampered the Revolution, they never took over the struggle. Patriotism, a sustaining and overriding belief in a future of liberty, fueled the fight and carried the contest through the hardest of very hard times.

REALITY CHECK
Extortion

Because the central government had virtually no fiscal authority, unscrupulous individuals could demand from individual commanders almost whatever price they wanted. These greedy men were not just wealthy speculators, but, often, ordinary farmers, who sold produce directly to army and militia units.

TAKEAWAY
Sabotage Within and Without

Benedict Arnold was motivated to turn traitor by a combination of resentment over his nation's ingratitude, financial need, and a general deficiency of character. Although his treachery was detected before it did harm, other subversive forces that undermined the Patriot cause were war profiteering and logistical incompetence. Moreover, want of clothing, shelter, food, and pay moved some units of the Continental army to mutiny.

PART FOUR

Most Glorious

Chapter 20

VICTORY AT SEA

The Surprising Story of the American Revolution at Sea, Including the Exploits of John Paul Jones

RITAIN, AN ISLAND NATION, was always first and foremost a sea power; its army, though formidable, was a poor cousin to its navy. Had the British used their fleet more extensively and effectively, it could have been the decisive force in crushing the American Revolution. The problem was that the Crown did not want to risk expanding what it considered a local rebellion into an international conflict by undertaking large fleet operations. So the role of the Royal Navy was initially restricted to supporting the efforts of the army.

Then came Washington's bold action at Germantown and the American victory at Saratoga (see Chapter 13), which encouraged France to enter the war in 1778. Back in 1761, during the French and Indian War, Spain and France concluded the Bourbon Family Pact, a military alliance. Britain's victory ended up costing Spain some of its North American and Caribbean holdings, and, when France joined in the American Revolution, Spain followed, hoping—like France—to recoup what it had lost in the previous war. Like France, Spain at first participated covertly, giving and lending money, but in 1779, Spanish forces opened a second front against Britain in present-day Florida and Alabama.

The "rebellion" had indisputably become an international conflict—one in which the mighty Royal Navy was now obliged to play a greater role. How would the United States, which barely had a navy, respond?

ASYMMETRICAL WARFARE, EIGHTEENTH-CENTURY STYLE

THE TERM *asymmetrical warfare* began to be used in the late twentieth century to describe conflicts in which small countries or even stateless groups (such as Islamic extremist groups) effectively confront great states (such as the United States) by using terrorist, insurgent, and guerrilla tactics that challenge even the mightiest conventional military force. The term was unknown in the eighteenth century, but it aptly describes the conduct of the American Revolution at sea. In 1775, the Royal Navy had 131 ships of the line—the battleships of the era, each of which mounted at least 64 guns (though some had 90 to 100 cannon). In addition, there were 139 craft of other classes, including many frigates. (If ships of the line were the equivalent of battleships, frigates were cruisers—lighter, faster, more maneuverable, but still packing plenty of firepower.)

Opposing this mighty armada was an American navy that, in 1775, did not even exist. In a letter of October 19, 1775, to James Warren, John Adams proposed funding what he called an "American Fleet," and the Continental Congress agreed on October 30. The first ships of this fleet were a collection of small craft gathered from various private sources during the siege of Boston (see Chapter 8). Congress resolved to create a national navy and to build thirteen frigates. That, of course, would take time. Strange as it sounds today, the national navy competed for scarce resources with various state navies. Eleven states had their own navies during the Revolution. In addition, there were privateers and commerce raiders. These were civilian vessels commanded and crewed by merchant sailors, who were authorized by Congress to commit acts of piracy against British shipping.

Patriot, silversmith, and engraver Paul Revere executed this view of Boston Harbor in 1770. The ships alongside or close to the wharves are merchant vessels, and the much larger ships lined up at the right are Royal Navy men-of-war—far more formidable than any colonial vessel.

Naval warfare, especially in the eighteenth century, was mostly a matter of cold numbers. The side with the most ships—and the most guns—almost always won. In a ship-on-ship contest, a vessel with sixty-four guns could pretty certainly be counted on to sink a ship of forty-four guns. How, then, did the Americans stand a chance in combat at sea?

The Earl of Sandwich and the Royal Navy's Decline

The lesson of the Penobscot fiasco would seem to be simple: It is better to have a lot of ships handled by professional military sailors than just a handful of ships sailed by amateurs.

YET THE DISPARITY OF NUMBERS between the great Royal Navy and the puny naval assets of the United States does not tell the whole story. When the French and Indian War ended in 1763 the Royal Navy was at its height as a military force. No other nation's navy could seriously threaten it. But that, as they say, was then, and the American Revolution was now. In 1771, the Earl of Sandwich, an exuberantly corrupt politician in an age celebrated for its corruption, was named first sea lord, the equivalent of secretary of the navy. Sandwich allowed the Royal Navy's ships to decay into what one historian of the period called "floating coffins." Even worse, he saw to the promotion of cronies, and officers were allowed to advance not on their merits but for their political connections. An acquaintance of Lord Sandwich once described him in a rhymed couplet:

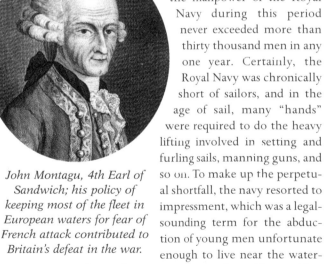

John Montagu, 4th Earl of Sandwich; his policy of keeping most of the fleet in European waters for fear of French attack contributed to Britain's defeat in the war.

> "Too infamous to have a friend,
> Too bad for bad men to commend."

The Duke of Richmond complained that "I would determine not to trust Lord Sandwich for a piece of rope yarn." When Sandwich was told that the Royal Navy was in acute decline, the "discipline of the service . . . entirely lost" and "the dockyards . . . in a wretched disabled state," he replied: "I have neither leisure nor inclination to enter into a discussion upon the subject."

Morale disintegrated, and between 1774 and 1780, sixty thousand sailors deserted or died from disease. This is a staggering number, considering that the manpower of the Royal Navy during this period never exceeded more than thirty thousand men in any one year. Certainly, the Royal Navy was chronically short of sailors, and in the age of sail, many "hands" were required to do the heavy lifting involved in setting and furling sails, manning guns, and so on. To make up the perpetual shortfall, the navy resorted to impressment, which was a legal-sounding term for the abduction of young men unfortunate enough to live near the waterfront. The captain of a vessel would assemble a "press gang" from among his crew and turn them loose on waterfront businesses and taverns. Sometimes, a Royal Navy vessel would intercept a British merchant ship, board it, and commandeer whatever crewmen it needed.

DONT TREAD ON ME

When the Second Continental Congress created the U.S. Navy in 1775, it also authorized five companies of Marines, some of whom carried yellow drums decorated with a coiled thirteen-rattle rattle-snake above the motto "Dont Tread On Me." Christopher Gadsden, congressional delegate from South Carolina and a member of the Marine Committee, presented Commodore Esek Hopkins with a yellow flag with the rattlesnake device and motto as his personal battle standard. Hopkins flew the flag on the 1776 mission to Nassau. Variations on the rattlesnake image and "Don't tread on me" motto were used on state and regimental flags throughout the Revolution and, later, in the Civil War. Although the original flag had a solid yellow background, it is traditionally recalled as having a backdrop of thirteen alternating red and white stripes. Since the terrorist attacks of September 11, 2001, the U.S. Navy has revived this so-called First Navy Jack, which is now flown from all active American warships.

The answer is that, sometimes, they stood almost no chance at all. Consider the Massachusetts state navy in 1779. Nineteen armed ships and twenty troop transports (carrying three thousand soldiers) were sent to Penobscot Bay in Maine—then part of Massachusetts. Penobscot Bay was a haven for Loyalists driven out of Boston, and the navy's assignment was to attack them and their fort. The Massachusetts transports disgorged their troops, but they failed to take the fort, and as they battered fruitlessly at their objective, the Royal Navy assembled a rescue fleet of sixty-four vessels. In the naval combat that followed, the Massachusetts fleet was overwhelmed. All of its ships either sunk by enemy fire or deliberately scuttled to prevent capture. The cost of their expedition was $7 million, which came close to knocking Massachusetts out of the war.

First Encounter

On June 2, 1775, the four-gun British schooner *Margaretta*, a pair of sloops, the *Polly* and the *Unity*, sailed into the Maine port of Machias to gather timber for the British garrison in Boston.

Lacking ships, local Patriots decided to do battle with the Royal Navy in church rather than at sea. Word was that the officers and crew of the *Margaretta* were a pious bunch and could be counted on to show up for worship. Therefore, on Sunday, June 11, the militia stormed the chapel. The sailors were not so far in the depths of spiritual transport that they failed to realize what was happening. Men and officers clambered through the church windows, dashed from the church, and made for their ship. Not to be defeated so easily, the militia took to the few boats they had, and some forty men gave chase, capturing the *Margaretta* after a brief skirmish. Two days later, the *Unity* also surrendered. The *Polly* got away. The *Margaretta* was duly rechristened as the *Liberty* and placed under the command of one Jeremiah O'Brien, who sailed it into battle against the schooner *Diligent*, capturing it as well. The *Liberty* and the *Diligent* became the first two ships of the Massachusetts navy. The disposition of the *Unity* is not recorded.

Bigger Game

The exchange off Machias had no appreciable impact on the American Revolution, of course, though it must have delighted the locals as much as it shamed a handful of Royal Navy personnel. Not content with such ad hoc operations carried out by state volunteers, the Continental Congress sent the newly created Continental navy on its first—and, as it turned out, only—major planned naval expedition in the Revolution.

Esek Hopkins had been raised on a Rhode Island farm, but he took to the sea and was judged by Congress to have acquired sufficient experience to justify his being given command of the first U.S. naval squadron. During March 3–4, 1776, Hopkins sailed to the British-held island of Nassau (then called Providence or New Providence) and, in a surprise amphibious assault, landed a force of Continental marines, who attacked Fort Montagu in what was *their* first action of the war. They acquitted themselves admirably, not only capturing the fort, but collecting one hundred cannons and mortars. Bagged as well was the island's royal governor, Montfort Browne, who was later swapped in a prisoner exchange for an American officer.

Esek Hopkins was the first commander in chief of the United States Navy. After scoring a brilliant victory at Nassau, he suffered a humiliating defeat against HMS Glasgow on April 6, 1776, which brought about his dismissal from command the following year.

A MAN NAMED JONES

THE EXPEDITION HOPKINS HAD LED to Nassau was made up of eight ships, the biggest of which were converted merchantmen mounting just twenty-four and twenty guns. Esek Hopkins had four officers ranked as captains: Dudley Saltonstall, Abraham Whipple, Nicholas Biddle, and John B. Hopkins, and a longer roster of lieutenants, including one John Paul Jones.

He had been born John Paul in Scotland in 1747. His father was a gardener in the employ of a Scots squire, but the boy was apprenticed to a shipowner. Paul discovered right away that he had a real taste for the sea, and on his very first voyage he was also able to get a taste of America; he visited his brother Paul (yes, Paul Paul), a Fredericksburg, Virginia, tailor.

After his master went bankrupt, Paul was turned loose from his apprenticeship and took a berth on a slaver. In 1766, the nineteen-year-old served as first mate on another slave ship, which was a lofty position for so young a sailor. But John Paul found it difficult to stomach trading in human beings, sold out his financial stake in the slaver, and booked passage—as a passenger—on the first ship back to England. En route, both the captain and first mate succumbed to a virulent fever, and John Paul stepped in to command. The owner, grateful for having his ship safe in port, rewarded him with a portion of the cargo. Word of his exploit quickly spread, and he was hired as captain of the *John*, out of Dumfries, Scotland.

The young captain seemed to lead a charmed life at sea, but, on his second voyage to the West Indies in the *John*, Paul had occasion to deal a flogging to the ship's carpenter for neglect of duty. The sailor collapsed and died. When this incident was duly reported, the man's anguished father charged Paul with murder. Arrested and briefly held, Captain John Paul was tried and acquitted. He returned to sea and was back in the West Indies during 1773 as captain of the *Betsy*, out of London. During an attempted mutiny, Paul killed the ringleader. Actually, according to eyewitnesses, it wasn't so much that he killed the man, as that the fellow rushed the captain and managed to impale himself on Paul's drawn sword.

Mutiny was a common occurrence in the eighteenth century, and few juries would have convicted a captain for putting an end to one, even if Paul had done more than just draw his sword. But having already come under a cloud for the earlier death of the carpenter, the young captain had earned a dark reputation. His friends suggested that he make himself scarce until a military court-martial—certain to be sympathetic to the commanding officer—could be convened. They advised him to take flight to America.

John Paul Jones was not only America's greatest naval hero, but must stand with Britain's own Lord Nelson as one of the most audacious and skillful naval officers to serve with any nation's navy—ever. This jaunty 1781 engraving is by French artist Jean Michel Moreau.

This he did and, without an excess of imagination, changed his name by adding Jones to the end of it. Unemployed, he lived on the charity of friends until the Revolution erupted. Borrowing funds, he traveled to Philadelphia, where he found work helping to fit out the *Alfred*, the first of the vessels purchased by Congress for the Continental navy. On the job, John Paul Jones got to know the leaders of the fledgling service, and, on December 7, 1775, he secured a berth as first lieutenant aboard the *Alfred*. The notion of ever returning to the islands for a court martial was set aside.

The *Glasgow* Affair

Around midnight on April 6, 1776, about a month after his victory at Nassau, Esek Hopkins led a five-ship Continental navy flotilla back from the West Indies and was intercepted by the twenty-gun British frigate *Glasgow*. Although outnumbered and outgunned, the *Glasgow* seized the element of surprise and attacked off Block Island, Rhode Island. After inflicting twenty-four casualties among the American sailors and seriously damaging the *Alfred,* the *Glasgow* withdrew. Hopkins hadn't managed to get a single hit against the enemy, and all that he had accomplished in the earlier engagement, at Nassau, was instantly forgotten. The damage to the *Alfred* could be repaired, but there was a serious question as to whether anything could fix the Continental navy. The incident seemed to break it apart. Officers resigned their commissions, and crews took to privateering. Hopkins endured the angry censure of Congress, and the fledgling American fleet was idled, then blockaded by the British in December 1776. Congress relieved Hopkins of command.

Every cloud, runs the cliché, has its silver lining. Another result of the *Glasgow* affair was the court-martial for cowardice of the captain of the *Providence,* who was relieved and replaced—by John Paul Jones.

Providence and *Ranger*

With *Providence* as his flagship at the head of a small flotilla, Jones quickly captured or sunk twenty-one British warships, transports, and commercial vessels, plus a Loyalist privateer—all before the end of 1776.

Like many aggressive commanders, John Paul Jones was hardly a modest man. His often-dismissive arrogance did not endear him to his brother officers, and, for his part, Jones objected to being classed as junior to seventeen other captains. The fact was that Jones was indeed junior to the others, and Congress was loath to offend these officers, yet its members were also aware that John Paul Jones was the best officer in the Continental navy—quite probably the best officer in any navy of any nation. Seeking to reward Jones even as it removed him from proximity to other officers, the Continental Congress, on June 14, 1777, assigned him command of the sloop *Ranger* and ordered him to sail to France, where he would

FORGOTTEN FACES
Honor Thy Father

Esek Hopkins was born in Providence, Rhode Island, in 1718, and skippered a privateer (state-sanctioned pirate raider) during the French and Indian War. At the outbreak of the American Revolution, he was made a brigadier general of the Rhode Island militia, in charge of coastal defense. He was given command of the squadron of eight armed merchant vessels chartered by the Continental Congress as the first ships of the Continental navy. Ordered to patrol the southern coast, he instead embarked on the spectacular Nassau raid; unfortunately it proved to be the high point of his career. Hopkins's ignominious defeat in the *Glasgow* affair earned him the censure of Congress in August 1776, dismissal from command in May 1777, and discharge from naval service in January 1778. Hopkins did not hang his head in shame, but served in the Rhode Island legislature for nearly a decade and was active in the state's affairs until his death in 1802. Nor did the U.S. Navy forsake the memory of its "father." Two destroyers—one serving in World War I and the other in World War II— were named for him.

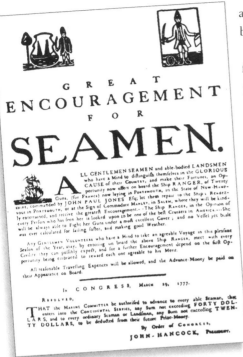

This recruiting poster calling for seamen to serve with John Paul Jones aboard USS Ranger was issued by the Second Continental Congress on March 19, 1777.

NUMBERS
Mother Lode

By the time he returned to Brest, on May 8, John Paul Jones had captured seven prizes (seven ships of the Royal Navy) and their crews.

assume command of the frigate *Indien,* which was being built in Amsterdam for the Continental navy.

When Jones arrived in Brest in December, he found that the *Indien,* delivered to France, had been presented to that country by the American commissioners who were negotiating the military alliance with the government of Louis XVI. Not one to be discouraged, Jones left Brest in the *Ranger* on April 10, 1778 with a crew of 140.

He then embarked on what might best be termed a tear.

On April 27–28, 1778, Jones raided Whitehaven on the Solway Firth in Scotland, personally leading a party from his crew in spiking the guns of two forts and burning three British ships. His plan had been to burn all of the ships in the harbor, but he ran out of time. Nevertheless, John Paul Jones earned the distinction of having executed the only American operation on British soil during the Revolution. He took the war—albeit briefly—to the motherland.

Jones had also planned to abduct the Earl of Selkirk and hold him hostage to secure good treatment for American prisoners of war. As luck would have it, Selkirk was away when Captain Jones came calling. But, still undiscouraged, Jones reboarded the *Ranger* and crossed the Irish Sea to Carrickfergus, where he captured the British sloop *Drake* in a battle less than an hour long. It was a sharp exchange, in which Jones lost eight men killed or wounded, but inflicted forty casualties on the British.

Career of the *Bonhomme Richard*

By the summer of 1779, the French had formally joined the war against Britain and delivered to the command of John Paul Jones five French naval vessels and a pair of privateers. Jones's flagship was an East Indiaman—a large merchant vessel built to endure long voyages between Europe and India—called the *Duras.* Refitted as a man-o'-war, it deserved a new name. Jones knew that the only American more popular among the French just now than he himself was Benjamin Franklin, whose *Poor Richard's*

Almanac was wildly popular even in the court of Louis XVI. Jones hit upon the happy idea of christening his new ship *Bonhomme Richard*—the Good Man Richard. The king and his courtiers were delighted.

Jones now embarked on an extraordinary mission of catch-as-catch-can raiding. Off Flamborough Head, along the North Sea's York coast, on September 23, 1779, he sighted two warships, the forty-four-gun *Serapis* and the twenty-gun *Countess of Scarborough*, escorting in convoy forty British merchant vessels. Despite its jaunty name, the *Bonhomme Richard* was a converted cargo vessel. It had been built for carrying capacity, not for speed or maneuverability. With forty-two guns, it was also slightly outgunned by the *Serapis.* Yet the prizes were too promising to pass up. Jones resolved to pursue the *Serapis* with his flagship while the three other vessels with him at the time—the *Vengeance,* the *Pallas,* and the *Alliance*—chased after the *Countess.*

The battle commenced well after nightfall under a bright moonlit sky. In the opening moments of the struggle, two of Jones's biggest guns exploded. Now the firepower gap between him and the enemy was suddenly widened. That gap would be narrowed, however, by Jones's genius at seamanship. Despite being heavier and clumsier than the British warship, the *Bonhomme Richard*, in Jones's hands, deftly outmaneuvered the enemy. Jones knew that broadside to broadside, he would come out second best to the forty-four guns of the *Serapis,* so, having outmaneuvered that ship, he now rammed its stern. This prevented the British vessel from firing a broadside, but it also put the *Bonhomme Richard* in a position from which none of her guns could be brought to bear, either. Doubtless noting this, the *Serapis's* skipper asked Jones if he was surrendering. The reply entered American history:

"Has your ship struck?" the skipper of the *Serapis* called out, meaning, *Have you struck (lowered) your colors?* Jones replied: "I have not yet begun to fight."

The two ships drew apart, and the Serapis, operating at close quarters, collided with the *Bonhomme Richard.* Jones seized this as an opportunity and ordered his men to lash on to the British vessel. This done, he began pounding the Serapis with his still-functioning

POP CULTURE

From the Harte

Bret Harte (1836–1902) is best known for his "local color" stories about rough-and-ready life in the California Gold Rush of 1849, but in 1878 he added his versatile pen to the many that had already celebrated John Paul Jones. "Off Scarborough, September, 1779" was written for the centennial of the *Bonhomme Richard*'s victory over the HMS *Serapis*. The poem's speaker is John Paul Jones himself:

IX

. . . Then I crept out in the dark
Till I hung above the hatch
Of the "Serapis,"—a mark
For her marksmen!—with a match
And a hand-grenade, but lingered just a moment more to snatch
One last look at sea and sky!

. . .

Then turned and down her yawning throat I launched that devil's pill!

X

Then—a blank was all between
As the flames around me spun!
Had I fired the magazine?
Was the victory lost or won?
Nor knew I till the fight was o'er but half my work was done:
For I lay among the dead,
In the cockpit of our foe,
With a roar above my head—
Till a trampling to and fro,
And a lantern showed my mate's face! and I knew what now you know!

cannon. The British returned fire, but it was too little too late. After two hours, the *Serapis* surrendered. The *Bonhomme Richard* had sustained so much damage that Jones abandoned it, transferring his flag to the prize ship, the *Serapis,* which he sailed into Texel, Holland. Jones turned over the prize, together with his other ships—except for the *Alliance*—to the French. In the *Alliance*, he continued to raid British shipping before setting off, in December 1780, on his return to the United States. He did so in a French military transport called the *Ariel.* En route, Jones captured the British ship *Triumph*—which, however, escaped before he could triumphantly haul it into an American port.

A hand-colored eighteenth-century etching depicts the epic North Sea battle between Bonhomme Richard, *under John Paul Jones, and HMS* Serapis, *commanded by Captain Richard Pearson, on September 23, 1779.*

JONES'S LUCK RUNS OUT

JONES SURVIVED THE MOST DARING and brutal combat at sea, only to fall prey to the envy of brother officers in the Continental navy. The Continental Congress wanted to promote him to rear admiral, but the other officers blocked it. Nevertheless, he was promised command of what would be the biggest ship in the Continental navy, the *America*. He waited a year while the ship was under construction, only to learn, shortly before it was launched, that it would be turned over to the French. Jones, too, was turned over to America's allies. He sailed with the French fleet until the end of the war.

The end of the Revolution brought no peace to John Paul Jones. In search of profitable adventure, he sailed to Russia, where he served as an admiral to Catherine the Great in one of her wars against the Turks. He defeated the Turkish fleet, but found himself the victim of envy once again—this time the envy of Russian officers. Disgusted, he settled in Paris in 1789, where, his spirit depressed and his health broken, he died in 1793.

FRENCH TRIUMPHS

UNDER ADMIRAL D'ESTAING, as we saw in Chapter 16, the French fleet floundered, and every engagement the French fought in American waters ended either in defeat or simply ended—inconclusively—through 1781. Elsewhere, however, under other commanders, the French fleet fared much better. In contrast to the Royal Navy, which had fallen victim to corruption and neglect by the time of the American Revolution, the French navy, which turned in a poor performance during the French and Indian War, had been greatly improved with new ships and better sailors.

Not that the British lacked magnificent naval commanders. George Brydges Rodney was one of the best, having become a national naval hero during the Seven Years War. A man of great character and ability, he naturally objected to the corrupt practices of Lord Sandwich, who responded by deliberately withholding from Rodney any command against the American rebels until 1779. By that time, Rodney was sixty-one-years old and hobbled by gout. Nor did Sandwich do Rodney any favor in the command he assigned to him. He was made commander in chief of the Leeward

---

DETAILS, DETAILS
A Hero Returns

It was not until 1905 that the remains of John Paul Jones, interred in Paris, were returned to the United States. In 1913, they were entombed at the naval academy in Annapolis, Maryland.

Admiral George Brydges Rodney was a superb naval commander who predictably ran afoul of the Earl of Sandwich, corrupt first lord of the Admiralty, and was not given a major role in the naval war during the American Revolution. He nevertheless scored a major victory against the Spanish at Gibraltar on January 16, 1781, but then became enmeshed in lawsuits over prizes of war and, because of this, faltered badly in the Caribbean.

Islands in the West Indies—a backwater in the war, which no other admiral would even consider.

As he made his way to the West Indies to take up his new assignment, Rodney was ordered to come to the relief of Gibraltar, which was under a Spanish siege. In a magnificent moonlight battle on January 16, 1781, he not only relieved Gibraltar, but sunk or captured seven Spanish warships in the process.

Once again, Rodney was hailed a new national hero. But then things started going terribly wrong.

He captured the island of St. Eustatius on February 3, 1781. A possession of Holland, which was Britain's latest enemy in this revolution that had turned into a world war, St. Eustatius was a place of considerable wealth, and Rodney looked forward to enjoying a substantial portion of this war prize (Rodney shared with America's Benedict Arnold an overweening fondness for living beyond his means). The problem was that British merchants greeted the capture of St. Eustatius with an avalanche of claims of their own. After all, it was their shipping that the Dutch privateers had raided. And that avalanche soon buried Rodney under a pile of lawsuits. More immediately, Rodney's focus on the bounty of St. Eustatius kept him from making a scheduled rendezvous with Admiral Samuel Hood, whose mission was to blockade Fort Royal off Martinique and keep the French bottled up there. Because Rodney failed to link up with him, the French fleet drove Hood off.

In 1778 and 1779, the French took the islands of Dominica, St. Vincent, and Grenada, while St. Lucia fell to the British. In 1781, France captured Tobago. Elsewhere in action remote from North America but nevertheless spawned by French involvement in the American Revolution, Admiral Pierre André de Suffren de Saint Tropez enjoyed victories off the coast of the Portuguese-held Cape Verde Islands and off the coast of India.

ALTERNATE TAKE

If the French Navy Fell . . .

Nothing Rodney might have done would have changed the outcome of the Revolution; however, as Admiral Hood complained, had Rodney acted more aggressively, he could have taken at least twenty French ships, thereby breaking the back of the French navy. This, surely, would have softened the blow of the British defeat in America.

THE ROYAL NAVY RECOVERS—TOO LATE

AS WE WILL SEE IN CHAPTER 22, the most consequential defeat the Royal Navy would suffer came during the Yorktown campaign in 1781, but even after this defeat—which presaged American victory in the Revolution—the Royal Navy recovered when Rodney returned to command in the West Indies. Crushed by disappointment over the St. Eustatius treasures, he had fallen ill and returned to England. There, however, his patriotic spirit reasserted itself, and, though still in poor health, he rejoined Admiral Hood in the West Indies on February 19, 1782. During April 9–12, 1782, in the epic Battle of Saints Passage, Rodney captured Admiral François Joseph Paul, comte de Grasse aboard his sumptuous flagship, the *Ville de Paris,* directly after his triumph against the British fleet off the Yorktown peninsula. The victory did nothing to blunt the effect of Yorktown, however, and Rodney's failure to pursue the bulk of the French fleet diluted the victory.

Another post-Yorktown British victory came at Gibraltar, when Admiral Richard Howe, called out of retirement, succeeded in breaking Spain's three-year siege of the British island fortress. This action gave the British a stronger bargaining position in the Paris peace conference that ended the Revolution.

THE PRIVATEERS' WAR

EMPLOYED MORE EFFECTIVELY at an early stage of the war, the Royal Navy might have crushed the Revolution. Had the Continental navy possessed more sailors like John Paul Jones, it, too, could have had a greater effect on the course of the war. In the end, it was the privateers who probably made the greatest impact at sea.

Most of the individual American states issued letters of marque and reprisal, which were, in effect, official warrants sanctioning piracy. The letters authorized some twelve hundred to two thousand privateers to prey on British merchant shipping. This would, first and foremost, interfere with the flow of supplies to British troops. Secondarily, it would provide badly needed supplies for the Continental army and the various militias. As for the privateers, they were paid by what they captured; they were entitled to a substantial share of whatever goods they appropriated. It is estimated that about six hundred British ships were captured by privateers—a record far in excess of anything the puny Continental navy achieved.

TAKEAWAY

Davy vs. Goliath

Although the Royal Navy was large, it was in decline during the period of the American Revolution. The American navy was diminutive, but John Paul Jones alone was probably worth a hundred ships. In addition, the Americans had an alliance with France, which operated a formidable navy, and had the services of a legion of daring privateers eager to capture prizes.

On April 3, 1776, the Second Continental Congress began issuing "letters of marque and reprisal," official warrants authorizing masters of civilian vessels to raid and capture the merchant ships of enemy nations. Recipients of such authorization were called privateers, and, in the American Revolution, they constituted the major naval force of the United States.

Chapter 21

ANOTHER SHIFT TO THE SOUTH

The English Move Inland to the Southern Backcountry, and the Fight for the Southern Interior Turns Ugly

AFTER FAILING TO STRANGLE the American Revolution in its Massachusetts cradle, the British decided early in the war to focus their efforts on regions believed to have strong Loyalist support, including New York and the South. During 1775–76, however, it was Patriot forces that either gained or maintained control in the South, and the British withdrew, leaving 1777 for the most part a very quiet year in the Southern theater. The calm ended in 1778, when Major General Robert Howe assumed command of Continental army forces in the South. He planned to capture St. Augustine, Florida, but could not persuade local militia commanders to cooperate. The British responded to American stirrings in the South by capturing Savannah (see Chapter 18, "The Fall of Savannah"), and, with that, the South once again became a hotly contested theater.

LOW COUNTRY DISASTERS

IN SEPTEMBER 1778, MAJOR GENERAL BENJAMIN LINCOLN took over from Robert Howe as American commander in the South. As we saw in Chapter 18, this courageous and hard-working officer was no great tactician. He failed to wrest control of Georgia from the British in 1779, and the Franco-American amphibious assault on occupied Savannah likewise soured.

The next year was no better. Through much of the war, the Americans had been the beneficiary of overly cautious, even lethargic British military leaders. An exception to the general run of British commanders was Banastre Tarleton. He had participated in the capture of General Charles Lee at Basking Ridge, New Jersey, in December 1776 (see Chapter 11, "The End of Lee") and, after that coup, made a meteoric rise from lieutenant to lieutenant colonel. He performed brilliantly during the Charleston Campaign of 1780. He understood that it was one thing to capture South Carolina's major city, but quite another to end all Patriot resistance in the Carolina hinterlands. He set about with relish the task of mopping up backcountry rebels, beginning, as mentioned in Chapter 18, with the Battle of Monck's Corner (April 14, 1780). This was followed by the Battle of Lenud's Ferry, South Carolina, on May 6, in which Tarleton fought the survivors of Monck's Corner, who had been joined by fresh troops under Colonel Anthony White. In an opening skirmish, White captured an officer and seventeen of Tarleton's men. In response, Tarleton led a stunning cavalry charge that not only liberated the captives, but killed or wounded five American officers and thirty-six enlisted men, and captured seven officers and sixty dragoons.

By the summer of 1782, when this cartoon was published in London, Britons generally regarded the American Revolution as a lost cause and had little patience with empty boasts concerning it. Brilliant and ruthless, Banastre Tarleton also had a reputation as a "thunderer"—one who expounds on his exploits with thunderous voice—and he is shown here, having apparently talked the head off the British heir apparent, the Prince of Wales. The pair is depicted outside of the Whirligig, whose exuberant whirligig sign announces it as a London brothel.

REALITY CHECK
Holding Fire

Military officers were trained to order men to hold their fire as long as possible, since firing at close range was so much more effective than firing at long range. Muskets and marksmen alike were notoriously inaccurate. However, this tactic worked well only when firing from a strong defensive position or when firing from a proper two- or three-rank formation. In a situation in which soldiers were spread out, holding fire was a disastrous tactic. Spread thinly, soldiers could not mass sufficient firepower to prevent being overrun, which is precisely what happened to Buford's command.

POP CULTURE
No Quarter

The phrase "Tarleton's quarter!" became a Patriot battle cry, much as "Remember the Alamo!" would become the cry of Texas independence in the next century.

Massacre at Waxhaws

Tarleton's willingness to break the rules of conventional warfare was shown to brilliant advantage at Moncks Corner and Lenud's Ferry. At Waxhaws, South Carolina, that willingness crossed the line into atrocity.

About three hundred men under Colonel Abraham Buford, the 3rd Virginia Continentals, were on the march to reinforce Charleston during Clinton's siege of that city. Before Buford reached it, however, Charleston fell, leaving him and his three hundred men the only organized American unit remaining in South Carolina. Cornwallis, having taken Charleston, ordered Tarleton (and others) to locate Buford and capture or kill his force. Tarleton quickly ascertained that Buford had bivouacked at Waxhaws Creek. Determined to bag him, he assembled 40 men of the 17th Dragoons, together with 130 cavalrymen and 100 infantry, mostly Tories of the Loyal Legion. There were more than a hundred miles to cover and to cover fast, so Tarleton ordered as many of the infantrymen as possible to ride double with the cavalry, two men to a saddle. In the Low Country heat of late May, many of the cavalry mounts collapsed and died under the added weight. No matter. Tarleton stole replacements and pressed the pursuit.

He made contact with the rear of Buford's column early in the afternoon of May 29, having pounded through 105 wilderness miles in just fifty-four hours. Wasting no time, he sent a messenger to Buford under a flag of truce, with a note demanding the American's surrender. "If you are rash enough to reject the terms," Tarleton wrote, "the blood be upon your head."

Buford handed the messenger his reply: "I reject your proposals and shall defend myself to the last extremity."

Tarleton received the reply, then attacked with utmost savagery. Buford had not had time to consolidate his position, and his men were strung out in a long column. His officers gamely ordered their men to hold fire until the British and Loyalist forces were within ten paces. The Americans were overrun. Buford had no choice but to give up and "ask for quarter"—that is, throw himself and his men on the mercy of the victor.

To justify what happened next, Tarleton later claimed that someone had fired a shot at him during surrender negotiations.

This was almost certainly a lie. What is known is that Tarleton ordered his men to put to the bayonet all of the Continentals who had surrendered to him. One hundred thirteen of Buford's men were killed in this manner. It was the bloodiest atrocity of the war, and if Tarleton had intended it to demoralize the southern Patriots, intimidating them into surrender, he was very much mistaken. It inflamed them.

Disgrace at Camden

The fall of Charleston and the other Patriot defeats in the Low Country put South Carolina in British hands. When General Lincoln was forced to surrender, George Washington selected the very capable Nathanael Greene to replace him, but the Continental Congress intervened and decided that the man credited with the victories at Saratoga, Horatio Gates, was just the commander to win back what had been lost in the South. Overruled, Washington had no choice but to acquiesce.

Determined to regain a foothold in South Carolina, Gates set out for Camden, South Carolina, which was held by 2,200 troops under Cornwallis's personal command. Gates collected militia reinforcements to augment his Continentals, which gave him a total force of 4,100. On the face of it, this was a great numerical advantage, but reality turned out to be more complex than simple arithmetic. First, many of Gates's men were suffering from ailments common to the Southern swampland and were not fit for duty. Second, Gates somehow inflated his estimate of the number of men he was leading. He believed he had not 4,100 men, but some 7,000. So what if a few were sick? The fact was, that about half of Gates's command was ailing, leaving him with perhaps 2,000 men fit for duty.

By the night of August 15, 1780, Gates confessed that his men were "much debilitated." But debilitated or not, they were soldiers, and he ordered a nighttime march on to Camden. By pure coincidence, Cornwallis had ordered some of his troops out of Camden to search for American forces. Cornwallis's troops stumbled upon Gates's column at about two thirty on the morning of August 16.

MEDICAL MATTERS
Devil's Drink

Horatio Gates had been trained in the British army, which held sacred the tradition of distributing a ration of rum to the troops. Rum, and alcohol in general, was believed to ward off and cure disease, improve discipline, and build courage. Lacking rum, Gates ordered as a substitute the distribution of molasses, which was plentiful in the Low Country. The laxative effects of the molasses, combined with the ingestion of food poorly stored in a hot climate, created an urgent epidemic of dysentery among the ranks.

The late nineteenth-century American illustrator Howard Pyle depicts "The American Colonist" enjoying a morning eye-opener: a carefully poured dram of rum.

DETAILS, DETAILS
Flight of the General

A Congressional inquiry in 1782 cleared Horatio Gates of wrongdoing, accepting his claim that his only purpose in departing the field so precipitously had been to reach safety so that he could rebuild his army. Whether it was the product of prudence or cowardice, the flight of the fifty-two-year-old general from Camden to Hillsboro—a distance of almost two hundred miles in three days—was truly remarkable. He made the first leg of the journey, sixty miles to Charlotte, on the fastest horse he could find. The rest of the trip was made on a relay of mounts.

Gates was pleased. To be sure, his men were sick—even those still capable of marching—but he believed he occupied advantageous ground. Nevertheless, he decided to hedge his bet personally by observing the battle from the rear, leaving other officers, including Baron de Kalb, to take charge from the front lines. But even the brilliant Kalb could do little with the sickly Virginia and North Carolina militiamen of the American left wing. They fell apart at the first British assault.

The right wing fared better. Consisting of veteran Maryland and Delaware troops, this force held its ground—at least until the two American commanders, Ortho Williams and Baron de Kalb were wounded (Kalb fatally). Now they fell apart as well, and the right wing was routed.

Only 700 of the 4,100 American troops Gates commanded reached the haven of Hillsboro three days after the battle. An estimated 1,900 died, and nearly 1,000 were taken prisoner. British losses were 68 killed and 350 wounded. Gates had not waited to see the outcome of the battle, but fled the field after the collapse of his left wing. The defeat at Camden effectively ended Gates's career, although he was permitted to rejoin the army at Newburgh, New York, for the final days of the war.

Eyewitness

On September 17, 1780, New York City Loyalist James Rivington published a mocking ad in his *Royal Gazette*:

REWARD

Strayed, deserted, or stolen, from the subscriber. On the 16th of August last, near Camden, in the State of South Carolina, a whole ARMY, consisting of horse, foot, and dragoons... with...baggage, artillery, wagons and camp equipage. The subscriber has very strong suspicions...that a certain CHARLES, EARL CORNWALLIS, was principally concerned in carrying off said ARMY with their baggage, etc. Any person or persons...who will give information... where the said ARMY is, so that they may be recovered and rallied again, shall be entitled to demand from the Treasurer of the United States the sum of THREE MILLION of PAPER DOLLARS As soon as they can be spared from the public funds...

RECOVERY

HAVING DRIVEN THIS LATEST AMERICAN ARMY out of South Carolina, Cornwallis left Camden on September 8, 1780, bound for North Carolina, which he also intended to clear of rebels. He advanced in three columns. He led the main force; Tarleton was in charge of the Loyal (Tory) Legion and the regular light infantry; and Major Patrick Ferguson led the rest of the Tories.

Battle of Kings Mountain

Cornwallis was shocked by the ferocity of resistance from diehard North Carolina Patriots. He did capture Charlotte, on September 26, 1780, but at an unexpectedly high cost in casualties. Then, having taken the town, he found his lines of supply and communication under constant attack. Hoping to screen his main column from guerrilla assault and snipers, Cornwallis sent Ferguson ahead to lead the Tories along the foothills. This tactic succeeded only in separating Ferguson from the main body of troops and exposed him to attack by militia under the command of Colonels Charles McDowell, John Sevier, Isaac Shelby, William Campbell, Benjamin Cleveland, James Williams, and Major Joseph Winston. The beleaguered Ferguson retreated to the Catawba River, then trekked up Kings Mountain, on the border between North and South Carolina. Believing he had found an advantageous high-ground position there, Ferguson took his stand on October 7—only to find himself enveloped by Patriot forces. In close combat, Ferguson was killed even as he was in the act of shooting an American officer. With the death of their leader, the Tories surrendered.

Kings Mountain was a glorious victory for the Americans, a badly needed tonic after a string of defeats. Cornwallis halted his advance, then withdrew back into South Carolina. Worse for the British, the Battle of Kings Mountain put an end to Tory influence in North Carolina for the rest of the war.

The Battle of Kings Mountain, October 7, 1780, was a welcome Southern victory for the Patriots after a string of ignominious defeats. This nineteenth-century colored engraving shows an early stage of the battle.

VICTORY AT THE COWPENS

AFTER GOING THROUGH TWO failed commanders in the South—
Generals Lincoln and Gates—Washington finally prevailed on
Congress to let him appoint Nathanael Greene to overall command of the region. Washington had great confidence in Greene,
who was a commander capable of handling conventional military
forces as well as exploiting guerrillas. He was appointed in October,
but did not reach the field until December 1780. While awaiting
their new general, South Carolina guerrillas continually harassed
the British forces. Cornwallis counted on Tarleton to dispose of the
guerrillas, but even he proved unable to do so.

When Greene finally arrived, he took note of the success of the
irregular forces. He also observed, realistically, that Cornwallis outnumbered him three to two. He therefore decided to avoid a major
confrontation and continue instead to employ guerrilla tactics.
Greene summoned the best guerrilla leader he knew: Virginian
Daniel Morgan. The trouble was that Morgan had resigned from
the Continental army on July 18, 1779. He pled ill health, but it was
an open secret that he quit because he had been passed over for
command of what became Anthony Wayne's Light Infantry
Brigade. The Camden debacle, however, awakened (or reawak-
ened) in Morgan a selfless patriotism, and he ungrudgingly
answered Greene's call to arms.

Greene assigned Morgan the mission of harassing the British in
western South Carolina while he himself supported guerrillas in the
north-central portion of the state. From Cornwallis's point of view, it
appeared merely that Greene had committed the military sin of
dividing his forces in the face of the enemy. He therefore sent Tarleton
to deal with Morgan while he mounted an attack on Greene.

On January 16, 1781, Morgan discovered Tarleton's approach
with eleven hundred Tories and regulars. Morgan's own command
consisted of about a thousand militiamen of varying ability and experience. Morgan was mindful of the recent disaster at Camden, which
he attributed less to Gates's cowardly incompetence than to the inex-
perience of the militia forces there. Morgan therefore decided to
arrange this battle so that his militia could *not* cut and run. He decided to deploy his forces at a place called the Cowpens, which, as the
name suggested, was little more than a backwoods South Carolina

REALITY CHECK
Master of War

Most military historians
agree that Daniel
Morgan was the only
out-and-out military
genius to emerge from
the American
Revolution. A lesser
commander than
Morgan would have
prudently retreated at
the approach of the
much-feared Banastre
Tarleton, but not only
was Morgan by his
nature disinclined to
withdraw from battle, he
also understood that to
retreat was to invite a
force of militiamen
simply to disband and
go home. As Morgan
saw it, the best time for
a fight was when a fight
presented itself.

cattle pasturage. In the disposition of his forces, he proceeded, quite on purpose, to break every rule of military common sense.

First, he positioned his men with their backs to the Broad River, so as to cut off any avenue of retreat. This left his men but two options: win or die. Second, he put his greenest troops in the front line. Behind them, he deployed his proven Virginia veterans and the Continentals. Then, farthest to the rear, he held his cavalry in reserve—whereas, any commander who had ever read a military manual would have put his cavalry in the most advanced position. Seeing the build up of American forces at the Cowpens, Banastre Tarleton was delighted. This, he thought, was the perfect place for a bayonet charge, the tactic that had thoroughly terrified the Americans at Camden. And so the battle began.

Morgan instructed his riflemen carefully: "Look for the epaulets! Pick off the epaulets!" (Epaulets were worn by the officers.)

As he advanced, it must have seemed to Tarleton that these Americans at the Cowpens were doing precisely what the Americans had done at Waxhaws: held their fire until it was too late. But there was all the difference in the world. At Waxhaws, the Americans had been thinly spread out. At the Cowpens, they were perfectly positioned to deliver deadly massed volleys. This they did, at close range. After firing the first volley, the raw recruits of the American front line sheared off to the left and around to the rear of the American lines. This put the British—their ranks diminished by the first volley—up against the second line, the seasoned veterans.

Tarleton's troops were—admittedly with good reason—arrogant. Confidence is a good thing in an army, but arrogance is disastrous. The Tories attacked without discipline, willy-nilly. Seeing this, Morgan acted quickly. He ordered his green troops, who had returned to the rear, to sweep out and behind Tarleton's approaching left wing while he sent his cavalry forward in a wheel around to the rear of Tarleton's right. This was a double envelopment, which is to battle what a checkmate is to chess: absolute victory for the enveloper; absolute defeat for the enveloped.

Morgan's victory at the Cowpens was more than a military masterpiece. It saved Greene's army and cost Cornwallis (according to Morgan's tally) 110 killed, 200 wounded (and captured), and 531 captured (unwounded)—a count U.S. Army War College scholars

DETAILS, DETAILS
Lessons of Cannae
Morgan was a self-educated general, but he almost certainly was familiar with the military masterpiece every eighteenth-century commander knew and admired: the Battle of Cannae. There, in southeast Italy, in 216 B.C., the Carthaginian general Hannibal had doubly enveloped the elite Roman legion and wiped it out. In the depths of the South Carolina backcountry, Morgan had wrought a second Cannae.

Swamp Fox

Despite his genius, Daniel Morgan never achieved the legendary stature of another frontier guerrilla leader, Francis Marion, better known as the Swamp Fox.

A MAN OF DIMINUTIVE STATURE—"small enough at birth to be put into a quart mug," it was said—he was an unlikely fighter, frail and sickly for much of his life. Yet during the French and Indian War he was a leader of militia—a fierce Indian fighter—and by 1775 he was a passionate advocate of independence and a delegate to the South Carolina Provincial Congress. In June of 1775, he was elected captain of the 2nd South Carolina Regiment and fought in the defense of Charleston in 1776, earning promotion to lieutenant colonel.

Marion served in the failed defense of Savannah and the fiasco at Camden. At Savannah, he led his regiment in a gallant but unsuccessful counterattack, and, at Camden, he furnished the only bright spot in the otherwise dismal encounter. On August 20, 1780, after the American defeat, Marion and seventeen men leaped out of the swamp and attacked a much larger force of Tories and reg-

ulars, who were escorting American prisoners. The attack was so sudden and swift that the enemy assumed it was the leading edge of a much larger force. Abandoning the prisoners, the Tory and British soldiers ran.

Most of Marion's actions were small guerrilla assaults, typical of which was the fight at Tearcoat Swamp (in South Carolina, where modern U.S. Route 301 crosses the Black River). On the night of October 25, 1780, Marion led 150 handpicked men against a much larger Tory militia force. The bewildered Tories were stunned by an attack that miraculously materialized out of the swamp. They ran, leaving behind three to six dead, and fourteen wounded. Marion took twenty-three prisoners and eighty muskets and horses. More important, the attack was widely talked about and not only suppressed a Tory uprising in the area, but converted a number of Loyalists to the Patriot cause.

The diminutive South Carolina Patriot leader Francis Marion earned his sobriquet—the "Swamp Fox"—with victories such as this one over British, Loyalist, and Hessian forces at Parker's Ferry, South Carolina, on August 30, 1781.

consider somewhat inflated. Whatever the precise figures, they tell only part of the story. The Cowpens was especially deadly for British and Tory officers. Of 66 officers engaged, 39 died. American losses were no more than 12 killed and 60 wounded. Combined with the triumph at Kings Mountain, Cowpens lifted the American armies from collective despair and dissolution. The aura of invincibility that had surrounded Banastre Tarleton had been shattered, and, from this time onward, American fortunes in the South were transformed.

A DRAW?

THE BATTLE OF THE COWPENS convinced Cornwallis that he had to adapt more successfully to frontier warfare. He therefore took the bold step of ordering his troops to shed most of the baggage that traditionally hobbled British armies in the American wilderness. His men were to march with only what they could carry on their backs.

Stripped down in this way, Cornwallis set out after Greene's army, pursuing it northward to the Dan River, near the Virginia border. Greene noted the uncharacteristic speed with which Cornwallis moved and correctly guessed that he must be traveling very light. The advantage of that was speed, of course, but the disadvantage was an acute shortage of supplies. Greene outran the advantage and exploited the disadvantage by crossing the Dan, being careful to take with him every boat in the area. By the time he arrived at the near shore of the river, Cornwallis was indeed desperately in want of supplies. Yet, without boats, he was unable to cross the river. He decided to turn back to Hillsboro to resupply his force. In the time that took, Greene recrossed the Dan into North Carolina and continually sniped at Cornwallis's lines of communication, further draining his supplies.

But Greene knew better than to provoke a full-out fight. He would wait until he had worn down Cornwallis some more and had collected enough men to outnumber the British commander. In the meantime, he directed operations against local Tories—including a massacre of four hundred Tories by forces under General Andrew Pickens—which eroded Cornwallis's base of Loyalist support.

On March 14, 1781, Greene decided that the time was ripe for a battle. The site he staked out was Guilford Courthouse, North Carolina. His plan was to repeat here what Daniel Morgan had

DETAILS, DETAILS
Deadly Grapes
Grapeshot was the antipersonnel artillery ammunition of the eighteenth and nineteenth centuries. Instead of a solid cannonball, a collection of small metal balls—like a cluster of grapes—was loaded into a canvas bag and shot out of the cannon. Once fired, the bag would quickly disintegrate, spreading the grapeshot from the muzzle, as if the cannon were a large shotgun. Grapeshot often passed through victims, shattering bones and thereby turning bone fragments into secondary projectiles, which multiplied the lethal effect of the shot. Grapeshot could be specially manufactured, or it could be improvised from a variety of objects, including chain links, scrap metal, glass shards, and rocks.

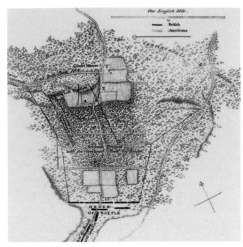

Nathanael Greene tried to duplicate Daniel Morgan's victory at the Cowpens by pulling off a double envelopment against the British at Guilford Courthouse. A combination of inadequately trained men and Greene's unwillingness to risk his reserves marred the execution of the tactic, and the battle ended in a draw: a tactical victory for the British, yet also a costly strategic defeat.

TAKEAWAY

Tide Turns in the South

Whereas the Waxhaws Massacre and the Battle of Camden were major American defeats in the Southern backcountry, the tide in the region was turned in the Patriots' favor by the battles of Kings Mountain and the Cowpens. The Battle of Guilford Courthouse was so costly a victory for Cornwallis that he withdrew from North Carolina and marched into Virginia. This set the stage for his final defeat at Yorktown, the culminating battle of the American Revolution.

achieved at the Cowpens, a double envelopment. On the next day, March 15, as Morgan had done, Greene put his rawest recruits in the front line, deploying seasoned veterans in the rank behind them up. He instructed the frontline militia to fire two volleys before withdrawing to the rear. They did just that, but then, instead of shearing off in good order—as Morgan's men had done—they fumbled back in chaos, stumbling all over one another. This prevented Greene from forming them up to bring off the kind of envelopment Morgan had achieved at the Cowpens. Despite this, Greene might have achieved a victory if he had sent his cavalry (like Morgan, he kept it in reserve) running around the rear of the British positions. But, capable as he was, Greene fell short of Morgan's genius—and, more important, lacked his willingness to go for broke. Not wanting to risk his cavalry in a single attack, he held back a portion of it—which gave Cornwallis the breathing space he needed to retaliate. The British general trained his artillery on the Americans, raking them with deadly grapeshot. He was firing at such close range that many of his own soldiers fell along with the Americans. Nevertheless, the artillery had the desired effect. It drove Greene from the field.

He who possesses the contested ground when the battle is over must be judged the winner. Guilford Courthouse was therefore a victory for the British. Yet the battle had cost Cornwallis a quarter of his army, a loss so devastating that he decided to clear out of the North Carolina interior. At best a tactical victory for the British, Guilford Courthouse was ultimately a strategic defeat. Cornwallis withdrew to Wilmington, on the Carolina coast.

Greene was frustrated that a triumph had slipped through his fingers, but he did not yield to the impulse to pursue Cornwallis for another showdown. He correctly assumed that Cornwallis intended to keep moving north, into Virginia, and there, he knew, he would meet Washington's much larger force. Greene decided to leave Cornwallis to the commander in chief while he turned south to recover South Carolina and Georgia.

Chapter 22

YORKTOWN: THE WORLD TURNED UPSIDE DOWN

How the Franco-American Yorktown Campaign Brought the War to an End

THIS WAS THE SHAPE OF THE AMERICAN REVOLUTION: the major action began in New England, moved south to New York, New Jersey, and Pennsylvania, and then down into the South. The Carolinas and Georgia experienced brutal frontier warfare, and the two chief cities of the South, Savannah and Charleston, fell to the British and remained in British hands until the end of the war.

If New England was the heart of the Revolution, Virginia was its soul. From this state came many of the founding fathers, including George Washington himself. Yet the war did not reach Virginia until 1779, when Lord Dunmore burned Norfolk (see Chapter 18, "The Southern Roots of War"). This was followed later in the spring by the capture of Portsmouth and a few other coastal Virginia settlements. But these were minor actions. Cornwallis was alone among the principal British commanders in believing that controlling Virginia would bring the Revolution to an end. He wanted to conduct a major campaign in the state, and he made bold to ask General Henry Clinton to pull out of New York and send everything he had into Virginia. This was, however, quite beyond the vision of Clinton, whose cautious and conventional nature made him loath to undertake such a daring move. Nevertheless, at the end of 1780, he finally agreed to dispatch a major force into Virginia.

IN HIS MAJESTY'S SERVICE

THE COMMANDING OFFICER OF THE FORCE Henry Clinton sent into Virginia was Benedict Arnold. True to his word, Clinton did not abandon Arnold, even after the collapse of the West Point plot. He saw to it that the turncoat general was compensated for property confiscated by the Continental Congress and that his family was provided for. But, most of all, Arnold had sought a high-level command in His Majesty's service—something grander than Washington and Congress had ever granted him. In this, he was disappointed, commissioned a brigadier general, one rank below what he held in the Continental army.

The problem with being a turncoat is that nobody ever trusts you much. It was clear to Clinton and Arnold's other "handlers" that he had not betrayed his country out of an overwhelming love of mother England. He had turned traitor for cash. The British recognized Arnold's skill as an officer, but they never embraced him, and they did not entrust to him a major command. Instead, he was given a detachment of sixteen hundred soldiers, told to augment this by raising a legion of Tories (and deserters from the Patriot forces), and raise hell in Virginia. Benedict Arnold was to be a raider.

He sailed from New York on December 20, 1780, with those sixteen hundred men, including John Graves Simcoe and his band of Tory Rangers. Stormy weather injured or sickened some four hundred of his men, so that by the time he reached Hampton Roads on December 30, Arnold had an effective strength of twelve hundred. Nor would he be very successful in raising Loyalist forces. He was told to recruit at least eight hundred, but all he could scrape together were 212 men.

The Virginia Raids

Despite his failure as a recruiter, Arnold proved to be more than competent as a destroyer. On January 3, 1781, he seized the battery at Hood's Point, which defended Richmond—at the time Virginia's major inland town. Arnold entered Richmond on January 5, the militiamen assigned to defend it having decamped without firing a single shot. Arnold dispatched Simcoe and his Rangers to nearby Westham, to destroy a key foundry and gunpowder factory there (and also to burn public records, which had been stored at Westham for safekeeping) while Arnold personally directed the burning of Richmond. With the town ablaze, he reboarded his men on their captured ship and sailed away.

LAFAYETTE FIGHTS BACK

FRIEDRICH STEUBEN, THE EUROPEAN OFFICER who had been instrumental in training the Continental army at Valley Forge (see Chapter 15, "The Forge"), was now in command of American forces in Virginia. His stern, by-the-book manner had been crucially important during the hard Valley Forge winter, but now, against Arnold in Virginia, it made him seem little more than a martinet. His troops and fellow officers disliked him, and when he tried to ambush Arnold along the road to Westover, he could not get his forces to move swiftly enough and was easily outmaneuvered. Worse, Arnold wheeled about and routed Steuben. This done, the turncoat set up winter camp at Portsmouth.

Arnold had done significant damage in Virginia. Yet, without a major command, he could do little more than make hit-and-run raids—and, for his British superiors, this was insufficient. They were stuck on his failure to rally the Tories, and, in spring 1781, he was relieved of command by Major General William Phillips, whose subordinate he became.

Steuben, too, was on his way out—at least for the time being. In June 1781, worn out and ailing, he would present the Marquis de Lafayette with his 450 Virginia Continentals and take sick leave until he rejoined Washington's forces for the siege of Yorktown.

Washington had sent Lafayette south at the start of 1781 to fight Arnold. The commander in chief gave his young protégé three light infantry regiments drawn from the ranks of New England and New Jersey Continental troops. The plan was for Lafayette and this force to link up with a French fleet, but the British blockade of Newport, Rhode Island, delayed the fleet long enough so that it was overtaken by a British fleet under Admiral Marriot Arbuthnot. This resulted in the Battle of Cape Henry at the mouth of Chesapeake

It is the fate of a turncoat to be trusted by no one, and the British never trusted Benedict Arnold with the major command he craved. Unable to do much more than make hit-and-run raids throughout the South, Arnold was relieved of command in the spring of 1781 and replaced by Major General William Phillips (pictured here), under whom he was now assigned to serve.

REALITY CHECK
Jefferson Takes Five

Arnold's raiding mission was made easier by the curious lethargy of Virginia's governor, Thomas Jefferson. A fiery radical in the independence movement, a man of enormous intelligence and passion, the author of the Declaration of Independence itself, and destined to become the nation's third president, Jefferson was inexplicably incompetent as his state's wartime leader. General Washington pleaded with him to prepare the state to defend itself, but Jefferson hardly stirred. The result was that Arnold had little trouble capturing American ships, sailing them up the James, and then visiting destruction throughout the state.

Bay on March 16, 1781. Although it ended in a narrow French victory, the contest took its toll and intimidated the French admiral Charles-René-Dominique Sochet, chevalier Destouches into giving up the notion of coordinating forces with Lafayette in the Virginia expedition. To compound Lafayette's problems, General Clinton was able to exploit the disruption of the Franco-American plans by shipping two thousand reinforcements to Benedict Arnold—along with Arnold's own replacement, William Phillips.

Richmond

Yet another Franco-American amphibious operation had fizzled, and this one threatened to be more than a mere disappointment. Steuben, awaiting the arrival of Lafayette, had just 450 Continental and militia troops to defend Virginia against what was now a force of three thousand British regulars and Tories. Lafayette at the time was at Head of Elk, on the Chesapeake, some 150 miles north of Richmond—without the transport Destouches was to have provided. Up north, things weren't much better, as Washington faced the familiar problem of having to stand by as his principal army disbanded for want of food and supplies. In the meantime, Phillips and Arnold raided more of Virginia, and on April 30, they were poised on the James River, at the head of twenty-five hundred men, ready to capture Richmond.

To study any eighteenth-century war, the American Revolution included, is to be struck by how arduous and time consuming it is to move masses of men and equipment. War generally proceeded at a stately, even lethargic pace, at least until the moment of actual contact between armies. Yet, sometimes, minutes counted. Lafayette and twelve hundred Continentals arrived in Richmond just hours before Phillips and Arnold were ready to invade the town. It had not been easy getting them there. His countryman having failed to bring the fleet, Lafayette had to summon all of his command presence to keep his little army from falling apart. When troops began to desert, he exhorted, he cajoled, and he executed—assembling his men to witness the hanging of a captured deserter. This done, he made a speech. What was to come, he explained, would demand great sacrifice, and those who did not want to make the sacrifice he now invited to leave, provided they submitted their resignation like soldiers, in writing. Lafayette received not a single request, and no one else deserted.

Now Lafayette made a sacrifice of his own. He personally borrowed money from Baltimore merchants to purchase cloth and pay tailors to make summer uniforms to replace the heavy winter garments his troops were burdened with. Properly clothed, they could better endure the series of forced marches by which Lafayette drove them to Richmond.

Although Phillips and Arnold outnumbered Lafayette's Richmond garrison, they knew how costly it was to storm a town in which even a relatively small unit occupied strong defensive positions. They turned their back on Richmond and marched away from the James.

Cornwallis versus Lafayette

It was not that Phillips and Arnold intended to let Lafayette go, but they knew that their commander, Charles Cornwallis, was intent on taking care of him personally. Cornwallis believed that Virginia was now the key to the American Revolution, and all that stood between him and control of Virginia was that miserable French boy. That, according to Lafayette's memoirs, is precisely what Cornwallis called him. He said: "The boy cannot escape me." In fact, Cornwallis was convinced of Virginia's importance and so determined to bag Lafayette that he defied the instructions of his commanding officer, Henry Clinton. That chronically cautious commander was afraid that Washington intended to mount an all-out attack against New York and therefore requested that Cornwallis return most of his army to the Northern theater. Instead, he assembled a force of seventy-two hundred men by the late spring of 1781—more than a match for the three thousand Lafayette was able to muster when he added local militiamen to his Continental contingent.

It was at this juncture that General William Phillips succumbed to a hazard of warfare in the Southern theater. He contracted typhoid fever and died. Cornwallis decided to assume direct command of Phillips's army, so that he now controlled—personally—all British and Tory forces in Virginia. He knew that he enjoyed overwhelming superiority of numbers over Lafayette and therefore advanced out of Petersburg and chased the

DETAILS, DETAILS
Je Ne Sais Quoi

Numbers, training, equipment, and tactical skill are all important to the successful conduct of war, but nothing is more important than the "command presence" of an army's generals. This leadership quality is quite intangible—it cannot be quantified, and it can hardly even be described—yet victory is almost impossible without it. Both Washington and Lafayette had this quality in abundance, and both admired it in one another.

Young and inexperienced, Lafayette nevertheless proved a gallant and highly intelligent officer. He was an important commander in the Yorktown campaign, in which he is pictured here in this print from the 1780s. The black man who holds the general's horse is neither a slave nor a servant, but, as indicated by his sword, a soldier.

DETAILS, DETAILS
Man without a Country

After he was replaced in the South by General William Phillips, Arnold raided his home state of Connecticut, putting 143 buildings to the torch in New London on September 6, 1781. In December of that year, he left America for England, settling in London until 1785, when he moved to St. John, New Brunswick, as a merchant shipper. He subsequently resumed his West Indies' trade business, without great success. Ultimately, Benedict Arnold became a man without a country. Subject to trial and execution if he ever returned to America, he was never embraced by the British. This must have taken a toll on him. In his late fifties, Arnold developed what was described by contemporaries as a "nervous disease." He died in London in 1801, aged sixty. His young wife, Peggy Shippen Arnold, died three years later, at the age of forty-four.

Eyewitness

"Lafayette was young, but he had no illusions about the seemingly impossible odds. Late in May, he wrote to Washington: "Were I to fight a battle, I should be cut to pieces, the militia dispersed and the arms lost. Were I to decline fighting, the country would think itself given up. I am therefore determined to skirmish, but not to engage the enemy too far." He then added a dash of fatalistic Gallic wit: "Were I anyways equal to the enemy, I should be extremely happy in my present command, but I am not strong enough even to get beaten."

Frenchman northward. Lafayette was well aware that he could not make a successful stand, so he concentrated on eluding the British commander. Overwhelming numbers were a great advantage in combat, but, in a chase, were a liability. A small, lightly armed force could run. A big, heavily armed force could, at best, crawl. Discouraged, Cornwallis broke off the pursuit and decided to let Simcoe and Tarleton run loose on the countryside, doing to Virginia's rebels what they had done to those in the Carolinas. In short, rather than consume resources chasing Lafayette, Cornwallis decided to punish Virginia.

With the pressure temporarily off, Lafayette had sufficient breathing space to receive badly needed reinforcements, three Pennsylvania regiments under a most splendid commander: "Mad Anthony" Wayne. This still left Lafayette outnumbered, but he now had forty-five hundred men, as well as Wayne and other officers very nearly of his caliber. He decided that it was time to stop running, and he stunned Cornwallis by suddenly turning on his army, which was marching down Virginia's York Peninsula. The Frenchman deployed his forces down as many roads as he could find in order to give the illusion of far greater numbers than he possessed. On June 26, 1781, members of the Pennsylvania and Virginia regiments overtook Simcoe's Queen's Rangers at a crossroads tavern known as Spencer's Ordinary. The fight was short and nasty, but not decisive. Still, it was the Rangers who decided to break free—and who left their wounded behind in the tavern.

AMBUSH AT JAMES RIVER

Cornwallis encamped the main body of his army around Williamsburg while he pondered his next move. He was too experienced a commander to have fallen for Lafayette's trick of sending his army down various roads. He knew that he enjoyed a substantial advantage in numbers over the Frenchman. But he also recognized that Lafayette was a skilled and bold commander. He needed to use his greater numbers to their maximum advantage. Cornwallis certainly did not want to get into another futile and exhausting pursuit.

It was Henry Clinton's growing anxiety that finally moved Cornwallis to action. Fearing an imminent American move against New York, Clinton changed his *request* that Cornwallis transfer men up north into an *order*. He commanded Cornwallis to send three thousand troops to New York immediately. As it so happened, three thousand was precisely Cornwallis's numerical advantage over Lafayette.

Cornwallis understood that tactical acumen sometimes had as much to do with outmaneuvering your own superior officer as it did with outmaneuvering the enemy commander. He decided to march his whole army out of Williamsburg and advance to the Jamestown Ford on the James River—the place where the three thousand troops would have to cross to get to Portsmouth, from which ships would take them to New York. Why move his whole army there? Cornwallis believed that doing so would make it look as if he were evacuating Virginia. He reasoned that this would lure Lafayette and Wayne into attacking him when they believed he was most vulnerable, while crossing the James—at a moment when the army was apparently divided on either side of the river. Having baited his prey, Cornwallis would attack from ambush.

On July 6, 1781, the two allies responded just as Cornwallis had expected they would. Wayne's men marched toward what they believed to be Cornwallis's rearguard—unaware that most of the British force was still lying in wait on the north bank of the James. If Cornwallis had attacked immediately, he would have overwhelmed the five hundred men of Wayne's attacking force. But he bided his time. He could not tell where Lafayette and the rest of the American force were. He feared that, if he attacked now, he would reveal himself—and "the boy" would elude him once again.

ALTERNATE TAKE
Total War

Cornwallis had chosen a highly dubious strategy. What the great military theorist Karl von Clausewitz would, in the nineteenth century, call "total war"—combat waged not just against armies, but against entire populations—was nothing new in 1781 and would be repeated in centuries to come, often on a horrific scale. Yet it is doubtful whether total war ever prevailed more quickly or more effectively than devoting all effort to killing the enemy army. This is a lesson Cornwallis should have learned. After all, most of America was in British hands—most major towns, most ports—and still the fighting continued. Why? Because there was an American army.

Cornwallis meant to destroy Lafayette as well as Wayne, and to do so in a single, terrible blow.

It had been a long war, but even in the longest of wars, there are decisive moments. This was one of them. If Cornwallis succeeded in defeating Lafayette and Wayne, Virginia would fall. With the fall of Virginia, the American Revolution might well end.

"Lord Cornwallis, when he commenced the pursuit of Lafayette, had written a letter, which was intercepted, in which he made use of this expression: The boy cannot escape me. He flattered himself with terminating, by that one blow, the war in the whole southern part of the United States, for it would have been easy for him afterwards to take possession of Baltimore and march towards Philadelphia."

Lafayette, Memoirs,
Correspondence and Manuscripts

Lafayette peered anxiously at the skirmish developing at the ford. As he watched, on the verge of committing the rest of his troops to the fight, he began to suspect that more than just Cornwallis's rearguard occupied the north bank of the James. He decided to investigate the situation by sending only a detachment, rather than his entire army, to reinforce Wayne. Now it was Cornwallis's turn to be fooled. The detachment Lafayette sent was enough to make Cornwallis believe that he was committing all he had. Accordingly, Cornwallis ordered his troops out of ambush, and they now fell upon nine hundred Americans.

Most commanders would order a general retreat—in effect, telling their men to run for their lives. But Wayne was not most commanders. He saw that he was overwhelmingly outnumbered, but instead of doing what was expected, he ordered a counterattack. And such unconventional, audacious action was precisely calculated to unnerve Charles Cornwallis. His troops stopped in their tracks— just long enough for Wayne to rally his men for an organized fighting retreat. He was able to disengage and withdraw in good order, with the loss of twenty-eight killed, ninety-nine wounded, and twelve missing in action. Lafayette had refused to send his army into a possible trap. Wayne had extricated his from that trap.

To Yorktown

CORNWALLIS CONTENTED HIMSELF with his minor victory, perhaps believing that he had at least chastised the two American commanders. He now resumed the advance to Portsmouth, presumably with the intention of obeying Clinton's orders to send troops to New York. But now Clinton gave rein to his customary indecision. He seems to have had second thoughts about relinquishing Virginia. On July 8, he issued new orders, directing Cornwallis not to Manhattan, but to Philadelphia. On July 12, he changed the orders back to New York. On July 20, he issued a completely revised set of orders. Cornwallis was to occupy and hold a position in Virginia, establishing his army at Old Point Comfort, on the north shore of Hampton Roads. This, Clinton determined, would make an accessible naval base for amphibious operations.

Given his superior's dithering, Cornwallis could hardly be blamed if he questioned Clinton's choice of encampment. He decided that Yorktown, a sleepy tobacco port on the York River, would make a better base of operations than Old Point Comfort.

The Allies Plan

On May 21, 1781, George Washington met with Jean Baptiste Donatien de Vimeur, comte de Rochambeau, at Wethersfield, Connecticut. The two men wanted to plan just how the combined French and American armies would coordinate operations with the French fleet, under Admiral François Joseph Paul, comte de Grasse, to strike a resounding blow against the British. Up to now, both commanders were well aware, Franco-American amphibious operations had failed. They hoped that, by careful planning, this one would break the streak.

Their objective was New York—just as Henry Clinton had feared—but whereas Washington left the meeting eager to begin, Rochambeau was not so sure, and he left to de Grasse the option of striking the British at New York—or Virginia. Early in July, the

In the comte de Rochambeau, George Washington found a most capable military partner. The Franco-American victory at Yorktown was decisive for the American Revolution. Rochambeau received not only the gratitude of Washington and Congress, but his own king, Louis XVI, lavished high military office on him. This earned Rochambeau an arrest during the Reign of Terror that followed the French Revolution, but he managed to evade the guillotine and lived out the rest of his life on a pension granted by Napoleon. This portrait was painted in the eighteenth century.

REALITY CHECK
Why Yorktown?

It is difficult to understand just why Cornwallis was attracted to Yorktown, which offered no advantage over Old Point Comfort and had two great weaknesses as a defensive position. First, it offered no high ground from which to defend against a siege. Second, it was a peninsula. If Gloucester Point should fall, there was no way out, except by sea. It is true that Cornwallis commanded a large force of some of the best soldiers in the British army. He also had Tarleton's excellent Tory legion and a substantial contingent of Hessians. Cornwallis had artillery, and he had every reason to believe that he could count on the Royal Navy. Perhaps all of this was sufficient to make it impossible for Cornwallis to imagine he could be trapped in the base he had chosen.

French army linked up with the Americans above New York City. Initial exchanges convinced Washington that Clinton intended to defend the city with everything he had. If this realization gave Washington pause, what he heard next forced him to change plans. Admiral de Grasse declared that the Chesapeake Bay offered the best approach to the mainland from the West Indies, where the French fleet was anchored. It would not be advisable to sail as far north as New York.

So Washington turned to Virginia. The plan was this: he would, with Rochambeau, reinforce Lafayette and Wayne against Cornwallis while de Grasse attacked the British fleet, cutting off all seaborne sources of reinforcement, communication, and supply. They would make it a very bad day to be caught out on a peninsula. In addition, de Grasse was assigned to land three West Indian regiments for use in the Yorktown campaign.

The plan was sound. As usual, however, all depended on execution. Washington and Rochambeau had to move their large forces south—fast—to cut off Cornwallis before he decided to advance out of the Yorktown peninsula. Additionally, de Grasse had to achieve control of the waters off the peninsula, and he had to do it before his time ran out. The American Revolution meant everything to America, but to France it was just part of what had become a far-flung war with England. De Grasse and his fleet were a priceless asset, and he was under strict orders to leave North American waters no later than October 15, mainly to ensure that the fleet would reach safe haven before the onset of hurricane season.

Advance to Chesapeake Bay

On August 21, 1781, the greatest operation of the American Revolution commenced. Washington and Rochambeau skillfully balanced the need for speed with the equally important necessity of deceiving General Clinton into believing that New York remained their target; therefore, after crossing the Hudson, Washington and Rochambeau divided their commands into three columns, which they sent in a less-than-direct line of march. This would keep Clinton in New York and buy time for de Grasse to get on the move.

It was September 1 before Henry Clinton realized that Washington and Rochambeau were headed not to New York, but to Virginia. It was by this time also apparent just where de Grasse was heading. British admirals Samuel Graves and Samuel Hood launched from New York to intercept de Grasse's West Indian fleet and a French supporting fleet, under Admiral Jacques-Melchior Saint-Laurent, comte de Barras, which had left Newport, Rhode Island. The British commanders understood that sea power was now more critical than ever, that both the armies of Cornwallis and Washington-Rochambeau needed a seaborne lifeline. They intended to furnish Cornwallis with his lifeline even as they were determined to prevent de Grasse from providing for his countryman and ally.

Based on French naval performance up to this point, the British admirals had every reason to assume that they would prevail. However, de Grasse was not d'Estaing. He outsailed the British, beating them to Chesapeake Bay. French cruisers took up positions in the James River, thereby preventing Cornwallis from escaping to the south. Additional French ships took up blocking positions at the mouth of the York River. The rest of de Grasse's fleet waited for the Royal Navy to appear at the mouth of the Chesapeake.

A 1781 map of the Battle of Yorktown: Until the comte de Grasse defeated the British fleet under Admiral Graves at the mouth of Chesapeake Bay on September 5, 1781, the French navy had performed poorly in the American Revolution. De Grasse prevented Graves from coming to the aid of Cornwallis, who therefore remained trapped on the Yorktown peninsula, his back to the sea.

The British and the French navies engaged on September 5, 1781, in Chesapeake Bay. In this, the Battle of the Capes (also known as the Battle of the Virginia Capes or the Battle of Chesapeake), de Grasse had more ships and more guns. Indeed, his flagship, the magnificent *Ville de Paris,* mounted 110 cannon, making it the biggest warship of its time. In train behind *Ville de Paris* were twenty-four more ships of the line, each with sixty-four to eighty guns. In addition, he had a half-dozen swift frigates. In opposition, Graves and Hood commanded nineteen ships of the line and seven frigates. They did, however, have an advantage of wind and position. The British could move faster and with greater discretion than the French, who were wholly within the bay. But the British fleet was outgunned, and, in this instance at least, it was also outmaneuvered. De Grasse directed the Battle of the

Capes with consummate seamanship. The firing began at about four o'clock in the afternoon and was over by six, when Graves and Hood beat a retreat from Chesapeake Bay and returned to New York. Cornwallis would have to face the enemy on land and all alone.

Siege

On September 9, 1781, Admiral de Barras linked up with de Grasse in Chesapeake Bay. This gave the French navy total control of the bay and enabled de Grasse to land enough troops to swell the Washington-Rochambeau expedition to sixteen thousand men. They assembled at Williamsburg and prepared to battle the army of six thousand Cornwallis had with him at Yorktown. It was a rare occasion indeed. Not since the beginning of the war did Washington command so large an army, and almost never did the Patriot forces outnumber the British at any one place.

On September 17, Washington and Rochambeau conferred aboard de Grasse's sumptuous flagship to plan the siege of Yorktown. The mission was straightforward, and so was the plan. Admiral de Grasse would prevent interference from the Royal Navy while Rochambeau and Washington would envelop Yorktown and bombard it with artillery delivered by de Grasse's ships. During these operations, allied engineers would dig siege trenches to provide cover for the army's approach to the Yorktown fortifications. It would be a slow, systematic "investment" of the objective, intended to strangle Cornwallis, who would have no place to go but the sea—a sea controlled by the French.

> *"If you cannot relieve me very soon, you must be prepared to hear the worst."*
>
> Cornwallis, letter to Henry Clinton,
> September 23, 1781

Washington understood that this campaign was his to lose. Cornwallis was so badly outnumbered that only a major blunder on the allies' part would forfeit victory. The problem was how to prevent Cornwallis from holding out past October 15, when de

Grasse had to leave, thereby opening the way for the British to receive reinforcements by sea or to escape.

Relief by sea is precisely what Cornwallis pinned his hopes to. On September 30, he began to consolidate his position at Yorktown by ordering the outer "works"—the outermost ring of entrenchments—to be abandoned. He reasoned that he could hold out longer by contracting his perimeter. Hold out long enough and surely the fleet would come through. But no sooner had he withdrawn from the outer works than the allies moved forward to occupy them—and not just to occupy them, but to use them as cover for close-range artillery. On October 1, American batteries commenced bombardment of Yorktown.

For the next six days the artillery pounded away. Then, on October 6, Washington made a ceremony of personally breaking ground for the first approach trench—a trench dug at an angle to the British fortifications in order to provide cover for advancing troops and artillery. After three days, additional artillery was brought forward through the approach trench. Once again assuming a symbolic role, Washington personally touched off the first shot. The Franco-American artillerists were able to position their guns exactly where they wanted them. Thus they were able to hit Yorktown as well as Gloucester Point, the position Tarleton was assigned to hold. Their range was such that the American guns even drove the last two remaining British frigates out of the river.

> *"The business with his Lordship in this State will very soon be at an end, for suppose you know e'er this that we have got him handsomely in a pudding bag with 5000 land forces and about 60 ships including transports.... I am all on fire. By the Great God of War, I think we may all hand up our swords by the last of the year in perfect peace and security!"*
>
> *Letter from Virginia militia general George Weedon to Continental army general Nathanael Greene, September 5, 1781*

ALTERNATIVE TAKE
Between a Peninsula and a Hard Place

By this point, Cornwallis must have been getting nervous. He was bottled up on the Yorktown peninsula and could not maneuver. There was nothing for him to do but wait for the Franco-American assault. However, had Admiral Graves come through—had he defeated the French fleet—he could have provided Cornwallis with transportation off of the Yorktown peninsula and then deposited him at a landing place from which he could have attacked Washington and Rochambeau from the flank or the rear. Despite the superiority of Franco-American numbers in Virginia, that would have prevented Cornwallis's defeat and, quite possibly, have been a disaster for Washington and Rochambeau.

A hand-colored French print, published in Paris about 1781, depicts the surrender of Cornwallis to Washington and Rochambeau at Yorktown.

The Noose Tightens

On October 14, Alexander Hamilton—future secretary of the treasury and now personal aide to George Washington—teamed with a French officer to lead a fierce nighttime bayonet attack against defenders of two redoubts (forward defensive positions) near the York River. Having routed these defenders, Hamilton reported the way clear to extend the approach trenches all the way to the river. Cornwallis was completely isolated. Realizing this, in utter desperation, he sent a sortie of 350 men against a line of allied trenches on October 16. The attack was unexpected, and the Americans pulled back—but a unit of stout French grenadiers soon repulsed the sortie.

Cornwallis had no good options left. A breakout across the York River under cover of darkness and to Gloucester Point might work. From here, he'd have to make a forced march clear up to New York. It was a very long shot, but the British commander felt honor bound to try. He began by launching his elite Guards and units of light infantry in boats. They would stealthily row out to Gloucester Point, then send the boats back for more troops. In this way, quietly, Cornwallis hoped his army would, as it were, leak out of the bag in which Washington and Rochambeau had it.

The first contingent made it across, but a sudden storm stranded the boats at Gloucester. There would be no escape.

Cornwallis Ends It

On October 17, 1781, a Lieutenant Denny of the Pennsylvania Line gazed upon Yorktown from one of the approach trenches. At about ten in the morning, he reported seeing "a drummer mount the enemy's parapet and beat a parley"—a signal requesting a truce. This done, "an officer, holding up a white handkerchief, made his appearance outside their works. The drummer accompanied him, beating." Washington ordered his artillery to be silent and sent an American officer out to meet the British representative. The officer tied a handkerchief over the redcoat's eyes, sent the drummer back to Yorktown, and took the man "to a house in the rear of our lines. Firing ceased totally."

The emissary asked for an armistice to discuss terms of surrender. He promised that, before the end of a two-hour cease-fire, Cornwallis would send his proposal in writing. Washington agreed, and before the armistice was set to expire, he had in his hands Cornwallis's surrender proposal. The British commander asked for the parole of his troops and their safe conduct to England. But Washington had no need to bargain. He replied that surrender must be without condition. Before the day was out, Cornwallis agreed.

On this very day—October 17, 1781—Henry Clinton launched a rescue mission from New York. Along the way, he received the news of Cornwallis's surrender and turned back. That was on October 19, 1781, the very day that the surrender was formalized with a ceremony. The Franco-American troops were arrayed in a double column one mile long, Americans on the

POP CULTURE
The World Turned Upside Down

Anecdotes of the Revolution, a little book published in 1828 by one Alexander Garden, carried for the first time the story that, throughout the surrender ceremony, the British regimental pipers played a tune called "The World Turned Upside Down." It would be nice to accept this anecdote as the truth—which it may well be.

If buttercups buzz'd after the bee,
If boats were on land, churches on sea,
If ponies rode men and if grass ate the cows,
And cats should be chased into holes by the mouse,
If the mamas sold their babies
To the gypsies for half a crown;
If summer were spring and the other way round,
Then all the world would be upside down.

Currier & Ives, about 1846, published this more intimate view of the surrender. Cornwallis, claiming to be too ill to surrender personally, sent General Charles O'Hara to convey to Washington his sword. As the print accurately depicts, Washington stepped aside to allow Benjamin Lincoln, defeated at Charleston, to receive the weapon.

right, Frenchmen on the left. At the head of the line, Washington sat astride his horse. At the foot of the line, Rochambeau was mounted on his. At an appointed time, Cornwallis's army began to march out of the fort, their colors cased—tightly furled in token of surrender. Sullenly, each soldier threw down his weapon. To a man, the troops directed their gaze to the line of Frenchmen. They refused so much as to acknowledge the presence of the Americans.

Pleading illness, Cornwallis did not surrender personally to Washington, but conveyed to him his sword by the hand of General Charles O'Hara. Washington stepped aside, allowing Benjamin Lincoln, who had been forced to surrender Charleston, to accept the weapon in his stead.

With that, the surrender was accomplished, and seven thousand British soldiers marched off to prison camps. Cornwallis, with his principal subordinate officers, was not imprisoned, but was paroled to New York.

What Yorktown Meant

The news of Yorktown did not reach London until late in November. Lord Germain reported that Prime Minister North took it "as he would have taken a ball in the breast." He gasped: "Oh God! It is all over."

Strange that North would say such a thing, seeing that thirty thousand British troops remained in North America, and the British held every major American port except for Boston. But the fact was that six years of costly war—a war that many in England protested—had drained even the stalwarts of their will to fight. The defeat of Cornwallis was the proverbial last straw. It was added to the defeat of the Royal Navy at the Battle of the Capes, and it was heaped upon the prospect of having to confront the combined fleets of Spain and France. Parliament had had enough. On December 20, the members concluded that continuing the fight for America was no longer viable. George Washington had been right. He knew he could not defeat the British military, let alone the British nation. But he believed it possible simply to outlast both.

TAKEAWAY
The Last Straw

Seeking a position from which he would have access to the British fleet, Cornwallis led his army to the Yorktown peninsula of Virginia. Once French admiral de Grasse defeated the British fleet, however, this point of access was transformed into a cul de sac, leaving Cornwallis no way to escape siege by a large Franco-American force under Rochambeau and Washington. Although a formal treaty would not come until 1783, the Battle of Yorktown virtually ensured Patriot victory in the American Revolution.

Chapter 23

THE PEACE OF PARIS AND
A NEW ORDER OF THE AGES

*Mop-Up Operations in the South and Momentous
Negotiations in Paris; What the American Revolution
Achieved As Well As What It Left Unfinished*

ON DECEMBER 20, 1781, THE BRITISH PARLIAMENT voted to make peace in America
and, accordingly, delivered its recommendation to George III. Enraged, the king
rejected the resolution, declaring that to relinquish the American colonies was
to surrender Britain's place as a world power. Lord Germain, however, had had
enough and tendered his resignation to the king. The monarch told him that
he would find someone else willing to continue the fight.

There was in these exchanges a colossal irony. To begin with, it had been George's total
unwillingness to compromise with his colonies that had driven them away. He declared
them to be in rebellion long before Thomas Jefferson drafted the Declaration of
Independence. And now, when Parliament and the king's own ministers recognized that
the war had been lost, that it was time to stop fighting, George III—as monarchs go, a
decent man much beloved by his people—behaved like the tyrant the colonial rebels had
insisted he was. Unlike their brethren across the sea, the people of England would not start
a revolution over this outburst of tyranny. They would, however, end one.

Parliament holds the purse strings. Without its compliance, there could be no war—
the royal will notwithstanding. George III could not resist the tide of history.

NUMBERS
Eutaw Springs Losses

Greene withdrew after suffering 500 casualties out of 2,000 men engaged. The British continued to hold their camp, but lost 693 killed, wounded, and missing. The magnitude of the losses on both sides made Eutaw Springs the last major battle of the Revolution.

On September 8, 1781, Nathanael Greene fought Alexander Stewart to a bloody draw at Eutaw Springs, South Carolina. In the last major battle of the American Revolution, Greene inflicted more casualties on Stewart's command than he suffered, but he failed to dislodge the British from their camp.

LAST BATTLES

MOST HISTORIES OF THE AMERICAN REVOLUTION blithely declare that the Battle of Yorktown ended the Revolution, usually adding the qualification "for all practical purposes" or something similar. To those still fighting and dying, Cornwallis's surrender did not seem like the end, qualified or unqualified.

Southern Endgame

Even as the Yorktown campaign was under way in Virginia, Nathanael Greene was fighting British forces led by Francis Rawdon-Hastings and, after Rawdon-Hastings fell ill, under Alexander Stewart. The British stubbornly held on to Savannah and Charleston, so Greene kept pounding away in the Carolina backcountry.

On September 8, 1781, reinforced to a strength of two thousand men, Greene felt capable of seizing the initiative. Stewart—camped with about two thousand men at Eutaw Springs, South Carolina, on the Santee River—had sent a foraging party to gather sweet potatoes. Greene fell upon them, then ambushed a Tory cavalry scouting party under Major John Coffin—who slipped away and alerted Stewart to the approach of Greene's army, thereby depriving Greene of the critical element of surprise.

Warned by Coffin, Stewart formed a line of battle in front of the Eutaw Springs camp. Greene's militia performed magnificently, firing seventeen consecutive volleys without giving way. Nevertheless, Stewart's men broke through the militia line—only to come against Continentals from Maryland and Virginia, who stood fast, then drove the British back at the points of their bayonets. Apparently stirred by their success, the Americans abandoned all discipline. They stormed into the British camp and fell to plundering the soldiers' tents instead of finishing off Stewart's army. Major John Majoribanks, in command of a British reserve force, sprang out of the thicket in which he and his men had been hiding and attacked the Americans. Stunned, many of the

Continental dragoons were cut down. Majoribanks led his men into a brick house, which became cover from which they poured musket fire and from which they plied a swivel gun—a small artillery piece—against the Americans.

Under this withering attack, many American soldiers snatched up British stragglers who had not reached the safety of the house before the door slammed shut. The Americans used these unfortunates as human shields and backed away from the gunfire.

At this, Majoribanks sortied out of the house, rushing those American soldiers who were still looting the British camp. Majoribanks himself fell in this skirmish, but not before having transformed a magnificent American triumph into something of a British victory.

Eutaw Springs demoralized Greene's army, which was cut in half through casualties, sickness, and the expiration of enlistments. While it was camped in the Santee Hills of South Carolina, mutiny was in the air. A believer in nipping these things in the bud, Greene had one Timothy Griffin, guilty of mocking an officer, executed by firing squad.

By December 9, 1781, the British presence in the South had been reduced to garrisons in Savannah and Charleston. The Savannah troops withdrew on July 11, 1782, and the Charleston contingent on December 14. Greene made his headquarters in Charleston and remained there, struggling to keep his army together, until August 1783, when news of the Treaty of Paris finally reached him.

Beyond the Appalachians

On the trans-Appalachian frontier, where the Revolution had never been about organized armies fighting one another, but was a struggle among whites and variously allied Native Americans, the surrender of Cornwallis had little effect. In Kentucky and the Ohio country war continued to flame.

After the Gnadenhutten Massacre in Ohio (see Chapter 17, "Massacre at Gnadenhutten"), the Delawares staged severe vengeance raids. These in turn provoked the so-called Second Moravian Campaign, led by militia colonel William Crawford, aimed at destroying all "hostile" Native American settlements. Crawford's command was a rabble of only 450 frontiersmen, who,

DETAILS, DETAILS
Quotable

At the Battle of Eutaw Springs, when an American captain named Manning roughly seized a British officer as a human shield, the latter responded by reciting his titles: "I am Sir Henry Barré, deputy adjutant general of the British army, captain of the 52nd regiment, secretary of the commandant in Charleston." Manning replied, "Are you indeed? You are my prisoner now, and the very man I was looking for; come along with me."

on the night of June 4–5, 1782, were surprised by Shawnees and Delawares near Sandusky (in present-day Ohio). Forty or fifty militiamen were killed or captured, and twenty-eight wounded. The defeat of Crawford's militia forces triggered additional raids led by Joseph Brant. Even after the Treaty of Paris officially ended the American Revolution on September 3, 1783, the country between the Appalachian Mountains and the Mississippi River remained at war and would remain so for more than a decade, until 1795, when "Mad Anthony" Wayne defeated the Shawnee and other hostiles at the Battle of Fallen Timbers.

TALKING IN PARIS

EVEN KINGS GET TIRED, and, on February 11, 1782, George III accepted Lord Germain's resignation. He continued to go through the motions of refusing to end the war in America, but his majority in Parliament was no more, and on March 4, the House of Commons passed a resolution to the effect that anyone who attempted to continue the war in America was an enemy of king and country. In the face of this, on March 20, the king's prime minister, Lord North, resigned—thereby avoiding the humiliation of a no-confidence vote in Parliament. All George III could do now was to form a new government with the opposition.

Charles Watson-Wentworth, the Marquis of Rockingham, once again became prime minister (he had a brief tenure in 1765–66). He pledged, of course, to serve his king, but he also demanded that the Crown now recognize the independence of the United States. Rockingham delegated Richard Oswald to treat with the American representatives in Paris. He arrived on April 12, 1782, and discovered that only Benjamin Franklin was present. Franklin's fellow treaty commissioner John Adams was in Holland, trying to negotiate a loan for the infant republic. John Jay, former president of the Continental Congress and now America's minister plenipotentiary to Spain, was in Madrid, dealing with America's difficult Spanish allies. Henry Laurens, the fourth commissioner, had been a British prisoner of war since 1780, when he was captured at sea on his way to Europe. Oswald, who liked Americans and even had a cousin in the Continental artillery, personally posted the staggering £50,000 bail necessary to secure Laurens's release from the Tower of London.

The American treaty commissioners had been instructed by Congress to do two things: first, to secure from Great Britain recognition of independence and, second, to faithfully follow the instructions of France, America's faithful ally.

Congress was in America. Benjamin Franklin was in Paris—and what he saw was that his country's "faithful ally" actually had far less interest in fostering the well-being of the new United States than in promoting the New World claims of its ally, Spain. Indeed, in Madrid, Commissioner Jay was rapidly discovering that Spain, allied with the French and the Americans against the English, was in no hurry to acknowledge American independence. It wanted United States territorial claims sharply limited and insisted on retaining its dominion over Florida and the entire Mississippi Valley, including navigation of the Mississippi River. A disgusted John Jay, arriving in Paris from Madrid on June 23, denounced Spain as almost as great an enemy to American liberty as Britain had been.

John Jay was delayed in his arrival at negotiations for the Treaty of Paris because, as U.S. minister plenipotentiary to Spain, he was engaged in long and frustrating negotiations with the Madrid government in an effort to define a Spanish-American alliance.

"The people in this country are in almost total darkness about us.... There are violent prejudices among them against us.... The King and Ministry are warm, yet I have reason to believe that the bulk of the nation is cold toward us. They appear to me to like the English, hate the French, and to have prejudices against us."

Letter of John Jay, in Madrid, to Samuel Huntington, president of Congress, May 26, 1780

The dilemma of Franklin (and the other commissioners, as they arrived in Paris) was to keep from alienating France while avoiding the sacrifice of hard-won American liberty and sovereignty either to France or Spain.

Franklin defined three objectives for himself and his fellow treaty commissioners: first, to obtain unconditional recognition of independence; second, to obtain significant continental territory; third, to secure a guarantee of access to international waterways and to the abundant fisheries of Newfoundland. France seemed increasingly unwilling to cooperate in attaining the second two objectives.

Breaking with an Ally

On September 9, 1782, John Jay discovered that Vergennes, the French foreign minister, had dispatched his private secretary to England to conduct peace talks with the British, separately from the Americans. Vergennes was offering a peace based on the map as it now looked. Britain would hold onto Maine, New York City, a large part of the Ohio country, and the cities of Charleston and Savannah.

For Franklin, this was the final straw. Urged on by Jay, he proposed that the Crown authorize Oswald to treat not with the thirteen colonies, but with the "United States." This would constitute a de facto recognition of American independence that would instantly free the United States from diplomatic dependence on France. The British agreed.

The peace talks proceeded remarkably smoothly, especially considering the length, cost, and bitterness of the war. By October 5, the negotiators had laid out an agreement, which specified U.S. boundaries, outlined a procedure for the evacuation of British troops, guaranteed access to the Newfoundland fisheries, and pledged free trade and navigation of the Mississippi. Days later, John Adams, having concluded a treaty of commerce and amity with the Netherlands (October 8), arrived in Paris (October 26). He agreed with Jay and Franklin that the treaty with the British should be finalized without consulting the French. By November 5, all the commissioners—Laurens having just arrived—agreed on a final draft of the articles of peace. On November 30, the four commissioners and the English representative signed a provisional treaty and submitted it for ratification of the governments.

Treaty Signed at Last

On September 3, 1783, the final Treaty of Paris, having been ratified by the governments, was signed. In addition to recognizing the independence of the United States, the treaty set boundaries that excluded Canada, but extended westward more or less along the forty-fifth parallel to the Mississippi, southward to the thirty-first parallel, and east to the Atlantic Ocean. The treaty gave the United States access to the

REALITY CHECK
Love Thine Enemy

Why did the British agree to recognize the "United States" even before signing a treaty? Had the Crown accepted Vergennes's proposal, it would have retained significant American territory, including western territory that would limit eventual American expansion. But the British government looked beyond these immediate territorial gains. By dealing directly with the Americans—with the United States— Britain would erode the Franco-American alliance, maybe even bring it to an abrupt end. In the game of world politics, instantaneous recognition of U.S. independence seemed a modest price to pay for this. Thus, on October 1, 1782, Franklin and Jay commenced formal negotiations with Oswald— without the French.

fisheries off the banks of Newfoundland and Nova Scotia. It pledged both countries to honor all legal debts. It disavowed any further penalties against citizens of any nation that had been involved in the hostilities. The treaty stipulated the evacuation of all British troops. It guaranteed to open the Mississippi River to navigation by the United States as well as Britain.

All of these points were readily agreed on. More difficult was the "Loyalist question." The Crown wanted the rights of the Loyalists protected and any confiscated property restored. The American commissioners, however, regarded the Tories as traitors, who had waged ruthless warfare. They balked, and, in the end, the British agreed that Congress would do more than "recommend" to the states that they "correct, if necessary," any acts of confiscation of the estates of British subjects.

Most Americans rejoiced at the Treaty of Paris. Franklin's emotions were more temperate. "There never was a good war," he declared, "or a bad peace."

The Treaty of Paris, signed on September 3, 1783, by the British treaty commissioner and three American commissioners— Franklin, Adams, and Jay—ended the American Revolution.

THE NEW ORDER

ON JULY 4, 1776, the Continental Congress not only adopted the Declaration of Independence, it also passed a resolution authorizing a committee that included Benjamin Franklin, Thomas Jefferson, and John Adams to design an appropriate national motto and great seal for the new nation. As it turned out, this took almost as long as the Revolution. The seal was not approved by Congress until June 20, 1782.

Most of us carry several copies of it in our pockets. It's on the dollar bill, and it bears the national motto—*E pluribus unum* ("From many, one")—and two more mottos: *Annuit coeptis*—"He [God] favors our undertakings"—and *Novus ordo seculorum.* That last one is the most ambitious of all. It means "A new order of the ages" or "A new age now begins."

The Treaty of Paris ended the American Revolution by securing a recognition of independence, setting boundaries, and getting some fishing and navigation rights—pretty routine stuff—but the *Novus ordo seculorum* was more like the Declaration of Independence and Paine's *Common Sense.* It was a very ambitious proposition, an assertion that the fight in North America had brought a new order to the conduct of human affairs.

Washington Bids Farewell For Now

On December 23, 1783, before the Congress assembled at Annapolis, Maryland, George Washington resigned his commission as commander in chief of the Continental army.

"HAVING NOW FINISHED the work assigned me," he tearfully declared, "I retire from the great theater of action, and bidding an affectionate farewell to this august body under whose orders I have so long acted, I here offer my commission, and take my leave of all the employments of public life."

Washington withdrew the documents of his commission from his pocket and handed them to the president of the Congress, Thomas Mifflin. He then set off for Mount Vernon, his beloved plantation on the Potomac. For Washington, as for everyone else, the American Revolution was over, but, his farewell notwithstanding, he would not long be absent from "the employments of public life." In 1789, Washington would begin his first term as the first president of the United States.

"With an heart full of love and gratitude I now take leave of you. I most devoutly wish that your latter days may be as prosperous and happy as your former ones have been glorious and honorable."

Washington's farewell to his officers at Fraunces Tavern, New York, December 13, 1783

Loose Ends, Bitter Ends

In America, the prevailing emotions at the end of the war were joy and hope, but there were also problems. The Continental army, underfed, undersupplied, and unpaid, nearly mutinied yet again on March 10, 1783. Washington quelled the uprising with his mere presence, but on June 17, disgruntled Continentals surrounded the Pennsylvania State House, where Congress sat. The Philadelphia Mutiny was peaceful—a matter of intimidation rather than violence—but it did not end until June 24, by which time Congress moved first to Princeton, New Jersey, and then to Annapolis, Maryland.

The veterans' problems were symptoms of a wider economic crisis. Under the Articles of Confederation, Congress had no authority to levy direct taxes and desperately groped for other ways to finance the debt incurred in fighting the Revolution. The Continental currency Congress issued was nothing more than a heap of bills of credit, backed neither by gold nor silver. Individual states also issued their own currency, some of which was backed by "specie" (gold or silver), but most of which was not. During and immediately after the Revolution, the United States was plagued by massive inflation. When the Revolution ended, a significant portion of the war's $170 million debt had been paid down, but $27 million remained—and many creditors demanded payment in gold. In 1786, the new United States defaulted on interest payments to Spain, France, and the Netherlands.

Struggling under the Articles of Confederation

As much as anything else, it was the financial crisis that motivated Congress to convene the 1787 Constitutional Convention, which replaced the Articles of Confederation with a document giving the central government the authority to levy taxes. The Articles had been drafted in 1777 and ratified in 1781. They purposely created a very weak central government, without the authority to levy taxes, precisely because no one wanted to fight a Revolution against tyrannical taxation only to end up with a new tax-mad government. The Articles of Confederation, however, did not even create a nation, but a "firm league of friendship" among thirteen sovereign states. There was a Congress, consisting of two to seven delegates from each state—although each state was given just one vote, regardless of its population. There was no executive branch—no president—and no judicial branch. Although charged with conducting foreign policy, declaring war, making peace, maintaining an army and navy, and so on, Congress, lacking the authority to tax, was entirely at the mercy of the states, which could choose to obey federal laws or not, and which could contribute funds to federal projects or not.

The Loyalist Question

That the Articles of Confederation failed to create a genuine nation was a major problem that remained to be solved after the

---

DETAILS, DETAILS
Bankrupt Financial Czar

In 1780, the worst year of the Revolution inflation, what had cost a Continental dollar in 1776 now cost more than $1,000 in "Continentals." In 1781, Congress appointed merchant and financier Robert Morris financial czar. Brilliant with money, he managed America's credit portfolio and was able to finance the later years of the Revolution. Morris was far less adept with his personal finances. Unable to pay his taxes or the interest on his loans, he was arrested in February 1798 for debt and spent three and a half years in debtors' prison.

NUMBERS

Slavery

In 1790, the first U.S. census counted 697,897 slaves. Although the Constitution specified that the importation of slaves was to be banned by 1808, by that time there was hardly any need to import slaves. The 1810 census counted 1,191,354 slaves, a 70 percent increase in two decades.

Revolution. Another problem was how to incorporate the Loyalists into the new nation. They had been persecuted throughout the Revolution, and they had fought back with an often-savage form of warfare. Most revolutions degenerate into civil war, and although combat between Loyalists and Patriots sometimes verged on just this, the Revolution never quite crossed the line.

During the fighting, most of the states confiscated Tory property. In 1783, as part of the Treaty of Paris, the British established a commission to examine the claims of 4,118 Tories. The Crown disbursed £3,300,000 to compensate Loyalists for their losses. But that was not the end of it. Despite the Treaty of Paris stipulation that no one would suffer further penalties for actions during the war, the persecution of Tories continued for some years after the war had ended.

Many Loyalists left the United States, some 60,000 to 180,000 fleeing to Canada or the West Indies. Others moved west, settling on the frontier and sometimes making alliances with Native Americans to fight the "Americans." In this was planted the seeds of the War of 1812.

The American Revolution failed to bring liberty to the nation's slaves, and the issue of slavery was destined to tear the Union apart in a civil war that began seventy-eight years after independence had been won. This abolitionist print is from the 1830s.

All Men Are Created Equal?

The American Revolution liberated white America from British "tyranny," but did nothing to liberate black America from white tyranny. Slavery would stand in this new republic—this harbinger of a new order of the ages—for some three-quarters of a century before it tore the nation apart in a civil war.

REBELLION AND REFORM

NOWHERE WERE ECONOMIC HARDSHIPS harder after the war than in western Massachusetts, where the government, dominated by coastal mercantile interests, levied heavy taxes to pay down state debts, even as it rejected paper money and suppressed all laws intended to provide debtor relief. The result was a torrent of foreclosures and imprisonment for debt, especially among the struggling small farmers in the west.

In August 1786, armed mobs of these men began forcing the closure of courts in Massachusetts's western counties. Daniel Shays, a veteran of the Revolution, emerged as the leader of this mass demonstration, which was accordingly dubbed Shays's Rebellion. The federal government was powerless to send forces to suppress the outlawry. Congress stood by as a combination of Massachusetts state militia and an army funded by private merchants put down the troubles during January–February 1787.

Constitutional Convention

Shays's Rebellion and the mounting financial crisis (with state after state starting to print mountains of worthless paper money) moved Congress to convene, in 1786, a convention at Annapolis, Maryland, to discuss problems of interstate commerce. The delegates to this convention were wise enough to see that these issues were merely part of a much larger issue, which required an extensive reform of government. The Annapolis delegates called for a constitutional convention, which met in Philadelphia in May 1787.

The fifty-five delegates in Philadelphia elected George Washington president of the convention. The Virginia delegation, led by Edmund Randolph, put forth the "Virginia Plan," which called for the creation of a central federal government consisting of a bicameral (two-chambered) legislature, an executive branch, and a judicial branch. It sounds like what we have today, but, the Virginians wanted a very strong central government, with a chief executive elected not by the people but by the members of the legislature (who had been popularly elected). Moreover, the chief executive would hold his office for life. Representation in both chambers of the legislature would be proportionate to state population.

Many delegates objected both to the power and tenure of the chief executive under the Virginia Plan and to a system of representation strictly tied to population. William Paterson of New Jersey proposed an alternative, labeled with the name of his state. The "New Jersey Plan" would retain most of the Articles of Confederation—including equal representation for each state—but it added a separate and independent Supreme Court.

With two alternatives to discuss, the debate intensified until Roger Sherman, delegate from Connecticut, proposed what historians later

DETAILS, DETAILS
Electoral College

As originally conceived, the Electoral College consisted of electors voted into office by the legislatures of each state, with each state entitled to as many electors as it had senators and representatives combined. This evolved into election by the people. Although we may think of ourselves as voting for a president every fourth November, we actually vote for a slate of electors pledged to cast their votes for a particular candidate. In some states, this pledge is backed by law. In others, it is backed by no more than tradition, so that—in theory at least—an elector in such states ostensibly pledged to candidate X could legally cast his or her vote instead for candidate Y.

DETAILS, DETAILS
Only Eight Years

The nation was grateful to FDR, but ratified in 1951 the 22nd Amendment, restricting future presidents—by law—to no more than two elected terms and thereby ratifying as well George Washington's early wisdom.

The chief objection raised against the proposed Constitution was that it failed to provide explicit protection of individual rights. To address this criticism, on September 25, 1789, the First Congress of the United States proposed a dozen amendments to the Constitution. The first two, dealing with the number of constituents for each Representative and the compensation of Congressmen, were not ratified by the states, but the rest were. They now collectively constitute the Bill of Rights— American history's greatest afterthought.

called the Connecticut Compromise or the Great Compromise. Sherman called for a bicameral legislature, in which the "upper house," the Senate, would provide each state with equal representation, and the "lower house," the House of Representatives, would provide representation proportionate to each state's population. There would be a strong chief executive, but he would be elected not by the representatives in the legislature, but by an Electoral College.

The Great Compromise provided the impetus required for William Johnson (secretary of the convention), Alexander Hamilton, James Madison, Rufus King, and Gouverneur Morris to draft the final document. After thirty-eight of the fifty-five convention delegates approved it, Congress submitted it to the states for ratification.

A new struggle began between those who supported the proposed Constitution—dubbed Federalists—and those opposed, the Anti-Federalists. Delaware, Pennsylvania, and New Jersey ratified the Constitution right away, but a total of nine states were needed for final ratification. To sway the national debate toward ratification, Alexander Hamilton, James Madison, and John Jay collaborated on a series of essays collectively called *The Federalist Papers* and published during 1787–88 in various New York newspapers under the collective pseudonym of "Publius." Perhaps the most brilliant political discussion of modern times, *The Federalist Papers* laid out the case for the Constitution, analyzing the weaknesses of the Articles of Confederation and explaining how a strong central government was best suited to governing a large and diverse nation because it would prevent any single special interest from taking control.

In the end, thanks in large part to *The Federalist Papers,* the new Constitution was ratified—but Virginia held out until the Anti-Federalist objection that the Constitution failed to guarantee individual rights was answered by a promise that a "Bill of Rights" would immediately be added to the document. Virginia's James Madison led the effort to create the first ten amendments to the Constitution, the so-called Bill of Rights, which was based largely on the Virginia Declaration of Rights, adopted back in 1776. The Constitution was ratified on June 21, 1788, and the Bill of Rights on December 15, 1791.

The First President

The new Constitution took effect on March 4, 1789. In April, the U.S. Senate convened to tally ballots cast by members of the Electoral College for the first president of the United States. The result was hardly surprising. George Washington had been unanimously elected, with John Adams as his vice president.

Indeed, it was with the firm understanding that Washington would be elected that the framers of the Constitution entrusted so much power to the chief executive. He had led the Continental army to victory, and that was important. He had presided fairly and skillfully over the Constitutional Convention, and that was important, too. But most important of all was what Washington did not do. As a victorious general, he could have proclaimed himself king—or the equivalent. He did not. His mission accomplished, he retired from command and withdrew to his beloved plantation, Mount Vernon, until his country called on him again. Whatever else he would be as the first American president, he would not be a tyrant.

George Washington was inaugurated in New York City on April 30, 1789, and set about creating the presidency. He built his cabinet, naming Thomas Jefferson as secretary of state, Henry Knox as secretary of war, Alexander Hamilton as secretary of the treasury, Samuel Osgood as head of the post office, and Edmund Randolph as attorney general. He then conducted himself with dignified restraint. He believed he should avoid conflict with Congress by leaving all legislation to that body. He declared his firm opposition to the formation of political parties—although, by the time of his second term, two opposing parties had already taken shape: the conservative Federalists, headed by John Adams and Alexander Hamilton, and the more liberal Democratic-Republicans, headed by Thomas Jefferson. He accepted a second term of office, but refused a third, establishing a precedent that was unbroken until, moved by the twin crises of the Depression and World War II, Americans elected Franklin Delano Roosevelt four times.

More than anything else, it was the character of George Washington that created the office of president and helped the United States to take its place among the other nations of the world. With a great document and a great man leading its initial implementation, the victory of the American Revolution was fully and finally secured.

TAKEAWAY
United at Last

The Treaty of Paris was speedily concluded in 1783 and formally ended the American Revolution, leaving the United States independent, but also burdened with a severe economic crisis, which the weak federal government was powerless to remedy. This coupled with the threat posed by Shay's Rebellion, motovated the Constitutional Convention of 1787 and the ratification in 1788 of the Constitution, which provided a much stronger central government and transformed a confederation of states into a truly unified republic.

American Revolution Timeline

1763
OCT. 7: George III issues a proclamation setting the lawful limit of western settlement at the Appalachian Mountains.

1764–65
The British Parliament passes or revives revenue acts and other measures regulating colonial trade, provoking the first colonial protests against "taxation without representation"—including a colonial nonimportation boycott against British goods.

1765
The Stamp Act—the first direct tax on the American colonies—prompts truly organized colonial protest and resistance, including the formation of the Sons of Liberty and other resistance groups.

1766
Parliament responds to colonial pressure by repealing the Stamp Act.

1767
Parliament passes the Townshend Acts, which include taxes on glass, lead, paint, paper, and tea. The colonies resume their nonimportation boycott.

1768
The "Massachusetts Circular Letter" presents Samuel Adams's and James Otis's argument against taxation without representation and calls for unified resistance by all the colonies. The royal governor of Massachusetts dissolves the colonial legislature, and British troops arrive in Boston.

1769
The Virginia House of Burgesses condemns the Crown's actions against Massachusetts and also asserts that only Virginia's governor and legislature may tax its citizens.

1770
Parliament repeals the Townshend taxes, except for the tax on tea.

MARCH 5: The Boston Massacre takes place.

1772
Samuel Adams calls for the creation of "Committees of Correspondence" as a means of communicating information and coordinating action among the colonies.

1773
The Tea Act gives British merchants a monopoly on tea, at the expense of colonial American merchants, provoking, on December 16, the Boston Tea Party.

1774
Parliament passes the Coercive Acts in response to the Boston Tea Party.

SEPTEMBER 5: The First Continental Congress meets.

1775
APRIL 19: The battles of Lexington and Concord are fought; these are generally considered the first battles of the American Revolution.

MAY 10: The Second Continental Congress convenes in Philadelphia.

MAY 10: The capture of Fort Ticonderoga, New York, is an early Patriot victory.

JUNE 14: The Second Continental Congress creates the Continental army.

JUNE 15: The Continental Congress appoints George Washington to command the Continental army.

JUNE 17: The Battle of Bunker Hill is fought.

AUGUST 23: King George III rebuffs the Olive Branch Petition.

DEC. 31: The Americans withdraw from Canada.

1776

JAN. 10: Thomas Paine publishes *Common Sense.*

MARCH: The British army evacuates Boston.

JULY 4: The Continental Congress declares independence.

AUGUST 27: The Battle of Long Island is fought.

SEPT. 15: New York City falls to the British.

OCT. 28: The Battle of White Plains is fought.

DEC. 26: The Battle of Trenton is fought.

1777

JAN. 3: The Battle of Princeton is fought.

SEPT. 11: The Battle of Brandywine is fought.

SEPT. 19: The Battle of Freeman's Farm is fought.

SEPT. 26: The British take Philadelphia.

OCT. 4: The Battle of Germantown is fought.

OCT. 7: The Battle of Bemis Heights is fought.

OCT. 17: British general John Burgoyne surrenders his army to American forces.

NOV. 15: The Articles of Confederation are adopted (ratified, March 1, 1781).

1778

MAY 4: The Franco-American alliance is ratified by Congress.

JUNE 28: The Battle of Monmouth Courthouse is fought.

NOV. 11: The Cherry Valley Massacre takes place.

DEC. 29: Savannah, Georgia, falls to the British.

1779

John Paul Jones begins his remarkable naval career.

MAY: Benedict Arnold turns traitor.

JUNE 21: Spain joins France as an American ally against Britain.

JULY 15–16: The Battle of Stony Point is fought.

SEPT. 23: The *Bonhomme Richard* (John Paul Jones) defeats HMS *Serapis.*

1780

MAY 12: Charleston, South Carolina, falls to the British.

AUGUST 16: Camden, South Carolina, falls to the British.

OCTOBER 7: The Battle of Kings Mountain is fought.

1781

JAN. 17: The Battle of the Cowpens is fought.

MARCH 15: The Battle of Guilford Courthouse is fought.

SEPT. 28–OCTOBER 17: The Yorktown campaign and siege takes place.

1782

While peace negotiations are under way in Paris, sporadic fighting continues in America.

1783

SEPT. 3: The Treaty of Paris is signed.

Live and in Person

YOU CAN VISIT SITES ACROSS the United States to see for yourself where history was made during the American Revolution. Note: If you are planning on visiting one of the below historic locations, please call or check their website for visiting hours; some locations periodically close for renovations.

ADIRONDACK PARK VISITOR INTERPRETIVE CENTER
Route 30
P.O. Box 3000
Paul Smiths, NY 12970
(518) 327-3000
www.adkvic.org
Six million acres encompassing 1,000 miles of rivers and some 2,500 lakes—the best way to envision the American Revolution as fought in upper New York State. Contact the Visitor Interpretive Center for more information.

BENNINGTON BATTLE MONUMENT
15 Monument Circle
Old Bennington, VT 05201
(802) 447-0050
www.dhca.state.vt.us/HistoricSites/html/bennington.html
Visit at night when the monument is dramatically lit.

BOSTON TEA PARTY SHIPS & MUSEUM
Congress Street Bridge
Boston, MA 02127
(617) 338-1773
www.bostonteapartyship.com
Museum with interpretive exhibits and living history programs, as well as tall ships with authentically restored ship's decks, crew's quarters, and cargo holds.

BUNKER HILL MONUMENT
Monument Street
Charlestown, MA
(617) 242-5641
www.nps.gov/archive/bost/Bunker_Hill.htm
Includes visitor lodge and changing exhibits.

CHARLESTON, SOUTH CAROLINA
Visitor Information Center
375 Meeting Street
Charleston, SC 29403
(803) 853-8000
www.charlestoncvb.com
Many of its revolutionary-era buildings survive here, especially below Broad Street.

COLONIAL WILLIAMSBURG, VIRGINIA
The Colonial Williamsburg Foundation
P.O. Box 1776
Williamsburg, VA 23187-1776
(800) 447-8679
www.history.org
The historic focus here is prerevolutionary, but the preservation included the House of Burgesses, where Patrick Henry asked for liberty or death.

COWPENS NATIONAL BATTLEFIELD
P.O. Box 308
Chesnee, SC 29323
(864) 461-2828
www.nps.gov/cowp/
Located on Route 11 it offers tours and staff rides (reenactment exercises) for military history students.

FREEDOM TRAIL
The Freedom Trail Foundation
99 Chauncy Street, Suite 401
Boston, MA 02111
(617) 357-8300
www.thefreedomtrail.org
A clearly marked 2.5-mile walking tour of Boston's most important revolutionary sites. The official start to the Freedom Trail is located at the Boston Common Visitors Center, 148 Tremont Street.

CLIVEDEN, GERMANTOWN

6401 Germantown Avenue
Philadelphia, PA 19144
(215) 848-1777
www.cliveden.org
The Philadelphia neighborhood that was
the site of the Battle of Germantown; the
Chew residence, Cliveden, still stands.

INDEPENDENCE NATIONAL HISTORICAL PARK

143 South Third Street
Philadelphia, PA 19106
(215) 965-2305
www.nps.gov/inde/
This square mile of Philadelphia includes
the First Bank of the United States,
Carpenter's Hall (where the First
Continental Congress convened), Army-
Navy Museum, Marine Corps National
Memorial, Independence Square,
Independence Hall; and the Liberty Bell.

KINGS MOUNTAIN NATIONAL MILITARY PARK

Superintendent
2625 Park Road (I-85)
Blacksburg, SC 29702
(864) 936-7921
www.nps.gov/kimo/
Visitor information center, films, and a
museum of period artifacts.

MORRISTOWN NATIONAL HISTORIC PARK

30 Washington Place
Morristown, NJ 07960-4299
(973) 539-2016
www.nps.gov/morr/
http://www.nps.gov/archive/sara/
tour-2.htm
Site of George Washington's winter
quarters in New Jersey during 1777 and
during 1779–80.

OLD BARRACKS

Barrack Street
Trenton, NJ 08608
(609) 396-1776
www.barracks.org
This museum occupies the building that
once housed the Hessians in Trenton,
New Jersey.

OLD NORTH CHURCH

193 Salem Street
Boston, MA 02113
(617) 523-6676
www.oldnorth.com
Site of Paul Revere's famous one-if-by-
land, two-if-by-sea lantern signal.

PAUL REVERE HOUSE

19 North Square
Boston, MA 02113
(617) 523-2338
www.paulreverehouse.org
Restored home of Paul Revere, plus
exhibits and gardens.

SARATOGA BATTLEFIELD

http://www.revolutionaryday.com/usrout
e9/saratoga/default.htm
http://www.nps.gov/sara/
Saratoga is located forty miles north of
Albany; visit these websites for information about the numerous battle sites,
monuments, and historic houses in and
around the Saratoga area.

VALLEY FORGE NATIONAL HISTORICAL PARK

1400 North Outer Line Drive
King of Prussia, PA 19406
(610) 783-1077
www.nps.gov/vafo/
Located at the intersection of routes 23
and 363 in Bucks County, Pennsylvania,
it includes exhibits commemorating
the endurance and sacrifice of the
Continental army.

WASHINGTON CROSSING STATE PARK

NEW JERSEY

355 Washington Crossing—
Pennington Road
Titusville, NJ 08560-1517
(609) 737-0623
www.state.nj.us/dep/parksandforests/
parks/washcros.html
Located at Route 546 and the Delaware
River in New Jersey.

PENNSYLVANIA

1112 River Rd.
Washington Crossing, PA 18977
(215) 493-4076
www.cr.nps.gov/nR/travel/delaware/
was.htm
Located at Routes 532 and 32 in
Pennsylvania.The site of George
Washington's Delaware crossing, both the
Pennsylvania and the New Jersey sides of
the Delaware River are now state historic
sites with the primary museum on the
New Jersey side.

YORKTOWN BATTLEFIELD

Colonial National Historical Park
P.O. Box 210
Yorktown, VA 23690
(757) 898-2410
www.nps.gov/york/
Ranger-guided tours of the battlefield
and town.

YORKTOWN VICTORY CENTER

Jamestown-Yorktown Foundation
P.O. Box 1607
Williamsburg, VA 23187-1607
(757) 253-4838 or (888) 539-4682
www.historyisfun.org/yorktown/
yorktown.cfm
Located near the Yorktown Battlefield at
Route 238 off Colonial Parkway, this museum offers indoor exhibition galleries, film,
and outdoor living history in the form of a
re-created farm and a army encampment.

Read More, See More

BOOKS

Bernstein, Richard B., with Kym S. Rice. *Are We to Be a Nation? The Making of the Constitution.* Cambridge, MA: Harvard University Press, 1987.

Boatner, Mark M. *Encyclopedia of the American Revolution.* New York: D. McKay Co., 1966, 1974.

Burnett, Edmund Cody. *The Continental Congress.* 1941. Reprint ed., Westport, CT: Greenwood Press, 1975.

Commager, Henry Steele, and Richard B. Morris, eds. *The Spirit of 'Seventy-Six: The Story of the American Revolution as Told by Participants.* New York: Harper & Row, 1958, 1976.

Gephart, Ronald M. *Revolutionary America, 1763–1789: A Bibliography.* Washington, DC: Library of Congress, 1984. 2 vols.

Jensen, Merrill. *The Articles of Confederation.* Madison, WI: University of Wisconsin Press, 1940, 1970.

———. *The New Nation: A History of the United States during the Confederation, 1781–1789.* 1950. Reprint ed., Boston, MA: Northeastern University Press, 1981.

Leckie, Robert. *George Washington's War: The Saga of the American Revolution.* New York: Harper Perennial, 1992.

Morris, Richard B. *The Forging of the Union, 1781–1789.* New York: Harper & Row, 1987.

Purcell, L. Edward, and David F. Burg. *The World Almanac of the American Revolution.* New York: World Almanac, 1992.

Rakove, Jack N. *The Beginnings of National Politics: An Interpretive History of the Continental Congress.* Baltimore, MD: John Hopkins University Press, 1982.

Rossiter, Clinton L. *1787: The Grand Convention.* New York: W. W. Norton, 1987.

———, ed. *The Federalist Papers: Alexander Hamilton, James Madison, John Jay.* New York: New American Library, 1961.

Smith, Page. *A New Age Now Begins: A People's History of the American Revolution.* 2 vols. New York: Penguin, 1976.

Smith, Paul H., ed. *Letters of Delegates to Congress, 1774–1789.* Washington, DC: Library of Congress, 1976.

Stokesbury, James L. *A Short History of the American Revolution.* New York: William Morrow, 1991.

Wood, Gordon S. *The Creation of the American Republic, 1776–1787.* Chapel Hill, NC: University of North Carolina Press, 1969.

WEBSITES

SITES WITH LINKS
http://americanhistory.about.com/cs/revolutionarywar/www.americanrevolution.org/

ART AND ARTIFACT COLLECTIONS AT THE SMITHSONIAN INSTITUTION
www.americanhistory.si.edu

BATTLES AND SITES
www.u-shistory.com/pages/h1197.html

www.srcalifornia.com/

DECLARATION OF INDEPENDENCE
http://lcweb.loc.gov/exhibits/declara/declara1.html

www.earlyamerica.com/earlyamerica/freedom/doi/index.html

www.archives.gov/exhibit_hall/charters_of_freedom/charters_of_freedom.html

www.archives.gov/exhibit_hall/charters_of_freedom/declaration/declaration.html

GLOBAL ACCESS TO EDUCATIONAL SOURCES: AMERICAN REVOLUTION
www.geocities.com/Athens/Academy/6617/amrev6.html

AMERICAN REVOLUTION TIMELINES
History Place:
www.historyplace.com/unitedstates/revolution/

PBS:
www.pbs.org/ktca/liberty/chronicle_timeline.html

Library of Congress:
http://lcweb2.loc.gov/ammem/bdsds/timeline.html

US History.org:
www.ushistory.org/march/timeline.htm

Index

Picture Credits